Autoaesthetics

Philosophy and Literary Theory

Series Editor: Hugh J. Silverman

Published

Stephen Barker
Autoaesthetics

Véronique M. Fóti
Heidegger and the Poets

* Wilhelm S. Wurzer
Filming and Judgment

Forthcoming

Robert Bernasconi
Heidegger in Question

Jean-François Lyotard
Toward the Postmodern

Gianni Vattimo
Consequences of Hermeneutics

* Also available in paperback

Autoaesthetics

*Strategies of the Self
After Nietzsche*

◆

Stephen Barker

Humanities Press
New Jersey ▼ **London**

First published 1992 by Humanities Press International, Inc.
Atlantic Highlands, New Jersey 07716, and
3 Henrietta Street, Covent Garden, London WC2E 8LU

© Stephen Barker, 1992

Library of Congress Cataloging-in-Publication Data

Barker, Stephen, 1946–
    Autoaesthetics : strategies of the self after Nietzsche / Stephen
Barker.
      p.   cm. — (Philosophy and literary theory)
    Includes bibliographical references and index.
    ISBN 0–391–03748–X
    1. Nietzsche, Friedrich Wilhelm, 1844–1900. 2. Self (Philosophy)-
-History—19th century. 3. Aesthetics, Modern—19th century.
    I. Title. II. Series.
    B3317.B36 1992   91–35840
    193—dc20   CIP

A catalog record for this book is available from the British Library.

Printed in the United States of America

For
Michelle

Contents

◆

Introduction

◆

> *Parable.*—Those thinkers in whom all stars
> move in cyclic orbits are not the most profound:
> whoever looks into himself as into vast space
> and carries galaxies in himself also knows how
> irregular all galaxies are; they lead into the chaos
> and labyrinth of existence.
>
> —*The Gay Science* 322

No careful reader of Nietzsche can miss his fascination with the power of parable. He dots his works with obscure and poetic mini-narratives like the one above from *The Gay Science*, in which he tests out the fit of parable to his perpetually central psycho-philosophical theme: the dedicated investigation of what it means to be a self-reflexive human being; that is, to the exploration of self. Nietzsche's parables reveal an absorbing dialectic of self-analysis oscillating between the Apollinian/Crucified,[1] the abstracted quasi-position of philosophical distance from which to contemplate the self, and the Dionysian, the radically profound "chaos and labyrinth of existence." Typically, as in his own self-defining parable from *The Gay Science*, these dialectical poles are shifting and chimerical, always forcefully but unreliably mutating, in that the abstract, contemplative pole of reflexive self-knowledge, the philosopher-pole, knows itself as "vast," carrying "galaxies" within it, even while at the same time it "knows how irregular all galaxies are"; on the other hand, intuitive self-knowledge leads to the opposite pole of the dialectical self, at which those metaphoric galaxies to which he refers, accreted formations of (self-)knowledge systems and (self-)assessment systems, lead not to systematic, Apollinian self-revelation but to Dionysian chaos, which as Nietzsche presents it is *itself* a richly paradoxical and self-contradictory binary opposition: the Dionysian labyrinth in Nietzsche is not *only* chaotic but rather a set of complex, structured systems from within which, as in the mythical Cretan one in which Dionysus lurks in the form of the Minotaur, the self-observer is threateningly and mortally unable

1

to discern a system, as in Lacan's version of the unconscious.

Self-reflexive existence is, for Nietzsche, a dense overlayering of systematic reversals caught or created, for the psycho-philosopher, in a structured system of parabolic reversals. The implications for contemporary theory and philosophy are enormous since Nietzsche's declaration that an inability to discern such a self-organizing system is not a manifestation of a conventional, constitutive chaos but rather a failure or disabling of perspective, or else a lack of facility with the systems of language that constitute it, not a failure of the labyrinth "itself." In what reveals itself as an obsession with self-declaration, Nietzsche works through linguistic labyrinths "toward" the metaphorized self seeming to lurk chimerically within them.

In Nietzsche's view, philosophy is revealed as a dialectics of self constituted as a strategic *passage* between these always shifting poles of self-analysis and self-assertion. As in so many other places in Nietzsche, in the parable from *The Gay Science* the thinker's thought is important because it occurs in the gaps/passages/crossings between chaos and system, not because thought converges on a regularity of self-interpretation. Nietzsche's orbit as a thinker (that is, as a fabricator of the self) is profound because of the gulf between the (Platonic) thought that would converge in a teleology of self-unity and the disparate and impossible thought that would seem to be required for understanding the chaos of living itself. And once again, Nietzsche's concern is grounded in self-reflection ("whoever looks into himself . . ."), with its penumbra of secondary associations ranging from the philosophical through the solipsistic.

Nietzsche's parabolic play is with the associative self rather than with the *subject*, because he is at play with the totalizing history of the idea of self and because "subject" is always determined in juxtaposition with "object," a distinction Nietzsche rejects summarily and repeatedly. "Self" has about it an in-built self-subversion that "subject," as a result of its history of disciplined usage, does not: while "subject" is filled with a long history of ontological validification, "self" is a volatile construction of unstable, evolving vectors, of mirrors and smoke. Nietzsche repeatedly asserts the primacy of the search for "self" as opposed to "subject"hood; he declares a vehement anti-dogmatism in terms of creative transference. Although this discussion in Nietzsche is often framed (parodically) in Kantian terms, it is more generally "against positivism," with its reliance on the "fact" of knowledge and indeed of self-knowledge. Nietzsche's introduction to the section of *The Will to Power*, entitled "Belief in the 'Ego.' The Subject," begins with a note "against positivism,"

which halts at phenomena—"There are only *facts*"—I would say: No, facts is precisely what there is not, only interpretations. We cannot establish any fact "in itself": perhaps it is folly to want to do such a thing.

"Everything is subjective," you say; but even this is interpretation. The "subject" is not something given, it is something added and invented and projected behind what is there. Finally, is it necessary to posit an interpreter behind the interpretation? Even this is invention, hypothesis.

Insofar as the word "knowledge" has any meaning, the world is knowable; but it is *interpretable* otherwise, it has no meaning behind it, but countless meanings.[2]

Counteracting what he considers to be a disastrously false sense of reality, even the enabling reality of what we call the "self," is a sense of reality as an eternally self-recreating artifact, a product of interpretation that is not "false" nor "true" but composed of the countless meanings of "art." In this passage on "subject" and "self," Nietzsche presents his case in the form of a dialectical discourse, an artful confrontation of voices.

Because Nietzsche's profoundly introspective anti-thought concerning the self is rather an "artist thought" engaging the thinker in a particular and powerful aesthetic way, and because it is so often alluded to in Nietzsche's writing, I take it as axiomatic. This is Nietzsche's final parabolic reversal, and central to my investigation here. Among the many radical, revolutionary, and astonishing things Nietzsche has to say to us and to our age, none is more astonishing than his commentary on the aestheticizing of the self-reflexive force. Although it is inherent in all his writings, within the context of his parabolic cosmos Nietzsche lays out this artist-thought most clearly in the succinct, elliptical speculation he sketched out while starting work on *Beyond Good and Evil* in 1886, a speculation whose form indicates that it was a passing thought, a musing, literally a sketch toward a statement or a note toward a manifesto:

> The work of art where it appears without an artist, e.g. as body, as organization (Prussian officer corps, Jesuit order). To what extent the artist is only a preliminary stage.
>
> The world as a work of art that gives birth to itself—[3]

What is astonishing about this speculation, hardly seeming to offer itself for serious consideration as the groundwork for a program or a work, let alone a life (or, indeed, all human lives) is its dramatic linkage of "artist" with artist's *work* and the assertion that the "world" (here Nietzsche is using the word in its Heideggerian sense—taken up by Heidegger, of course, from Nietzsche) is nothing other than a self-reflexive work of art in itself. Nietzsche's extraordinary assertion gives us a deep insight into a new kind of philosophy, a philosophy of the aesthetic self, and particularly into Nietzsche's own very complex attitude toward human life, the world, and philosophico-aesthetic discourse. The abysmal distance opened here between "knowledge" and "truth," already much discussed elsewhere, whose convergent identity had been since Plato the philosopher's grounding discourse, let alone the revamped place of "art" in Nietzsche's *schema*, operates in two ways:

1. art *displaces* knowledge/truth as a grounding criterion for "world," consisting of association and fabrication,
2. "self," like art, cannot be "itself."

That is, art must always be, and is always identified as, distanced and perpetually distancing from itself. In both of these senses, art is a departure from the traditional Platonic activity of philosophy and anathema to it.

But if the world "gives birth to itself" perspectively, Nietzsche implies, that world (the world of artful construction and fabrication—of creativity) must have a self, or at the very least a sense of self, to which it can give birth.[4] Without this teleological image, indistinct as it might be, the *passage* or process of world-invention cannot take place, and the world cannot be what it purportedly is, according to Nietzsche. In Nietzsche's philosophy, the agency for an artful inception and growth of world-creation is the self, producing and produced by the self-fabrication, self-imaging, and self-imagining that philosophy has become in Nietzsche. This is the basis for what I here call autoaesthetics, a problematic and self-contradictory term for the very problematic and fundamentally self-contradictory ideas of the self and art Nietzsche manifests, which for the artist mirrors (but never could create) that autonomous art he envisions and that contains the same schism. Nietzsche acknowledges that the aestheticizing of life entails its artful, stylish disappropriation, a free fall into metaphor and un-self-ness. Autoaesthetics, the artful and chimerical fabrication of the (un)self, means development of strategies of self-mastery, power over one's art and production, a convergence with self at the *locus* of the creation (and interpretation) of art, and a complex, tendentious metaphorical *dis*-unifying of the artist-self. Autoaesthetics contains the seeds of its own denial, simultaneously announcing and cancelling one of our most fundamental hopes, and persistently reopening the gap between the unity "self" implies and the radical disunity contained in any perspectival gesture.

Autoaesthetics' strategic disunification, with its privileging of perspectival duplicity, however, is among its most provocative traits. As the implications not so much for a self-produced art as for an art-produced self manifest themselves, so do those of the produced, aestheticized artist, whose new centrality eclipses philosophy and subsumes it in parable, but whose radical displacement threatens to cancel inspiration, creativity, imagination. Autoaesthetics reverberates not only with heavily ironized self-revelatory possibilities but with automatism, mechanization, syntactic predeterminations, and a violently displaced narratism—that is, with a divergence and disunity in artist as well as in art.[5] Both of these tendencies are immanent in the idea, though to follow Nietzsche's lead I would rather call it a convocation of forces, of autoaesthetics.

Indeed, my chief interest here is to show that while what I call autoaesthetics comes to its fully articulated theoretical power in Nietzsche, this floating sense of mechanized semiology, of *étrangeté* and engagement, is inherent in Modernist as well as Postmodernist writing; the effects of the autoaesthetic turn can be seen before and after Nietzsche—in such works as Stendhal's *Red and Black*, in unexpected places like Hardy's *Jude the Obscure*, and in the high Modernists of the twentieth century, James Joyce, William Faulkner, and John Fowles, who are seen and who claim to be doing something quite different from what Nietzsche lays out.

But if we continue to follow the autoaesthetic line we have seen Nietzsche take in *Beyond Good and Evil*, we perceive him going even further toward a cancellation of humanistic Modernist centrism: the world, he says, is a work of art that *gives birth to itself* without the agency or intercession of the artist, who is a "preliminary stage." Dispensing for a moment—but only for a moment—with a powerful play on the notion of theatricalization announced in this very dramatic claim, Nietzsche indicates here the atmosphere of tendentiousness and of tentativeness in which all art, and all selves, must be produced. Artistic confidence is, for Nietzsche, a rhetorical strategy in the face of the preliminary nature of the artist—and of the artist's work, a parodic rhetorical turn, parodic because it undermines the structures of Modernism on which it comments. One sign of Nietzsche's parodic turn is the organic nature of the image in which he defines the world, as "a work of art" that "gives birth to itself." This imagistic conundrum underlies the aesthetic conditions in which *all* artists, very much including Nietzsche, will produce their tentative works. To say that the world is *sui generis*, and a work of art, is quite different from saying that it is a work of art produced by a thoughtful mind out of a set of preconditions defined by a culture or a set of laws; any revelation of this art-world must be seen as a radical assertion of a different kind of will to power. Not only does this nascent world create itself out of itself, but it does so according to no a priori set of aesthetic doctrines or principles, creating any such principles out of itself as well.

The autoaesthetic artist orchestrates that cornucopia of inner and outer forces, the undifferentiated plenitude of that primal human chaos we call conscious/unconscious life. Insofar as autoaesthetics remains aesthetic, it can thus be seen as a reorganization of the idea of beauty. For the autoaesthetic artist, "beauty" in Nietzsche's sense is "the expression of victorious will," by which he means a "harmonizing of all the strong desires."[6] Likewise, "ugliness" is "the decadence of type, contradiction and lack of coordination among the inner desires."[7] In this elusive self-reference, Nietzsche presents a new model for aesthetic evaluation, one that parodies Enlightenment and Classical ideals of art and aesthetics as well as Enlightenment models for the definition, perception, and interpretation of both self and art, and brings us into a newly defined "world" with a new idea of beauty.

The medium in which Nietzsche transforms art and world, and simultaneously transforms any notion of beauty, is the ephemeral one in which "humanness," "nature," and "art" identify themselves in the most complete and sophisticated way: language. For the world to be a work of art giving birth to itself, it must be able not only to be born but to declare or articulate that birth—it must work through and transcend the mundane semiosis of the linguistic to become symbolic in the grammatological sense. As the tool with which the world is perpetually remade, language contains the power to which the human will aspires, the search for which produces such intense self-absorption. The way in which Nietzsche activates this self-absorption is a drastically revised treatment of the Enlightenment grounds on which it is built. As a deconstruction of the ideas of self he and we inherit from the eighteenth century, Nietzsche's trinity of grounding terms, as I will suggest extensively in chapter 1, is a revision *in transmuto* of the Enlightenment one consisting of Reason, Nature, and Progress, themselves written out of the Renaissance *humanitas* from which notions of the self continue to spring.[8] For the Enlightenment thinker or artist, philosopher or *philosophe*, these terms are detached from their human manifestations, corrupted by the cultural forces in which they occur. Right Reason can only occur if those distortions can be corrected; to paraphrase the great *Encyclopédie*, "reason is to the Enlightenment what grace is to the Christian"; and what will-to-power is to Nietzsche.[9] Nature, the Enlightenment concept of which flows out of the nature of Reason, is to be seen as the essential conceptualization of the beautiful and the good, the Golden Mean revealed. Progress is equally detached from experiential life, a mechanical process of improvement brought about by adherence to self-serving notions of Reason and Nature. The Enlightenment's closed, self-perpetuating metaphysical system is the rigidified basis on which Nietzsche works his disruptive strategies, which must be understood as generally parodic of that structuration and those structures. Indeed, Nietzsche's revisionist autoaesthetics operates within the detached, illuminated space of Enlightenment values in which he gives birth to his world and to himself as artist, as poet-philosopher, as aesthete.[10]

Of course, Nietzsche's concentration on style, his self-citation, and his undermining of the traditional role of *philosophe* were hardly new and hardly finished with him. Starting with Heidegger's rehabilitation of his work, Nietzsche has been treated to an astonishing array of responses, ranging from the historical to the radically theoretical. His work has found itself at the center of wildly disparate theoretical frameworks and dogmas, as well as in the midst of reasoned and careful scholarly treatments. The extensive attention such philosophers and critics of philosophy as Walter Kaufmann, Arthur Danto, and Richard Schacht have shown Nietzsche's work in recent years has enhanced rather than prevented its use by Foucault, Derrida, Lacan, Deleuze, and many others. In a stricter sense, the idea of self Nietzsche espouses has shown itself throughout the history of his use by literary and scholarly responders from Gide to Mann to Kundera, Sartre to Kaufmann to Derrida. In this set of treatments, the so-called self is, as Alexander Nehamas says, "not a constant, stable entity. On the contrary, it is something one becomes, something, he would even say, one constructs."[11] This radical self-separation is always a "testament" to grammatological distance, as Lawrence Rickels points out:

> The metaphors of writing and language that crowd around Nietzsche's characterization of the constitution of acts of will shift the genealogy of nihilism into a grammatological register. Because it never goes without saying, willing is also always differentiated with each verbal expression into a will and a separable act of willing.[12]

This "causative or grammatical split-level construction—language's resentment towards the will," according to Rickels, helps articulate the Derridean component into consideration. Nietzsche's own grammatology, a defense "against all our defenses,"[13] provides powerful evidence "that language always has the last word—behind the back of writer or interpreter,"[14] in an obsessive play with identity that Nietzsche posits in language. Thus the "artistry of thought" takes on (constantly) new meaning; indeed, thought itself is artistry, as Daniel Breazeale suggests: "Knowing always involves the kind of creative transference of meaning which we associate with *metaphors*; indeed, it is nothing but working with one's favorite metaphors."[15] Reality is for Nietzsche "an appropriation of an unfamiliar impression by means of metaphors; stimulus and recollected image are bound together by means of metaphor."[16] Logic itself, Nietzsche declares, and even the concept of logic, "which is as bony, foursquare, and transposable as a die—is nevertheless merely the *residue of a metaphor*."[17] Far from being a ratification of the "text" of phenomena, then, language, as the conduit of the interpretive self, produces at best a paradoxical confirmation of the concrete *by means of* its mediated evocation. This self-text is always something to be consumed, ruminated over, *produced*.[18]

Finally, Nietzsche's autoaesthetic strategy is interrogative. For Nietzsche, all self-assertions are interrogations of the texts of selfhood, a distancing and an undermining. The more Nietzsche exhorts us to "believe" in the self, the more he is suggesting that we disbelieve; the more Zarathustra affirms, the more we are to doubt. Interrogation breeds both energy and doubt, and this is merely the beginning of the grammatological conundrum of the self, the autoaesthetic strategy Nietzsche bequeaths to contemporary fiction and theory. Only in light of this constant threat of reversal can Nietzsche's seemingly categorical assertions be seen and assimilated.

This autoaesthetic strategy of self-subversion and interrogation, which has been subsequently identified as "Postmodern,"[19] is first articulated—a Post-modern strategy before Modernism!—in Nietzsche; that familiar twentieth-century Modernism with which we are most familiar and which seems initially so different from Nietzsche's *cosmos*, in which the entire idea of the self is rewritten, develops out of or parallel with that alternative, autoaes-thetic Nietzschean strategy. Peter Ackroyd, in his *Notes for a New Culture*, contends in this regard that in terms of the creation of an "adequate" *gestalt* of the self, a reaching beyond "Modernism" "first appeared in the writings of Nietzsche,"[20] born directly from Nietzsche's re-constellated forces, even-tually to become the movement in which "created form began to interrogate itself."[21] This is a release and, simultaneously, a loss, whose apparent polarity manifests Nietzsche's revolutionary "process of unfolding,"[22] the inception of that *articulation* on which I will spend a good deal of time in chapter 1.

Again, however, I want to go a step further here. Ackroyd's claim that Nietzschean thought lies behind the Modernist effusion of "the novel idea of literature"[23] leads directly to the question of mastery and "the novel." My own interrogation will fabricate a dialectical association between Nietz-schean interrogation and the novel as genre. The five modern/Modernist novelists treated here, Stendhal, Hardy, Faulkner, Joyce, and Fowles (and this is already a thesis), span in the five novels treated here more than a century and a half, yet they are all obsessed by an urgent need for self-validation in a world they no longer control, the assertion of an autoaesthetic force; further, they manifest common strategic responses to that urgency. All five of these novels, like Nietzsche's writings, respond to the Enlighten-ment assurance of self-identity, but in a world without any support for such assurance. All seem to ask the endemic contemporary question: "What am I to do with a world that treats me—and whatever it is or may be that is writing this 'me'—in a way I cannot recognize and from which I can seem to take no final satisfaction?" My strategy here will be to reveal some of those "defenses against all our defenses," both as Nietzsche employs them and as they appear in some appropriately critical examples of the modern novel. Nietzsche's most pressing question, the final words of his penultimate book, *Ecce Homo*—"Have I been understood?"—becomes in light of the critique he offers of the self, of questioning, and of understanding a complex and frustrating one whose answer writes itself in the space of the typical Nietz-schean affirmation of life. The Modernists I will treat here recede from the relentless critique of logic and of the self Nietzsche offers in this light.

To "interpret" Nietzsche, then, is to confront the threshold between an impossible explanation of the self and an acknowledgment that *no* understanding of the self, in Nietzsche's terms, is possible, an alternative smacking of the nihilism Nietzsche abhors. Indeed, this is the *gouffre* in which Stendhal, Hardy, Joyce, and Faulkner are perpetually caught and from which certain corners of the Postmodern emerge; I will here try to show ways to think about and use Nietzschean terminology *according to Nietzsche* and *beyond Nietzsche*. This is what I mean by "strategies of the self *after* Nietzsche": the "after" serves myriad purposes ranging from the (undermined) chronological one to the aesthetic one (as in "after Raphael" or "after Picasso"). In terms of both time and space, strategies of the self "after" Nietzsche provide the grammatological opening between interpretive modes required to place these works in a Nietzschean context. The aesthetic, (quasi-)mimetic implications of that "after" ought to reverberate suggestively through the discussion of Nietzsche's treatment of the project of Western philosophy and its application to aesthetic theory and criticism. Nietzsche is a good student of Zarathustra, following that hallowed and weighty figure down the mountain and then up the mountainside toward an evaluative gateway only the very convincing dwarf of gravity/history discourages him from reaching and comprehending.

In the following examination of Nietzsche's thought on aesthetic self-fashioning, I want to burrow into five facets of this autoaesthetics, which are announced by the "section titles" of my (dialectically) paired set of chapters. The first chapter of each pair addresses the Nietzschean context directly, setting up some possible conditions by which to engage in the autoaesthetic strategy of reading and incorporating a text (that is, of making the world). Once those suggestions for possible context are made and developed, a second chapter follows in which the reading of a text manifests the autoaesthetic strategy I have discussed and demonstrated. The contexts themselves, then, remain embedded in the "interpretive" chapters.

In some sense, this format is itself a dialectic between the more Apollinian treatment of Nietzschean text itself and the interpretive use of that treatment in a critique of the literary art it has "produced." Throughout his writing life, Nietzsche's produced view of Dionysus evolved, from the rich but divisive and dialectical one of *The Birth of Tragedy* to the unified and unifying one of *Twilight of the Idols*. While one might initially see the Dionysian as a Hegelian synthesis of seeming opposites, as Apollo is subsumed into Dionysus, even in the "earlier" Dionysus this is precisely what does *not* happen—indeed, the opposite happens: instead of a "simple" dialectic between the dream and intoxication, between reason and unreason,

Nietzsche evolves more and more toward a view that all these dyads are themselves chimerical, in light of the myriad forces out of which we construct our selves. This anti-dialectical view, which is in actuality another *Jenseits*, grows more and more compelling as we look at the way in which the Dionysian, the Apollinian, and the aesthetic interact. In this light, any notion of the self remains at once a unifying theme and a chimera.

In chapter 1, I examine ways in which Nietzsche's trinity of terms builds toward this ironic *aufhebung*, and how the terms with which I will work in the book engage in a Nietzschean deconstruction of Nietzsche's own terminology. Starting with one of the seminal novels of the Modernist tradition, Stendhal's *Red and Black*, I proceed, in the second chapter, to show how the dilemma of this self-assertion is a fundamental building block of the Modernist aesthetic, born from the proto-Nietzschean doubt about the nature of the aesthetic self. Julien Sorel's wrenching search for grounding validification, for a pedigree on which he can rely, only to discover the politicization of the chimerical self, is one of the most poignant statements of Modernist assertion's darker side.

One of the most controversial aspects of Nietzsche's life-program was and is its attitude toward suffering. I have already pointed out how one of the most fundamental sources of contemporary *angst*, in Nietzschean terms, is precisely the knowledge that self is chimerical. This is at once a source of power (in a Nietzscheanized Postmodern world) and of pain (for the Modernist intent on self-harmonics and organic unity). Autoaesthetics produces a framework for the dilemma of pain and suffering in Nietzsche that allows it to be constitutive and coercive at once—that is, to compound itself out of its own (satisfying) suffering. Self-identification is at once a menace, an incursion, and an empowering. In chapter 3, I address ways in which the invasive metaphors of danger and suffering can be aesthetized and drawn into Nietzsche's artistic purview, suggesting that the images of the mirror and the dagger, of reflection and the threat of invasion set up poles by which the acknowledge artistic suffering. Frameworks of both reflection and incursion pervade my reading of *Jude the Obscure*, in which, I contend, Hardy's own autoaesthetic is heavily though invisibly influenced by the Nietzschean one as constructed.

In the third section, which directly confronts the issue of writing, here in terms of Zarathustran autoaesthetics, I examine Nietzsche's notion of the spiritual as a self-overcoming, a sublimation to metaphor. This sublimation has for Nietzsche a highly spiritualized nature always undermined by Nietzsche's heavy irony in the face of any seemingly placid spirituality not susceptible to ironization. Inherent in spirituality, Nietzsche declares, is the healthy reversal of metaphoric dialectics. Rising into metaphor, Zarathustra attempts to become himself by overcoming himself; he inhabits his story in order to be himself. Nietzsche subtly shows the prophet disappearing into his own self-reflection, yet unaware of its detachment. The eschatology of *Zarathustra*'s Book Four is among the most incisive and scathing parodies of conventional Modernist spirituality in Western literature. But it is even more than this: in it Nietzsche shows Zarathustra, the man, subsumed by his own poetic flight; the remainder—what is left behind—is an ironic allegory of supplementarity. For William Faulkner, try as he will, language cannot be made to reify Ike McCaslin as both of them would wish—indeed, as both of them need it to do, and as a result Ike's world itself floats in a genealogical narrativity that gives him nothing but pain. Ike's analysis of his past, his memories, and his values permit him only the most cursory satisfactions. Ike's inability to accommodate the autoaesthetics Nietzsche points out destroys him.

Following (and of course questioning) the Grand Design of Western narrative structure, my trajectory reaches its nadir of subverted self-empowering in Ike; the concluding fourth and fifth sections suggest an ironic emergence from the wilderness. Having explored some of the implications of autoaesthetics for the positivist Modernist project in the first three sections, the concluding two explore something of the "yes-saying" to which Nietzsche's autoaesthetics might lead us. Since "truth" is replaced by Nietzsche with what I have called "empowering," which is always based on strategic and teleological forces, and since that empowering is always a function of self-creation and the cancellation of threat, the fourth section begins with a treatment of the work in which Nietzsche most vehemently turns toward the positive strategy of Zarathustran empowering. To go "beyond good and evil," for most of us, prospectively the source of ultimate anxiety—in a world where no rules protect us, where morality and ethics have abandoned us, is truly a frightening prospect, as Nietzsche points out in his discussions of the "last man." But this fear, of course, as we have already begun to see earlier, is a part of being oneself. This is what Nietzsche does in *Beyond Good and Evil* and what John Fowles does in *Daniel Martin*. The acknowledgment of "self-lack" is not the negative and nihilistic thing it might seem to be, but the beginning of self-discovery and self-empowering. To be "reduced" to metaphor is to overcome the self by becoming the self as Nietzsche conceives it. The entire strategy of Fowles' novel about a playwright *manquée* is to show Daniel Martin as self-empowered in just this way. Fowles uses the traditions of narrative practice in the novel to weave a complex fabric of autoaesthetic empowering which does not reveal its strategy until the final page.

The grounds of Nietzschean autoaesthetics having been laid out in the previous chapters, Section Five concerns itself with the play of language and legitimacy in the Nietzschean anti-tradition. This last section explores the "graphtings," both graftings-on and graphings, by which Nietzsche's idea of self-creation emerges. Chapter 9 explores the origins of some of Nietzsche's own legitimizations in Heraclitus, analyzing some Heraclitan aphorisms and the aphoristic strategy adopted so effectively by Nietzsche in most of his writing. Heraclitus' self-empowering is quintessentially Nietzschean, I contend: one might say either that Nietzsche was influenced by Heraclitus or that Nietzsche found a ratification of his *Weltanschauung* in what we presume to be Heraclitus' remnants or fragments. Either way, Heraclitus provides keys to Nietzsche's sense of the self through but beyond dialectics. To "open the dialectics of writing" is to be aware of the metaphoricity through which we are empowered, but also to be lost in those dialectics, as a play of forces rather than as material or essential unity. In the play of Joyce and Beckett, with their obverse purchases on the metaphorical coin, we can see the final working out of that Modernist life-wish, the writing of the self. The ways in which Joyce *does* this and Beckett energetically *does not* demonstrate the dialectical confrontation of the internal struggles of Nietzsche's self-empowering: for Joyce, the writer/thinker may write, or even apotheosize, the self, while for Beckett that is not only impossible but purely chimerical.

A number of concealed, allegorical structural strategies lurk behind the organization of the material I want to juxtapose with and present next to Nietzsche here; one would find it impossible to read and respond to Nietzsche without delighting in such ironies and ironizations. As a result, one will find a "shape" here that might have been dictated by Aristotle, Dante, or Augustine (a Grand Design). These structural strategies open and reopen the issues Nietzsche takes up and which are worked out in the *art* with which Nietzsche's art is confronted. To call them intentional is tantamount to saying that uttering or writing a proper sentence is intentional, or that wanting to "know oneself" is intentional; it goes without saying. Intentionality, however, complex and unguideable, is one of the bases of the auto-aesthetic.

With Mallarmé's cyclic orbits in *Un Coup de dés*, an autoaesthetic apotheosis occurs. The integration of the poem's pages with the "galaxies" that wheel across them and spill out of the book's very binding, in the form of Mallarmé's poem, suggests the wealth of strategic discursive practices Nietzsche initiates. On this cusp of the Postmodern, my reflections on the Nietzschean self pass into the "chaos and labyrinth of existence." Finally, in exhibiting and exploring the incipient Postmodernism of Mallarmé and Beckett, I intend to direct Nietzsche toward a future critique of the written self, one I do not intend to engage here but merely to suggest and to portend.

Part One

◆

DIONYSUS AND THE CHIMERICAL SELF

The desire for destruction, change, becoming *can* be the expression of an overfull power pregnant with the future (my term for this, as is known, is the "Dionysian"); but it can also be the hatred of the ill-constituted, disinherited, underprivileged, which *has* to destroy, because what exists, indeed existence itself, all being itself, enrages and provokes it.

—*The Will to Power* 846

1

◆

Nietzsche's Trinity of Terms and Mine

A coming-to-be and passing away, a
structuring and a destroying, without any moral
additive, in forever equal innocence, shows itself
in the play of artists and of children.
Only aesthetic man can look thus at the
world, one who has experienced in artists and in
the birth of art objects how the struggle of the
many can yet carry rules and laws inherent in
itself, how the artist stands contemplatively
above and at the same time actively within his
work, how necessity and random play,
oppositional tension and harmony, must pair to
create a work of art.

—*Philosophy in the Tragic Age of the Greeks 7*

Nietzsche's radical re-writing of the very idea of philosophy into an active, aesthetic psycho-philosophy, from one of metaphysical and even mystical certitude to one of deep questioning and the active absence of certitude (from a convergent model to a divergent one), is continuously tested out against and implemented by his equally radical re-writing of the idea of what it is to be human. Here, Nietzsche invents many new processes of self-assessment and self-reflection; he is obsessed throughout his work with the fabrication of the self and the power accruing to the idea(s) of the self he holds. In the evolution of the Dionysian Man[1] we can see the return not only of what we would now call the repressed self[2] but of a self-assessment that posits "self"-ness at the very threshold of the unknowable, either in the form of that which is unaccessible to philosophy, on the one hand, or the unconscious, on the other. This conundrum of liminality allows Nietzsche to proceed energetically with his moral and ethical project regarding the aesthetic context for human culture. Nonetheless, Nietzsche's concern for the molding, indeed the inventing, of the self pervades his work. Self-fashioning occurs in the shadow of the chimerical Dionysian self-apotheosis that is, in Nietzsche, as ironic as it is powerful. This "shadow" of the self, explored so elliptically and so fully in *Thus Spoke Zarathustra*, a shadow both because of its uncanniness and its persistence, is central to Nietzsche's view of the self. Each purported self we manifest is in fact a shadow of other past and future selves, as well as of other present ones operating parallel to the one we call the shadow.

The idea of the shadow, for Nietzsche a shadow which creates and identifies the self, is the idea of language. Humankind's sophistication and power, its self-creation as a work of art, which can and must be translated into self-interpretation and "self-knowledge," begin and end with the realization of the extended power of the overt and the sublimated (Dionysian) word; such is the fundamental thread of Nietzsche's auto-inventive and contentious philosophy. Although this contention evolves, undergoing numerous subtle and dramatic changes, during Nietzsche's work, whatever its guise might be its obsessive articulation as a function of the Dionysian word never flags. And Nietzsche does not, in his concern with the extended power of the word, mean to posit some domination of/over the word, nor a control of its functions. Nor does he mean that we gain or create power (the power of self-declaration) when we objectify the word either "possessed" or "given." Far more appropriate as an image of the way Nietzsche looks at words, their energy and their tensions, is not in terms of the way we play with words but how *words play with or on us*—how we are fabricated, forged, or created by them. This aspect of the Dionysian is one of play, always a *tracing out* and a distancing. At the same time as they identify what they signify in the way we are used to thinking about and using them, Dionysian words, however problematic, are always pointing toward a dimension beyond what we mean when we simplistically say "understanding" or "appropriation." This distancing has been the object of much scrutiny in contemporary theoretical and literary discourse, of course, in its own right. In much of this recent analysis, however, language is still seen as a kind of opaque transcription of reality—as casting a shadow in the conventional sense; indeed, the archaic suppositions we still make about language control the greater part of our discourse. These notions are not completely denied by Nietzsche any more than they are by contemporary theory. Nietzsche's claim is that we "forget" that the associative security of language is not its *only* use, and treat language as a mere functionary of explanation. It is only when we look at the inherent metaphoricity of language that we begin to question this simple, utilitarian equation of word and thing or of word and state or condition.

But (Dionysian) language is also not "simply" a set of integrated Saussurean differences in whose magnetic tensions words are to be recognized and understood only by their nature as signs and their differences from other words, although, in defense of both of these methods of understanding language, it must be said that they see language as the vehicle by which we identify ourselves with a culture, a way of life, a civilization, and a tradition. A vital and "real" part of this enculturation is language's functioning to produce (discover? create?) a dialectical sense of self. My exploration of Nietzsche and some literary works overtly or covertly influenced by the Nietzschean autoaesthetic will concentrate on ways in which this awakening to the radical power of self-declaration takes account of the innate differentiation *within* the word, when we use and integrate it, but this exploration *occurs* differently: since Nietzsche's articulation of the Dionysian word, we can no longer expect words to act as the meta-corporeal extensions of human consciousness nor as the disclosers of the plan (Great or merely great) of the intellect; after Nietzsche, not only does the subject come fairly violently into question, as contemporary theory now considers axiomatic, but so does the *object* we regard as the word.

Or rather, if the word (whatever it may be thought of as being) can in any way be meaningfully objectified after Nietzsche, it is only within a field of forces of which the words are held momentarily in tensions produced by other forces acting on them, most centrally the force of *other words*, and of writing itself. Tensions within language itself, between subject and predicate, noun and adjective, etc., as well as between page and mind, come under new scrutiny in Nietzsche, for whom language (particularly written language) is at once radically privileged and displaced. At the same time, Nietzsche's aphoristic obsession with style makes us re-appraise the tensions of connotation and denotation as well as of the fundamental exchange-value of language's inherent metaphoricity. For Nietzsche, the so-called outer reality of the world we experience is dissolved and transformed in the multi-vectored Dionysian word: the world as we "see" it or "know" it is fabricated out of language, the raw material of known experience and the empirical existence of things showing themselves as secondary to the "ordinary" signification language/writing seems to produce.

Ironically, here at just the place where for Nietzsche the positive power of language begins and contemporary post-Nietzschean theory[3] opens out, Nietzsche must face the charges of nihilism that have (so incorrectly) dogged his work since the 1870s and which have been in such high relief since at least the 1890s, when his books became more widely available and therefore more widely responded to. "Nietzsche" has been displaced *and therefore* at least partially understood by and in his own reception—fitting, in a way; indeed, the initiatory displacement of the Dionysian word must certainly be understood in part as a loss, in that the much-desired unified sense of self, the integrated complacency and certitude with which the Judeo-Christian tradition so badly wants to view its relation to cognitive reality (what Nietzsche calls the "Apollinian," and of course elsewhere the "Apollinian fiction"), is reduced to shards by Nietzsche and the literary, semiotic, and linguistic theory that has followed him.

Along with Nietzschean interrogation *everything*, from chaos to certitude, as well as the conceptual bases on which such concretions are founded, comes into question; Nietzsche declares that even the most categorical assertions language can make (for example, those made so ironically throughout *Thus Spoke Zarathustra*) reveal at the same time their necessary corollary, inherent in the force-structure of, and always present within, any declaration as a shadowy question and one that brings into question the nature of assertion itself.[4]

This built-in interrogative strategy has from the beginning been grounds for a charge of nihilism against Nietzsche, resultant from what J. Hillis Miller has called Nietzsche's "disarticulation" of the self. Miller points out how Nietzsche deconstructs both inner and outer worlds in a "systematic putting in question of the idea that the self is a substantial and integral entity."[5] Since all interpretation is in some sense a falsification of experience and of *force*, any identifiable notion of an identifiable self is necessarily also a false one. But this is far too simple; Nietzsche is purposive here: the creating of an idea of the self, he says, albeit inherently riddled with shadows and falsehoods, makes human (as opposed to unhuman) life "possible," and provides what Miller calls "the pleasure of an exercise of the artistic will to power over things."[6] We adopt certain styles of language, in the strategic disarticulation of the self, to "make the regularizing and equalizing of our collective dreamlife possible,"[7] Miller tells us—that is, to further falsify it. This extended falsification, an interpretive reversal and inversion of the traditional order of cause and effect, unties the "knots" of which we seem to be constructed. Nietzsche's chief strategy in this elaborate undermining of traditional human ontology is to undo the idea of the will itself, as Miller further suggests, disconnecting will from intentionality or causality and "returning" it to the status of force or drive, unknown and unknowable. Thus language, as the catalyst for any autoaesthetics, is at the same time its jailer, the ultimate (human) displacement.

But in terms of strategic Nietzschean self-declaration, understood as containing its own impossibility, such a displacement is also a gainful substantiation. It is in this final reversal that Nietzschean autoaesthetics takes place, providing us with a strategy for reading a compelling contemporary view of what it is to be human. Nietzsche offers no less, though the path to this strategy is dogged by metaphorical distancing and overlayering. The movement away from the convergence of language on any utility of meaning and toward the openness of dispersive metaphoric tension is, as Nietzsche repeatedly suggests, the closest we can come, bound by the limits of consciousness and the reductive need to communicate in our discourse, to the exercise of free will. Consciousness itself, so to speak, is never self-consciousness but, as Gilles Deleuze says, "the consciousness of an ego in relation to a self which is not itself conscious"(39).[8] Yet here, of course, Deleuze articulates the disturbing non-identity of the Nietzschean self, which persists in trying to understand the implications of its having acknowledged cancelling out and reversing the traditionally static nature of language, at the same time asserting (and also questioning) its dynamics.

Nietzsche models and (ironically) structures this displacement on the adoption of a trinity of terms, the existence and thematics of which must come under the same scrutiny as all other discourse in the Nietzschean mode, within the chimerical Dionysian context.[9] Nietzsche's central terms, Overman, Eternal Return, and Will to Power, are modelled on (Dionysian versions of) the Father, Son, and Holy Spirit just as powerfully as Nietzsche himself modelled his own (dis)course through language and life on "the Crucified."[10] At the same time, as a result of their disruptive ground, his terms are a categorical denial of the ordinary place of these terms.

In Nietzsche's topography of the self, this placement/displacement is an energizing rather than a dissipation. It is precisely in this syntactical gathering of forces, emblemized in the *active* triangulation of his key terms, that the chimerical Nietzschean self moves toward emergence. That triangulation requires further exploration, in light of the theme of self-fabrication. As Nietzsche points out, triangulations are everywhere in our tradition. For Nietzsche, the world of human becoming is a play of tensions,[11] resultant from the displacement that characterizes all incipient meaning. Nietzschean triangulation is therefore not that found, for example, in Girard's *Deceit, Desire, and the Novel*, in which the object of desire is displaced by another, in a narrative setting, in order that the desirer may have a surrogate object through which to deal with that desire.[12] Nor does it have to do with the sort of Freudian surrogation that finds objects for desires that displace the "real" (albeit concealed) object to assuage desire or to make it palatable.[13] Triangulation in the texts of Nietzsche, and in those of some writers who take it up, consciously or not, before and after him, does not place *objects* in a relationship but *dis*places the objects entirely: Nietzschean triangulation is a play of forces, not of objects.[14] Nietzsche sees the thinker—and the poetic artist—as a juggler; for him, however, the juggler does not have three *objects* with which to create his theatrical effect but myriad *movements* or forces.[15] Nietzsche's trinity, his triangulation of forces, is one in which, while the flow of displacement is privileged, displacement itself as a term is displaced; in which the possibility of stasis on the page or on the mind's page is an impossible fiction; and in which the so-called object—which after Nietzsche includes also the "subject," as he declares first in "On Truth and Lies in a Nonmoral Sense"—is always moving and transmuting, metamorphosing and metaphorizing, so that a structuration made up of the shifters called "objects" (including words) radically slips out of the relationships providing what Nietzsche attacks as "metaphysical comfort," becoming in the process a subversion of the very process by which they are articulated.

For Nietzsche, then, objects-in-language, including concrete or abstract ideas of the self, are always chimerical. This is what Poststructuralism means by the object *mise en abîme*, divorced from comfortable and static definition. The abyss into which meaning is thrown is literally that: bottomless, dimensionless, wholly open; Nietzsche's abysmal language is a *return* (an Eternal Return) to Hellenic plenitude or "creative chaos."[16] The Nietzschean Will, and what Michel Haar calls "its need for a demonstration of the continuous growth of its power,"[17] provides a new definition of "Nietzsche's concept of *chaos* also—it is 'Proteus,' the 'primordial *indetermination* of the Will of Power.'"[18] Nietzschean chaos is, however, according to Haar, "not at all disorder, but rather the multiplicity of impulses, the entire horizon of forces, within which knowledge and art are to delineate their perspectives."[19] Any safe or rigid equivalency of word and thing, word and single concept, is cancelled. No longer do "things" (including things like "me") "mean" as they have appeared to.

In other words, the play among Nietzsche's central terms invents a new way to see oneself. As in Nietzsche, the terms in which this inquiry is couched are nourished by that rift, what Derrida calls the "interval,"[20] between so-called things and so-called meaning, in Nietzsche's energizing and enervating displacement into and through language. The very terms in which my project declares itself, "articulation," *étrangeté*, and "self" or "power," are functions of this word-play interval. Words, for Nietzsche, are always in a hermetic dialogue which we overhear, simultaneously reversing and affirming our expectations of them. His writing from "On Truth and Lies in a Nonmoral Sense" (which concerns this issue specifically) through *The Antichrist* demonstrates this preoccupation. Words for Nietzsche are refections, parabolic curves turning back on themselves ("Beware the *straight!*" Nietzsche warns us). But Nietzsche sees the sheer joy in this play; his rich working-out of those central (anti-)conceptual terms constantly insists on and endlessly rewards interrogation.

The purpose of my Nietzschean interrogation, then, is to explore a set of terms parallel to Nietzsche's, laid out as a shifting of thought about the nature of writing and the force of literature, as a strategic force of self-declaration in some contemporary literature. Nietzsche's inquiry and my own do not reject traditional meanings, do not even reject the idea of the importance of the localized closure of meaning, but rather throw them into their Dionysian (interrogative) context. The point is that a Nietzschean investigation never arrests itself at those meanings, which while co-opted and used no longer exercise any "final" or categorical power, an Apollinian construct (Apollinian fiction). Nietzsche's co-option of the paradigmatic traditional foundations of discourse *includes* the use of paradigmatic structures, such as trinities, shown so clearly and so repeatedly in *Thus Spoke Zarathustra*'s preoccupation with cabalistic or gnostic numbers, with prophetic tradition, with repetition as a function of structure, and with the (mock-)eschatological issue of *conclusion* itself.

But because of his multiple ironies, Nietzsche can still easily be misunderstood. Precisely because it is so easy to misunderstand Nietzsche's terms—and we are still freeing ourselves from the disastrous interpretations Nietzsche's sister[21] and the Third Reich anointed for them, and *their* repudiation by another generation of misinterpreters such as Heidegger—I want to open a new avenue of use for them—an avenue into an aesthetics of self-reflection, in order to be able to read a body of (Apollinian) literature through them. In translating Nietzsche's constellation of terms into another one, I try to maintain the subtle relationship in which these three terms move and interrelate, in palimpsestic echoes of Nietzsche's. *Die ewige Wiederkehr*, the Eternal Return, is echoed as "articulation"; the *Übermensch*,[22] so maligned, mistranslated, and misunderstood, receives a kind of existential apotheosis as *étrangeté*, itself an untranslatable *crossing-over* of the abyss of language and of meaning; and what I have called "the self," or "power," in what looks like a fairly straightforward way, is at the pole of Nietzsche's *Wille zur Macht*. But self/power is a becoming that is no more than what it can claim for itself; among the infinite things it can claim—*being*.

My own transference is at the heart of the Dionysian possibility, since whatever Nietzsche "meant" by his three central terms, he concealed that intention in richly metaphorical *Dichtungsprosa*. No record exists that anyone actually asked Nietzsche what the *Übermensch* meant, as many asked Beckett what *Godot* meant (Beckett's answer was always that if he had known he would have said); and Nietzsche *did* vouchsafe that he saw himself as the Dionysian melding of thinker and poet, requiring no explanation, revealed only in his concealment, as Alphonso Lingis asserts:

Nietzsche conceived of thought itself as an artistry. The world is full of beautiful things, but nonetheless poor, very poor in beautiful moments and beautiful revelations of these things. What is needed is to locate oneself at the right spot from which the summits can be seen gleaming through the mists and veils. Not a dissipation of those mists and veils . . . not an ordering, dominating as from a point of origin, but the very sense of chance, fragment, enigma; the surprised, fragmented, stupefied view held by the veils and surfaces.[23]

Taken in this metaphoric sense, the very act and surface of writing (of writing the self) *is*, in its very action, the full plenitude of Dionysian meaning, at once chimerical and magically substantial. This is a dangerous and beautiful idea, which Nietzsche perceived as being utterly liberating and energizing, defying the understanding and eluding (though courting) rational thought. Nietzsche's abysmal, Dionysian thought of Dionysian language is the transference of which the convocation of truly human forces consists, one of whose dimensions is its declaration, as in Lingis' comment above or in what we will see of Nietzsche's poetry. The tensions ranging through the multifarious strands of meaning interconnecting Nietzsche's central terms, like an ethereal spiderweb, produce the power of the self, which must always and which cannot be declared.

But this non-declaration, the elliptical working out of the web of terms on which Nietzsche builds and which so centrally identifies Nietzsche's most dramatic self-absorption, cannot withstand the transference into my terms without comment—to be read usefully, constellations require star charts. I cannot presume to claim Nietzsche's license in strategically neglecting to provide one; and lacking my own para-Zarathustra (which, however, my own writing aspires to become), my para-terms need some grounding, as follows.

ARTICULATION

In Arthur Danto's *Nietzsche as Philosopher*, a very compelling link between Nietzschean thought and analytic philosophy, he declares:

Eternal Recurrence is the idea that whatever there is will return again, and that whatever there is, *is* a return of itself, that it has all happened before, and will happen again, exactly in the same way each time, forever. Nothing happens that has not happened an infinite number of times and which will not happen again, for all eternity, in exact iterations of itself. There is no beginning and end, and no middle either to the story of the world; there is only the monotonous turning up always of the same episode, time and again.[24]

Danto goes on at length about this, quoting extensively from *Zarathustra* to show that Nietzsche is not being approximate, vague, nor obscure about this recurrence, but quite exact. No doubt there is a powerfully mystical element, as Danto and others report, about the so-called revelation of the Eternal Return to Nietzsche, "six thousand feet beyond man and time" near Sils Maria in August 1881; on the other hand, emphatically, this mystical and metaphysical element is balanced, as everything is in Nietzsche, by its metaphorical and declaratory other: *behind* the fairly obvious notion of cyclic return, an indigenous fertility notion (and therefore purely Dionysian), is the grounding idea of metaphoricity, literal and figurative, the transference of meaning/energy from one form (or word) to another. *This* is the basis of the Eternal Return—not that everything repeats itself in history but that everything is eternally doubled and redoubled in language— simultaneously. This not to say that, for Nietzsche, language is mimetic, providing a representation of what is rendered into discourse *à la* Plato, but that, as we have learned and re-learned many times since Nietzsche (but didn't quite know before him), inherent in language itself is the otherness, the *étrangeté*, by which discourse operates. A further element, the ethical or moral one (that is, the notion that certain metaphorical transferences are worthy of eternal repetition, within the context of the establishment of a self-power) will be explored in due course. The Parmenidean view of the Eternal Return, myopia intact, has carried through to many, indeed most, contemporary accounts of it.

Nietzsche's Eternal Return is often grotesquely misunderstood. Philosophers, critics, and theorists have, for example, debated whether Nietzsche "seriously" means by the Eternal Return that all events melt together in a pastless, futureless present in which all events repeat themselves endlessly and in which no distinction between what has been and what is to be can be validly made. Given Nietzsche's problematics of action as the foundation of the self, this static, enervated universe is emphatically not his. And yet here again, in the theme of (self-)articulation, Nietzsche recapitulates the first great *historical* conundrum of Western philosophy, one with which he was famously and obsessively concerned. In the great question of the nature of stasis and motion (in language, for example), both Heraclitus and Parmenides find their way into Nietzschean discourse: atemporality is just the kind of metaphysical trap Parmenides found himself in when he tried to refute Heraclitus' idea of flux; treatment of Nietzsche often collapses together the two polar positions and mixes them together in a comical, Jarry-esque cyclone. But Nietzsche's Eternal Return, borrowed from Heine[25] out of Pythagoras, Parmenides, Vico, and (negatively) Hegel's notion of the Bad Infinite, and transfigured in *The Gay Science*,[26] is of a different order. Nowhere else has Western philosophy seen the irony, the playfulness that Nietzsche infuses into the Eternal Return which, though it is as serious a concept as is imaginable, is still perpetually at play with its own articulation, "the Dionysian faith."[27] From its first recording as such in

The Gay Science (its declaration formed the concluding two sections of the first edition of that book), the Eternal Return is associated with overabundance and madness—with the Dionysian, and of course with the very formulation of the self. We must remember that Nietzsche chose to introduce the Eternal Return in a section of *The Gay Science* entitled "Sanctus Januarius," in which he sees himself as the legendary saint whose blood re-liquifies on a particular feast day (the Dionysia?), indicating that Nietzsche himself felt him*self* re-animated through the "Dionysian faith" he had in the Eternal Return. In the penultimate section of Book Four we find a "demon" telling us (Nietzsche works, in this section as in so many others, in the second person) that "the eternal hourglass of existence is turned upside down again and again," and us with it. From this section alone, one might suppose that Nietzsche sees a straightforward Viconian circularity in the temporal, albeit at the level of macro-experience. But by the end of the section, the devil, the Dionysian messenger, has explained in much clearer detail what "the greatest weight" (*Das grösste Schwergewicht*), which is the process of this hourglass inversion, introduces. This further explanation leaves no doubt that Nietzsche's parabolic and parodic intent is to take that Dionysian leap of faith, to re-metaphorize his proceedings:

> The question in each and every thing, "Do you desire this once more and innumerable times more?" would lie upon your actions as the greatest weight. Or how well disposed would you have to become to yourself and to life *to crave nothing more fervently* than this ultimate eternal confirmation and seal?

At just this point, with the introduction of Zarathustra into the text, Nietzsche floats out of the historical terms in which the Eternal Return has appeared and transmutes the issue into one of ethico-aesthetics: the moment *worthy* of eternal repetition is the moment of the advent of the Eternal Return; the criteria for that worthiness are determined by the power of transference itself, by Dionysian faith, as autoaesthetic articulation.

Articulation presents, engages, and declares the presentation and the reversal in which words are always engaged. Nietzsche perceives this ironic tendency as inherent in language, throughout history. He discusses it in terms of Homer's *agon*, part of which is the joy and fear of articulating a/the *epos*; when Aristotle encourages the rhetorical use of language to articulate a goal and a strategy for reaching it, he makes good Nietzschean sense. These are indeed ways in which "articulation" is generally and correctly, according to Nietzsche, used, although in its simplest and most straightforward sense articulation means speaking (or, secondarily, writing) about. But we must, he says, be forced along with Homer, Aristotle, and Hegel to see and acknowledge not solely the Platonic serenity and stability *behind* this definition, both of the spoken word's primacy and of an idealized view of both communication and *idea*, of a "mind" seeking out and finding another "mind," the very play of words itself. Nietzschean articulation is both joining and division, "straight talk" and radical deviation, not only a spoken sound but also the way sounds as things relate and are juxtaposed, the *idea* of such a juxtaposition, and naturally the link between the spoken word, the written word, and their stable/unstable systematics of joining and difference, association and dissociation. Though it sometimes seems as though this issue is settled, of course it isn't: the questioning of the primacy of speech begun by Nietzsche and most dramatically foregrounded in our time by Derrida remains, for the majority of the academic establishment and the public at large, an unacceptable deviation from humanistic norms, and Nietzsche a nihilist. In some respect, Nietzschean articulation inhabits straightforward philosophic terrain, as the very principle of association and dissociation.[28] To articulate *at all* in the way Nietzsche suggests is to acknowledge the syntactic tensions that both produce and prevent what we conveniently call communication. This great Nietzschean legacy is visible, ensconced in pervasive Nietzschean perspective, as Derrida opens his discussion of the language-place, quoting Saussure in Part I of *Of Grammatology* on the notion of articulation:

> The question of the vocal apparatus obviously takes a secondary place in the problem of language. One definition of *articulated* language might confirm that conclusion. In Latin, *articulus* means a member, part, or subdivision in a series. . . . Using the second definition, we can say that *what is natural to mankind is not spoken language* but the faculty of constructing a language; i.e. a system of distinct signs corresponding to distinct ideas.[29]

It is out of this opening, a declaration of what is *natural* (that is, here, Dionysian) to man, that Derrida initiates the discussion of the *trace*, out of what Gayatri Spivak calls "Nietzsche's pervasive strategy of intersubstituting opposites."[30] Articulation is herein not merely a system of closings, of definitions, but, as we shall see in the final section of this book, of openings, a dialectical Eternal Return. The *trace* as laid out by Derrida is the eternal echo of articulation, inherent within articulation itself—the phoneme and grapheme resonating within itself, from its re-articulated *nature*.

But even more provocatively for Nietzsche, as we see in Derrida's treatment of the Nietzschean theme, articulation is a joint between different parts, a *fold*.[31] This is Nietzsche's own word, from the Preface to *The Gay Science*, in that remarkable passage, through which I will work at length in chapter 3, which begins

Oh, those Greeks! They knew how to live. What is required for that is to stop courageously at the surface, the fold, the skin, to adore appearance . . . .[32]

This most literary of metaphors, addressing the codex of the self, is at the center of Nietzsche's strategy of self-declaration. Nietzsche does not mean merely that we tell stories about ourselves, fabricating an idea of self out of these epic narratives (though that is part of the nature of the fold), but that the very *thought* of the self, the abysmal thought that underpins all narrative, itself consists of this fold of articulation, a textualizing fracture. This opening out of textuality, for philosophy and for literature/poetry (these, working in tandem and fulfilling each other's aims, constitute the *gaya scienza*), as articulated by Nietzsche, provides a context for a/the reading of literary, psychoanalytic, and philosophical texts. Nietzsche declares that texts submit to this self-interrogation willfully or not, and that the most convergent, un-interrogative of texts finally must be seen in light of these strategies of self-formulation and textualization. He sees articulation, then, as a folding and a tearing, implicated in the initiatory formation and substantiation of a sense of self, which originarily creates and divides flesh and spirit. Michel Haar tells us that Nietzschean language is "a machine fabricating false identities,"[33] "explosions" of "metaphorical transpositions (so primeval that they are always forgotten)." Haar's comment occurs within the context of the Nietzschean sense of forgetting, in which R. J. Hollingdale points out that the "key" to Greece and the answer to the greater question, "What is real?" lies in the concept of *agon* born out of Nietzschean articulation, the fundamental motivating force; Nietzsche saw himself as the recreator—the re-articulator—of this force,[34] which he had (re)discovered in Heraclitus. Only in Nietzsche do we see revealed what is inherent in Heraclitus, that flux is not only chronological and metaphysical but dialectical as well—not only a flowing "river" of divergences but a contest of dialectical differentiation. This strife of eternal contestation, Nietzsche's key to understanding the nature of articulation, is born out of the *metaphor* of Heraclitan warfare, of which the world is constructed:

> The strife of opposites gives birth to all that comes to be; the definite qualities which look permanent to us express but the momentary ascendancy of one partner . . . . Everything that happens, happens in accordance with this strife.[35]

Dionysian strife places language, the cornucopian cradle of the self, in a new relation to the world. The escape from (or abrogation of) metaphysics, like the entirety of Nietzsche's project, occurs in the giddy and impossible realm of ubiquitous reversals and contradictions inherent in autoaesthetic articulation. All assertions contradict themselves; for example, what is employed to cancel metaphysics is itself metaphysical. Nietzsche's comment in *Twilight of the Idols* that we continue to believe in God because we have not lost our faith in grammar attests to this reversal. Articulation can declare its own nature into existence, just as it can declare that its own nature cannot (and can only) be declared. Nietzsche's strategy of articulation is inductive, presenting specificity *before* generalization. This is evidence of the poet (= *gaya*) in him, the writer for whom the image engenders the idea, and at the same time the *eiron* mocking the inner philosopher, the man of science who sees evidence and generalizes from that to the *abgrund*.[36] *Zarathustra*'s message, for example, is articulated in such parabolic terms that it must finally remain invisible until one sees him come out of his cave for the final time (though that egress will ostensibly be repeated infinitely), eager yet again to bless the day, his disciples at the ready, aware and yet utterly unaware that he himself has only begun to learn about discursive self-reflection by coming down into the world and language of men—his message has not been any more nor less articulated than any other's: however much Zarathustra believes that he has achieved the heights, his lesson is that the *Übermensch* cannot come down to the *mensch*—and can do nothing else; cannot be the physical manifestation of his *articulated* ideals—but can be nothing else; that it exists only in the articulation that forms it and by which he forms himself. This becomes more urgent in that, like a Platonic dialogue, *Zarathustra* is to be read but is to be *heard* at the same time; it relies on its *folding* of speech around the axis of writing, its poetic condensation assembling, disassembling, and dissembling out into a mock-spoken discourse that behaves like an Old Testament prophet-tale but that is rhetorically encoded as a written narrative, compact, harmonious, and opaque.

Nietzsche aspires, in the wealth of his strategies for writing, to an assimilation of the breadth of possibilities for rhetorical structure. Though he does on several occasions employ Aristotelian deduction (as in the three surprisingly conventional essays that comprise *On the Genealogy of Morals*), Nietzsche's induction is a vital part of his self-exploration.[37] Articulation is not affected by this format: the reversal inherent in language operates despite the format by which it is ordered. It seems impossible to read Nietzsche without wanting to imitate his play with the forms of discourse, his mixing of forms, and his reinvention of them. He shows that it is not only permissible to think and write aphoristically, but that we capture *most* about ourselves when we do so. Every writer, Nietzsche argues, knowingly or unknowingly walks the tightrope over the abyss in his search for self, his tightrope stretched between obfuscation and the obvious, between an urge to innovate and an urge to suppress the urge to let it have full rein.[38]

Here, at the core of his teaching, Nietzsche acknowledges his debts. In his analysis of its most famous usage in *Thus Spoke Zarathustra*, Nietzsche declares that the doctrine of the "Eternal Return," that is of the unconditional and infinitely repeated circulation of all things—this doctrine of Zarathustra *might* in the end have been taught already even by Heraclitus.[39]

I will develop these Heraclitan connections at greater length in chapter 9; my intention here is to show the acknowledgment of priority Nietzsche accords to Heraclitus, a first hint of the wealth of inter-textuality Nietzsche deposits in this central concept. It is vital to remember in this regard that what Heraclitus teaches, in his concept of constant flux, is not nihilism and not devaluation but constant and unremitting revaluation, a condition of eternal (aesthetic) *judgment*, on which Zarathustra capitalizes in *his* assessment of this concept. Having acknowledged the antecedence of Heraclitus' complex legacy, Nietzsche continues his exploration of the Eternal Return, as introduced in *The Gay Science*, in Part Three of *Zarathustra*, in one of the pivotal sections of that pivotal text, "On the Vision and the Riddle."[40] The effort and force of Eternal Return is to evaluate each moment in order to find, or at least to search for, a moment *worthy* of eternal repetition.[41] But here the Nietzschean triangulation that never permits meaning to arrive is at work again: any understanding of the idea of the Eternal Return is to be had through a fuller understanding of the *Übermensch* and the forces that bind and enfold (*articulate*) it.[42] Only in an appreciation of the *Übermensch* does Eternal Return have weight; without the Overman it is merely *ressentiment*. Thus valuation is always cross-valuation; Nietzsche sets up conditions for evaluation and for revaluation that themselves must constantly undergo (as in Zarathustra's *untergehen*) the scrutiny that will make them, though never constant, at least abundantly significant.

ETRANGETÉ

In one's growing perception of the magnetic connections among Nietzsche's central terms, one also sees the strategic development, the additive and cumulative energy, of the (de)construction Nietzsche makes of the self. His terminology is a key to this spiraling upward of self-discovery, self-creation, and autoaesthetic self-articulation, which forms the basis of human life lived at its best and to its fullest. Understanding the fundamental nature of articulation for human life, Nietzsche begins to develop the purely metaphorical idea (though it is much more than an idea—it is the action of metaphoricity) of the *Übermensch*. This Overman is pure otherness, pure transcendent difference, and therefore always chimerically absent from, but free to be universally present in, Nietzschean self-creation. The ideal self, which is, provocatively, potentially human as well, establishes the highest goal for humankind, but always estranged, absent, and distant, mirage-like. Ironically, we know this because Nietzsche declares the *Übermensch* so emphatically in his central texts; once he has begun to define it, the Overman lies at the center of Nietzsche's energy in all his remaining works. Beyond its energy of self-declaration, the Overman is a strategy of distancing from mundanity, from aspiration. As much as it may seem to desire the static, it avoids change by manifesting the uncanniness of pure change. The Overman is the principle of poetic license, aesthetic distance; it is the Ideal Other, pure *étrangeté*.[43] In positing the Overman, Nietzsche shows the articulate artist the second part of the drive necessary for creativity and therefore for life. And like *ressentiment*, that gnawing resentment that Nietzsche assiduously referred to only in French, my insistence here on the strangeness of *étrangeté* echoes and manifests that cosmopolitanism that made Nietzsche a stranger to German Idealism, philology, and philosophy, first professionally, then philosophically, then polemically. *Etrangeté* is, in my usage of it, a very specific term with a very specific locus of meaning not to be found in—or out of—translation. It is the chimerical position in which the writer writes, the position of the text relative to the writer (who is then a reader like all others), and it is the position of the text relative to the *écriture* of self of which the text consists and out of which the text is fabricated. Although it is wrong (and tendentious) to say that such words as *ressentiment*, *force*, and *étrangeté* are untranslatable, it is equally wrong to say that much is not changed when they are translated; for example, Gilles Deleuze's *force* is not ours: to translate (French) *force* as (English) "force" is to lose its more disturbing and invasive overtones of physical interference (including rape) and dynamism, as opposed to its more abstract or generalized English meaning. My use of *étrangeté* is an attempt to maintain the invasive, Dionysian *force* of articulation. Nietzsche's own strong, life-long sense of isolation, and of the more general *issue* of "outsideness" and "insideness," on which Derrida so tellingly picks up in his considerations of the *parergon* and, earlier, the *hors d'oeuvre*—that which is related or connected to but supposedly outside the text, whatever they both might be—is brought to bear in this "foreignness," "outsideness," "strangeness." None of these single definitions is identical with any other; but the phenomenon of *étrangeté*, desire for inclusion and the inherent "distance"—the metaphoricity without metaphor—of writing, becomes with Nietzsche the acknowledgment and the situation of the writer *when writing* and *when being written*.[44] *Etrangeté* is at once an ensconcing and an aftermath, algorithms of space and time. The final distancing of human intelligence, of the aesthetic and critical self-fashioning of which our lives consist at their clearest, is that *étrangeté* could only be "understood," to echo Nietzsche's own fundamental worry, by the *Übermensch*.

The fact that the *Übermensch* is impossible even while always emergent is a function of its (and our) *étrangeté*. As Nietzsche develops the concept of the Overman, particularly through Zarathustra's (eternally) repeated going under, a descent into the mundane corporeal world, he shows us that the achievement of the Overman is a question of what he calls the *Überwindungsmotif*, the action of overcoming, and its necessary corollary, *Selbstüberwindung* or *Selbstaufhebung*, the self-overcoming that is the requisite for any part of that discovery.[45] It is up to us to interpret what this self-overcoming consists of. My contention is that Nietzsche's sense of this phenomenon is that of what Derrida will later (out of Nietzsche) call the *relevé*, a heavily ironized version of *aufhebung*. That is to say, when Nietzsche urges us to overcome ourselves, he means that we come to see ourselves as a function of eternally defining metaphoric tensions. His view, developed from his earliest essays, is that *Homo sapiens* has no relevance if it does not incorporate its life into the language of which it is constructed—not the other way around.[46] This construction *in* language, adumbrated in "On Truth and Lies in a Nonmoral Sense" and continuing forward through the famous section of *Twilight of the Idols* cited above, as well as throughout *Ecce Homo*, is a self-construction which also self-deconstructs. It is a suspension of self—truly a self-overcoming—we attempt to *overcome* ourselves in order to *be* ourselves; growing out of Heraclitan ambiguity and the radical displacement of the *thing*, our non-artist selves are undermined and made chimerical by these Nietzschean semiotics of proximity and distance.

Our (and Nietzsche's own) relation to the Overman is itself *étrangeté*. In this respect, the Overman is an emblem of the Lacanian Full Word, the "final" (that is, chimerical) statement of the Self after which nothing more need be said.[47] The strategy of *étrangeté* is an overcoming of banality[48] and at the same time an aknowledgment of our capitulation into the habits of speech, writing, and life that frame, define, delimit, and preclude originality, which is always *other*.

But the Overman *can* exist, according to Nietzsche. It can be reified in the *articulation* with which it is created in writing, by the poet-philosopher, even though it is not and cannot be fleshly nor wordly. That he cannot *be* the Overman causes Nietzsche to posit a new interpretation of the Fall ("falling short") which must always be his lot. The descent into life and death is at the same time, in Nietzschean eschatology, the Fall. Just as Zarathustra *goes down* from his mountain top, and just as the tightrope walker falls from his rope out of narrative *into* life (and thus into death), mankind ineluctably imitates the fall of the *Übermensch* into writing. The nature of *étrangeté* is such that it persists in and underlies all writing and the crossing-over of articulation/folding inherent in what amounts to the general human grammatology. The Overman is not writing itself but a mimesis of its substance and its master, one of its myriad potentialities. The conundrum of the Overman as Nietzsche perceives it, like that of *étrangeté*, is that crossroads, the *carrefour* at which Nietzsche works, and over which he worries until it yields its most contentious forces. This is the autoaesthetic process, the crossroads of a set of tendentious vectors on which we travel and of which we are more or less aware.

Indeed, Derrida's positing of *différance*, as for example in his interview with Henri Ronse in *Positions*, provides the opening for *étrangeté*. Ronse references Derrida's essay "Force and Signification" in *Writing and Difference* and points out that it is *différance* that led Derrida "back to Nietzsche (who linked the concept of force to the irreducibility of differences)."[49] But we are all "led back to Nietzsche" when we perceive the grounding nature of *étrangeté*, through articulation, in an autoaesthetic strategy. Ofelia Shutte approaches this idea in her discussion of "Nietzsche's Critique of Metaphysics,"[50] in which she sees Nietzsche as offering an antidote to the "ego-world disjunction" in the form of the *positive* and *continuous* experience of becoming in the world, which leads us back to Nietzsche's will-to-power.[51] Shutte interprets Nietzsche as saying that "in the world of becoming there is no such thing as a detached self," that the "self is rooted in a world which, like the self, consists of a play of forces" (47). The advantage of this position, particularly in light of Gilles Deleuze's sense of force, is that it can allow us to see Nietzsche's will to power as a play of life-forces, a metaphor for vitality; the disadvantage of Shutte's position is that it does not take into account Nietzsche's own comments on the subject; on the nature of subjectivity and on the nature of subject as a function of writing. For example, in "On Truth and Lies in a Nonmoral Sense" Nietzsche claims that

> between two absolutely different spheres, as between subject and object, there is no causality, no correctness, and no expression; there is, at most, an *aesthetic* relation, I mean, a suggestive transference, a stammering translation into a completely foreign tongue.[52]

Subject is itself a function of the language in which it is declared. As though anticipating Heidegger's (mis)interpretation, Nietzsche then declares in *On the Genealogy of Morals* that "there is no 'being' behind doing; effecting, becoming; the 'doer' is merely a fiction added to the deed."[53] Deeds are always at a distance from our autoaesthetics of interpretation; efforts to "re-attach" the self to the world must always fail because of the Zarathustran path toward life's dilemma of *ironic* self-discovery. For Nietzsche/Zarathustra, this is the process of advancing toward becoming the loneliest man, then man who perceives the Overman as the solution to his own conundrum of clarification.

That the Overman is pure *étrangeté* is not to say, as Shutte does, that mankind, nor indeed the highest goal of mankind, represented by the

Overman, is merely *alien*. Alienation occurs relative to something, to a fixed point of reference.[54] Alienation can orient itself relative to religious, social, or philosophical systems or it can manifest itself as a function of individuals. Alienation is always pejorative, a condition of undesirability: alienation, as Sartre says, is condemnation. This introduces a central aspect of *étrangeté* in the strategy of Nietzschean autoaesthetics: it is a judgment. But *étrangeté* is not Sartrean condemnation; it is a position of power *because* of its distance, and it contains all of and only the relationality of alienation.[55] The *unheimlich*, like the *étrange*, must always be simultaneously self-sufficient, contained, *and* other. Claude Levèsque's discussion of this phenomenon shows that

> this outside-thought would be essentially a thought about the limit and transgression of the limit, a thought at the limit of thought. More affirmative than negative, it would go overwhelmingly toward affirmation. . . . Thought of *étrangeté* not negative.[56]

Levèsque links this Nietzschean discussion to the issue at hand directly through "son article intitulé *Das Unheimliche* (L'inquiétante *étrangeté*),"[57] which he incorporates into his claim that

> in the disturbing *étrangeté* the "originary" *différance* is affirmed in whose interior unfolds our gestures, all of our acts, and even the possibility of our language.[58]

Indeed, the discussion reveals itself as being of "la dangéreuse ambivalence lexicale de l'*Unheimlich*,"[59] the "original repetition." Levèsque points out that for Nietzsche, as for Blanchot, the "same" is not the identical, the Eternal Return is not a return to the same. To be consigned to language, according to Blanchot (out of Nietzsche), is to "répète ce qui n'a pas lieu, n'aura pas lieu, n'a pas eu lieu" (repeat what does not take place, will not take place, and has not taken place) (108–109).[60] *Etrangeté* reveals itself as the condition of the neutral and strange as well as the "other," of the displacement marked out by the radically *positive* force of language, linked to "death" but only to affirm "life."

SELF/POWER

Through the complex agency of articulation, with the impossible goal of the *Übermensch* before us, our chart of Nietzschean autoaesthetics grows. Though his poetico-philosophy remains obdurately apolitical, its teleology is clear. Nietzsche is centrally concerned about that final goal: self-creation. Once one has perceived one's textual nature and its ramifications, one is poised at the threshold of self-declarative power. This threshold is akin to that at the brink of consciousness, the Dionysian crossing-over from the unconscious into the ego-state. Thus, power never "arrives"; the self is a function of repression and sublimation. In his language of self-creation, Nietzsche subverts his own *telos*.

Michel Foucault's idea of power is instructive in forming an understanding of autoaesthetics: Foucault's interpretation of this particularly Nietzschean idea of power takes its discursive impetus from the *étrangeté* we have been examining. Foucault, like Nietzsche, perceives the *naiveté* of what we call knowledge, but since for Foucault all power is dialectical (and ironically more political than Nietzsche's, though Foucault wants to go beyond "simple" Hegelian or Marxist dialectics), its relationality gives it a greater and more direct social component than Nietzsche's more rigorous and more solipsistic investigation. Like Nietzsche, Foucault derives his power from his style, rather than from the rigorous argument or logical structural of traditional philosophic discourse. Foucault's discourse about discourses is (de)structured on a principle of free play, controlled only by the consistency of his (often) elegant style and forceful rhetoric.

Unlike Nietzsche, however, Foucault is not concerned with an abiding notion of the self.[61] His discourses, as Hayden White points out, "begin in paradox and end in negative apocalypse,"[62] but his is an apocalypse that arises in the purely "tropological space" in which language manifests an absolute vacancy of being. Despite his sense of enervation redeemed only by style, Foucault has a very "positive" sense of power, which is always power *over*. Power over others, over goods, over cultural structures, and finally over authoritative discourse itself is, for Foucault, the desire for power and the power of desire.

Yet, for Nietzsche, the autoaesthetic power of *étrangeté* is also indeed *beyond* desire, the force behind the force[63] of *étrangeté*. Power is that which accrues from an understanding of the force of articulation and of *étrangeté*. In this Nietzschean sense, it is the impetus toward proper understanding and implementation of *étrangeté* in articulation; it has nothing to do with domination, everything to do with relation and hierarchization. Power is the internal relation of the so-called writer to the so-called text, of text to writing, of writing to the possibilities of its exegesis. At each level, something is *withheld* and cannot cross over; in this withholding occurs the inception of power, working as an accumulation of understanding and a boundary of identity: it permits the crossing over, however incomplete, that forms the relations between writing and interpreting, word and metaphor. It is, as Alphonso Lingis points out,

> the force behind all forms. . . . It is not an essence; it is neither structure, *telos*, nor meaning, but continual sublation of all *telos*, transgression of all ends, production of all concordant and contradictory meanings, interpretations, valuations. It is the chaos, the primal fund of the unformed—

not matter, but force beneath the cosmos, which precedes the forms and makes them possible as well as transitory.[64]

Echoing both Deleuze's *force* and Derrida's *différance*, Lingis points to the dialectical impetus of the will-to-power. Indeed, Lingis goes on to emphasize this grounding (what I would call culminative) nature of the will-to-power, which is therefore simultaneously "plural."[65] That is, will-to-power is differential and distinctive, not a comprehension nor co-option of *étrangeté* but its affirmation and implementation. When Nietzsche describes this ultimate force, he does so in its own terms, introducing (the differentiation of) metaphor into it at the very point of signification. He does so in an extensive section of Book Four of *The Gay Science* which conflates metaphor, self-awareness, self-overcoming and *étrangeté*, a section so rich and dense that it deserves quotation in full:

> *Excelsior!*—You will never pray again, never adore again, never again rest in endless trust: you do not permit yourself to stop before any ultimate wisdom, ultimate good, ultimate power, while unharnessing your thoughts: you have no perpetual guardian and friend for your seven solitudes—you live without a view of mountains with snow on their peaks and fire in their hearts—there is no avenger for you any more nor any final improver; there is no longer any reason in what happens, no love in what will happen to you; no resting place is open any longer in your heart, where it only needs to find and no longer to seek; you resist any ultimate peace; you will the Eternal Return of war and peace; man of renunciation, all this you wish to renounce? Who will give you the strength for that? Nobody yet has had this strength! There is a lake that one day ceased to permit itself to flow off; it formed a dam where it had hitherto flowed[66] off; and ever since this lake is rising higher and higher. Perhaps this very renunciation will also lend us the strength needed to bear this renunciation; perhaps man will rise ever higher as soon as he ceases to *flow out* into a god.[67]

Like the lake rising out of its sedentary nature, properly self-reflexive *Homo sapiens* must autoaestheticize, rising out of its imprisonment in dogmatic (for example, religious and conventionally metaphysical) thought. No longer can we count on the "metaphysical comfort" in which we have languished (and in which we have found only the comfort of *ressentiment*). When we deny this tyranny and assert our own power, we move toward rebirth in another dimension. Not only does this emblematic section rely on the will-to-power-as-transference to achieve itself, and not only does it declare the solitude and separation in which this condition can be born and understood (it also contains the first use of "eternal return"). Movement toward the solitariness of the Overman is also toward an understanding of the evaluation within which he is manifest. Will-to-power is not power, for Nietzsche. The tendentiousness of the *Wille zur Macht* sets up the conditions of desire within which the poet operates. Nietzsche here refers to the perpetuity of difference and of the *Entsagung*, the renunciation which facilitates such a fundamental struggle. In this renunciation, this withholding, are the concentration and accumulation that form writing's power. It is in metaphor that "power draws its ultimate consequences at every moment (Macht in jedem Augenblicke ihre letzte Consequenz zieht)."[68] Inherent in renunciation, metaphoric distance, and their "ultimate consequences" are the revaluation and the critique of which Nietzsche's writing consists.

This ironic and solipsistic power of detachment[69] provides the ground for all of Nietzsche's operations of language and, according to him, for that of *all* language-fabricators (*poiētēs*). This autoaesthetic triangulation, an elemental cluster of discursive forces, is the impetus for *their* operations as well. Nietzsche's sense of the growth to a sense of self, through his tangential triangulation, provides armament for life. Having established this schema, I want to repress it, to sublimate Nietzsche's trinity of terms and my own "below" the surface of *this* text, and to allow them to surface only intermittently, deprivileged intruders on the autoaesthetic scene of reading.

For example, these and other trinities lurk "below" or "behind" the story of Julien Sorel, the quintessential proto-*Übermensch-manquée*; Stendhal intuits them as setting the stage for the powerful but disastrously unsuccessful conclusions the fictions of self-identity can produce. Julien's *histoire* is an apt embarkation toward an exploration of a covert Nietzschean autoaesthetic.

2

◆

La Métaphysique du soi: Julien Sorel's Echoing Voices

My first solution: Dionysian wisdom. Joy in the destruction of the most noble and at the sight of its progressive ruin: in reality joy in what is coming and lies in the future, which triumphs over existing things, however good. Dionysian: temporary identification with the principle of life (including the voluptuousness of the martyr).

—Nietzsche, *Will to Power*, 417

We find at the base of sincerity a continual game of mirror and reflection, a perpetual passage from the being which is what it is to the being which is not what it is and inversely from the being which is not what it is to the being which is what it is. . . . Bad faith is possible only because sincerity is conscious of missing its goal inevitably, due to its very nature.

—Jean-Paul Sartre, *Being and Nothingness*, 66

Différence engendre haine.[1]

—Stendhal, *Le Rouge et le noir*, 203[2]

Although first published in 1831, thirteen years before Nietzsche's birth, *Red and Black* is a novel about Dionysian distances and the many ideas of

35

difference within the (proto-)Dionysian; it is about voices, about hearing and not hearing them, and about the way in which the ear produces and distorts the voices from which (an) accurate and powerful self-reflection might be constructed. Although they are often palimpsests of a dead past and a moribund future, these voices nonetheless offer the only possible opportunity for self-constitution available to the latent self. Stendhal's novel makes of these voices, with all of their inherently insoluble problems for protagonist and reader alike, nothing less than a metaphysical construction designed as a potential formation of a sense of identity adequate to deal with—indeed, to survive in—the world. Julien Sorel is throughout the novel concerned, obsessed, with who he is both for himself and in order to ratify that sense in the world around him. He is an aspiring noble in the ruin of nobility, to paraphrase Nietzsche's epigram, and a man of the and our future. To accomplish both of these goals, Julien relies on a series of chimerical voices to guide and strengthen him, and to provide him (and us) with a means of interpreting him. We must turn to these voices, of fathers and of authority figures, of mentors and anti-mentors, and the impossible, Dionysian voices of feeling itself, to understand Julien's trajectory and his martyrdom.

In like fashion we ourselves, as readers, interpreters, inheritors of the paradigms of self-identification through which Julien goes in the novel, must *add* voices, our own and those of other interpreters to whom *we* have listened, to Julien's in order to understand and assess *his* plight and resolution. Like our own, Julien's voices are impossibly disparate, brittle, and unreliable, and at the same time exercise a terrible power—they are voices within Julien's own fictive narrative; as a result, the critical response within the novel, which for Julien comes from "outside," like that which is at work in the surface of the narrative, is diverse beyond our ability to homogenize it. Voices, for Julien as for us, are the voice of difference.

It is in this recognition of the primacy of voices and their chimerical homogeneity that we recognize Julien as a prototype of the Nietzschean man; only as Julien recognizes the necessary error of his dependence on these voices to cover over the sense of etiolation he experiences in the world, and so ends his dialogue with it, does he emerge into what we might call the modern world from the Romantic one. In this tension of (self-)reflective surfaces, in the echoes of the active yet static forces of language, the novel achieves and retains its currency and its power.

This *différence*, the linguistic ground of *étrangeté*, acts in a positive fashion on the text, in several ways. It acknowledges and deepens the diversity of the levels of discourse apparent in *Red and Black* and causes a cross-fertilization of extraordinary intricacy. By virtue of its enigmatic surface, superstructure, and sub-structure, the novel's ambiguity produces a theoretical matrix of vast, potentially unlimited, proportion. At the same time it goes on acknowledging its remarkably disparate elements. In this respect, the multilevel interpretive possibilities of the text and the many voices that can be and have been applied to it act as *openers* to a further, meta-textual investigation, in which that diversity itself, as *différence* and as *différance*, becomes a central textual strategy. Julien's voices, both his own diverse ones and those to which he listens, break up the surface of the novel, at the same time disguising themselves as integral parts of Julien's (hi)story. By the same strategy as Stendhal's in the novel, the reader/interpreter is both free and constrained to apply his or her own voices to the text. In fact, and uncomfortably for any orthodox or singular critical approach, the more diverse these voices the greater the interpretive yield. Thus does Stendhal, like Nietzsche, undermine the very nature of critical response and the idea of the singular subject. The anti-orthodoxy Stendhal employs to create the mirage of grounding that plagues (even while it creates) Julien can fruitfully cross over into the actual experience of reading Julien's narrative, in an exercise of imitative form. My strategy here will echo Stendhal's/Julien's: to apply disparate voices to the chimera of a text,[3] make it reveal this other level of discourse, and show in a new light a central strategy of Julien Sorel's Dionysian autoaesthetic, in which we perceive that, as Hillis Miller points out, there is no "entity of the self,"[4] that, rather, styles of language determine what we call the "self" and give it its power.

HEGIRA

Like the theoretical and critical perspectives within which Julien lives, the novel is pervaded by concern not just with the passive question of identity but with the active quest for it as the principle of life, with the establishment of a metaphysic of self which will finally seem, in some hypothetical future, to substantiate him and it. This action must finally be seen as, in addition, a kind of *hegira*, an attempted exodus or escape from the (dis)comfort of a sense of homogeneous selfhood, though not to safety. Julien can be seen, as in the epigraph from Sartre, as sincerely concerned with the internal forces he thinks will constitute him as a whole being, substantial and real, *beyond* his deeds. In this respect, Julien is "a continual game of mirror and reflection, a perpetual passage," like the mirroring and echoing convolutions of Sartre's words that for Sartre (and for Julien) yield only bad faith. This is precisely Nietzsche's formulation of the result of *ressentiment* as a motivator: since there is no "subject" except that, as in "the subject of a story," of "becoming," since "'the doer' is merely a fiction added to the deed"[5] the "being" is faced with an endless quest for a stasis that is purely chimerical. The subject, taken in this autoaesthetic way, literally triumphs over and takes "real joy" in triumphing over, "existing things, however good." Julien does this repeatedly in his social and psychological actions. This quest which is also an escape is always dialectical and, as a result of its very nature, is always deffered. Like the Dionysian Overman its consummation is absented to a chimerical future.

This dialectical quality of overlapping voices forces a sense of the self's truncation at just those moments in which its illumination seems most promising, from the very start. Though we will soon enough "escape" into Julien's consciousness in what has become standard omniscient narration, the novel begins in the first person: the first voice we confront is that of an anonymous figure in a curious relationship to the town, an unidentified figure who is local but an outsider, whose voice in the novel is that of the region and its (human) culture. This voice is the controller of the description of the town in which we find ourselves: "How many times, my mind still dwelling on the balls of Paris which I left the night before, have I leaned on these great blocks of bluish-gray granite, gazing deep into the valley of the Doubs!,"[6] the voice muses. Having established not only the physical setting of the story but the cultural nexus as well, the voice introduces Sorel, whose entrance into the novel, confronted by the mayor and the dignified M. de Rênal, who are seeking the "useless" Julien, is literary and autoaesthetic: "At first, Sorel replied by reciting at length all the formulas of polite conversation he knew by heart. While he was repeating these empty phrases with an awkward smile which emphasized the air of falsity and almost of trickery natural to his features,"[7] Sorel is thinking something entirely different. Entering the allegorical mill, Sorel seeks out his youngest son. The Dionysian imagery continues: "Approaching his mill, old Sorel bellowed for Julien; nobody answered."[8] The increasingly invisible narrator's Odyssean reference to Julien's polytropic nature, to his "nobody"-ness in the mill setting where his elder brothers, "a couple of giants," were working "with heavy axes," produces a deepening sense of the primitive and archaic nature of Julien's world. In fact, the gigantic brothers, Titans to Julien's Olympian guile, are busy with a kind of inverted writing (in contrast to the sophisticated reading the invisible Julien is doing, high above them at that moment): "They were intent on following exactly the black lines drawn on the wood; at every blow of their axes huge chips flew through the air. They did not hear their father's voice." The manual and verbal labors of self-creation are all around us as Julien is introduced. When old Sorel spies his errant son in the rafters and shouts for the boy to come down, Julien still *cannot hear him*; the unheard shout has been the first Dionysian reference to Julien in the novel: "Get down from there, animal, I want to talk to you,"[9] Sorel has shouted. But Julien does not have ears for this voice; Sorel is forced to whack Julien with a long staff to get his attention. The blow knocks Julien's favorite book[10] into the river and returns him to the standard relationship with his father Julien must manifest: anger and fear. But in contrast to the Cyclopean singularity and stature of his father and brothers, Julien is "weak" and "pallid," only his dark eyes manifesting the Dionysian *and* the Apollinian in him; they are described as eyes of "fire and reflection," but which at this moment are filled "with the most ferocious hatred." Julien shows himself as a worthy avatar of the evolving Dionysian life.

As Julien sits in the loft of his father's mill,[11] it seems as though we have a clear insight into his condition and his position; instead, at the moment at which a "zoom in" to Julien seems inevitable, the narrator swerves aside, forcing us away from the image of the chimerical Julien into the surrounding scene and into the text Julien makes of the scene, never letting us partake of Julien in more than a reflective and therefore chimerical way. This narrative distancing is the first of the many displacements of Julien with which the reader is faced. The reader's attention is at a distance, looking on, not knowing where to locate itself in this room in which the mechanization of Julien's father meets with the resistance of Julien's detachment. The overdetermination of the voices present, in that first sight of Julien, will not permit the reader's eye to come to rest. And Julien's location, his aloof position, is itself displaced. Julien's father knocks him from his lofty perch, then picks up a long pole and strikes his son with it: in the noise of the mechanization in the mill, confrontation of an identity forged from labor (the Sorel men) and one of reflection (Julien's), the tenor of the relationship between Julien and his (genetic) father are such that this is the only communication possible. We will see again and again the impossibility of communication between fathers and sons as the novel progresses. Old Sorel has knocked Julien down, in fact, to bring him back to another world, unwittingly tossing the *text of the rival father*, the literary past, into the (Heraclitan?) river and displacing that text with his own inarticulate one, but as always old Sorel fails; as the two of them walk toward the house, Julien's thoughts turn to the book (of Napoléon),[12] now sunk in the canal (which turns out not even to be a "natural" river—this world of seeming nature is literally entirely autoaesthetic and anthropocentric); the narrator turns to a physical description of Julien, and the promise of clarity in identity is denied. Thus is the pattern of the novel established: here, Stendhal is the reader's *professeur des polarités*: in his world of anti-heroism the lesson is to remove oneself from any fixed position, to become autonomous and unconflicted, to acknowledge one's otherness in order to be neutral (above contention) and, ironically and contradictorily, to excel. Stendhal and his hero want to rise above this sordid world's terrain, even if it is merely in the rafters of the father's work-barn, in a kind of melding of Daedalian soaring and Dionysian overcoming that allows a potentially clearer sight of that surface.

REFLECTION

Julien, however, like Stendhal, can never escape sufficiently from this sordid world; his dialogue with it can be momentarily quieted only by action that transcends the language in and of which he constitutes himself. Time and again in his story, Julien displays his inability to escape from the world of "existing things" and a concomitant inability to leave behind his rarified rhetorical world. Dramatic events, ranging from his fall from the rafters to his shooting of Mme. de Rênal to his execution, acknowledge this dilemma of the reflective and the anti-reflexive moment. Throughout the novel, as Julien tries to substantiate himself in the world around him, he must *insert* himself into his own story, adopting the impersonal, stereotyping linguistic mode of the *jugement*. Julien's self-assessment, based on codes of behavior and thought he has gleaned from his multiple literary fathers, is always a reevaluation of the idea of the self, as such. Like Nietzsche, Julien engages in the perpetual eternal return of self-assessment.

Even judged and sentenced finally, however, Julien is never what he seems to be, doomed from the beginning only to *react* to a hostile world. This hostility is in part a historicization, in which Julien is caught in the events of his time. Even he can see that "his time" is *no* time, that the time in which he lives consists in its essence of the voices of other times. His age, according to Julien, is a diminished one: the voices to which he pays heed are always of another age. Julien is perpetually caught between Foucaultian *epistémès*, not part of the aristocratic world of the eighteenth century but violently eschewing that of the mechanistic and basely opportunistic nineteenth. He is not able to escape the grounding conditions of his age (he too is base and opportunistic), but he perceives beyond that age, in both directions.

Through the texts by which he knows the outer, other world, Julien can see that the glory and power of the *will*, however chimerical for him in actuality, of Napoleonic France has been supplanted by the disillusionment, alienation, and requisite accompanying nostalgia of the Revolution of 1830. Julien's sense of powerlessness is pervasive—and always textual:

> Man's will is powerful, I read it everywhere; but is it strong enough to surmount disgust like mine? The great men of history had it easy; however terrible their test, they thought it beautiful; and who but myself can understand the ugliness of everything that surrounds me?[13]

Julien does not *feel* the power of the will, he *reads* it, but as directed toward a successful self-definition: he is "caught" out of his time with only the vestiges and echoes of a lost, past age. Ironically, Julien's concern with history provides him with a distance not only from the contemporary, fallen world but as well from the imperfections of the world he nostalgizes; both thus become more satisfying. He is able to glimpse in the voices of his mentor texts worlds of scintillating social structures as found, for example, in *Les Liaisons Dangéreuses'* "terrible sociability," as Baudelaire calls it (Brooks 288), created out of a need for an order which can generate no inherent energy but which relies on its form, a kind of formal exoskeleton, for its perpetuation—though Julien glimpses this world only from the impossible distance of the following half-century, even though it is only the next generation. The terrible sociability of the age is a layered *étrangeté*, fraught with theatricality and the distance of the gaze.[14] Because of his constitution in voices, for Julien "l'histoire c'est du théâtre,"[15] both immediate in his desire for it and distant because of his sense of deep alienation. Julien is literally caught between the cultural paradigms of two ages, as Peter Brooks indicates when he tells us that Stendhal was "the last major novelist to have a direct and important relationship to the French 18th century":[16] *Red and Black* occurs at a moment of "insurrectionary imbalance" comprising both the "old" valor and the "new" hypocrisy.[17] Even within the novel one can see this operate, as Julien stands out from the other (particularly younger) people portrayed. But not only is Julien disenfranchised from the process of historical change; Jean-Pierre Richard claims that Julien's heroes themselves, the sources of Julien's voices, "possess against those of Mathilde the immense advantage of not having been engulfed by history: as a participant in a living myth, Julien does not need, as Mathilde does, to admire those temporary altars nor to go into mourning to celebrate the past."[18] Julien's entry into Paris, the center of the world's stage and itself a kind of character in Julien's living myth, is marked not by a freedom from history but by a very history-oriented journey of what amounts to a mourning for a past Julien has indeed missed, a journey in which Julien, deeply moved by the place he has finally reached, is not moved by the voices nor the histories of the great psychic mentor (Napoléon) who has drawn him there, but rather by their absence, "only by the monuments bequeathed by his hero";[19] indeed, these monuments and their deathly voices are what Julien has come to Paris to experience. From start to finish, Julien's dialogues are stillborn, his voices those of a machine fabricating false identities out of a dead past. Julien cannot, Stendhal insinuates, really live among them, any more than can a Jude Fawley or Ike McCaslin or Gabriel Conroy. Theirs is an articulation which attempts an eternal return of the conditions of *perpetual* life which, although greatly to be desired, like Zarathustra's cannot be met.

NOBLESSE

Nonetheless, despite the moribund, abrogating impetus of the world caused by its creation in a complex series of dialogues with the dead, Julien must attempt to discover and control "how men are" in order to see who (or how) *he* is. He must articulate those voices, in a condition of *étrangeté*, in order to have even the most minimal sense of self. For Julien, this articulation is accomplished by the "interior" running monologue he has in that inner voice Julien cannot escape, the voice of the *Moi* that Michel Crouzet juxtaposes (anticipating Lacan) with that of *l'Ordre*, in his introduction to the novel, as constantly struggling with(in) that order. Crouzet's depiction of Julien is precisely that of the poet *manqué*; his inner voice, however, that of difference and negation, the abrogation of a meaningful connection with the world around him. It is the voice of the *non* with which Julien must confront the world. This is not a nihilist voice, a general "no" with which to measure life, but as in Nietzsche a resounding *"no"* in response to the herd, to the normalizing urge, a nobility of *independent* selfhood formed in *étrangeté*. In this light, Crouzet tells us that Julien's *noblesse* is his

> power to deny the social, and to die *saved*, intact, true to his contempt. He is, then, the Promethean hero of Revenge; in him, in his denial, he distills all human traits. Julien, by his *élan*, by his mask, by his nearly deliberate failure, is the symbol of the energy of opposition, who grounds the sovereignty and the purity of self [*Moi*] on his irreducible power of non-participation.[20]

The non-participation Julien manifests is one born of the very dialogue in which he lives his "principle of life": Julien is always the respondent, the reflection of his surrounding voices. He is a new kind of embodiment of will and energy, one that must be *re*active, the living manifestation of the discourse between what Nietzsche will call "intrinsic impulses" and "conscious volition." Although Julien acts in society, from the moment he is knocked from the beam in the sawmill to that at which his head falls from his shoulders in imitation of that other Revolutionary father, Danton, he is seeking the Full Word from which to fabricate a meaningful life, and yet, as Nietzsche shows us in *Zarathustra* and elsewhere, he is at most a *noble parvenu*,[21] attaching little social value to making his way in society. His solipsistic ambition aims to prove his personal worth *to himself*.

Julien's index of personal worth, his constant self-reevaluation, stems from his sense of a lost scene of origin itself, produced *through* his grounding voice-texts. This is a scene he re-envisages repeatedly: if he can rediscover (or reinvent) what it is to be "natural," a quality with which he feels completely out of touch, he can conquer that naturalness (can this be natural?) and become, ironically, a closed system of self-sufficiency.[22] But for Julien, the voices directing him always contain that elusive but powerful quality of *étrangeté* with which he cannot naturally join, which by definition cannot be joined; there is always another, an Other, and the voice of that Other, in the voice he hears or reads. As Sartre (out of Nietzsche) shows,

> whatever or whoever he may be, whatever may be his relations with me, and without his acting upon me in any way except by the pure upsurge of his being—then I have an outside, I have a *nature*. My original fall is the existence of the Other. Shame—like pride—is the apprehension of myself as a nature although that very nature escapes me and is unknowable as such. Strictly speaking, it is not that I perceive myself losing my freedom in order to become a thing, but my nature is—over there, outside my living freedom—as a given attribute of this being which I am for the Other.[23]

For Julien as for Sartre, the primal interrogation of such a formulation concerns itself with the "I" speaking, as in Nietzsche's rephrasing of the "Who am I?" to "Who is the 'I' asking the question 'Who am I?'" No sincere (in Sartre's sense), confidently felt final location for this ghostly presence can be charted. Julien's sincerity, his nature, apart from its earnest search for itself, is always a function of the sometimes momentary Others from whom his nature reflects itself. This is why the novel begins within the framework, the contextualization, of Verrières and the Rênals, and why Julien is introduced into the text by the call of the problematic father. Julien is always listening for himself in others and in the roles those othered voices expect him to fulfill. The warp of this texture of *étrangeté* is established before the narrative shuttle moves. Julien is concealed, not revealed, in "the conflict between *role* and *nature*."[24] His autoaesthetic is like a manifesto: "to foil the temptation (and the fascination) of the theatrical scenario to rediscover beyond the mimetics of imitation [*sic*] that language conforms to authentic being."[25]

This is established from the moment Julien's reading of the *Mémorial* reveals him in the rafters, and is concretized for the reader of Julien's book in Part I, Chapter 5, "Haggling," in the appropriate form of a dialogue. This chapter begins in conversation, as Julien's father, that man of such an utterly different manner and nature, tells him about the position M. de Rênal has offered. Julien's first response to this opportunity to enter the world—the theatre—of another class, to become more nearly what he feels himself to be, is not what we expect. Rather than embrace a life he might feel destined for, Julien turns away unexpectedly, wanting to run away to Besançon to become a soldier. To become what he wants to become is deeply problematic, since it is not nobility of social place he desires but nobility of selfhood: his autoaesthetic, potentially fulfilled, must be averted. In the roseate haze of the first sign of a response from that glowing world beyond the sawmill and

Verrières, Julien cannot see, momentarily, beyond the indignity of eating with the servants; he cannot imagine a world in which he is one of the privileged (that is, powered). Life in the loathsome Verrières has "chilled his imagination."[26] Rather than eat with the servants (that is, be a servant himself), he would prefer to run away and join the army (to choose anonymity). Obduracy in the face of a potential frustration of his goals is not a sign purely of vanity nor of irrational ambition, however, but textual, deriving from Rousseau's *Confessions*, which, along with "a collection of bulletins from the Grande Armée and the *Mémorial de Sainte-Hélène*, is "the only book his imagination had made use of in constructing a picture of the social world" and "filled out his Koran."[27] We are told that "he would have gone to the stake for these three works";[28] and we are left without any doubt in the end that, like the other great textual martyrs whose voluptuousness Nietzsche suggests to us, in every sense "he died for them." These texts establish the nature of the world and of what Julien is capable of doing and is prepared to do in it.

ORAGE

The build to Julien's end is careful, stylish, and deliberate. Stendhal carefully nurtures Julien's sense of autoaesthetic genealogy through a series of radically different sorts of voices. Julien moves from paradigm to paradigm, showing us that what matters to him is not a particular "calling" in life, though the phrase is perfectly apt, but a powerful style. The sources of those paradigms are also disparate. Books are sometimes primary in his chorus of mentors, but his hidden, protected "nature," that which Julien considers to be "himself," has been established in the purported warmth of conversation with the old surgeon-major, whose stories of the Napoleonic campaigns have filled Julien with envy. But Stendhal's story of Julien begins with the old man dead, already a textualized part of Julien's past, at a critical point when the active glory of the sword, in the Napoleonic tradition, has been supplanted by the textual glories of the soutane. When those paradigms of hero-worship change, so does the manifestation of them in Julien's *Weltanschauung*. He is able to see that "the uniform of the century" is no longer that of the soldier, but Stendhal allows Julien only the barest vestiges of this grounding in the cloth.

Having agreed to work as a tutor, Julien escapes from his father's sawmill and decides that "it might be useful to his hypocrisy" to stop at the church on the way to the mayor's house. Rather than opt for the old church of the tradition of his forefathers, Julien goes to the magnificently nouveau riche church in Verrières, whose very walls, hung with red for a religious festival, reflect his entrapment in the unsubstantiated, the unfledged, and the raw, to speak with the abbé, M. Chélan.[29] Rather than receive the expected religious instruction he receives quite another kind, a secular and cryptic multilayered message he will take the rest of his life to decipher and to articulate.

Finding the church "deserted," in the eerie scarlet glow of the cloth hanging over even the windows, he discovers on the lectern a scrap of paper, "set out there as if for him to read."[30] His sense of destiny quickened, Julien peruses the sheet, a broadside announcing the recent execution of a criminal, one Louis Jenrel. Turning the paper over, Julien discovers the cryptic message there, "the first step [le premièr pas]."[31] His head swimming, confronted by multiple layers in the little scene, Julien swims through a series of reactions. He has unknowingly discovered the edge of a conspiracy very much of the "present" political world, but he does not perceive it directly. His concern is predictable, after the initial bafflement: "Who could have left this paper here? thought Julien. Poor fellow, he added with a sigh, his name has the same ending as mine."[32] Julien senses, vaguely and subconsciously, that he ought to recognize himself in the executed man (though he does not recognize the man's name as an anagram of his own—that is left to the reader), and in the broadside indeed his own conspiracy of martyrdom has now begun. He too has taken the first step toward execution. Immediately after seeing the paper, in his agitation and with his imagination transported beyond his ability to control it, Julien has a vision of a pool of blood near the baptismal font, and though it turns out to be spilled holy water on the surface of which the church's crimson curtains have thrown their blood-red reflection, it stands as a prescient, symbolic reminder of the "natural" course Julien will follow. It is a secular "quotation" of a religious experience, but is exactly the opposite of the calling Julien, like Stephen Dedalus, might expect. Everywhere here, as later, Julien's autoaesthetic nature is *reflected*, from the note and its name, from the water's shining, sinister, misleading surface. In this private scene, the purportedly pacific power of the church is subverted and transmuted into the first step toward Julien's self-discovery and self-overcoming, in his voices and his imagination.

The *next* step, literally the next stop in Julien's journey, cements his vocation and his fate. It is his introduction to the *other* for whom still more fatal steps will soon be taken: Mme. de Rênal.[33] For her, as for himself, Julien is and remains *Cet étranger*. Therefore, ironically, it is before her that Julien plays and betrays his *rôle naturel*,[34] which is reachable only through his "vain projects": for Julien, sincerity and the natural are corollary attributes, but always to be discovered in interaction with a world constantly making itself *in*substantial, though the former is public, the latter private.[35] Julien's natural role (an autoaesthetic oxymoron) constantly frustrates itself and makes him increasingly a stranger to himself.

But before the arrival on the stage of Mme. de Rênal, a further word about mentors. We have already seen hints of the way in which Julien's duplicitous and problematic relationship of the public to the private, of his sense of himself and his placing of that self in a world of his construction and ratification, is a function of his problematic paternity, an inner and outer dialogue with fathers. Julien himself questions whether it is possible that he is the son of Sorel the sawyer, whose "nature" is seemingly so different from his own. Indeed, later in the novel, for the chevalier de Beauvoisis, Julien's "breeding" *seems* to show; the nobleman wonders if Julien is not "the illegitimate son of one of the Marquis de La Mole's intimate friends,"[36] and indeed the marquis, who nearly becomes Julien's *beau-père*, treats him "like a son" himself; the marquis is told by the abbé Pirard that "they say he's the son of a carpenter in our mountains, but I rather suspect he's the natural son of some rich man."[37] And the fact is that Julien's program is to invent himself out of the idea of the "son" and "surrogate" standing in for those to whom he owes his sense of himself: Napoléon, the old surgeon-major, abbé Pirard, the marquis.

Ironically, this overdetermined paternal genealogy serves as much to mask Julien as to identify him. He does not seek *a* role, but the power of role-playing in the theatre of life. He feels that lineage must be transcended in order that one not be constrained by it, but that role-playing is the necessary staging platform for autoaesthetic—and politico/social—power in the world. Julien's revolt against his genetic father, for such it is according to him, is staged not so much against the brute whose genes he carries but against the constraint of the un-theatrical, the singular existence of the man with one circumscribed identity. Julien, as a result of his autoaesthetic, is a "son of no one," as Crouzet calls him, who is only visible in "an originary void." Resulting inevitably from this stance is "the urgency of the mask."[38] The mask (and the masque), a defense and a social formula, covers Julien's concern for his lost and always absent father(s), and at the same time offers defense against a world in which "among the cheats it is necessary to be a cheat-and-a-half, and offensive, because hypocrisy reverses the inferior situation that inflicts Julien."[39] The mask saves, hides, and cancels Julien, protecting and de-substantiating him as a function of his will-to-power. Part of the constraint of Julien's masks is the requisite element of duty, which Julien sees as a debt to an invented social code applicable to the great ones among whom he counts himself. Julien feels that it is his duty to seduce Mme. de Rênal—it's in his books—just as it is his duty to remain outside the world of ambition. This aloofness results from Julien's having no lineage; since his father *never exists* (thus becoming, ironically, a proper father), he must be constantly and unsuccessfully reinvented. Julien is allowed the "originality" of the bastard whose origins are romanticized. But Julien does not have "solid" fathers, in the texts out of which he makes them. We have seen how, in the scene in which Stendhal introduces Julien to us, two fathers,

Sorel and Napoléon, "compete" for him; but it is not a competition of the textual father and the genetic one. Rather, *both* fathers, then as later, form a textualized voice which calls to Julien to identify with it.

This problematic paternal context is the only explanation we need of Julien's formation; by the time we meet him, at nineteen, the world is a language, a syntax one must assiduously respect. This world-language proceeds from one relationship to another, from the anagrammatic (Julien Sorel = Louis Jenrel = *je lis un rôle*)[40] to the far more complex one between Julien and Mme. de Rênal, about which we are told that

> in Paris, Julien's position with regard to Mme. de Rênal would quickly have been simplified; but in Paris, love is the child of novels. The young tutor and his timid mistress would have found in three or four novels, or even in the couplets of the Gymnase, a clarification of their position. The novels would have outlined for them the roles to be played, provided them with a model to imitate; and this model, sooner or later, though without the least pleasure and perhaps even reluctantly, vanity would have forced Julien to follow.[41]

Particularly when it is most ironic, as here, the precision of Stendhal's language is remarkable. It is exactly correct to say that Mme. de Rênal and Julien would *re*-discover themselves in the novels they might use as the models for their affair; the texts would indeed trace the role they might play: they would become yet another facsimile, another set of offspring of the constitutive texts. But Mme. de Rênal and Julien *haven't* read, not in the way Stendhal means. If the sort of love they need to experience is like a novel, they are already doomed to miss it: Julien translates his love into *devoir*, the only text he knows, and in his fumblings for Mme. de Rênal's favors (literally her hand[42]) he demonstrates how this writing-over of duty obscures and vitiates his feelings, his "nature." Julien, of course, is not aware of this process; after his success with her (literal and literary) hand, while Mme. de Rênal is in a state of deep agitation, Julien, satisfied, "sleeps like a log,"[43] not from love but from being mortally exhausted by "the struggles which pride and timidity had been waging all day in his heart." He wakes the next morning having done "his duty," "a heroic duty." This is the only language he knows.

THEATRICAL TENSIONS

But this is not enough. Julien's *devoir* is also to name (himself). In the full flush of his conquest (of Mme. de Rênal's hand), refreshed by the deep sleep he has had, Julien locks himself away in his bedroom and, as if confused by the initiative he has taken, and in reflection on the correctness of his present state, in a strategy of consulting a higher authority, he *reads* about the exploits of Napoléon. The only "naturalized" element of this activity is the *rôle naturel* of Julien's autoaesthetic. Later, in further imitation of his most romanticized master-father, as the campaign to conquer Mme. de Rênal continues, Julien/Napoléon writes down a battle plan for the conquest, a plan with which he is so taken up that when Mme. de Rênal interrupts, he cannot conceal himself:

—Don't you have any other names besides Julien? she asked him.

The question was flattering, but our hero knew not what to answer; there was no room for this episode in his plan. If he had not been so stupid as to make up a strategy beforehand, Julien's quick wit would have served him very well; his surprise would only have added to the brilliance of his phrases.

He was awkward, and exaggerated his awkwardness. Mme. de Rênal pardoned him quickly enough; she saw in his clumsiness the effect of a delightful simplicity. And the only thing she had found lacking in this man, to whom everyone else attributed a great genius, was precisely an air of candor.[44]

It is exquisite irony that the question of his *name* should destroy Julien's composure and that the question's awkwardness should so completely negate the "surprise [*esprit vif*]" Stendhal ironically imputes to the hidden Julien. The text of that most contemporary and still-heroic struggle, the *devoir*, becomes itself an autoaesthetic process, in fact, a process of naming and therefore of otherness. Derrida's remarks on the proper name, for example, throughout *The Post Card*, bring the nature of the name-claim into high relief;[45] Julien has shown us this powerfully. Jean Starobinsky remarks that

a name is situated at the confluence of existence "for itself" and existence "for others." It is an intimate truth and a public thing. In accepting my name I accept that there be a common denominator between my inner and my social being. . . . Confined to our name, our identity becomes alienated; it comes to us through and from others.[46]

Although Starobinsky's language is geared to the sort of inner/outer discussion Julien might make of his own personal emergence, rather than to a larger sense of the name as a sign of the absence, of *étrangeté*, out of which Nietzschean power is to be born, and although inherent in the notion of an "inner and a social being" is a schematic simplicity Stendhal undermines and denies continuously, the thrust of Starobinsky's point, that our identity comes to us through the self-naming of others, passed on to us, echoes Julien's strategy. Julien is indeed caught in the play between private and social, but never captured there. In his very attempts to name himself, a process in which he must continually reconstitute himself, doing violence to others, whether fathers or lovers (both figures of the encroachment of external authority and therefore threats), Julien undercuts all of his own potential for overcoming his self-limitations.

Julien's senses of history and his place/name in it both ground and alienate him; by extension, that part of him which privileges the process of naming is equally historically oriented. According to Julien, he is to be seen as *sui generis*, created through a kind of parthenogenesis which, like a parody of the medieval idea of God, is textualized everywhere but fully realized nowhere. In this respect, both his historical origins and his so-called nature are thrown permanently into question. This paradox results from a dialectic between what Starobinsky calls the "inner" and "social," which is Julien's formulation can be translated into "imagination" and "memory." Julien's memory is purely Nietzschean, rich with strategic forgetting, fabricated wholly from his need for protection against a strange world out to do him harm (by denying him autonomy). Truly, for Julien, *différence engendre haine.* He has, as Crouzet suggests (following a Hegelian model), engaged in a battle with a world "already made and badly so [*déjà fait et mal fait*],"[47] in which his tumultuous course is "the gallop of a black horse," full of morbid and paranoid, as well as constructive and liberating, concerns. Memory protects him time and again by providing a context in which to deal with the world's hostility. One of the clearest and most dramatically persistent ways in which this hostility manifests itself is in Julien's feeling of provinciality: Julien cannot conceal the (correct) feeling that he has "lived among yokels" and therefore "never studied the great models" for the invention of "the language of a sly and prudent hypocrisy,"[48] except for his few coveted books. This accretion of memories of historical deprivation continues, to be clearly seen by Chélan's successor, abbé Pirard, a man of faith whose (Nietzschean) view of language is wholly cynical: when Julien faints in his presence, the abbé asks if he faints regularly, and when Julien says he does not, Pirard responds, "Such are the effects of the world's vanities; you seem to be used to laughing faces, theaters for the display of falsehood."[49] Julien has learned his lesson well enough to have his "word of honor" doubted by the abbé, for whom the history of words is the history of a lack of essential validity. The abbé, in his own way, provides another aspect of the strategy of detachment autoaesthetics employs, though in a fascinating multiperspectival way; while for Julien this strategy is a gateway to the self, for Pirard it leads to a tragic loss of soul.

Pirard's complaint is that language is insubstantial, always an echo; this is precisely its strength for Julien and for autoaesthetics. The "few great models" Julien has had have been and prove continually to be no more but no less than echoes. Among the most obvious, if Napoléon has been his *professeur d'énergie*, Tartuffe has been his *professeur d'hypocrisie*.[50] The values of these figures and their ghostly lessons lie in their creation of a substitute and perpetually substituted reality. "Beyond" the earthly, on first entering Paris, like Jude Fawley Julien attempts to read a validity into the very stones of the historic city: as Richard put it, the "stones of the Malmaison, Ney's tomb, are all warm with disrupted presences, with scarcely stifled memories, of a story more real than that of the age in which they had the misfortune to live."[51] The so-called real exists only in a cryptology of shadows Julien has *missed* in fact but assimilated in fiction. Dead history, both political and cultural, is the social and psychological milieu out of which Julien's self-articulations grow.

Imagination, on the other hand, purports to come from an "inner," that is, "living," voice, a voice that is not memory and therefore not gregarious. At first this would seem to be a clear advantage, but for Julien the difference between the social and the inner voice is that the latter is the product of unmediated desire that plunges Julien into a world full of realities modeled closely after those desires. This is a thrusting of the conventional world of imagination (like that, for example, of Romanticism) back out into a hostile world, in a teleology of ambition that remakes the world in its own image and distorts vision. In fact, Julien experiences two kinds of imagination. One progressively obscures the "real" as seen by reverie (as when Julien comes to Paris), producing a world in which dreams, of the past and of the putative future, are the current coinage and in which the outer world is abrogated. The other imagination never leaves the world, but completes, corrects, and enhances it (as when Julien himself becomes an *orage*). Richard contends that the second imagination "naturalizes" the first,[52] but this process is complex and involves a series of patently *un*natural elements. In both cases, imagination acts as an expropriation of the world. This can be most clearly seen in Stendhal's imagery. Walking through the countryside near Vergy, Julien climbs onto a rock and looks out across the countryside, where he has an imaginative vision of a sparrow-hawk[53] circling above the sleepy fields: "Julien's eye followed mechanically the bird of prey. Its calm, powerful movements struck him; he envied this power; he envied this isolation. Such had been the destiny of Napoléon; would it some day be his?"[54] The flight (*vol*) of the bird of prey becomes imaginatively symbolic of his own flight. But this flight is also, again, an expropriation, a theft (*vol*) of the text of the absent heroes who inform Julien's imagination: he steals their valor, words, and presence, but can finally see himself only as a surrogate Napoléon, and one all too earthbound. The appropriation of the hero is never seen as even imaginatively successful.

Ironically, Julien places himself, impossibly, at the still center of this swirling structure of imagination and (increasingly) memory-language. This positioning is vital to his project. Only near the end, when his chosen *telos* has been cancelled, in his condemnation and incipient death, does he seem to change. He becomes more and more the poet, less and less wordly: he sinks (or rises) increasingly into language; the circles of the hawk are revealed as being the solipsistic, rippling circles of his own "nature" around himself, and as imagination takes over from memory he seems to relinquish his projected goal structure, his ambition (though, of course, not his need for the mask). But this too can be seen as an interpretation from "outside," as the dissemination of Stendhal's own circles around Julien's "nature": Napoléon replaced by Danton, "merely" another of the martyred shadows of the past. Danton surfaces again and again, a fragrant shade embodied in Julien and whose version of heroism is as powerful as the more openly accessible Napoléon's. After delivering his diatribe against the bourgeoisie at his trial (an exercise that seems to involve the voice of a character we have met nowhere before in the novel), Julien remakes himself finally in the image of the Danton that Altamira has depicted, musing on the fact that one cannot *subjectively* conjugate the verb "to guillotine" reflexively into the past tense, unless there is *another life*,[55] or unless life is a function of language. But Julien has already entered that other life several times, and less than a page later he thinks to himself that "truly, man has two beings in him,"[56] that "I alone know what I might have done.... For the others, I am at most nothing but a PERHAPS."[57] Julien has used his customary devices to fly out of the unacceptable region in which he found himself and which he has inhabited. Then he can admit to us that, "Since I was condemned to death, all the poetry I ever knew in my life comes back in my memory. It must be a mark of decadence,"[58] but the decadence to which he refers in his only possible language is no more than the upsurge of the "inner" voice, to return to Starobinsky's distinction, and it is in this state that Julien can shortly thereafter embrace Mme. de Rênal "with a pleasure that was quite new to him," as Stendhal says, "no longer the intoxication of love, but rather a profound gratitude."[59] The energizing of the imaginative powers in Julien, no matter how inadequate their expression, changes him "for the last time" into someone for whom the present finally seems to exist. Although it is still in and of the world of language, imagination works as a *pretext* for a new vision of that world.

Closely related to it but underlying this dialectical tension between imagination and memory in Julien's autoaesthetic structuring is that of sensation and perception. The "inner" voice is still recognized, existing alongside the "social" in a rational and teleological Kantian grid; to displace it, one must discuss physics (forces of and in the world), not the metaphysics of self-overcoming. The (dangerous) self of *force*, with all its implications of intrusion, lies for Julien in the sensations' "intrinsic, nonvolitional nature" of "impulsive sensitivity."[60] Pervasively, sensation denotes immediacy, while perception is linked with the kind of teleology Julien has already investigated. Perception judges, "distinguishes what one feels."[61] Such concepts as "duty" and "honor" cannot exist without such a distinction, since the projects of self-definition are always textually perpetuated value judgments. Julien *must*, for example, make Mme. de Rênal submit to having her hand held, in that first scene between them, because that is the duty Julien's texts enforce ("Je lis un rôle."). Of this inversion, Georges Poulet claims that the notorious resolutions made by Julien are not evidences of energy but confessions of weakness. The person who calculates the future is one who, in his or her depths, does not find the resources necessary to face blithely the unpredictability of the present moment,[62] and since Julien deeply doubts his own depths (even that they exist, given the Nietzschean shallowness of the autoaesthetic), his effort is always to "transcend the moment and project himself into the future," where "the awareness of a fleeting happiness [is] glimpsed, so to speak, inadvertently."[63] This is the joy-in-ruin about which Nietzsche speaks, the triumph over what *is*. The power of Julien's grounding texts is such that sometimes he is able to gloss over the gaps and lacks of which they are constructed.

Sometimes, he sees clearly but is not able to manufacture such glosses, and "failing" (which is really succeeding), submits to the (impossible) raptures of the moment. As he makes love to Mme. de Rênal, Julien gives

> no further thought to his black ambition or to his projects, so difficult to realize. For the first time in his life he was carried away by the power of beauty. Lost in a vague delightful dream, wholly foreign to his character, gently pressing that hand which seemed to him perfectly beautiful, he only half heard the rustling of the linden tree in the light night wind and the distant barking of dogs by the mill on the Doubs.
>
> But this emotion was a pleasure, not a passion. Returning to his room, he thought only of one happiness, of getting back to his favorite book; at the age of twenty, the idea of the world and the effect to be produced there is more important than anything else.[64]

A momentary step "down" into Julien has been taken, but his weakness has been covered over quickly, almost invisibly, and retextualized; appropriately, the "text" of the subsequent passage abounds with the key words of Julien's dialectic: *pouvoir, perdu, rêverie, étrangère, plaisir, passion, livre, idée du monde*. But then, following his conquest of Mme. de Rênal, eight short chapters later in one appropriately entitled *Penser fait souffrir*, rendered passively into English by Adams and others as "To Think Is to Suffer,"[65] the dialectic has become very clear indeed. After transports of unanticipated and even unimagined passion, Julien and Mme. de Rênal have seen, at their passion's very height, the perfect immorality of their affair: perception has interceded, and this is not just a social or even moral perception; it goes to the very root of Julien's self-metaphysic. When intellectualization/perception itself intervenes, feeling becomes impossible for Julien. He sees himself as incapable of feeling and thinking simultaneously. Poulet agrees, declaring that "to perceive is almost to render oneself incapable of feeling. But the reverse is almost equally true. To feel, at least to feel too intensely what one feels, is to render oneself incapable of perceiving. . . . A man 'in an ecstasy of passion' distinguishes nothing at all."[66] One must constantly attempt to objectify formulation, to step back and *perceive* one's dilemma, to see the impossibility of simultaneous thinking and feeling; to separate *what*-one-feels (perception) from *that*-one-feels (sensation). Julien's dilemma is literally meta-physical, trapping him in the cognitive and the rational. But this very entrapment enforces the perpetuation of a Julien other than the one he is seen to be and needs himself to be.

CLIMAX AND GAZE

Nowhere is this more true than in the climactic sections of the novel, as Julien's projects come to fruition only to be destroyed. Having managed to remain aloof from the world and to feel that he is manipulating it, having recaptured the errant Mathilde, Julien is prudent, having learned well from Korasoff: he "never abandoned himself to the full sense of his joy except at times when Mathilde could not read the expression of it in his eyes. He carried out with exactitude the duty of every so often saying to her something disagreeable."[67] "Familiarité engendre différence engendre haine." The autoaesthetic force surges up at the moment at which Julien is able to suppress his feelings, his unmediated sensitivity.

In the chapter entitled "A Man of Spirit,"[68] Julien achieves what he has come to believe must be his final autoaesthetic force: he becomes Monsieur le chevalier Julien Sorel de La Vernaye. But this does not make him a "real" nobleman but, in Stendhal's words, a man of "spirit," a *false* "natural son," *ex nihilo*, insubstantial, ghostly, a walking uniform. His dialogues with perception and sensation, with memory and imagination conflate in this title, the signature of his absence. Julien literally becomes a trace. Nonetheless, one might say *as a result*, he has achieved his projected goal. He is seemingly in control of the world *from outside it*, but has managed to make the kind of marks on it he has desired: Mathilde is pregnant with his ("noble") son, Julien himself is rich, accomplished, accepted—identified. The man of spirit has settled into the existence he has been destined for all along, according to the texts of which he has been the agent. And yet, in the very way in which he formulates this world of voices we can see the final phrasing of his dilemma: "Now at last, he thought, the novel of my career is over, and the credit is all mine."[69] It is not a *life* he has lived, but a novel, the novel of his life.

This *roman* has culminated in a series of texts/letters between Mathilde and her father, and finally in a letter from her to Julien himself, announcing the apocalypse. In fact, this entire section announcing his spiraling rise is presented to the reader as a concentric series of texts centering in and on Julien; the fact that "the credit is all mine" and that he must account for the novel of his life becomes an economics of the artistry of thought to construct a viable way out of insubstantiality. As Stendhal chronicles the breakup of Julien's apotheosis, he artfully deprives us of salient and pivotal moments in the trajectory. The Full Word is, of course, never spoken by nor of Julien, and in his guise as nobleman he is even more ripe for trimming than he was as the aspiring student. The firmer his identity seems to be, the more precarious it becomes from the autoaesthetic point of view; the more he claims closure on his sense of self, the greater the danger of its being torn open again. Self-articulation is indeed, as we see in Julien, a tear in nature, a product of the false-identity machine which, as Julien's purported identity begins to unravel, behaves in very Kafkaesque fashion. At the end of the novel, a sense of the inevitability and despatch of Julien's exposure/explosion grows more and more powerful. Stendhal even contrives to make Julien's fall *incroyable*, suspending the mimetic narrative time-frame in favor of a condensed reportorial voice that cannot be believed. The reader is not, just as Julien is not, privy to his reactions at the pivotal moments here. Having read Mathilde's letter recalling him to Paris from Strasbourg, Julien proceeds with "almost unbelievable rapidity" (361) to his fall, one that moves more rapidly than does his narrative or our understanding of him. This "unbelievable" speed is the result of a withholding of narrative, a mimesis by the narrative voice of Julien's own lack of total, unified consciousness. It is, fittingly (because impossibly), the welling up of something like "pure feeling." The only reportable aspect of Julien's personality during the journey is "the frightful doubts [*l'affreuse inquiétude*]"[70] with which he proceeds. After he has read Mme. de Rênal's letter, there is nothing for the narrator to report but pure action, uninhibited by analysis or perception.

But in the autoaesthetic paradigm, we have been carefully prepared for this *orage* at Julien's downfall. We have been warned sufficiently that the world is not what Julien (having metamorphozed from a child of voices to one of apocryphal nobles) has deemed it to be. The chapter appropriately entitled "The Hell of Weakness"[71] ends with the prophetic declaration that "we must give up prudence! The age was created to bring everything into confusion! We are on the march toward chaos!"[72] The chaos is more than that of a world in which a La Mole can love and determine to marry a Sorel, and in which a Sorel's ambition can actually be attained *in that world*, that is more than the distinction between Starobinsky's inner and social. Most centrally, Julien's is a chaos that will not permit him to "hear" himself correctly *outside* the life he is living: his removal to a place of safety is unaccomplishable. But Julien has gone on fabricating his will to overcome his own and the world's obstacles, determined that only in the completion of the project can he articulate that the *volonté* of the bourgeoisie is translatable into a flight upwards: if Napoléon is the *"professeur d'énergie*, he is also that of *"volonté."* Julien has come to believe in his own fictions, a fatal flaw, as Nietzsche has shown us. For Julien, the evidence is seemingly in his favor: he has become a natural son of the aristocracy, he has a new name (which reconstitutes both his inner and outer, social beings), he is rich, he thinks he has and will have power. And yet the nature of Julien's voices deny him this triumph before it is had. The "originality" attributed to him by the Marquis de La Mole derives not from any power Julien has but from his pure *étrangeté*; indeed, all but Julien should instantly see *from his language* the nature of the originality the marquis bestows:

> One becomes fond of a fine spaniel, the marquis told himself, why should I be so ashamed of my fondness for this young abbé? He is an original. I treat him like a son; well, where's the harm in that? This notion, if it lasts, will cost me a diamond worth five thousand louis in my will.[73]

The implication in the marquis' likening him to a spaniel is that of Julien's being of a different species at which, in some minimal way, one might marvel. Julien's originality, for the marquis, might well be tinged with the danger one should see lurking about this strange beast, the danger manifested by a will capable of breaking into *action*. In his depiction of Julien by the marquis, one must remember the name Sorel-*père* has called Julien from the beginning: "animal." The chaos we have seen adumbrated earlier in the text is that of the non-essential self breaking through, unpredictably and dangerously. This exploding into the world of an unformed and unformable self is the singular, "original" quality with which the self-evaluations of the perception are juxtaposed, and which brings the idea of meaningful action into question. Indeed, Julien's culminative action, the one with which he seals his fate and caps his existence, is the *negation* of action—the silence of Julien's speechless head standing on the table before Mathilde. Having achieved the (false) nobility he has so sought, and treating this as a total statement of him—as his Full Word—and then seeing its inadequacy to the chaos of which an autoaesthetic life consists, Julien must renounce his false discoveries and return to his *real* nature, the trace or echo. As Julien has moved through society, ascending the social ladders and transcending (or diving beneath) his disastrously completed "project-orientation," he discovers that he has not advanced but regressed to action:

> Since making up his mind to act, he no longer reasons; he does nothing but pursue an image. . . . The time of those endless oscillations is over. . . . There is no more need for these great soliloquies: henceforth we have nothing but the silence of a lucid hypnosis.[74]

The autoaesthetic hypnosis Julien experiences throughout his novel is one in which perception is subjugated to sensation, in which he makes no decisions; what is called "making up his mind" here, a step at a time, is really the fabrication of the mind as an entity within the echo-chamber of voices.

But even in this most crucial set of episodes, Julien remains textualized. It is not from the moment of his "fatal" gunshot that Julien renounces his future and hence his project, and not from his prison, but from the moment of reading the *letter* in which Mme. de Rênal *exposes* him, and even this is occurring during a state of suspended animation which has begun when he receives a note from Mathilde. By the time of his trial, he has collapsed into his texts. All he longs for is a "noble [literary] death." He has joined Louis Jenrel, Altamira, and the spiritual presence of Boniface de La Mole in being "the [textual] man with the death sentence." But one suspects that there was no character equivalent to Valenod in Boniface's story nor in Altamira's; no wonder Julien is forced to relinquish the heroic stance, to replace Napoléon with Danton in his resignation and irony at the end. Poulet points out that "to live from day to day, to renounce the future and one's ambition, is thus to give up all plans, and in general, even the plan to live. Life is now without design";[75] Julien has caught sight of the void beyond the "cover of his novel."

When Julien's dialogue with society and himself ceases, he must cease to exist: he suffers execution long before his physical head falls. Like Nietzsche's Hamlet, he has seen and understood. This visionary motif is more than metaphorically linked to the novel's obsession with autoaesthetic vision. From the outset, Julien's dialogue with power has centrally involved itself with the scrutiny of others and its formative role in his sense of self. The truth is that the "resignation" Julien manifests in prison is not success: etiolation is not unity nor wholeness. Just as for Fabrizio in *The Charterhouse of Parma*, safety from the world is largely a question of distance from it.

But Julien has never been able to remove himself entirely from that world. Even at the end he is not "unseen": he must maintain his name and is concerned about the public accounts being made of him. He is also obsessed with the future of his son. Since the world's gaze has its reality, its operation, in his perception, we can see that this very attention is a confusion of his teleology. This process never completes itself: Julien always feels himself encroached upon by the world, always a prisoner of its gaze and therefore doubly imprisoned. For Julien, the gaze of the world is itself always a voice, an active participant in the text he makes of himself. The effect is that as Julien's agitation increases, his mobility decreases; the more tormented he is the more indifferent he appears.[76] Action always precipitates a complex interaction between reflexiveness and the prevention of reflection, since only in self-contemplation does the voice of the narrator participate in the process of character-building. When consummate action begins, self-reflection is impossible.

Very early on, Julien has decided what direction his hypocrisy will take, nurturing it like a ward. We have seen how Stendhal demonstrates this in his very choice of words: Julien "thought [*jugea*] it might be useful to his hypocrisy to stop off in the church."[77] His social identity is constructed of self-judgments throughout the novel, until the judgment moves elsewhere (in "Le jugement"). Paradoxically, the static nature of judgment is for Julien, as Nietzsche tells us, always in the future, always a function of the joy of that future and its "destruction of what is most noble and at the sight of its progressive ruin." He is constantly striving toward a chimerical goal, experiencing the present "only as a bridge to something that lies ahead."[78] Although sensational action cancels the power of the gaze, it also cancels self-reflection—and therefore the future.

Since Julien is obsessively autoaesthetic, he must find a way to deal with his text of the gaze of others, despite the fact that this gaze and the strategies he uses to deal with it provide finally nothing but distance from his texts and from others. We have seen how, at the textual level, Julien masters imagination and makes it a servant of memory; at the level of sensation and perception, where Julien must determine himself by action or inaction, he feels and experiences reality as a "resistance,"[79] which makes hypocrisy necessary, its cultivation a product of ambition but also of self-protection. Julien comes to realize the power of the gaze early on, "neutralizing" the enemy by appropriating its views and biases and ironizing them in the game of supremacy at hand. Love itself, with all of his love-objects (as they must be called, in a relatively clinical way), is a function of this struggle with the *agon* of the self. After his first touch of the hand with Mme. de Rênal, having now adopted as his *duty* her subjection, Julien approaches her the next day in a new light:

> His glances the next morning, when he saw Mme. de Rênal, were remarkable; he looked her over like an enemy with whom he was bound to fight. These glances, so different from those of the evening before, drove Mme. de Rênal to distraction; she had been kind to him, and he seemed annoyed. She could not turn her eyes from him.[80]

Julien's gaze does to Mme. de Rênal what ours does to him: it functions as the sign of a mysterious judgment and evaluation, a distancing at precisely the moment at which Mme. de Rênal and we as readers most need reassurance. By means of that distancing gaze, in some real respect Julien is cancelling her out, dismissing her, and co-opting her into himself. She is no longer what she seems to be to the reader, but has become a facet of the very difference Julien perceives and makes his own strategy. She might well say, in Sartre's words,

> I grasp the Other's look at the very center of my *act* as the solidification and alienation of my own possibilities. In fear or in anxious or prudent anticipation, I perceive that these possibilities which I *am* and which are the condition of my transcendence are given also to another, given as about to be transcended in turn by his own possibilities. The Other as a look is only that—*my* transcendence transcended.[81]

But this Nietzschean gaze is not "natural" to Julien. Later, Julien actually practices the look that has thrown Mme. de Rênal into such agitation. Having met Altamira at a ball, Julien returns to the Hôtel de La Mole convinced of his own increasingly Dantonesque nature and, contemplating the possibilities of *la tempête* such a man might create, he confronts Mathilde in the library. She looks into his fierce eyes, but she "could not sustain his gaze, and stepped back instinctively. For a moment she looked at him; then, ashamed of her fear, turned and left the library with a light step."[82] Through his own gaze, Julien imagines he can master the significant world; he is able to make use of the power of otherness *over* another. Later, when he is in the final stages of recovering the love of Mathilde, going to and from the Hôtel de Fervaques, he realizes that Mathilde is watching him return to the stable each night.[83] She stands behind the thin curtain of her window, watching. Significantly, in this play of glances, he has been forbidden to look at her there, as though in some totemic way such a look would violate or entrap Mathilde in itself. But Julien is able to autoaestheticize the gaze in its imaginative use without her knowing:

> The muslin was so flimsy that Julien could see through. By looking in a certain way from under the brim of his hat he could see Mathilde's figure without seeing her eyes. Consequently, he told himself, she cannot see my eyes, and this does not amount, in a way, to looking at her.[84]

This activity bears fruit. On the night on which, at the Hôtel de La Fervaques, "he placed himself in such a way as to catch sight of Mathilde's eyes";[85] he is mesmerizing her, aware that "the appearance of the Other causes the appearance in the situation of an aspect which I did not wish, of which I am not the master, and which on principle escapes me since it is *for the Other*."[86] Shortly thereafter, following the performance of *Manon Lescaut*, in the moments before Mathilde throws herself at Julien's feet in the library, "she could not bring herself even to look at him; she was afraid of encountering an expression of scorn."[87] He has her. But instants later,

> she turned her head slowly toward him: he was staggered at the extremity of greed he read in her eyes; he could scarcely recognize them as belonging to her.
> Julien felt his powers slipping away, so deadly painful was the act of courage he required of himself.
> In a minute those eyes will express nothing but icy disdain, Julien told himself,[88]

and he must leave the room in order to *stay in control*. As soon as the gaze is returned, Julien once again feels the loss of power that always accompanies his own subsumption into the power of the other, the gaze, the voice.

Whatever the power he may momentarily have over others, it remains, as we have seen, potentially mortally threatening to his own sense of himself. The effect of this radical subsumption and differentiating is to cancel Julien out, to make him *nothing*. Julien's struggle through this dilemma is echoed in Sartre:

> Thus not only am I unable to *know* myself, but my very being escapes—although I *am* that very escape from my being—and I am absolutely nothing. There is nothing *there* but a pure nothingness encircling a certain objective ensemble and throwing it into relief outlined upon the world.[89]

Julien, as Sartre suggests, disappears into a two-dimensional world (that is, into a kind of text, an "objective ensemble"), throwing any sense of being into an ironic mode of chimerical loss. This occurs to Julien repeatedly, as when he enters the office of abbé Pirard and faints under the intense pressure of his self-concealment, or more subtly when he fears the ridicule of the alien glance of Mme. de Rênal at Vergy or of Mathilde in Paris. Julien constantly attempts to escape definition for this reason; when he becomes the object rather than the subject of the analytic process he feels observed and judged, and he must escape this effacement. Crouzet points out that Julien's uniform response to this apparently disparaging judgment is to allow *son angoisse* to overflow and humiliate him.[90] The threat of the enervation the world's glance can effect is fundamental, since "the world is frozen, emptied by a look: it is the eye which, after having separated things and partitioned them off, reins henceforth over a lifeless populace, on a soulless desert."[91] So strong is the cancellation Julien feels that the world itself is rendered barren by it.

DEATH MASK

No wonder the mask of hypocrisy is necessary for Julien to form a sense of himself (despite the inherent hypocrisy in this very strategy), to combat his own cancellation. He makes use of any aid he can to avoid being appropriated. We have seen that his myriad masks serve to deflect the world's expropriating power by ensuring him that the Other does not know who he is. Importantly, at Vergy he employs the very darkness of night as a protective shroud. Night—any mask—permits Julien to feel as though he has become "himself," that he has been freed by the mask, be it the veil of his language or the roles he plays in the Hôtel de La Mole (the blue suit and the black suit). Finally, all other mentors are fundamentally threatening to his sense of himself. Even Korasoff becomes a book of impersonal love-letters, copied out without thought, nothing more than a convenient, opaque mask. His dead heroes form an important part of Julien's hypocrisy, which is itself the enemy of spontaneity, finally "shriveling"[92] the self.

No wonder, then, that Julien's idolatry shifts from the brilliant figure of Napoléon to the dark, mysterious one of Danton, the man of chaos, a kind of anti-hero. But even anti-heroics will not hold. In his dialogue between "community" and "ambition," Julien's *étrangeté*, whether it be expressed in terms of social class or psychological distance, renders him incapable of maintaining his project in the face of the world. Finally, he repudiates the social milieu for which he is unprepared from the outset and toward which he has the vantage point of the perpetual outsider. Since he must operate within the world's sphere, literally and metaphysically, he is forced to make concessions to its hypocrisy. He is not able to act the part of Napoléon *or* Danton, any more than he can be Boniface de La Mole. Julien rises to meet his fate, finally, because he *has no choice*. In the tower to which he has been consigned, above the world (compare *The Charterhouse of Parma* and its dialogue with withdrawal from the world), resigned to his execution (the *real*, physical one), Julien has eschewed all ambition except for a noble death and feels only remorse for the choices he has not made, the voices he has not heard. It is in this *process* that we may look for deeper understanding of the problem of Julien Sorel's metaphysic of the autoaesthetic self. For Julien, "energy" is always desire to rest in a substantial world of identity, but always he is a function of "passage, this passage from self to self,"[93] and whether Julien is noble, rising above others by "virtue" of his desire[94] or sinking below them through its imprisonment and blindness, this ascendency of *passage* defines Julien. He tries to harness this caught-between-ness in order somehow to ratify himself, to make it stand still so that he can control it. *Red and Black* is largely an effort to crystallize desire, to make it "heard."

Ironically, Julien calls this accretion "love," but not "the strict desire of possessing a particular woman," as it seems even for him to be, but an attempt to "lay hold of the world in its entirety through the woman."[95] Mme. de Rênal is Julien's passport to humanity; this is his tragedy. Since real love is always here a ratifier of the distance between the self and others, not a sign of community, Julien must acknowledge its phantom nature.[96] When the mask is down and Julien is "honest" with himself about his love, for example, in the moments at the end of "The Morning After,"[97] immediately after his first seduction of Mme. de Rênal, he instantly discovers that he loses all sense of role and becomes a "nothing struggling to be something," in this scene confessing all his *inquiétude* to Mme. de Rênal and then, in response to his own vulnerability, transmuting this openness into the joy of possession (114). Julien's love is always either textualized as part of his project, as in the love letters he exchanges with Mathilde, or serves as a prolegomenon to his project, as in the ideal of love he has established for himself, his *ambition*.[98] Generally, love is a tool for power, not a reifier. Once it ends in Julien's almost killing Mathilde with a sword (ironically, to her *delight*, given her role: Julien becomes for that moment the heroic Boniface); in the end it ruins and kills *him* (since it is Mme. de Rênal's madness of love—her sensation—that causes her to be manipulated into writing the final, fatal letter to the marquis). Love is always "un modèle qu'on imitait qu'une réalité."[99] This process, always a displacement of the traditions of which Julien feels himself to be constructed, can finally produce only that mimetic model.

Predictably, Julien's happiness in love increases as it becomes more *remote*. He tries to fix his love in memory, in images, in verse, in objects such as the exotic antique (empty) vase he breaks, but love, since it must always be translated into role and sensation, can never satisfactorily ratify or realize Julien. Love only develops in a condition of mutability, as a "passage." Trying to feel love and nothing else, Julien feels nothing. Because it must escape him, love becomes the equivalent of his own death in a *sacrifice divin*.[100] Death, being the absence not of life but of self, becomes the great neutrality in which the *moi* is no longer even *peut-être*. Stendhal is true to this cognitive self-definition in reporting Julien's final moments. Stendhal has left Julien's death scene out of his novel, but in the absence of the death scene we see Julien not "dead" but absolutely "receded," otiose in our omniscient gaze, his *étrangeté* complete. In the final scene Mathilde and Mme. de Rênal aimlessly ride through the countryside in a carriage, the world barren and deserted, and we, with an "almost unbelievable rapidity," find ourselves with Fouqué over the headless corpse of Julien, who lives on in Mme. de Rênal's sensations and Mathilde's perceptions.

Julien's *moi*, now in its Lacanian formulation, can never unite with his ultimate, complete, and therefore impossible sense of *fully articulated* self, the *je*. He can know himself only in terms of his textuality, past and future. This interweaving of the patterns of judgment and response to an alienated and distant world incarcerates Julien in a "happy prison" in which no real community (beyond the verses in his head) is possible; he has truly been, from the beginning, "the man with the [Dionysian] death sentence." Julien composes himself of a contiguous series of death sentences in each of his utterances and in the texts with which he constitutes himself. His is not a social but a psychological withdrawal. Julien realizes that he himself is negation, that in his self-abrogation in the act of being looked at and judged, he alienates the world he has organized.[101] In this light, he can see that even his heroes have been charlatans, voices of nothing: "O dix-neuvième siecle!" he cries. Even Napoléon has been false in pretending—in Julien's fictions of him—to be substantial. But it is *Julien's* flight, not Napoléon's, that is culpable. His has been a theft and a transmutation of ironic, autoaesthetic truth, sincerity, "nature," a shifting of these into the insubstantial, the chimerical. Julien's *passage* has been that of literature itself, in that he has produced the idols that have sustained him, but that very sustenance has been and is as problematic as the texts and the figures *he* has produced. As the *creator* of idols Julien must acknowledge their, and his, insubstantiality. If the novel is a mirror carried down the road of life, as Stendhal claims it is, Julien must accept finally that the mirror reflects (creates) the anomalies, the faults, and the ephemerality of world *and mirror*. The "harsh truth" with which Stendhal introduces us to the novel is not a static presence but "the lightness, the riskiness, the energy" that must accompany the task of self-searching.[102]

Julien's metaphysic is finally revealed as, in the positive and constitutive sense, a Dionysian fiction: his "natural self" is fabricated out of a vital mutability, the sense of loss that results from isolation, and the energy of *étrangeté*. Julien is a layered series of echoes emerging out of a seeming chaos of forces. Stendhal himself, in the short epilogue to the novel he appends to "clarify" Julien and his *histoire* after the novel's conclusion, shows that he is aware of the vital cancellation of the individual that the Dionysian entails, asserting that he has done everything "to avoid laying a finger on private life."[103] This curious, short epilogue is worth quoting, constituting as it does a "strange ceremony" of celebration in which Julien is re-contextualized as martyr and Dionysian power. The novel's closing sentence informs the reader that Mme. de Rênal, three days after Julien's death, "died in the act of embracing her children."[104] "The End." And then:

> The great advantage to the reign of public opinion, which does indeed achieve *freedom*, is that it meddles in matters where it does not belong. For example, private life. Hence the gloom of America and England. To avoid laying a finger on private life, the author has invented a little town, *Verrières*, and when he had need of a bishop, a jury, a court of assizes, put the whole thing in Besançon, where he has never been.[105]

Stendhal, obsessed by the idea of history, avoids history and insists on his own autoaesthetic strategy, undermining the pathos and theatricality of the novel's conclusion by creating a deliberate alternative theatricality that deconstructs the mimetic effect. Apollo is undermined by Dionysus in the narrative strategy of the novel's conclusion. The Nietzschean dialectic of private and public world, of the psychological at the expense of the political (in the broadest sense), of inner and outer (and therefore of the substantial and the insubstantial) is one that expends great efforts to achieve a balance between Apollinian narrative and Dionysian energy. This effort adumbrates a pure Nietzschean autoaesthetics, formulated by Sartre thus:

> The sincere man constitutes himself as what he is *in order not to be it.* . . .
> Total, constant sincerity as a constant effort to adhere to oneself is by
> nature a constant effort to dissociate oneself from oneself. A person frees
> himself from himself by the very act by which he makes himself an object
> for himself.[106]

This self-objectification, a manifestation of the attempt at balance, follows the martyrdom of Julien's body, fragmented like that of Dionysus, fetishized by Mathilde as she worships Julien's severed head, which—shades of Zarathustra—is taken to a "little cave magnificently lighted by innumerable candles," "near the peak of one of the highest mountains in the Jura in the middle of the night,"[107] while "twenty priests celebrated the service for the dead," and buried with great circumstance by Mathilde and Fouqué, who "almost went mad with grief at the sight" of Mathilde's scratching out a burial place. Lest we are in doubt as to the marriage of Apollo and Dionysus in this gesture, orchestrated by Julien, narrated by Stendhal, carried out by Mathilde and Fouqué, Stendhal informs us that "this savage grotto was adorned with marbles sculpted at great expense in Italy."[108] Julien has atoned for the Dionysian force that has driven him toward selfhood and destruction, and in exchange for his martyrdom he becomes a shrine to autoaesthetic force.

This is, no doubt, a freeing up, a creating *for* oneself of the illusion of being alive, Julien's ultimate goal. Since one always depends on the fictions of the textualized world for perception, all one can capture is a series of fragments of a self that is constantly transmuting into what looks like something else. Julien is obsessed by the "horizon" of himself, which is constantly disappearing out of sight ahead of him, out of his control and threatening to vanish. Only superhuman effort maintains his illusions of selfhood. He is always different from himself. As a result, he adopts the persona of the chaotic accepter of his "reality," without a future, and thus is able to neutralize (or to *become*, in Nietzsche's word) the nothing. In the end he becomes a synecdoche, a head, just as Mme. de Rênal had been only a hand: "Never had a head been so poetic as at the moment when it was about to fall,"[109] Stendhal tells us, as Julien's last memories of moments in the

Vergy woods, memories which "came crowding back into his mind, and with immense vividness,"[110] seem to revitalize him; then, at his death, "everything proceeded simply, decently, and without the slightest affectation on his part."[111] To the end, Julien vacillates between autoaesthetic energy and enervation, torn between world and nothing.

The irony of these last narrative reportages should convey something of the problematic reliability of Julien's (and Stendhal's) fictions—"without affectation" indeed: Julien is pure affectation, or he is nothing. In his own assessment of the nature of self-fabrication, Julien concludes first that there is "no law of nature"; he then amends that chaotic judgment to the view that if there is it is "the need of a creature that is hungry or cold, *need* in a word . . . ."[112] And Julien's voice(s) fade away. "Need *in a word*" is for Julien always the primary need, *his* need, the reflection of the insubstantial substance he attempts unsuccessfully to reify. With that ellipsis, "need in a word . . . ," he can say no more, although he continues talking; only the need for and in a word, the echo of the world and of its condition, remains. In acknowledging that grounding need for need, in textualizing and therefore fictionalizing it, and in constituting the "world" *as* that need for need, searching for himself, Julien acknowledges his *étrangeté*, his own ineluctable difference. More than this, in allowing his voices to fade and vanish Julien cancels his own process of evaluation.

The disparate voices that here act upon Julien and his text/textuality, like those precursors on whom he unsuccessfully depends for ratification, voices of philosophy, society, literature, criticism, demand attention and interpretation, and finally still act as a constellation: they seem to present a certain shape of discourse only if one reads them through the dimensionality of *Red and Black*. Their distance from one another, like the stars in a constellation, does not diminish, but their parallactic configuration creates nonetheless a symbolic homogeneity of the same sort as (and with more success than) Julien's voices. He interprets the world as we and *our* voices interpret him; his dilemmas and the chimerical *métaphysique* they generate are his and ours.

Part Two

◆

TEXT AND THE
FRAMEWORK OF SUFFERING

Art and nothing but art! It is the great means
of making life possible, the great seduction to
life, the great stimulant of life.

. . . .

Art as the *redemption of the man of
knowledge*—of those who see the terrifying and
questionable character of existence, who want to
see it, the men of tragic knowledge.

Art as the *redemption of the man of action*—
of those who not only see the terrifying and
questionable character of existence but live it,
want to live it, the tragic-warlike man, the hero.

Art as the *redemption of the sufferer*—as the
way to states in which suffering is willed,
transfigured, deified, where suffering is a form
of great delight.

—*The Will to Power* 853

3

◆

The Mirror and the Dagger: Nietzsche and the Danger of Art

The world as a work of art that gives
birth to itself—

—*The Will to Power* 796

Although I spent some time on it in the Introduction, this remarkable phrase needs further comment, since throughout the hyperbolic density and complexity of his writing no part of Nietzsche's philosophy requires so much attention and yields so much insight into the revolutionary nature of his view of the world as his thoughts related directly to art[1] and aesthetics. In his relentless questioning of the value of *all* values, Nietzsche reveals himself as the explorer not only of what we might now comfortably call Modernist privileging of action but also of the so-called Postmodern disillusionment with action and indeed with value itself, both of which, as I mentioned in the Preface, are contained in Nietzsche's aesthetic. In art we embrace and elude ourselves; these simultaneous opposites are endemic to autoaesthetics. Mankind frames itself. Nietzsche does not obey any of the traditional relationships between artwork and artist;[2] for Nietzsche, art (including the artistry of thinking—and of thinking the self) as such destroys the complacency and serenity of any possible aesthetic balance or closure. Art is a testament to what *cannot* enter the mind, an alien intruder. Despite our Apollinian notion of it, Nietzschean art is not to be mastered nor controlled, but glimpsed, felt, sensed—as glimpse, feeling, sensation of the self. We, as artists and perceivers of art, are outside it and within it. In the richest and most enigmatic parable of this irresistible dichotomy, Nietzsche in the epigraph to *The Gay Science* lays out this ironic autoaesthetic:

66

> I live in my own house,
> Have imitated no-one nor nothing
> And—laugh at any Master
> Who cannot laugh at himself.
>   Over my doorway.[3]

The *Meister* here being potentially laughed at, from the confines of "my own house," could as well be an Old Master as a dignitary, in a first subversion of the traditional in art. Nietzsche identifies himself—as the artist—outside of himself assessing his relationship with his own values and those of others, within an autoaesthetic context. And further—Nietzsche's implication is that to be able to laugh at oneself is to be able to hover at the threshold of one's house, of oneself. This is the Dionysian laughter, emblem of a Dionysian art, that overcomes the Apollinian artist-self unable to perceive the danger of real self-scrutiny. The ironic laughter with which any "Master" is greeted who cannot laugh at himself (that is, hover outside his own door) is reserved for those who do not value the Dionysian but are trapped in an Apollinian, a Socratic or Platonic, interpretation of self and life.

We have begun to see how the autoaesthetic impulse, for Nietzsche, lies at the very foundation of man; as the multiplicity of forces at work in us it urges and manifests our complexity and our aspirations. As Nietzsche points out in *The Will to Power*, "It has been the aesthetic taste that has hindered mankind most: it believed in the picturesque effect of truth, it demanded of the man of knowledge that he should produce a powerful effect on the imagination,"[4] a demand which Nietzsche says the "man of knowledge" (the Apollinian Man) cannot comprehend, let alone accomplish. We have seen how Stendhal explores beyond the Apollinian art in the disastrous autoaesthetic of Julien Sorel; Nietzsche is repeatedly concerned with this "aesthetic taste" and its "hindrance" of mankind. Throughout his work he returns to it, devoting a central place to his thoughts on the aesthetics of the self, within the context of the dilemma of "hindrance/help." He states this dilemma succinctly later in a famous passage in *The Will to Power*:

> One is an artist at the cost of regarding that which all non-artists call "form" as content, as "the matter itself." To be sure, then, one belongs in a topsy-turvy world: for henceforth content becomes something merely formal—our life included.[5]

In this vertiginous and inverted world, in which what we call content (the substantial, even the essential) is revealed as "something merely formal" (no more or less than a question of style), lies the problem and the value of art—and its power of (and for) self-creation. Indeed, as Alexander Nehamas points out, "Nietzsche looks at the world in general as if it were a sort of artwork; in particular, he looks at it as if it were a literary text."[6] Though I would disagree with what I perceive as the *single script* Nehamas seems to think Nietzschean life consists of, and have begun to argue for a disparate welter of "literary texts" which underwrite our lives (Nehamas' thesis requires us to stay closer to the Apollinian than Nietzsche would like us to, I think), nonetheless we have begun to see the context in which the intent of Nehamas' comment, as well as much of his treatment of the narratological self in *Nietzsche: Life as Literature*, bears fruit.[7] For Nietzsche, art and artfulness (a complex Nietzschean kind of word) are always signs and even signatures; indeed, the most important of signs and signatures: art and the "inner" process by which it is produced (and which produces us) are signs of life itself for Nietzsche, as Richard Schacht and others have suggested.[8]

Though it is always in a dialogue with the nihilism Nietzsche sees as everywhere threatening the value of human discourse, and which can only come about as a result of art without Dionysus and the "yes," as he points out so extensively in *The Will to Power*, art always dependably provides, for Nietzsche, the potential antidote for the nihilistic impulse;[9] this antidote to nihilism is the aesthetic survival urge. Indeed, this fundamental signification of art is the final ratification of the "ultimate self-referential application of the knowledge drive"; Nietzsche posits art as the sole agent for "the philosopher's chief function": "to break the hegemony of pure knowing, not from without but from within,"[10] since that (false) drive has only a chimerical hegemony as the drive for self-protection against external and internal threat. Art attacks the panacea of knowing at its source, translating a false solution (however powerful) into a true one (acknowledging, as we shall see, its incompleteness in a perpetual tumult of desire). The disruption of "knowing" by art[11] entails a transcendence of the state in which knowing is or seems to be sufficient; it entails what Nietzsche calls *becoming creative*. This is the lesson that Julien Sorel can never learn, not ever being able to perceive nor trust in his artistry sufficiently to have it bring him positive results. Since, in keeping with the centrality of art, for Nietzsche, everything good and beautiful depends on (art's) self-professed signification, its illusion, art acts as the manifestation *and the imitation* of its own power to create. In creating an idea of the self art creates everything of value. In *The Will to Power*, Nietzsche establishes the framework for this transcendent creativity: "The world," he says "is a work of art that gives birth to itself." I want to analyze how and on what terms this typically hyperbolic and ostensibly extravagant claim—surely one of the most audacious of metaphors—is possible, and how, if at all, it can be defended. Working toward an aesthetic taxonomy, I want to look at Nietzsche's view of art and aesthetics as an index of human life, then, as a result of this perception, at art as an index of suffering, then at the nature of art as metaphor, and finally and more directly, at the constitutive and activating danger of art, for Nietzsche, all within the context of what Nietzsche calls the "redemptive" power of art.

ART AS AN INDEX OF HUMAN LIFE

Nietzsche's strategy is to posit that art, like that metaphorical doorway in the epigraph to *The Gay Science* that frames his experience, is an *index* (an informer, a pointer), and that this framework or index is a function of human *difference*, that is, the way human life is *not* other life. Art, for Nietzsche, acts as a species-identifier. We, as humans, may conceive of life by and because of the art that results from our interaction with our specifically human life.[12] As Nietzsche shows elsewhere, from his early essays on, this perception of the difference of human life is not in itself a qualitative judgment, not an evaluation per se. It simply is. As humans, however, in our last-man anxiety, we transmute this difference into the familiar value judgment we make of our own superiority, and at that moment we are no longer merely naive autoaesthetes fabricating ourselves out of nothing, but ideologues with our own political agendas for self-creation and self-preservation. At that moment, a certain kind of redemptive power of art is born, along with the world. At that moment, all of our aesthetic claims alter radically, becoming aggressively self-protective (the current discussions concerning the arts and politics are cases of this self-preservative moral judgment that accompanies self-creative art); Nietzsche mirrors and, with his typical expertise, mocks this ideological self-ratification in his familiar hyperbole: "Nothing is beautiful," Nietzsche declares in *Twilight of the Idols*, "only man: on this piece of naivety rests all aesthetics—it is the first truth of aesthetics."[13] Human life, in other words, is distinguished from "life in general," and privileged—an index of the closed system of the beautiful. This is a particular kind of aesthetic judgment, wholly without the notions of "beauty" to which it is usually attached. In this categorical definition, and elsewhere in Nietzsche, we can see the strong suggestion that the distinction between human life and "life in general" is precisely the aesthetic faculty, that aesthetics redeems human life from being inhuman and us from being merely *unmenschen*. But this particular kind of redemption cannot be permitted to stand unquestioned, as Nietzsche shows—its strategies must be co-opted for a different kind of autoaesthetic struggle toward humanness. In this struggle, Nietzsche's comments on Kant in, for example, *Ecce Homo*, in which Nietzsche claims to go beyond Kant's rational teleology, are particularly indicative of the revolutionary nature of the autoaesthetic power to create the so-called "human." Clearly delineating in these references to the tradition of aesthetic philosophy his break from traditional German philosophy, Nietzsche focuses on the reactionary and deleterious effect on philosophy of Kant's model of anti(-Nietzschean) aesthetics, as for example here:

The theologian instinct in the German scholar divined *what* was henceforth possible once again. . . . A secret path to the old idea stood revealed, the concept *"real* world," the concept of morality as the *essence* of the world (—these two most vicious errors in existence!).[14]

Kant comes in for such a drubbing at Nietzsche's hands because of that onesidedness Nietzsche finds manifested in Kantian "theological morality," which Nietzsche refers to as "the erring instinct in all and everything, *anti-naturalness* as instinct, German *decadence* as philosophy—*that is Kant!*"[15] Kant's pseudo-redemptive aesthetic is revealed by Nietzsche as being no more than *ressentiment,* indeed as inhuman. In place of this theological rationality, Nietzsche proposes a "strength which prefers questions for which no one today is sufficiently daring; courage for the *forbidden*; predestination for the labyrinth. . . . New ears for new music."[16] Nietzsche, as the Orpheus of this new music, clearly and repeatedly—and increasingly shrilly in his later works—demands a radically new path for the discovery of the truly autoaesthetic experience, beyond the pseudo-redemption of the theologico-moral aesthetics of classical philosophy and its German descendants. He will not allow art to be a mere appendage nor adjunct to reason; art is a positive confusion to the fearful order of the cognitive mind, an active and dangerous disruption of that serene predictability of the un-gay science of philosophy; it is a discrete, fundamental power. This is what Nietzsche means by "art as the *redemption of the man of knowledge*"; it transforms the knowledge man has of himself into "tragic knowledge" of the "terrifying and questionable character of existence, accessible only through art."

Nietzsche thus suggests that aesthetics and its result, art, are dialectical, which for Nietzsche means oppositional, agonistic, a struggle against the enervation of the static, of death-in-life. Discussing Nietzsche's aesthetics, Theodor Adorno addresses this schismatic tendency by directly paraphrasing and commenting on Nietzsche's statement above: "Art is beautiful," he says in *Aesthetic Theory,* "by virtue of its opposition to mere being."[17] This is Adorno's version of Nietzsche's claim that man vies with *himself* to make his aesthetic truth-claim. In *Beyond Good and Evil,* for example, Nietzsche says that "in man *creature* and *creator* are united: in man there is material, fragment, excess, clay, dirt, nonsense, chaos; but in man there is also creator, form-giver, hammer hardness, spectator divinity, and seventh day."[18] This familiar bifurcation *in man* gives rise to art which "commands, wills" that one "become master of the chaos one is; to compel one's chaos to become form."[19] "Truth" is the will to master the multiplicity of sensations, of forces, at work within oneself. Art is that "form" which gives validity to the reflection of human life. According to Nietzsche we are all at work framing ourselves as self-reflexive works of art, created out of that will-to-form within which we see ourselves, whether or not we are able to achieve through our efforts what others might call art; once again, consistent with Nietzsche's psychologization of the world, the evaluative nexus of aesthetic energy is internal and solipsistic, sufficient unto itself. Its only criterion for "validity" is that it be dangerous and subversive (no mean feat, and one requiring real creativity as opposed to slavish or unimaginative mimesis or representation).

Art, then, as an index of human life, acts in two ways. The first is as a mirror; but here, as we have seen, Nietzsche does not infer Aristotle's economy of mimesis to be our "natural state" nor the act of reproduction of an image of our ideal state, which is to be taken as art. Aristotle's mimesis, like Plato's, is the impossibly and undesirably (because falsely) "pure" Apollinian world, a dream of equivalences in which a work of art mirrors and re-presents either the universe (mimetic theory), the audience (pragmatic theory), or *itself as an artwork* (objective theory). Ironically, Nietzsche's structure for art only tangentially encompasses art which reflects the artist himself (expressive theory), since this too is reflective from outside, though expressive theory is by far the closest to Nietzsche's of any mode of art production. These four are the forms of art-as-mirror traditionally constructed around the logocentric serenity of order. But when Nietzsche makes the seemingly categorical declaration, in *Twilight of the Idols*, that "man really mirrors himself in things; that which gives him back his own reflection he considers beautiful,"[20] he re-initiates the question of the nature of the mirror and the artist's power and desire to reproduce himself. Nietzsche's view of this reproductive faculty is that it is not *re*-production at all, but production. The "mask" or framework of art is, actually, *is*, what is seemingly "beneath" it. In one of his most prophetic aphorisms, Nietzsche declares that "without a mask one has no face to present"; appearance is (human) life. This is the index and the dilemma of art: "If one has a talent, one is also its victim: one lies under the vampirism of one's talent," Nietzsche says in *The Will to Power*.[21] "One does not get over a passion by representing it; rather, it is over *when* one is able to represent it." The artist is caught within an animating but morbid dialectic: by becoming, the artist moves toward absence, by being, the artist would disappear (what would Heidegger think of that?). By this measure, the artist who can *truly* represent a passion causes it to cease to exist, makes it inhuman. The human artist, because he goes on living, or at least existing, goes on producing imperfectly, falsely, or partially; the conundrum is that according to Nietzsche the closer the artist comes to the perfection of creation, the more "falsely" that production will be accomplished, given that the artist creates himself as he produces works. For Nietzsche, the seemingly ironic mimetic power of art is precisely its ability to reproduce falsehood, "only" appearance. As Gilles Deleuze states it,

> it is *art* which invents the lies that raise falsehood to its highest affirmative power, that turns the will to deceive into something which is affirmed in the power of falsehood. For the artist, *appearance* no longer means the negation of the real in this world but this kind of selection, correction, redoubling and affirmation. The truth perhaps takes on a new sense. Truth is appearance.[22]

The artist is *truthful*, according to Nietzsche, precisely "in his recognition of illusion and lie for what they are";[23] thus he gains a strategic affective freedom. Only the artist who can conceive of the entire world as appearance, who can see appearance *qua* appearance, can make a truth-claim for art, and only this autoaesthetic figure is correct and accurate in so doing, since only art, of all human activities, can facilitate this truth-claim.

Deleuze' comments about appearance echo the passage I mentioned in chapter 1, discussion of which I have deferred until now, of the closing section of the Preface to *The Gay Science*, in which Nietzsche goes further than anywhere outside of *Zarathustra* to explicate his autoaesthetic strategy. So much is contained in the passage, so many themes so richly laid out, that it must be quoted again; it is always a joy to encounter it:

> "Is it true that God is present everywhere?" a little girl asked her mother; "I think that's indecent"—a hint for philosophers! One should have more respect for the bashfulness with which nature has hidden behind riddles and iridescent uncertainties. Perhaps truth is a woman who has reasons for not letting us see her reasons? Perhaps her name is—to speak Greek— *Baubo*?

The suggestion that "truth" is the prehistoric personification of female genitalia, an "obscene female demon," according to Kaufmann's footnote,[24] and the further implication that we should conceal this truth behind the veils of "riddles and iridescent uncertainties" is almost unbearably tantalizing, and therefore typically Nietzschean, in its suggestion of the complete evasiveness of the nature of truth, despite the personification that nature too acquires in the passage. Nietzsche's typical anti-Christian theme here, claiming that the all-seeing is indecent and unnatural, is that it is in the concealed that we perceive truth—not a concealed truth, but truth-in-concealment.[25] Nietzsche's desire to "speak Greek" at the moment of defining truth, and defining it by avoiding definition, is the desire to enter the autoaesthetic abyss.

But Nietzsche goes further. Following this "Baubo" passage comes another, which is a kind of Koran (like Julien's) for autoaesthetics:

Oh, those Greeks! They knew how to live. What is required for that is to stop courageously at the surface, the fold, the skin, to adore appearance, to believe in forms, tones, words, in the whole Olympus of appearance. Those Greeks were superficial—*out of profundity*. And is not this precisely what we are again coming back to, we daredevils of the spirit who have climbed the highest and most dangerous peak of present thought and looked around from up there—we who have looked *down* from there? Are we not, precisely in this respect, Greeks? Adorers of forms, of tones, of words? And therefore—*artists*?[26]

The complete inversion of the Platonic image of rational human life, with its vertical orientation and depth-metaphors, pervades this passage, which echoes away from the "Baubo" paragraph preceding it so as to make it impossible for the reader to come out of the book's Preface, dedicated by Nietzsche to a description of the poetic philosophy he champions, without an elusive autoaesthetics fresh in mind. The poem about living in one's own place, without laughable so-called Masters, with which the book begins, must also be reinterpreted in light of this ironic displacement. Nietzsche is here introducing an anti-Platonic world view by which to read all of *his* works of art and those of others, a world view that cannot be thought about but which escapes thought, a non-ruminative world view. We must constantly strive to remember that for Nietzsche truth is not *concealed* but *concealment*, not hidden behind appearance but *appearance itself*, constitutive superficiality.

Historically, it is the turning away from this notion of truth as appearance that led the most human of humans, the Greeks, into the error from which Nietzsche is attempting to awaken us. The (Socratic, that is, culturally victorious) Greeks' error began with the privileging of reason of the knowing subject, which was the death knell of the extra-cognitive or intuitive aesthetic judgment employed, in Nietzsche's scheme of things, before Socrates. And so, as Nietzsche declares in *The Birth of Tragedy*, the Greeks lost their fuller or more complete framing strategy, trading it in for a less complete but safer and more accessible criterion by which to gauge themselves. Nietzsche asserts repeatedly that the pre-Socratic Greeks engaged in just the play with appearance he wants us to reconsider, before its consummate death in the advent of Aristotelian subordination of mimesis to the "real." The Greek tragic drama's sense of the tragic is precisely the redemption of those able to see "the terrifying and questionable character of existence," indeed, to "want to live it," while Aristotle's interpretation of this sense is no longer tragic but political. Nietzsche's concept of the human is radically different from Aristotle's, as from Kant's (Nietzsche sees them as committing the same error, Kant merely recapitulating Aristotle's), and will not permit this subordination of the aesthetic to the rational. Nietzsche considers art and "nature" to be complements, mirror-states in a quite different way from that of traditional mimesis. Freed from the constraints of referential truth, the artist is empowered with the ability to pursue *life*, human life, which requires art for its existence.

This "fold" of Nietzschean aesthetics, however, is a many-layered dialectic that creates an edge, an incision, at the point(s) at which it occurs. The fold is a reflection and an invasion; the second way in which art is an index of human life, in keeping with this fold, is as the image of a dagger: in "creating" human life, art is dangerous to it, since to be properly mimetic is precisely to mirror or represent the brittleness and danger associated with life, its ephemerality and incompleteness. Nietzsche saw his own life as being lived on this dangerous and troubling edge, as that of the harbinger of suffering. In just this spirit Nietzsche's school friends of Pforta called him a *Qualgeist*, literally a "pain spirit," a thorn-in-the-flesh—a pain in the ass. Thomas Mann, James Joyce in the Stephen Dedalus of *A Portrait of the Artist as a Young Man* and *Ulysses*, and more recently Milan Kundera in *The Unbearable Lightness of Being*, and many others have faithfully followed up on this aspect of man's (redemptive) learning about and suffering through himself.

This second index of art, as the invasive, is not simple nor straightforward. The "coming-within-ness" of art and of the aesthetic criteria for it is very problematic in Nietzsche. The incision of art, painful as it may be, requires a simultaneous objectification, a "point of view." This is one of the most significant aspects of the *index* of art. In providing an index, a gauge or measure, of the difficulty of becoming human through creativity, art—by virtue of its status as index—remains apart, aloof, reveals itself as an entry into—indeed a creation of—the suffering of human life.[27] As such, it is an index of the life of the *Übermensch*, man's struggle to overcome himself. This is, for Nietzsche, according to Adorno, a posture of eternal (self-)cruelty.[28] Art mirrors the power of man to attempt to overcome himself; art is great in proportion to its ability to signify an approach to its achievement.

ART AS THE INDEX OF SUFFERING

This cruel posture of self-incision and self-overcoming is the positivity of suffering, as opposed to the no-saying suffering of the Christian world-view. As Gilles Deleuze points out, "Art does not heal, calm, sublimate, or pay off, it does not 'suspend' desire, instinct, or will,"[29] but fosters them. In one of the most significant passages of *The Will to Power*, Section 1052, Nietzsche declares that art's affirmation is of a "being counted *holy* enough to justify even a monstrous amount of suffering."[30] Just in this way, the incision—the dagger—of art is an operation whose *telos* is the preservation of a certain type of man, the exceptional or Overman.[31]

This man, the highest artist, provides our index of the greatest "good":

"The beautiful and the ugly are recognized," Nietzsche claims, "relative to our most fundamental values of preservation."[32] The issue of preservation is fundamental for Nietzsche, particularly in terms of the crisis precipitated by notions of the "modern." Indeed, one of Nietzsche's favorite and most used puns is that on *moderne*, which as a German noun means "up-to-date" and as a verb means "putrefy, decay, rot." Nietzsche plays on the double meaning of *moderne* devastatingly against Wagner in *The Case of Wagner*, to describe "the modern artist par excellence," a term of execration unparalleled in Nietzsche's writing. Interestingly, Nietzsche describes "modernity" in *The Will to Power* as an "atrophy of types" in which "the overlordship of the instincts . . . has been weakened."[33] This enigmatic declaration shows how "the modern" confuses the issue(s) of Apollo and Dionysus and vacillates between up-to-dateness and rottenness. This slippage within a word, as well as the strategic indeterminateness of such a loaded word, is the emblem, Nietzsche shows repeatedly, by which to capture the ambivalence of life-and-deathness with which Nietzsche wants to invest "modernity." The last man, fading from the world like a ghost in the daylight, disappears within this ambivalence. But the *pharmakon* of art makes man "sick," as Nietzsche often says, in order to make him more than healthy. Nietzsche always uses this word, "sickness," to describe the enervation of the last man, who can no longer will, no longer perceive (let alone aspire to) the condition of the Overman.[34]

In terms of art, Nietzsche is operating at another level of "sickness." Man is sick with regard to art because art always demonstrates, in its very existence, man's inability to achieve transcendence, his imprisonment within the dilemma of finite life and finite energy. Again, the word "sick" is caught in a double bind of sickness and health; indeed, in this adumbration of Derrida's double bind of the *pharmakon*, this relationship of art to sickness and health results directly from the "extreme sharpness"[35] of the artist's self-perception and, more generally, of the psychological state of the artist as such.[36] We have seen how, from his earliest writings, Nietzsche characterized this conundrum in the evolving figures of Apollo and Dionysus. In terms of this framing of the artist in the suffering by which he comes closer to knowing himself, the artful Apollo represents deception, as the impossible eternity of beautiful form. Apollo is the legislator of aristocratic stasis, declaring "Thus shall it be forever!"[37] The cruelty of Dionysus and the suffering introduced by the artist's self-reflexive immersion in that cruel suffering occur in forcefully and forcibly reminding us of the morbidity, the brittleness, and the transitoriness of life's forces *in us*, the continual creation and death in which we live. The artist, like Nietzsche, is forever trapped between what Ronald Hayman calls "passive acceptance and violent rebellion, between *amor fati* and outrage."[38] This psychological state, along with the will to mimesis and intoxication, forms the marriage of the Apollinian and Dionysian and gives birth to artistic suffering:

> Life itself, its eternal fruitfulness and recurrence, creates torment, destruction, the will to annihilation. . . . One will see that the problem is that of the meaning of suffering. The tragic man affirms even the harshest suffering: he is sufficiently strong to do so.[39]

The artist's mimesis is of the suffering life formally offers up. Then, in terms of the incursion of art, Nietzsche provocatively continues: "Dionysus cut to pieces is a *promise* of life: it will be eternally reborn and return again from destruction."[40]

The harshest suffering, art's dissection of life, in which the artwork (and the artist's work) is left behind as a memorial, a cryptographic sign, occurs when the extraordinary man "breaks his will to the terrible, multifarious, uncertain, frightful upon a will to measure." The actual work of art is an "'eternalization' of the will to overcome becoming";[41] it is an index of suffering because the artist leaves it behind as a mark of a life-and-death struggle, a mark of difference, in a process of self-preservation in which "we possess art lest we perish of the truth."[42] "Art" and "truth," as we have begun to see, are not in opposition in life any more than in the preceding statement itself; the opposition of art and truth gives way to the key-word, "perish." Nietzsche's concern is that the truth of art reveal itself in order to allow man not to perish of false truths, which we call "facts." It is always a life-and-death dialogue. "Dionysus cut to pieces" is its emblem; the Dionysian force, which Nietzsche calls a "temporary identification with the principle of life (including the voluptuousness of the martyr,"[43] as we have seen in Julien and will see in Jude), is the "*aesthetic justification*"[44] for juxtaposing the will to preservation and recuperation with the eternal-creative's compulsion to destroy: the will to pain, the state of animal vigor.[45] Art is lost and life becomes *ugly* when we view them with a will to implant a singular interpretive meaning which finally denies art.[46] Thus do Apollo, the interpretive, and Dionysus, the eternal-creative, vie and merge in a perpetual state of agitation.[47] The *étrangeté* of this vying and merging establishes the context for creative suffering and for its celebration. For Nietzsche, the framework of suffering is truly celebratory, since it allows us to begin to know ourselves, whatever the cost. The celebration of suffering leaves in its wake a hallowed satisfaction.

In fact, the notion of the "wake" is vital to Nietzsche's autoaesthetic. The parable at the opening of "On Truth and Lies in a Nonmoral Sense" captures just this sense of the wake, in its several meanings. Like the conclusion of the *Gay Science* Preface, the opening of "On Truth and Lies" is Nietzsche at his most parabolically pungent:

Once upon a time, in some out of the way corner of that universe which is dispersed into numberless twinkling solar systems, there was a star upon which clever beasts invented knowing. That was the most arrogant and mendacious minute of "world history," but nevertheless, it was only a minute. After nature had drawn a few breaths, the star cooled and congealed, and the clever beasts had to die.

Here Nietzsche captures and reflects the art and the artifice, the life-and-death-ness, of man's aesthetic dilemma. In the "wake" of this parable, we cannot help but be thrown into a new relationship with our sense of self and of life, whatever we may conclude for or against the powerful Nietzschean attitude. In this "fable,"[48] as Nietzsche calls it in the next sentence, art and the art of telling about art congeal in a parable of man's significance and insignificance: the story is that of signifying per se, but it is also "about" the autoaesthetic (in)significance of the teller relative to the tale, of the dead person relative to the corpse, let alone relative to the wake. It is a "true story" about mendacity; that is, it is an articulation of story, a sign, a metaphor.

ART AS METAPHOR

Nietzsche, in the parable from "On Truth and Lies in a Nonmoral Sense," resorts to a metaphor of the *arche*, the world-origin, to define man's aesthetic dilemma.[49] And it is precisely here, in metaphoric transference, that Nietzsche sees the emblem of reflection and incision as constituting a transcendence. Nietzsche's privileging of style—and his own aphoristic and highly allusive poetic style—attest to the *étrangeté* of metaphoricity, of the fold of articulation as a (false) grounding of the sign. This is where the morbidity of art reaches its apogee. It is here that Nietzsche constitutes his greatest *philosophic* dilemma and his own estrangement from the philosophic establishment: "philosophy" for Nietzsche cannot escape its own suicide, as Paul de Man points out, turning out to be "an endless reflection on its own destruction at the hands of literature."[50] Literature, in its turn, is the metaphoric collapsing together of the active-creative and the reactive-creative. Literature, and even poetry and music, represents the "wake" of creativity, its sign, and therefore the sign of truly human being. Art catalyzes its own reactive impulse, which Gilles Deleuze has discussed.

Nietzsche claims that "the essential thing remains the facility of the metamorphosis, the incapacity *not* to react"[51] both with the eye (the Apollinian) and the "entire emotional system" (the Dionysian). Metaphoricity in this sense constitutes *what is*, beyond good and evil, the framework for man. Nietzsche never posits in his work a "self" being explicated by an artistic text, nor does he build a sense of self *through* a work; rather, he acknowledges the radical alterity and genealogical power of metaphor *as* the power of self-searching. Metaphor, in all its duplicity, is the articulation of "pure" self-ness.

In this respect Nietzsche redefines, for the twentieth century (the "modern" age), the concept of the "aesthetic." In the face of this fundamental power of transference, aesthetics is no longer "about" beauty, because "in beauty opposites are tamed": art is "the power over opposites,"[52] not their cancellation but their subsumption into a system (art itself) of suspension in which "violence is no longer needed."[53] Violence perpetuated cancels violence. Nietzsche's own art entails a new and different sort of violence, still being explored in many versions of so-called Postmodernism. In its "power over opposites," art transcends its more conventional specular role, familiar to us as the mimesis of the "real," and becomes the self-creating value of difference itself.

THE DANGER OF ART

Art, for Nietzsche, then, is the constant danger to which one always says YES. Aesthetics, insofar as it deals with art, its creative sources, its forms, and its effects, is always an analysis of distress. This framework, which redeems suffering so that it becomes a source of "great delight" rather than of *ressentiment*, of a self-constitutive *étrangeté* rather than merely of a dark alienation, Nietzsche seems to have perceived from his earliest writings,[54] and it is a pervasive theme. He is quite specific about the *étrangeté* of that danger. "The greatest danger," he declares in the section of *The Gay Science* by that name,

> that always hovered over humanity and still hovers over it is the eruption of madness—which means the eruption of arbitrariness in feeling, seeing, and hearing, the enjoyment of the mind's lack of discipline, the joy in human unreason.[55]

Remembering here the parable of the tightrope walker from the opening sections of *Zarathustra*, Nietzsche is extraordinarily clear about how he intends madness (*Irrsinn*) to be taken, in the string of appositives he uses to define it: "the joy in human unreason" (*die Freude am Menschen-Unverstande*) in the eruption (*Ausbrechen*) of arbitrariness (*Beliebens*, which although Kaufmann translates it as "arbitrariness" is more usually "choice" or "will") is the index of the exceptional man: Indeed, he concludes the section with an underlined rallying call to "artists": "We others are the exception and the danger." Unreason and art are metaphorically conjoined, and the danger that links them is positive, a YES-saying; to be exceptional is to be dangerous.

This metaphoric relationship between distress and art, which Nietzsche had treated directly in *The Birth of Tragedy* and to which he makes reference as early as the opening of "On Truth and Lies in a Nonmoral Sense," finds its fruition in the "unreason" of his own art—his poetry. In *The Gay Science*'s opening section, following the Preface at which we have already looked, an opening section entitled, in the Dionysian way, "Joke, Cunning, and Revenge," a poem entitled "The Wanderer" appears; its parabolic depiction of the danger of transference distills Nietzsche's argument for (the danger of) art and artistry:

> "No more path! Abyss encircling and dead still!"
> You willed it! Left the path by your own will!
> Now, wanderer, you have it! Now see cold and clear!
> You are lost if you believe—in danger![56]

The narrativity of the poem captures in metaphor the non-position, the *Unverstande*, from which Nietzsche approaches art, ensconced within the autoaesthetic *dein Wille*, the will-to-power, of the artist's framing method. The "path," like the tightrope for Zarathustra's tightrope walker, as we shall see in chapter 5, provides a link with the rational world of man; but the wanderer has left the path in favor of the "abyss [*abgrund*]," just as the tightrope walker precipitously leaves his rope in Zarathustra's story of him. The danger of art entails both the wanderer/poet's fighting for his existence and his alienation from the world of men, his passionate involvement and a dagger-coldness and clarity in examining and invading that world. The danger lies in allowing the frame but never fixing it, and permitting Dionysian free play within it.

At the other end of *The Gay Science*, an appended sequence of poems entitled "Songs of Prince Vogelfrei [*Lieder des Prinzen Vogelfrei*]" is further explication of Nietzsche's aesthetic framing, ostensibly *by* the poet, although this is suitably indeterminate in the title. The poet's name, *Vogelfrei*, means "free bird" or "free as a bird" but connotatively signifies, at the same time, a capital criminal at large who may be shot on sight with impunity. The metaphoric and imagistic process of "unreason"—of pure metaphor—by which this name is conferred portrays a life-and-death danger for the potential victim of the free bird and for the assailant, the *vogelfrei*, him or herself. The dramatic combination of the free and the vertiginously and fearfully threatened aptly indicates the oppositions contained in the dense metaphoricity of Nietzsche's autoaesthetic. This constant and dramatic crossing over echoes the extended motto Nietzsche declares in *The Will to Power*:

> To spend one's life amid delicate and absurd things: a stranger to reality; half an artist, half a bird and metaphysician; with no care for reality, except now and then to acknowledge it in the manner of a good dancer with the tips of one's toes . . . .[57]

The remarkable (but finally chimerical) privileging of the "inner" life, itself as undermined ontologically and rhetorically as any purported outer reality, without a care for the external mundanity of a "reality" constrained by general agreement, makes Nietzsche not only a product of the Post-Romantic nineteenth century; he carries this solipsistic sensitivity much further. "To spend one's life among delicate and absurd things" is to be constrained only by the limitations and strategies of *figuring* (framing) the Dionysian abyss, of rendering what is "off the path" pathful and articulate. One must note that Nietzsche's mathematics, in dividing himself into parts, is also indicative of that overabundance, that self-overcoming of which the autoaesthetic is constructed. To be half an artist, half a "bird and metaphysician," is to be more than oneself, to be a self-and-a-half, to dance across the idea of defining oneself as the artist dances across the canvas, the marble, the stage, the paper. The "free [jail]bird" is Nietzsche's heavily laden depiction of the autoaestheticist manifesting itself floating free of traditional self-identification.

But the metaphoric vertigo of the artist, while vital to artistic self-construction, is only part of the danger he both feels and offers.[58] Even more vital to the artist is his dilemma with the faculty of the understanding—not, ironically, with being misunderstood but with being understood. If "Have I been understood?" is the great cry of *étrangeté*, Nietzsche must continue to be able to answer in the negative—he must be misunderstood in order to be an artist. What is susceptible to the understanding is not and cannot be art, and the understanding has only tangentially and faintly to do with the autoaesthetic Nietzsche proposes. It can be religion, literary theory, philosophy, criticism, scholarship, education, etc.—pure frame—but it cannot be art. Nietzsche sees the role of the artist as that of the teller of parables. Parable, trope, the turning aside of meaning, all are vital metaphoric dialogues of the immanent self in Nietzsche's autoaesthetic. "The artist who began to understand himself," Nietzsche declares, "would misunderstand himself."[59] Richard Schacht's gloss on this troubling and dangerous idea, "art is not to be thought of as having to do with the revelation of fundamental truths about reality,"[60] is a pale understatement of Nietzsche's dramatic and poetic language. But Schacht's enervated comment reminds us that *Nietzsche*'s rendition is itself stylistic, a great and magnetic danger. Here again we must read Nietzsche's autoaesthetics with attention to its rhetoricity; if we were to continue the investigation we would find, according at least to de Man, that "the general structure of his work resembles the endlessly repeated gesture of the artist."[61] As we saw in chapter 1, this reading of the Eternal Recurrence, as rhetorical articulation, is more and more compelling as we explore the nature of autoaesthetics. This endlessly repeated gesture of self-creation is not one that privileges understanding but rather misunderstanding. Nietzsche's style is a strategy of transference that takes us toward not closure but *méconnaissance*. Art allows us to live at the highest levels of this creative misunderstanding by strategically allowing us a glimpse of the web of forces by which we turn aside from the (perpetual) death of reason. Within this web we are constrained and free, simultaneously, in being metaphorized. Gary Shapiro has pointed out that after *Zarathustra*, that is, by early 1885, Nietzsche turned his attention to an increasingly select audience which *would* misunderstand. In *The Gay Science*, this takes the form of a short, parabolic poem in the opening section, "Joke, Cunning, and Revenge," a poem that echoes the epigraphic doorway:

> "Fastidious Taste"
> When one is left free to choose,
> One would gladly choose a spot for oneself
> Right in the middle of Paradise:
> Gladlier still—before its door!

This poem throws the epigraph into a new light: now "Paradise" is not in the house from which we laugh at Masters, but in the position of the Masters themselves, *outside* the doorway in a condition of desire for the closure we never and could not reach. Since Plato, reason has taught us the opposite; Christianity urges us to accept the illusion of "ignorant faith" that also stifles interrogation and free play. In both rational thought and dogmatic religion, Dionysus is not martyred but transformed into demon or misfit. To (mis)understand autoaesthetic human life, one must give up understanding and live in its danger; one must come to see and value that danger for what it is.[62] One must appeal to art, to (mis)understand the fluidity of transference, the nature of parable, the activity of metaphor; art always, to use Mallarmé's words, *évite le récit*. Nietzsche's truth-claims are for an art that embodies and encompasses truth precisely in the danger and suffering of its never being what we—however we define it—seem to want it to be.

4

◆

Jude the *Camera Obscura*

> Jude is simply an endeavor to give shape and
> coherence to a series of seemings, or personal
> impressions, the question of their consistency or
> their discordance, of their permanence or their
> transitoriness being regarded as not of the first
> moment.
>
> —Thomas Hardy, *Jude the Obscure*, xx

> In vain do we surround modern man with all of
> world literature and expect him to name its
> periods and styles as Adam did the beasts. He
> remains eternally hungry, the critic without
> strength or joy, the Alexandrian man who is at
> bottom a librarian and scholiast, blinking
> himself miserably over dusty books and
> typographical errors.
>
> —Nietzsche, *The Birth of Tragedy*, 112

Thomas Hardy had a good deal of trouble naming the hero of his last novel, a work that convinced him finally of the futility and even the danger of extended character investigation. When one realizes the overdetermined nature of Jude Fawley's burden, one can see Hardy's dilemma. Although Jude stands for certain very un-Nietzschean "cathartic, Aristotelian qualities"[1] that Hardy had himself made the center of his fictional and metaphysical program, and although those qualities are everywhere in a fundamental dialectical struggle with the "hungriness" of which Nietzsche speaks, this very tension makes Jude a perfect autoaesthetic subject. However hard Hardy may have tried to avoid the Nietzschean autoaesthetic, Jude, for all his guilt and agonized, stalwart searching, remains a "typographical error," caught between the mirror and the dagger of an incipient artistry that never quite happens. His very ambiguity is profoundly Nietzschean, I would maintain, always perceived by the reader and by himself obscurely and with difficulty because he feels and appears to be concealed, veiled behind his own "pretexts," which in turn result from *his own* Nietzschean blindness. Jude is always and everywhere a kind of penumbra, a series of seemings or appearances, literally a trail of impressions looking desperately for some (im)possible grounding in his own social and metaphysical vacuum, caught outside the conventional but within the archaic world of conventions. He is a compendium of autoaesthetic forces whose only framework is his misperceived suffering; never able to "enter his own house," Jude is always in the thrall of the Masters on whom he relies for identity. Further, Jude is the *artist manqué* of Nietzschean autoaesthetics, unable to comprehend the power of autoaesthetic art and so doomed to live a last-man existence of guilt and morbidity. Jude's considerable energy cannot find the path to self-creation; his no-saying art is a burden to him rather than a release.

In this respect, Jude is the opposite of some of Hardy's other central characters, not only, as J. Hillis Miller otherwise very convincingly suggests, their final descendant. In "Tess's Lament," a later poem cited by Miller, Hardy reflects on just the problems of existence being discussed here, as (the equally blind) Tess has seen it:

> I cannot bear my fate as writ,
>   I'd have my life unbe;
> Would turn my memory to a blot,
> Make every relic of me rot,
> My doings be as they were not,
>   And gone all trace of me.[2]

The *amor fati* manifested here, which overwhelms the sense of life, is characteristic of Hardy. But Jude manifestly and increasingly through his short life does not want to "unbe." He engages in a Dionysian struggle, however vain and nauseating it turns out, for "real" or "valid" existence until the absolute end of his story, when, having been unable to prevent his recalcitrant body from contracting a fatal case of pneumonia, he still rails at the obscurity that has enveloped him from the beginning of his story. His is a tremendously forceful suffering, a true *agony*; he has fought with all his might to "be," and in the process has inscribed himself on the world, leaving traces in the very fabric of the walls around him. He has gone one step beyond the monument-worship of Julien Sorel, creating his own monuments to his lost and undiscoverable self. He has built monuments to his struggle to exist beyond the texts by which he, like Julien, has been constructed. Every endeavor of Jude's, from his desire for inclusion in the "timeless" confines of Christminster to his stonemasonry, leads him toward, if never to, an autoaesthetic resolution.

Hardy's frame for Jude is a denial of the Nietzschean yes-saying: in his Preface to *Jude* we learn that this story is all a function of failure (both Jude's story and Hardy's story of Jude), but that the failure is a noble one that comes about not for lack of effort, on both Jude's part and Hardy's. Jude experiences a loss of power, of validity, essence, and therefore of identity. His concern with his origins, with his social role, and with the texts on which he bases his life all point to a desperate struggle with the inertia and the suffering of loss and with the dangers of self-fabrication. His position is, however, quite clear: he is always caught between stories, perpetually attempting to fill the gaps with stone wedges that he chisels.

Just as the biblical Jude, his namesake, is both a disciple (Judas Iscariot) and the "author" of the penultimate book of the New Testament, itself a short and enigmatic letter warning the faithful against false teachers and "worldly people, devoid of spirit" (19), so Jude Fawley is "pseudonymous," everywhere attempting to write his own fate but, as a creature of *étrangeté* with no redemptive sense of his Dionysian self, born doomed. In Jude Fawley, Hardy shows not only a character at war with social convention, nor a pioneer of emancipation, but an explorer of the abjectness of "modern man," at once up-to-date and putrescent. Jude's ever more limited framework (and he is disastrously always working to make it more limited) only allows him glimpses of the enervating discovery that the conventions which ground us are no more than traditional writings-over—that to *stop* "writing-over" is to die. For Jude, a much-desired integrated identity is displaced, as it is for Julien Sorel, by a miasmic sense of "significance"; he is composed of a series of seemings or signs in which a sense of personal validation cannot exist, but the search for which cannot be cancelled.

I want here to work back and forth through the novel's dense thematic texture to unravel some of Hardy's, and Jude's, vivid autoaesthetic threads and to explore ways in which Jude's autoaesthetic, an object lesson in negativity, pessimism, and *angst*, confronts and denies the Nietzschean, with such disastrous results, in terms of Jude's self-conceptualization and self-construction as functions of articulation and of *étrangeté*.

ARTICULATION

IMAGED LIFE

Jude Fawley is as close to being an artist as one could be without being aware of what artistry is. Hardy's and Jude's own fascination with the "graven image," whether photographic, painted, carved in stone, or narratized, frames a desire to provide Jude a resting place, a static existence in which that fatal "caught-between-ness" can be arrested.[3] Images are precisely the beginnings and the ends of Jude's problem: his frantic attempts to capture and possess his own image, which nonetheless remains a Dionysian mirage, create of Jude a *camera obscura*, producing a faint, inverted, silhouetted and chimerical self-image. Indeed, Jude sees himself as literally a *camera obscura*, imprisoned inside his own body (and consciousness), encased in his own self-awareness, looking at what is *outside*: the geometry of his perspective is oriented to his sense of obscured enclosure, of always being cut off from any validation, which is always external even if metaphysical.

Jude energetically sets up a series of frames in which to image forth the world and himself, but in which, because of the inversion (*étrangeté*) of the reflected images, everything is "turning to satire."[4] An autoaesthetic ontology has become a series of false etiological puzzles centering on the theme of suffering. For Jude, no longer are such things as origins possible; now, given that like the camera Jude is confined to reaction and reflection, only causes—the causes of suffering—exist. All so-called originality, and thus authenticity (in the sense of author as creator), has been erased. Immediacy is impossible, and even mediated existence is obscured by veils. Jude is a personification of the Dionysian/Nietzschean man's antithesis, the last man, for whom reward is not Schopenhauerian union with the Will nor Hegelian synthesis but a failed Nietzschean autoaesthetics, seen in a series of frames that range from the literal to the purely figurative.

Jude's is an imaged life. Jude's multiple framing devices take many forms, from the literal to the literate. Photographs and their frames form a vital link in Jude's autoaesthetic narrative.[5] The study of Shaston, for example, is dotted and in some way held together by photographic images and photographs. Inadvertently in a junk shop, Jude discovers a photograph of himself he had given his wife Arabella. But Jude's use of it is oddly telling: he takes the photo home, removes the likeness of himself, and burns it, then saves the *frame*. Given the opportunity to save "himself" or the frame around him on which he counts for identity, he saves the synchronic ratifier and controller rather than the disturbing likeness, which is diachronic and, indeed, dead. When, eventually, Jude and Sue are married, instead of exchanging wedding bands they exchange photographs. Most telling of all, in this literal version of the *camera obscura*, is that moment in Shaston, after Jude has left Sue on the evening of his visit to her and Phillotson's home, when he returns invisibly in the middle of the night to Old-Grove Place to have what he thinks is a last (clandestine) look at Sue—through the window. He finds her there, framed in the light of the old house:

A glimmering candle-light shone from a front window, the shutters being yet unclosed. He could see the interior clearly. . . . Sue, evidently just come in, was standing with her hat on in this front parlour or sitting room whose walls were lined with wainscoting of panelled oak reaching from floor to ceiling, the latter being crossed by huge moulded beams only a little way above her head.

She had opened a rosewood workbox, and was looking at a photograph. Having contemplated it a little while she pressed it against her bosom, and put it again in its place.

Then becoming aware that she had not obscured the windows she came forward to do so, candle in hand. It was too dark for her to see Jude without, but he could see her face distinctly, and there was an unmistakable tearfulness about the dark, long-lashed eyes.[6]

Sue is framed by the formal wainscoting of the inner room, just as she has admitted being framed, that is, named, by the formal and conventional Phillotson. Next, from Jude's perspective, she is framed by the window itself, and further enclosed by Jude's conceptual framework for her. Within these frames, she holds the photograph, not only framed but contained in a box, a frame which completely obscures it. Sue's conceptualization of the photo provides a last, tantalizing frame, and one we are not party to. Jude sees and contemplates Sue, and at the same time does not see and cannot contemplate her. The photograph, taken from its box/frame, caught within its own frame, within Sue's gaze and thoughts, within the window frame, within Jude's conceptual framework and that of the narrator, and finally of the reader and his or her image structures, a final frame, is smothered by the attention to framing it receives. Appropriately, Jude has (and we have) no idea whose is the image in the photograph, and as Jude is leaving—in an agony of uncertainty over whose photo Sue has revealed to him and us—we hope as much as Jude that the mysterious photo will be brought to light. But Hardy does not lift the veil from the photo; his final framing never opens, and we never know whose portrait Sue has been looking at. Like Jude, we agonize over the identity of the figure (if the photograph is a portrait and not an image of the pyramids or the Parthenon), sharing the framing devices through which Jude has seen Sue and the enigmatic photograph. Like Jude, we are frustrated and unsatisfied.

This fascination with the photographic image is preceded by a kind of narrative photography. In his effort to write an essence out—or across—his existence, Jude is fascinated, as is Hardy in his narration, with dialogic images of an eternally elusive "inner sanctum." Jude and Sue Bridehead, for example,[7] have their most successful conversations, throughout the novel, when they talk to each other through a window, Jude generally the outsider. If Jude's late-night visit to Old-Grove Place gives us a sense of his photographic, image-oriented framework, the earlier visit, on the same night, is more complex. The scene reveals Jude standing at Sue's window; standing in the window frame, Sue directly addresses this framing device and uses it to characterize herself and Jude more candidly than she knows, in terms of the texts and frameworks of suffering. Notice in the following passage the ways in which Sue acts as an autoaesthetic photographer, creating a series of Judes that metaphorically transmute from martyr to martyr while never abandoning the particularity of her own autoaesthetic suffering:

> "I can talk to you better like this than when you were inside. . . . You are Joseph the dreamer of dreams, dear Jude. And a tragic Don Quixote. And sometimes you are St. Stephen, who, while they were stoning him, could see Heaven opened. O my poor friend and comrade, you'll suffer yet!"
>
> Now that the high window-sill was between them, so that he could not get at her, she seemed not to mind indulging in a frankness she had feared at close quarters. "I have been thinking," she continued, still in the tone of one brimful of feeling, "that the social molds civilization fits us into have no more relation to our actual shapes than the conventional shapes of the constellations have to the real star-patterns. I am called Mrs. Richard Phillotson, living a calm wedded life with my counterpart of the same name. But I am not really Mrs. Richard Phillotson, but a woman tossed about, all alone, with aberrant passions, and unaccountable antipathies."[8]

Sue's own articulation, a refrain of Hardy's narrative structuring, frames her in this window scene as more Dionysian than one would notice at a glance. Sue, in investigating her own "antipathies," becomes as much of an instructor to Jude as Phillotson had been in Marygreen, speaking to an important and ever-growing part of Jude that will come to obsess him as much as it does Sue. Jude, too, as we have begun to see from early on, is "tossed about" in "unaccountable antipathies." Sue can articulate, as Jude cannot, the so-called "actual shapes" she and Jude possess, somewhere "behind" the socially acceptable shells by which they are framed. This is a pure play of appearances. Like photographs of the (apparent) constellations, Jude and Sue are composed of "patterns" of parallax and narration. Sue's artistry, like Jude's, can only indicate that neither she nor Jude is identical with appearances, and that the terminally elusive happiness they hope for is not possible in a world of candor—even through a window frame—they want to inhabit. Ironically, the physical frame they construct for themselves and to which Sue calls attention serves to make them more aware of the impossibility of identity and thus of happiness.

The accumulated effect shows Jude's concern as being with the devices he utilizes to form frames, not with the image itself. These layered framings provide Jude with a kind of pseudo-clarity, as though a certain thickness of appearance might establish ontological satisfaction, but still protects the obscurity he requires to "be himself," free of the delimiting frames within which he works. After seeing Sue with the mysterious and unidentified photograph, Jude walks home, feeling suddenly freed (redeemed?) in the darkness from his dependency on seeing the world through Sue, who has reminded him, repeatedly, of the figures on whom he has depended for his framework, and that his reliance on Sue was something that

> those earnest men he read of, the saints, whom Sue with gentle irreverence . . . called his demi-gods, would have shunned such encounters if they doubted their own strength. But he could not. He might fast and pray during the whole interval, but the human was more powerful in him than the Divine.[9]

But humanity, for Jude, is an unframable free play of Dionysian articulation, indeed, the very denial of frames, incapable of being contained successfully by the rigid wainscoting that "conventional life" around him wishes to impose;[10] in search of this elusive humanity of framelessness, Jude will discover his most exquisite suffering.

NARRATIVE REALITY

Jude escapes the rigidities of self-definition not because he is able to transcend conventional society but because all such incorporative structuring, as we have seen, is composed of failed or successful autoaesthetic literary fictions, in Jude's case stories he hears—and tells—of the "earnest men he read of." Jude, like Julien Sorel, frames himself within a set of literary discourses which, because they are his own monologic voices masquerading as discourse, are already falsehoods, and finally are as ephemeral and insubstantial as Jude himself. It is in terms of these narrative frameworks that Jude must make the most telling and painful decisions about the nature of his suffering. Seeking the "Divine" (static, dependable, like a captured photographic image), hoping to balance it against the "human," on which he cannot rely, Jude resorts to a narrative framing that proceeds from "inner rooms" and "casements" to inner texts and a highly coded language of the self. Jude's self-textualization is a function of the literature, sacred and profane, that in Jude forms a metaphysical extension of the physical framing with which we have seen him surround himself.

For Jude, to frame is to suffer; this is more than a small part of his link to Sue, Jude's subtlest and most complex mentor, who, despite her ability to disregard convention to live unconventionally with Jude—for a while—represents in the context of the novel the force of what Nietzsche calls "European nihilism," that greatest suffering, which he characterizes as "denaturalization of values. . . . Scholiasticism of values," in which "detached and idealistic, values, instead of dominating and guiding action, turn against action and condemn it."[11] Nihilism is a turning away from the Dionysian humanity that demands action. As Jude begins to realize that he and Sue must take action against social convention (directly Sue's marriage to Phillotson, but indirectly Jude's demi-gods), he—talking to Sue through the open window at Aunt Drusilla's house—articulates unwittingly Sue's phantom-like inhumanity; in seducing her to his plan, Jude frames Sue as a "spirit," not knowing that in such a framing she must, indeed has, become in turn one of his demi-gods, that of nihilistic inhumanity.[12] In his address to her at this pivotal moment, he frames her in terms of her distant spirituality and *his* need for the autoaesthetic suffering that results from a denial of the human:

> It is more than this earthly wretch called Me deserves—you spirit, you disembodied creature, you dear, sweet, tantalizing phantom—hardly flesh at all; so that when I put my arms around you I almost expect them to pass through you as through air.

Through the *camera obscura* of nihilistic interpretation, Sue is apotheosized into a wraith beyond the body. Her response to this otherworldliness in Jude's judgment of her is to compound the textuality of her framing. She replies to Jude's airy flight:

> "Say those pretty lines, then, from Shelley's 'Epipsychidion' as if they meant me!" she solicited.[13]

The complexity of this exchange is monumental. The "tantalizing phantom" Sue seems to Jude is to be imagined in a narrative image, to be made to settle down, textually, in Shelley's lines. The "Epipsychidion" is made to detach itself in truly autoaesthetic fashion from the disastrously ephemeral social radical who wrote them, to exile itself, as Shelley did and Jude and Sue soon will, from all convention, and to set itself adrift on a sea of unconvention (where it, like Shelley and Jude, will surely drown). Shelley and his great work of the spirit are the perfect framing for Jude and Sue in their endeavors to break convention. But Hardy shows again, here, Jude's many options for suffering in the ephemeral insubstantiality of this literary framing: he does not know the Shelley. He hardly knows any poetry at all, he confesses in response to Sue's query, and so Sue is left to define herself, as *she* proceeds to recite Shelley's apt lines:

> There was a Being whom my spirit oft
> Met on its visioned wanderings far aloft. . . .
> A seraph of Heaven, too gentle to be human,
> Veiling beneath that radiant form of woman. . . .[14]

The nihilistic frame of inhumanity, "veiling beneath that radiant form of woman," is a further echo of the phantom of identity.[15] This play of textualization and improvisation continues in the scene. Sue importunes

Jude to say that the vision of the poem *is* her; Jude replies, *precisely*, "It is you, dear; exactly *like* you!"[16] For Jude, the slippage from metaphor to simile is endemic to identity—to be like is to be, and to be like a text, that is, framed by it, is to be so even more solidly. At what seems to be his most candid moment of insight into Sue's character, Jude translates identity into a trope, actual into metaphorical.

This relation to the Shelley image reveals a fundamental aspect of Jude's framing strategy and its imagistic, even photographic, nature. In declaring what Sue is "like," Jude characteristically gestures toward "freezing" himself and others in space and time. From within the *camera obscura* Jude seeks a still, inner core caught in a frozen image.[17] This is true from the first moment of the novel, images of Phillotson's leaving Marygreen, to Jude's last in which, alone in his inner room in Christminster, he calls out to and engages in discourse with his literary progenitors, present in (literary) spirit. Just as Jude and Sue are "like the lovers in a tragic version of the scene on Keats' urn, in which even the immediate moment of bliss is frustrated and finally denied,"[18] Jude's life is an attempt to capture the ephemeral and already absent, or else that which was *never there* outside of some Hardy-esque, Romantic "great memory."

ENTRAPMENT AND ISOLATION

Incapable of producing a sense of self, Hardy's anti-autoaesthetics does produce a sense of entrapment, as though caught between the suffocating pages of a closed book. This entrapment produces a gnawing *abîme* which deepens the sense of the *camera obscura*. As with all of Hardy's framing strategies, this abysmal sense is itself ironic, as J. Hillis Miller points out:

> Each of Hardy's protagonists has . . . the sense of a void within. This inner emptiness is the absence of any absolute ground for the self. These characters seek escape from their ontological insufficiency. . . . In this world, the gap always remains, that pain of loss or sense of hollowness which the permutations of the game of love can never more than momentarily ease. His characters, in a world without a center, a world without any supernatural foundation, seek unsuccessfully to locate a center and a foundation.[19]

Desire to locate a foundation, for Jude, is always escaping in the very strategies by which he seeks it.

BACK TO GENESIS

Indeed, this isolation appears in the first scene of the novel. Richard Phillotson, the beloved teacher, is leaving Marygreen for Christminster—leaving Jude behind.[20] As a boy of eleven, Jude stands in the middle of the village at the precise spot of the "still center," the well at the heart of Marygreen, after

Phillotson has departed, looking down into the "long circular perspective ending in a shining disk of quivering water" with "the fixity of a thoughtful child who has felt the pricks of life somewhat before his time."[21] The inverted framing of the sky and the sun's light, in the deep well's obscure depths and the tunnel-frame through which Jude must peer to see that light reflected below, are the boundaries of his initial and initiatory auto-aesthetization. Jude, in this first great suffering, peers into the center of things—Hardy is not being subtle here—and sees life as a shimmering image of reflection, not of disclosure or hermeneutic incursion; his peripatetic search for *other* mirrors and frames begins, and Jude will never be at rest again. He will always be trapped between perception, a Dionysian force, and reflection, the emblem of the Apollinian.

Although Phillotson's departure from Marygreen catalyzes the Nietzschean frame in which Jude will see(k) himself thenceforth, and although this scene is a welling up of autoaesthetics, the disruptive event breaks a frame within which Jude has unwittingly operated. The "old" frame, at the novel's inception, is one of simple village life (which has not altered much, as we shall see, between Hardy and Fowles, and which is used in quite similar strategic ways). The breaking of this frame requires not only the setting up of another (or others) but the setting up of others that can compensate for the remnants and memories of that broken one. For Phillotson's departure, in other words, Jude must construct a set of interacting frames, each insubstantial and tentative, which in their discourse will serve as the much more complex conceptual frame within which Jude functions. Because of the growing complexity of those frames, Jude's efforts to make himself less obscure become increasingly a need to discriminate within this multi-frame dialectic. This means that Jude's *étrangeté* is increasingly enhanced by the very circumstances within which he tries to overcome it. And Jude is conscious of this layered *étrangeté*, as Hillis Miller shows: "To be conscious is to be detached. Consciousness is a passive power of observation which cuts a man off from everything"[22] and this dual sense of self-awareness and *étrangeté*, what Jude would call "dream" and "sensuality," or spirit and flesh, since his terms for these conditions are taken from the text that is his namesake, the Bible, concludes in his realization that to see the world "clearly" is already to see the folly of this chimerical clarity.

But an inevitable (Nietzschean) undermining precedes or accompanies Jude's fragmented self-inscriptions. In that first, seminal scene, during which the credentials for the semiology of both articulation and *étrangeté* are set in place and in motion, Hardy declares that Jude is already, at eleven, "an ancient man in some phases of thought," though he is "much younger than his years in others";[23] that is, he is a palimpsest of stories from the past and naiveté about the present and future. In sum, Jude is a "man" for whom as you got older, and felt yourself to be at the centre of your time,[24] and not at a point in its circumference, as you had felt when you were little, you were seized with a sort of shuddering, he perceived. All around there seemed to be something glaring, garish, rattling, and the noises and glares hit upon the little cell called your life, and shook it, and warped it. If he could only prevent himself growing up![25]

All around the young(/old) Jude is the world's glaring *étrangeté*, shaking and warping the *camera obscura* of one's life, conceived spatially like a camera, as a little cell in which one passively resides, experiencing not the peace of the innocent but the shuddering and shuttered isolation of the trapped, displaced, and endangered. "Being at the centre of your time" is for Jude the definition of the "promised land" of eternal and perpetual "youth," avoiding the complexities of active adulthood within a conventional (that is, single) framework.

METAPHYSICAL SUFFERING

Although Miller and others have reminded us of the conscious nature of much of Jude's self-fabrication, other of his frames are not so clearly of those kinds. Even when they are physical, of course, Jude's frames are not merely to be seen. His metaphysical framing and the suffering resultant from it are even more binding than the physical. His strategies, like Julien Sorel's, are thematic[26] ones of the loss of authentic voices, beginning with Phillotson's, which vanishes to the "place that teachers of men spring from and go to."[27] From the moment of looking down the well at the chimerical disk of the lost sky, Jude becomes increasingly aware of the loss of origins and the need for their reinscription. Jude is, of course, an orphan; he has had to construct a metaphysical mother and father to replace the lost originals. We have seen that when Phillotson, the surrogate father, leaves Marygreen, Jude's first resort is to the well, the surrogate mother, as a symbol of constancy. He weeps into the well, "the only relic of the local history that remained absolutely unchanged,"[28] at the thought of Phillotson's departure. The stones of the well, adumbrations of the stones with which Jude will work as an adult, are the only constant frame in Jude's absolutely relativized world.[29]

Jude's sense of himself in the midst of the physical evidence of the past's enervation is as a kind of remainder, an empty camera. Aunt Drusilla calls him a "poor, useless boy" who would have been better off if "Doddymight had took thee too, wi' thy mother and father."[30] Cut off from an acceptable genealogy and its accompanying sense of continuity, the only real monuments Jude counts increasingly on are the ephemera of narratives and narrative frames. He must rely on unreliable stories of his origins and his past, his parents, his surroundings. Like the truncated and misquoted Shelley fragment with which Sue characterizes herself, Aunt Drusilla's stories of

Jude's origins are fragmented and incomplete.[31] Jude is here, again, the emblem of Nietzsche's last man, that other teller of false and enervated stories: he is part of "a culture without any fixed and consecrated place of origin, condemned to exhaust all possibilities" of self-substantiation.[32] For Jude, as for Nietzsche's last man, the question of parentage, literal and figurative, is indeed beggarly. Jude is a member of "our present age, the result of a Socratism bent on the extermination of myth. Man today, stripped of myth, stands famished among all his pasts and must dig frantically for roots."[33] Jude obsessively desires that lost unity, the mother, and that naming-power, the father, both of which have been lamely re-mythologized in Jude's pessimistic metaphysics.[34]

Jude has mistakenly thought that, Adam-like, he could name the world correctly, but his early exchange with the quack physician Vilbert enlightens him on this point. Asking Vilbert for the Latin and Greek texts of the Bible, because those who read Greek "may be able to read the New Testament in the original,"[35] he discovers that "there was no law of transmutation,"[36] that he cannot understand the "original" language intuitively and that he will have to memorize all the words he needs to translate correctly the unoriginal original. Having misunderstood this is to Jude a "gigantic error,"[37] and as he returns from Vilbert's house he grows more and more agitated by his discovery, longing for someone to come down the road to relieve him of the intensity of feeling, but "nobody did come, because nobody does."[38] Again, Jude confronts his *étrangeté*, the blinding crossover from innocence to difference and isolation, the failure of his autoaesthetic.

Jude's displacement from "old texts" manifests itself relative to three particularly Nietzschean frames: Christian dogma, rational inquiry, and (auto)aesthetics. We have seen how biblical imagery controls much of Jude's search for identity and how, embodied in Phillotson and Christminster, reason/education occupies such a central and powerful place for him. In order to understand the enervation Jude feels in the face of these determiners we must remember the place they occupy in Nietzsche's own autoaesthetic: they are the *most dangerous* frames by which one can endeavor to define oneself, involving endless life-and-death choices, made from the point of view of a value system of *ressentiment*. Jude is defined by Hardy as a "hungry soul in pursuit of a full soul,"[39] a perfect integration of the Nietzschean motif of "good" physical forces (here, hunger) and "bad" metaphysical forces. Since, for Nietzsche, autoaesthetic "knowledge" is based not on the fact of birth nor learning but on what Edward Said calls "transpersonal, natural, and 'prehistoric' forces like the unconscious or the will,"[40] Jude's course away from aesthetics predestines him to frustration and failure: his glimpsed autochthonous self is increasingly destroyed as his learning increases.

THE WIDENING GYRE

Misunderstanding the artful self-denial on which he is launching himself, Jude grows increasingly enamored of the *idea* of Christminster, which, as the seat of learning, is from the distant hills of Marygreen "a faint halo, a small dim nebulousness, hardly recognizable save by the eye of faith."[41] The subversion of Jude's autoaesthetic sense means the strengthening of reason and faith in his last-man dialectic. He feels, because of his attachment to Phillotson, that in Christminster he would "come to rest." Even the "old track," the prehistoric road that, although increasingly obliterated by modern innovation, runs through the middle of Marygreen, seems to point him in the direction of the chimerical, haloed city. In Marygreen,

> he could not realize himself. On the old track he seemed to be a boy still, hardly a day older than when he has stood dreaming at the top of that hill, inwardly fired for the first time with ardours for Christminster and scholarship.[42]

But were Jude to be able to come to rest in "the ardours of Christminster and scholarship," he would be Phillotson, not Jude. Like Zarathustra, but literally, Jude philosophizes with a hammer (and chisel), punishing the stone for *his* anomie, still focused on Christminster:

> A little further on was the summit whence Christminster, or what he had taken for that city, had seemed to be visible. A milestone, now as always, stood at the roadside hard by. Jude drew near it, and felt rather than read the mileage to the city. He remembered that once on his way home he had proudly cut with his keen new chisel an inscription on the back of that milestone, embodying his aspirations. . . . He wondered if the inscription were legible still, and going to the back of the milestone brushed away the nettles. By the light of a match he could still discern what he had cut so enthusiastically so long ago:

> The sight of it, unimpaired, within its screen of grass and nettles, lit in his soul a spark of old fire. . . . He might battle with his evil star, and follow out his original intention.[43]

In this pivotal scene, Jude's aesthetic sense quickens as he sees that figure in the stone, as Hardy says, "embodying his aspirations." The eternal return to the milestone is Jude's mirrored Gate of Moment, lighting in his soul "a spark of the old fire." While this is an old sign of his ardor for learning,[44] for the reader the obscured inscription, like its creator, is a fresh, momentary, and fleeting illumination, a marker for what is gone, like all artworks. But for the reader and for Jude, the objective rekindled at the touch of the grooved letters is not what he thinks it is: the hand points to Christminster (the sign of the hand is absent from many editions of the text, in which case the reference to Christminster is further obscured) but the message is one of *peripetaeia*.

THE HALOED CITY

Not until Jude commits himself to Christminster[45] do we see his dangerous art at work. In fact, Christminster is *not* pointed at by Jude's sculpted hand, but the falsehood of that marker is its truth. Moving away from "the centre of his time" takes the form of a crossover from the village environment in which he has grown up to that of the "city" to which Phillotson has gone. Marygreen represents for Jude the inchoate possibilities of the unformed self, the swirl of past forces of the unconscious he wishes to transcend; Christminster, which in his ruralized frame Jude has imagined with a mixture of rapture and suspicion, becomes the source of light and enlightenment in his new autoaesthetic, the haloed "outer" version of that disk of light he saw at the bottom of the Marygreen well; Jude's autoaesthetic *hegira* begins in his contemplation of Christminster:

> Jude continued his walk homeward alone, pondering so deeply that he forgot to feel timid. He suddenly grew older. It had been the yearning of his heart to find something to anchor on, to cling to—someplace he could call admirable. Should he find that place in this city if he could get there? Would it be a spot in which, without fear of farmers, or hindrance, or ridicule, he could watch and wait, and set himself to some mighty undertaking like the men of old of whom he had heard? As the halo had been to his eyes when gazing at it a quarter of an hour earlier, so was the spot mentally to him as he pursued his dark way.
> "It is the city of light," he said to himself.
> "The tree of knowledge grows there," he added a few steps further on.[46]

By shifting his frame from the city, Jude "grows older," growing indeed *into* his autoaesthetic suffering.[47] But for Jude to be given "real" entry into the promised land of suffering, rather than merely a metaphoric vision of it, he would have to explode his *camera obscura* of physical stasis. As Michael Millgate points out, "Jude is permitted visions of the promised land, but he is himself forbidden to enter it."[48] In fact, the reader can see that the so-called promised land of which Jude has become aware is not Christminster but the aestheticized dialectic of suffering between discovery and disillusionment, within the slipping frames of Jude's autoaesthetic. Jude locates Christminster as the ontological focus of the fictional *arche*; we have begun to see already, before he attempts to reach it, how for Jude

Christminster as *arche* is the now familiar Derridean *arche-trace*, displaced and distanced in space, time, and narration from any originary validity.[49] "Thither, J. F.," indeed.

PHARMAKON EYES

With Jude suspended on the brink of Christminster's terrifying promise, I want to look for a moment at the nature of these signs by which Jude marks his way. From within the *camera obscura*, Jude's signs, such as Christminster, become or include their opposites, cancelling their impetus and rendering themselves ironic markers incapable of being read as Jude wants to read them. In containing their opposites, Jude's signs form ongoing and ineradicable dialogues. In this, Hardy is a Nietzschean. Revising Kant, for whom "a collision of duties is unthinkable," Nietzsche shows that every thought, feeling, and impulse must operate in a conflictual association with another. This duplicitous irony instigates the rebellion against markers of entrapment that Jude needs and tries so diligently to overcome. Signs of *étrangeté* act as *pharmaka*, a dilemma for Jude as he strives to make monoleveled frames with a singularity they inherently lack.

As for Stendhal, Hardy's women often signify the Dionysian spirit struggling against the stultifying Apollinian. Such is certainly the case with Jude's wife Arabella, who is at once the freer of Jude's emotional life and the "belladonna" that induces a kind of amnesia in him. Jude sees that Arabella throws his scholarly aspirations into eclipse, but he sees this fact

> with his intellectual eye, just for a short fleeting while, as by the light of a falling lamp one might momentarily see an inscription on a wall before being enshrouded in darkness.[50]

The "falling lamp" by which he sees himself sinking into oblivion is a vital frame for Jude: it is the lamp of consciousness and, more importantly, of self-consciousness. Jude's autoaesthetic requires close scrutiny of his frames, and Arabella undermines this reflexivity. The sepulchral language in which Jude describes Arabella's effect on his literary aspirations marks the death of those aspirations while he is with her. Jude's relations with Arabella, as with Sue, are a sign of his *étrangeté*. Jude knows that his self-consciousness is composed of texts inscribed across that "wall," that inner wall always fleeing into the darkness of Jude's black little cell, his existential *camera obscura*. Because of his depth-metaphor orientation, Jude cannot see nor understand that it is not *behind* the wall on which the Arabella inscription is written that Jude "himself" is to be found; Jude perpetually fails to see that the metaphorical wall itself, the surface of appearance on which his perceptions and narrations are written, is his substance.

But the Ara-bella-donna that closes Jude's ambitious literary eye opens another Nietzschean/Derridean eye/frame: the complex set of reversals and conundrums represented by woman in the novel. Woman, for Jude, is the death-in-life tomb of emotional (sexual) life, from which man must escape, and she is the emblem of aesthetic perception from which all aesthetics, including autoaesthetics, evolve. Woman's power to corrupt pervades *Jude*;[51] in this Augustinian framework, woman is seen as an eternal trap, in the traditional Christian sense, preventing man from seeing clearly. The "feminine" in Jude, which would allow a vital autoaesthetic, is suppressed as he thinks through the question of his relations with woman as carefully as he can. Hardy's strong implication, however, is that the contamination of woman's—here, Arabella's—sexuality has made Jude incapable of clear and careful thought:

> There seemed to him, vaguely and dimly, something wrong in a social ritual which made necessary a cancelling of well-formed schemes involving years of thought and labour, of foregoing a man's one opportunity of showing himself superior to the lower animals and of contributing his units of work to the general progress of his generation, because of a momentary surprise by a new and transitory instinct which had nothing in it of the nature of vice, and could be only at the most called weakness. He was inclined to inquire what he had done, or she lost, for that matter, that he deserved to be caught in a gin which would cripple him, if not her also, for the rest of a lifetime.[52]

Marriage is a test of one's nature, a litmus for rebellion, against both the formal constraints of the "social ritual" and its more insidious secondary effects, most notably the sexual urge. Arabella causes Jude to forget his "fervid desires to behold Christminster,"[53] as sexuality eclipses intellectual energy, as if for Jude the two are mutually exclusive. And yet it is Jude who insists on marrying Arabella "to do the honorable thing"; and Jude badgers Sue for years about marrying until she acquiesces, when they go through a mock wedding to satisfy the community (and Jude).[54]

In *Jude*, Hardy portrays marriage itself as the *pharmakon*. It both liberates and constrains; it is a romantic fantasy and a crashingly real limiter. Of course, for Jude the "marriage question" is further divided in terms of its frameworks. Arabella and Sue represent two very different dialogues within Jude, Arabella signifying "the world of the flesh,"[55] her dark beauty a sexually attractive enticement to oblivion, Sue and her lightness representing all that is "disembodied."[56] Arabella opposes, by her nature, Jude's quest for knowledge and learning. Hardy handles this polar opposition between Arabella and Sue so broadly that the possibility of satire is prominent. Jude meets Arabella when he is struck in the face by a pig's penis she has (accidentally) thrown in his direction. He is enthralled by her mesmeric physicality, which cancels his "higher" thoughts. But Hardy cannot help endowing Arabella with a certain autochthonous power. She is an "original,"[57] embodying the "unvoiced call of woman to man" that "holds Jude to the spot against his intention—almost against his will, and in a way new to his experience."[58] Her attraction to Jude is very precisely described as "unvoiced."

Heavy irony attaches to the nature of Arabella's role in Jude's life. While it is true that she inhibits his intellectual activity (according to Hardy's scheme for her), she gives him a sense of stasis that *ought* to be attractive, were Jude seeking a conventional or traditional identity. Only because Jude's intention is to be *dialectical*, not static, is Arabella not constructive in forming Jude's sense of self. She provides Jude with the Dionysian "pole": it is "better to love a woman," he says about Arabella, "than to be a graduate, or a parson; ay, or a pope,"[59] words the *other* Jude would and could not utter. Zarathustran (and biblical) symbols abound in this dialectic of the body and the mind for Jude, as he describes himself, caught in the thrall of Arabella, as "a snake" "who has sloughed off his winter skin, and cannot understand the brightness and sensitivity of its new one."[60] As Adam *and* the serpent, quintessential man and evil spirit, Jude impossibly overlaps the frames within which he works, articulating his elation and his unease. The sensitivity of his very skin is affected by his passion for Arabella. Later, with Sue, although Jude will regain some of his love of learning, he will never be free of the serpent-like feeling that arises with his sexuality. The Freudian nature of the imagery associated with the sexuality of marriage, from the pig's pizzle to the serpent's shape to Jude's skin and body itself, are sufficiently schematically obvious to need no elaborate comment; Hardy's sexual-symbol system in the novel is such a straightforward Freudian one, at one level, that it needs very little discussion. The Zarathustran interpretation of the imagery is more suggestive and allusive. The serpent in *Zarathustra* is always associated with the eagle, the two being dialectical opposites conjoined by the prophet to represent the search for totality of humanness. The eagle represents pride in humanness, and the serpent is "the wisest animal under the sun."[61] "That I might be wiser! That I might be wise through and through like my serpent!" Zarathustra exclaims.[62] "But there I ask the impossible," he replies to himself, reinstating the dialogue between wisdom (the serpent) and pride (the eagle). Yet Zarathustra's semiotic associations of serpent and eagle are themselves subject to inversions of a telling sort. Zarathustra asserts that it is impossible to be as wise as his serpent because his wisdom "loves to fly away"[63]—like an eagle, and that his pride is rooted in his physical life, which is earth-bound (life the serpent). Nietzsche's animal symbolism is clearly not only complex but ironic, a constantly warping framework within which to see the ever slipping Zarathustra. Jude's serpent-nature is nearly as complex as Zarathustra's. Jude, too, sees his plight as being caught between the animal, as in his relationship with

Arabella, whom Jude describes as "a complete and substantial female animal—no more, no less,"[64] and otherworldly, as with Sue.

PHARMAKON EYES AGAIN

Jude and Sue are indeed "of one flesh" from the beginning, and though "flesh" is the key word, now that flesh is the symbolic one of narratives. Jude and Sue are lost and found in the stories of their common (obscured) origins in Marygreen, "twinned" orphans. Sue is the ethereal side of the Eternal Feminine with which Jude must wrestle, and which he misunderstands as badly as he has Arabella. Sue comes into Jude's life not through the blatant and symbolic sexual agency of the pig's pizzle but in a photograph, which provokes Jude into his journey away from the (symbolically) fleshly Marygreen and toward the dream/nightmare of Christminster.[65] We have seen how, from the beginning of his attraction to it, Christminster has been the focus of "abstract desire" for Jude, the goal of his search for self and excellence, the catalyst for all that might give him a sense of unity, and while it is true that Phillotson's departure for Christminster catalyzes Jude's interest in going there, Sue's photograph has begun the journey, reported to us in terms of Jude's inquisitiveness:

> The ultimate impulse to come [to Christminster] had had a curious origin—one more nearly related to the emotional side of him than to the intellectual, as is often the case with young men. One day while in lodgings at Alfredston he had gone to Marygreen to see his old aunt, and had observed between the brass candlesticks on her mantlepiece the photograph of a pretty girlish face, in a broad hat with radiating folds under the brim like the rays of a halo.[66]

All the framing devices we saw in the window-frame confrontation between Jude and Sue are here, frame within frame. The photograph is framed on the mantle, the frame for the hearth; Aunt Drusilla's heavy brass candlesticks frame the photo's frame. Within the photograph's frame, Sue's ethereally pretty face is framed by her broad hat which gives her the quality of an angel (like Christminster, Sue is framed by a halo). The "emotional" side of Jude attracted by Sue's photograph is quite different from that addressed by Arabella's earthiness. But Sue is not "merely" an angel; her double nature is revealed in Jude's obsession with the photograph after he has seen it. The specular power Sue's image has on Jude is ethereal, but its effect is physically powerful. Jude asks for the photo; Aunt Drusilla will not give it to him— and so Jude must have "the original," as though ironically the photograph has renewed the "old intentions" Jude has given up for Arabella. Sue's (image's) power over Jude is as an anamnesis in which he remembers something about himself he has lost and which quickens the aesthetic ghosts within him. Hardy describes the photo's effect exactly in these terms, with all of Jude's keywords present: the photograph "haunted him; and ultimately formed a quickened ingredient in his latent intent of following his friend the schoolmaster thither."[67] Sue is the catalyst of desire, not its object, producing in Jude the requisite re-awaking to his own fragmented self. The two of them together form a *doppelgänger*, "one person split in two," as Phillotson says about them.[68] Sue produces and, finally, *is* the image of Jude's wanderings. She calls herself "the Ishmaelite,"[69] the lost and wandering one, and indeed she is like a chimaera, always disappearing as one pursues her; as Hardy says, "there was nothing statuesque about her; all was nervous motion."[70] Her seeming insubstantiality comes from the fact that she is part of Jude's dreams. She is the subtler autoaesthetic intellectual side of Jude emblematized and then veiled behind the Goethesque figure of woman, the Eternal Feminine who is siren and detached symbol at once. When, later in their relationship, Jude and Sue agree to no further physical contact, Jude declares conclusively, "then let the veil of our temple be rent in two from this hour."[71] While Sue represents a dialectical opposition to the world of raw feeling and animal passion into which Arabella plunged Jude, a world in which inscriptions on walls or veils is no longer visible, her irony is that the so-called enlightenment Sue brings is itself a veil. Indeed, everything about Sue turns out to have been a veil: their "modernity" in eschewing marriage, their lovemaking as the approach to a "temple" of purer love within the spirit. In fact, Jude's frustrated, morbid autoaesthetic, his denial of any possible Dionysian fusion, depends on these ethereal veils. The many-framed image Jude has of Sue as his spiritual counterpart, a very complex *pharmakon*, sets up criteria of self-evaluation by which Jude frames himself, and this is the real meaning of any autoaesthetic. Jude's Nietzschean humanity is denied by his aesthetic idealism; he judges himself as being an "imposter" because of his love for Sue.

But Jude's relationship with Sue evinces a very complex anti-Dionysianism. Having relinquished his intention of becoming a minister— for Sue, Jude finally burns the books that would have defined him in that role, in so doing attempting a validity with Sue *beyond* those texts, in what Jude calls "actual feelings" produced in his vision of the spiritual Sue. Jude claims to rise above the texts that would have prevented that ascendancy, and sees in the flames of the books a momentary purgation of passion for anything other than Sue; one might say that the flames of Jude's passion for Sue are misdirected and consume the texts out of which he has tried to fashion himself.

ETRANGETÉ

Jude takes up the mantle of the will as a cancellation of Dionysian forces from Julien Sorel, and cements them in a culture only too ready to deny the will's errant physicality. Jude's constant avoidance of his own emotional life, his denial of the imagination in favor of *copying texts*, and his pervasive dialogue with cultural mores demonstrate this throughout the novel. Since all themes lie side by side with their dialectical opposites in Jude's world of unmade choices, it is natural that at the center of the novel's metaphoric thematics are oppositions between marriage and divorce and between harmony and *étrangeté*. Jude transforms the theme of divorce-as-*étrangeté*, elevating it to truly Nietzschean proportions and locating it at the center of his autoaesthetic dilemma. Divorce, always a form of *étrangeté*, is at the core of Jude's suffering. He translates this into not only an autoaesthetic theme but an aesthetic one as well. Since all art(work) is a tombstone of its creativity, a cryptographic sign, Jude's frustrated autoaesthetic art is a dramatic sublimation of his creativity, a true divorce from the (redemptive) art Nietzsche would urge him to pursue.

Divorce from self is balanced throughout *Jude* by divorce from others. Edward Said points out three kinds of divorce in Jude's story, in addition to the end of the marriage contract, which lead to the frustration of Jude's self-creation: "the divorce of man from his generative role either as man or as author; the divorce of man from time; and the divorce of man from his 'natural' intentions."[72] In Christminster, the desired place of unity and harmony, Jude finds only an overdetermined and depressing deadness, but Jude has no context in which to treat his malaise; he simply does not and cannot understand his condition. His *étrangeté* leads him to attempt desperately to divorce himself from surrogate fathers and achieve autonomy, but all he can manage is to see himself as the Crucified, a martyr to lost hopes and lost causes. Jude's tragedy is that he cannot settle into this too intense surrogate martyrdom. His mounting desire to become autonomous leads to a dismal return to Marygreen, to the original symbolic *camera obscura*: "Weary and mud-bespattered, but quite possessed of his ordinary clearness of brain, he sat down by the [Marygreen] well, thinking as he did so what a poor Christ he made";[73] in the clear reflecting surface of the well Jude can see himself as nowhere else.

Unable to accept surrogate martyrdom, Jude plunges back into a kind of surrogate autoaesthetic *aus dem Geiste der Musik*. He has heard a hymn, entitled "The Foot of the Cross," and feels a paternal kindred spirit for the composer. Jude's impossible dream, yearning for a surrogation that would at once relieve him of his *étrangeté* and allow him a double, a shadow, who would be able to relieve him of the burden of his own self-fabrication, lights on the composer of the hymn, because "he of all men would understand my difficulties. . . . If there were any person in the world to choose as confidant, this composer would be the one, for he must have suffered, and throbbed, and yearned."[74] Jude's identification with the unknown composer reveals his powerful aesthetic framework. The fact that the composer looms up as the one person who might serve in this role is telling in a Nietzschean way: only through a sublimation of the Christ-identity with which Jude has been struggling, that is, through the death of God/Christ as the salvation of his identity, can Jude adopt the composer as alter ego. Jude, the "last man" sufferer, chooses as confidant and mirror an avatar of the absent father who is distanced through the filter of a liturgical text. It is almost ironic that he so strongly desires to meet the composer in the flesh, but Jude carries through, finding and making a pilgrimage to the composer's house. Eager to hear that the composer has all the answers to his dilemmas of self, he is further disillusioned to find that the man is about to give up music, "that poor staff to lean on," altogether, and is about to open a wine distributorship, since "you must go into trade if you want to make money nowadays."[75] Not only has the composer radically undermined his own autoaesthetic but he is about to do so in absolutely ambivalent terms: he will purvey the symbolic blood of Christ—and the nectar of Dionysus—for profit, doubly undermining the autoaesthetic image Jude has had of him. Jude's frames have once again been disrupted, shifted, and overlapped: the spiritual savior has become a captain and a product of industry, a commodifier and a commodity. Embarrassed and confused by the turn of events, Jude stammers out a hasty and muted congratulations to the composer for his insights in the ethereal hymn and takes his leave, having discovered once again the chimerical inadequacy of the textual framework within which he thinks he is working.

Jude's *étrangeté* extends through the divorce theme to his divorce from the sons with whom he ought to have a close genealogical relationship. Indeed, one of the most telling aspects of autoaestheticism for Jude is his genealogical isolation in a *camera obscura* that does not produce the artful self, empowered in the world, he has hoped for. Jude actually *has* a son, a "natural" son by Arabella—but he must bring the son back from another country, from the strangers who have raised him, and adopt him even to give him his name. Going by one of the most heavily over-determined nicknames in all of literature, Little Father Time,[76] Jude's natural son, and surely one of the darkest of literary characters, comes to stay with Jude and Sue. But Little Father Time presents a counter-lesson to Jude's autoaesthetic: he does not tax Jude for an identity, as Jude has done with his father surrogates, but seems content with his anonymous lot. While it is true that Little Father Time is like Jude, he is an enigma:

> He was age masquerading as juvenility, and doing it so badly that his real self showed through crevices. A ground swell from ancient years of night seemed to now and then lift the child in this his morning-life, when his face took a back view over some great Atlantic of Time, and appeared not to care what it saw.[77]

As we remember that Jude himself was referred to as being not "of his time" from the beginning of the novel, we begin to see Hardy's message: Little Father Time's real self *is* history, the stories of the past. He is exactly like Jude. The "ancient years of night" in Father Time are the ground swell of ineluctable Dionysian *étrangeté* and isolation. Father Time's seeming selflessness is a complex business: on the one hand, Father Time is a kind of *tabula rasa* who must depend on Jude and Sue for his sense of self; on the other hand, he is not at all dependent on them, since any sense of identity Jude and Sue offer him seems to slide off his timeless exterior. Father Time, who embodies the Nietzschean idea that to be exceptional is to be dangerous, is an even darker *camera obscura* than Jude, who, perceiving this dark, blank quality as the perfect opening to produce in Father Time the person he never has been, misunderstands Father Time even more completely than he has misunderstood himself. "We'll educate and train him with a view to the University," says Jude with a forced naiveté.[78] "What I couldn't accomplish in my own person I can carry out through him." Jude sees Little Father Time as not merely a surrogate of his own failure but as the repository of possibilities of what Jude might have been and could still be through him; Sue replies "O you dreamer!" Jude's plan that the surrogate son will become the father's other self, or will become what the father desires, is set up and then undermined in the most dramatic of ways. Father Time's "education" is in fact *dis*integrative, drawing him further and further from his malleable passivity and into his Dionysian self, capable of taking the most terrible of actions.

This discussion takes place in Jude and Sue's residence in Christminster (appropriately in Mildew Lane), in a house which shares a (windowless) wall with the outer wall of a college of the university but which has "no communication with it,"[79] and while Jude inadvertently attempts to undermine his autoaesthetic possibilities by being "worthy" of the university life he has come to desire so deeply, Father Time appropriately instinctively distrusts these halls of learning. The old houses of the colleges seem like "gaols" to Father Time, not the sources of scholarly and imaginative liberation they seem to Jude. Everything about the life of suffering Jude and Sue live urges Father Time to consummate action. When it comes, ghoulish and shocking, his killing of the two infants and his own suicide result from the texts of the world Sue and Jude have given him. Hardy's final epitaph for Father Time leaves us in no doubt of this: "For the rashness of those parents he had groaned, for their ill-assortment he had quaked, and for the misfortunes of these he had died."[80] Another martyr, Father Time is Hardy's bleak marker for a Nietzschean view of the Christian dogmatist of the clearly post-Christian era. He is an autoaestheticist of a completely new sort, who rewrites in his own mortality the old testaments of radical *étrangeté* Jude and Sue strive to make theirs.[81]

The relationship between Jude's framework and that of Father Time is precisely that dialectic about which Nietzsche wants us to be so concerned. Father Time is turned into the nihilist Jude can never be. It is at the moment when valuation seems to empty out that nihilism rises up: "What does nihilism mean?" Nietzsche asks at the beginning of *The Will to Power*.[82] "That the highest values devaluate themselves. The aim is lacking; 'why?' finds no answer." This is the point at which Father Time's textual frameworks, imparted to him by Jude and Sue, cease to function successfully. Now the lesson is beyond the pessimism of which Father Time might fabricate a meaningful dialogue with the world, beyond any positive use-value. Father Time might, along with Nietzsche, declare that "I am full of suspicion and malice against what they call 'ideals.'"[83] Nietzsche goes on to account further for the kind of action Father Time commits:

> Christianity, the revolution, the abolition of slavery, equal rights, philanthropy, love of peace, justice, truth: all these big words have value only in a fight, as flags: *not* as realities but as *showy words* for something quite different (indeed, opposite!).

Indeed, Father Time fights for the balance of things in an intolerable world. He is what Nietzsche calls a "blind disciple," as in this passage from *Human, All-too-Human*:

> As long as one knows very well the strengths and weaknesses of his teaching, his art, or his religion, its power is still slight. The disciple and apostle who has no eye for the weakness of the teaching, the religion, etc., blinded by the stature of his master and his own piety towards him, for that reason generally has more power than his master.[84]

Because of his trust in the validity of Sue's and Jude's frameworks, Father Time is capable of things such eternal doubters could never do. This fervent discipleship is ironic, as well, however: not only is Father Time controlled in his actions by those binding lessons but he is also free from any other index of judgment than his own as to how they should be interpreted. Indeed, Father Time will not permit anyone but himself to have the final word on his life. The note pinned to his shirt, "Done because we are too menny,"[85] at once tragic and comic, is a horrific pun on the nature of the all-too-human, as Edward Said points out.[86] He discovered something about "men" from which he could not recover, with which he could not live, love, nor labor.[87]

DIALECTICS

Although it is always impossible to know what dialectical perspectives Father Time is adopting as the "successful Dionysian man," Jude's are much less problematic to ferret out, isolate, and define. Discourse itself, and dialectical discourse in particular, as we have seen, is vitally important to

Jude's autoaesthetic. Seeking integration through the tools of dialectic, he finds that he is always talking to himself but that his interlocutor is an echo of a lost wholeness that can only be remembered through the oxymoron of a ghostly presence. Beginning in Aunt Drusilla's old texts and in those of the countryside around Marygreen, it extends to the Bible (whose letter killeth), to the world of scholarship through Phillotson and Christminster, and to the very novel we hold in our hands. The biblical Jude warns us against "false teachers" who "revile what they do not understand,"[88] but then goes on to become himself a function of dead letters, declaring that "by those things that they know by instinct as irrational animals do, they are destroyed."[89] The biblical Jude is the champion of learning so long as it is the learning of grace through Scripture. Hardy's subtitle for *Jude*, from II Corinthians 3:6, tells us that the letter kills because it arrests movement, fluidity, difference. The letter is that of the law, of society, and of a kind of realization that adherence to texts of any kind places one outside of "nature," of "life." Written codes bring nothing but despair in Jude's world. Jude tries to believe in the life of the spirit, championing the Creed, doing paintings of the Ten Commandments (then checking to make sure he included all the "not"s), renewing the façades of Christminster buildings.

But Jude's dialectics are always turning aside, as is their nature. The tropic nature of Jude's sense of himself cannot permit Jude to be unitary in any way. Jude quotes himself into existence, just as Phillotson has taught him to do. Jude has tried to react to the constricting outer world as Nietzsche would want him to:

> A man who is truly noble is incapable of sin; though every law, every natural order, indeed the entire canon of ethics, perish by his actions, those very actions will create a circle of higher consequences able to found a new world on the ruins of the old.[90]

Jude tries so hard to be the modern man, founding that new order on the ruins of the old, that like Raskolnikov he tries to privilege and destroy the past at once, even as he frames it. He wants to think that the past is dead, "overgrown and irrelevant,"[91] but since his connection to it is tropic it can never die. In his exposure of the grammatical forms that imprison him, Jude not only loses meaning but explodes it into fragments, which at first seems to free him from the logic that is what Derrida calls "enslavement" within the bounds of language, since "language has within it . . . an illogical element, the metaphor. Its principle force brings about an identification of the non-identical; it is thus an operation of the imagination,"[92] and thus a fiction. Jude is caught in the multilayered circularity of his own dialectics, in which the towers of Christminster become gingerbread cookies, Remembrance Day becomes "Humiliation Day" for Jude and "Judgement Day" for

Father Time.[93] In his always inadequate framing, Jude tries to remember "the appearance of the afternoon on which he awoke from his dream,"[94] declaring vaguely that

> I may do some good before I am dead—be a sort of success as a frightful example of what not to do; and so illustrate a moral story. . . . I was perhaps, after all, a paltry victim to the spirit of mental and social restlessness, that makes so many unhappy in these days.[95]

Jude cannot say what victimizes him, because the discourses available to him do not yet articulate what Nietzsche has begun to define for us.

GENEALOGY AND DEATH

Genealogical and autoaesthetic power, for Hardy, is always in a dialogue with death, whether of the father(s) or the son(s). For Jude, children always die—not just those who are hung but those who grow into the dead adulthood of *fin de siècle* England as well. For Jude, the act by which Father Time transcends his father is not nihilistic but fraught with a kind of pure generosity. He has perceived the futility of the world and has shown himself able to refute and combat it. Both Sue and Jude react to Father Time's autoaesthetic solution to the conundrum of humanness as though it were an invasion of *their* lives, a text for *them*. Sue feels that "now Fate has given us this stab in the back for being such fools as to take Nature at her word";[96] Jude is even more literary in his response. His lament at the death of the children, quoting from the chorus of Aeschylus' *Agamemnon*, "things are as they are, and will be brought to their destined issue,"[97] is not so much a lament as yet another frame within which to see and deal with the world. It is classical, rich with allusions to a pre-Christian, actively Dionysian tragic notion of Fate. In the death of the children, Jude rises to a new tragic feeling. And Jude apparently cannot avoid the play on words his quotation of the telling passage brings into new perspective: what is brought to Jude's "destined issue" (the children as his and Sue's issue) is not merely the "issue" of birth and adoption into Jude's coded frameworks but death itself. Both Jude and Sue reel toward conventionality as a result of the shock following the children's deaths, Sue in her desire to "die" back into her relationship with Phillotson, which she does successfully in the end, fulfilling her contract with the teacher and excluding Jude. Jude's attempt, through drink and passivity, to return to Arabella results in another, more literal death—Jude's own. The "free instincts," themselves tightly controlled frames, by which Jude and Sue have pretended to operate have been abrogated by the tragedy of misplaced patriarchy and ill-fitting frames.

In this respect, death is the final freeze-frame Jude seeks. As he has seen his children destroyed, their destinies complete (he might have quoted the opening of the final chorus from Sophocles' *Oedipus Tyrannus*), Jude must realize the list of Jude's mentors has come to include Father Time himself.

Indeed, death has been a pivotal framing device for Jude since early in his story. Like Father Time, Jude has attempted suicide, but his attempt had not been desperate nor passionate but curiously circumspect, as though a calm acknowledgment of *étrangeté*. The suicide attempt takes place in the novel immediately after Jude's first "divorce" from Arabella, after Jude has gone to Aunt Drusilla's and heard for the first time about the enigmatic suicide of his mother, who has drowned herself after a quarrel with and subsequent parting from Jude's real father. This narration, added to Jude's building autoaesthetic narrative, precipitates action:

> Jude walked away from his old aunt's house as if to go home. But as soon as he reached the open down he struck out upon it until he came to a large round pond. The frost continued, though it was not particularly sharp, and the larger stars overhead came out slow and flickering. Jude put one foot on the edge of the ice, and then the other: it cracked under his weight; but this did not deter him. He ploughed his way inward to the center, the ice making sharp noises as he went. When just about in the middle he looked around him and gave a jump. The cracking repeated itself; but he did not go down. He jumped again, but the cracking had ceased. Jude went to the edge, and stepped upon the ground.
>
> It was curious, he thought. What was he reserved for? He supposed he was not a sufficiently dignified person for suicide. Peaceful death abhorred him as a subject, and would not take him.[98]

The obvious link between the isolated pond, the surface of which is glazed and reflective, impenetrable, with that of the water in the Marygreen well and with the image of the living and the dead mother forms a multifarious emblem of what is to follow for Jude, for Father Time, and for the novel. The round pond, the same in which his mother had killed herself, is an enlarged version of that silver disk in the Marygreen well in which Jude sees his ambiguous future reflected; it is a genealogical lens of Jude's restricted possibilities. That he cannot break through but remains on the surface of the reflecting, glass-like ice condemns Jude to a life of appearances he does not understand.[99] The retreat from the center of the frozen pond is the beginning of wandering through the vast array of insufficient frames with which he will surround himself.

But although he cannot be its agent, "peaceful death" is always hovering at the brink (threshold?) of Jude's horizon. Rejecting the voluntary physical death the frozen pond will not afford him, Jude must accept another kind of death—the *figurative* death of the *sparagmos*, of difference. It is in the framework of death, in its various forms in the novel, that Jude shows himself most clearly as being at the *Hausthür* of the Nietzschean autoaesthetic. Death pervades Jude's world, from the multilayered morbidity of Marygreen to the "mausoleum"[100] of Christminster, whose many voices are incapable of anything but "copying, patching, and imitating,"[101] writing over a ghostly absence with new ghosts. Jude clearly sees and expresses this morbidity, claiming that he is not merely another of Christminster's ghosts but "almost his own ghost."[102] Jude finds himself repeatedly speaking to the Christminster[103] ghosts, including Matthew Arnold, who mourned Christminster/Oxford as "the home of lost causes" (94). The spiritual city Jude *thought* he saw in the ghostly distance did not and does not exist; it is the framed emblem of *différance* and of Jude's *étrangeté*, both of which are euphemisms for a dialogue with death.

The final Dionysian conundrum Jude must face is that, as *étrangeté* is a death of any unified self, so is the hypothetical unity of self that would provide stasis. Since stasis is rigidity and rigidity is death, to find that static resting place where Jude would know himself would be to find death. The effort to find such a resting place, a *single perspective*, which would result in the stopping of the unbearable motion of Jude's otherness, is outlined in *The Birth of Tragedy*:

> Indeed, the myth seems to wish to whisper to us that wisdom, and particularly Dionysian wisdom, is an unnatural abomination; that he who by means of his knowledge plunges nature into the abyss of destruction must also suffer the dissolution of nature in his own person.[104]

Jude feels, in a penetrating adumbration of Sartre's Roquentin, the searing split between consciousness and being, Nietzsche's "wisdom" and "nature." The guilt Jude feels, however ghostly, is a product of this turning edge of wisdom, an inversion of the world's image that Jude, the *camera obscura*, always perceives.

Enigmatic scenes of death and remembrance haunt and crowd the conclusion of *Jude*. Jude dies because his autoaesthetic strategies fail him, having merged in a vortex of suffering from which Jude cannot rescue his "original intention" from the restored façades of colleges, churches, and graveyards. Jude is finally a pastiche of the old and the new, like the church he was restoring[105] when he and Sue met, in which everything is new (the implication is that "new" = "degraded") except a few pieces of "the old carving," which Jude defines for us as "traces of the original idea,"[106] *arche-traces* of the apocryphal but satisfying text from which Jude will increasingly distance himself as he tries to preserve and approach it. Those traces, "now fixed against the new walls"[107] of the church, are *both* old and new, not capable of offering fixity but also incapable of vanishing. This ought to provide Jude with solace, even strength, but it does not, as Hillis Miller points out:

Nothing dies. This includes all moments of shame or pain as well as times of tenderness, of joy. . . .The Imminent Will has blindly and unintentionally brought Jude into existence and. . . . Having occurred once in time, each moment enters again that universal space or simultaneity where those things which once having been, can never cease to be, move endlessly in chaotic drifting.[108]

What ought to open new possibilities for the self instead restrict Jude to "chaotic drifting," in which detached and ghostly voices accost him from without. As he treks back to Marygreen for the last time, dying, to that problematic "center," to see Sue, the consumptive Jude, now almost unable to breathe, tries to lose the sense that "everything is turning to satire."[109] Since suffering *from the letter* is Jude's design, in order to right the world he relinquishes it, though his ensuing death at the hands of elements is not, as Bert Hornback suggests, a "winning of dignity he has lost in his fights with himself and this world,"[110] but a final acceptance of Dionysian *étrangeté.* Jude capitulates to his reliable frames of suffering. His last imitative voices, including cries of "Father!" at the end (borrowed from Job, not from Jude), continue to reveal him as *un*original. Those final calls across the "all-embracing spatialized time of the void" cannot escape the "embracing anonymous wakefulness which surrounds him and keeps everything alive" in a "memory as wide as the whole expanse of time and space."[111] Although Jude has wanted to localize and specifize himself, he succumbs in the end to an opening out into the indeterminacy of the texts he has carved and which have carved him.

Jude, the *camera obscura,* sees this opening out as an "enslavement to forms,"[112] which are "true religion."[113] Fictions of a world/frame in which "minds were clear and love of truth fearless"[114] have turned to parody: the frames by which Jude has operated invert themselves into ironic and risible imitations of substantial forms. In telling Sue that "we are acting by the letter, and the letter killeth," Jude reveals his own adoration of appearance, his belief in "forms, tones, words, in the whole Olympus of appearance" as the "series of seemings" Hardy calls Jude in his Preface to the novel, and which is my epigraph above.

Lying in the rain beside his fateful milestone, a fitting gravestone, the dying Jude feels for the inscription on the back, hidden from all worlds but "his own"; he finds it "still there, but nearly obliterated by moss."[115] Jude's texts are failing as he realizes that "we story-tellers are all Ancient Mariners,"[116] doomed to our round of stories of death. When Edmund Gosse instructs us that "we rise from the perusal of [*Jude*] stunned with a sense of the hollowness of existence,"[117] we must see this hollowness in a new way—in terms of the Dionysian suffering of the *camera obscura.* The chimerical "inside" is finally as hollow as Jude's black-box perspective, a cross-referencing of chaotic frames, as Millgate claims: "If the intellectual concepts embodied in *Jude* do not cohere, that is perhaps because they were never intended to do so, because Hardy conceived and composed his last novel as a comprehensive image of intellectual and social chaos."[118] The gradual decay of Jude's hope ("the one thing in which he had been rich when the novel opened")[119] for a (fictional) return to (fictional) solidity is perpetuated by Jude's hollowness, his inability to be original.

But such a comfortable, if uneasy, and conclusive suffering would be most un-Nietzschean. Even Jude's death is not his own: it is incomplete and unoriginal, a derivative text of borrowed pain, ringing with the (creative) hollowness of *étrangeté*. The reader's sense is that Jude is finally free of the overwhelming pain of attempting to enter the vital human world he imagines around him. It is not so much that Jude has wanted to enter a world of *enlightenment* at Christminster,[120] but that having realized his "error" in making Christminster the focus of his illusory hopes,

> the expression on Jude's corpse-like face in the watery lamplight was indeed as if he saw people where there was nobody. At moments he stood still by an archway, like one watching figures walk out; then he would look at a window like one discerning a familiar face behind it. He seemed to hear voices, whose words he repeated as if to gather their meaning.[121]

Like Hamlet, Jude has seen the enormity of the ironic maze in which he is caught and "the progressive increase in the clarity of the final illumination,"[122] which is the final chord of Jude's life just as it is of Hardy's novel writing. Jude has become a disbeliever in enchanted texts even though he knows he is constructed of them. He has told Arabella, in their last walk together through the haunted streets, that "as Antigone said, I am neither a dweller among men nor ghosts. But Arabella, when I am dead, you'll see my spirit flitting up and down here among these!"[123] Jude cannot live and he cannot fully die. He knows that while the letter killeth, it gives the illusion of life. That is the source of its *real* pain. Nietzsche tells us in *The Antichrist* that God—and we—cannot be pronounced dead so long as we maintain a faith in grammar, that in our constituting of linguistic or narrative continuity we create and recreate the world, but Jude reminds us, as does Nietzsche elsewhere, that the letter itself is an endless series of ghosts who kill by imitation and emulation—and by absence. Although Jude has been "callous to the shabby trick played on him by the dead languages,"[124] in the end he sees the conundrum of his learning—that all of his scholarship, so pains-takingly acquired, only sharpens the focus of his *étrangeté*.

Jude's physical death is shown clearly by Hardy as an effacement into ghostly language. His final dialogue is not with the ethereal learning of "Bibliol" college and the timeless wisdom of Christminster but with the desperate Job, for whom man is not "the master of his fate nor the captain of his soul," as Jude had hoped at the novel's outset;[125] rather, as Nietzsche declares, "we knowers are unknown to ourselves."[126] We are caught at Jude's end in an absolute ambivalence between a "will not to will, the will to remain quietly watching on the sidelines,"[127] that desire to "sink without trace into the unconscious heavings of the impersonal force that stirs and urges everything,"[128] and the heroic acknowledgment that we are all traces, no more nor less, painful shards of old and new texts sewn together like Frankenstein's monster, traces that can never be eradicated any more than they can be whole. While muffled sounds of "Remembrance Day" festivities penetrate the "common wall" into Jude's black little room, his body, now nearly a corpse, is laid out and his death is only moments away. Outside and below, a speech can be heard. In this scene, Hardy's juxtaposition of obscurity and clandestine squalor with the empty rhetoric of hope is not lost on Jude, as he smiles for the last time before giving up the ghost. The monster that is Jude Fawley at the end of his story is made up not only of Job (and his "Why did I not give up the ghost when I came out of the belly?") and Hamlet (for whom "Since no man, of aught he leaves, knows what isn't to leave betimes, let be") but of all those carved, painted, written, and spoken memorials he has left behind. The last of these—Sophocles' at the conclusion of *Oedipus*, that we should "call no man fortunate that is not dead. The dead are free from pain"—chronicles a man unable to live in the world before him but, for all his learning, ignorant of an alternative.

Part Three

◆

SPIRITUALITY, IRONY, AND THE AUTOAESTHETIC SELF

> The "spirit," something that thinks: where
> possible even "absolute, pure spirit"—this
> conception is a second derivative of that false
> introspection which believes in "thinking": first
> an act is imagined which simply does not occur,
> "thinking," and secondly a subject-substratum
> in which every act of thinking, and nothing else,
> has its origin: that is to say, both the deed and
> the doer are fictions.
>
> —*The Will to Power* 477

5

◆

Zarathustra as the Shadow of the Shadow: Philosophy/Poetry/Power

—*Ensphinxed*, thus do I in one word
Stuff many feelings:
(Forgive me, God,
This language-sin!)

    —Nietzsche, "Among Daughters
      of the Wilderness," 2[1]

In some respects apparently the least spiritual of philosophers, in the wake of the Madman in the Marketplace who proclaims the death of God in *The Gay Science*, Nietzsche spent the better part of his writing cataloguing the exploded or ironized spirituality of so-called modern humanity; Nietzsche's concern was with the impact of the autoaesthetics of spirituality in a harshly solipsistic and de-spiritualized (psychologized and biologized) world. In the welcome absence of archaic absolutes, even such eternal ones as materiality, in a world Nietzsche saw as one in which any truth-claims could only be made through a ubiquitous and tenacious—and always ironic—"faith" in rhetoric, the very nature of mankind's spirituality, individually and cultur-ally, is brought critically into question. What is possible, Nietzsche shows, is an inverted spirituality or, said in another way, a spiritualization of irony itself. At the center of this re-spiritualization, Nietzsche saw *Thus Spoke Zarathustra*, on which I want to focus here, as a mock-spiritual, though very serious, gift to mankind that might show it how to *become itself* in a time of critical spiritual enervation. Although Zarathustra's[2] complex figure packs ("stuffs," to use Nietzsche's word) many apparently contradictory aspects of this complex and chimerical Nietzschean self into one image, in the *ensphinxedness*—the iconic and idealized figure—of Zarathustra we can perceive, if we have ears to hear and eyes to see, not only the fixed ideal of the (impossible) Highest Man but, even more interestingly, the tendentious figure of Zarathustra as the failed *Übermensch*, striving for but never achieving the self-overcoming out of which he constructs his life. In Zarathustran autoaesthetics we can see a significant deepening of Nietzsche's poignant and obsessive search for the meaningful self, caught obscurely between ratification and erasure. Seen as the quintessential *Künstlersroman* of the autoaesthetic, *Thus Spoke Zarathustra* is a schematic depiction of the growth toward self-awareness of that deeply troubled and troubling type Nietzsche calls "modern humanity." In exploring Zarathustra's idea of *weight*, discovering it to be less substantial than a shadow, I want to set up a framework for looking at some conclusions of the "modern" autoaesthetic dilemma, in Faulkner's Ike McCaslin.

Though Zarathustra is forty at the beginning of Part One, he is a metaphorical infant *born* out of his cave, whose suggestion of Plato (the Apollinian) and of pre-humanness (the Dionysian avatar) is aesthetically vital to the dialectical discoveries he and we will make. Nietzsche's Zarathustra is the paradigmatic desert wanderer who from his womb/tomb-like cave awakens and awakens us from a solipsistic negation to an awareness of self; like the recurrent stages of Zoroastrianism[3] in his *untergehen*, his descent into the world of men (and language), Zarathustra shows us vital aspects of our own desert existence. Though he first appears as original and unique, Zarathustra ends as a convocation of often overripe epigrams, obscurely quoted poetry, and vivid (borrowed) imagery. We discover—as he does not—that we are reading Zarathustra's story tangentially and through complex parabolic mirrors: the *ur*-voice, the author(ity) "behind" the figure of Zarathustra, is revealed as the autoaesthetic power Zarathustra thinks he represents.

But this ironic central theme of chimerical authorial or autoaesthetic power is only gradually revealed in the narrative. My epigraph above, taken from near the end of *Zarathustra*, demonstrates the height of irony to which Zarathustra's book aspires: from start to finish it is not Zarathustra before us but that *shadow*-self by which he is gradually supplanted, one of a succession of eternally interim identities imposing themselves between the figure of Zarathustra and the reader of his tale.[4] Although Zarathustra is ostensibly, as a prophet, a preeminently oral character, he is at the same time framed, like Jude, by the *prior* text in which his orality functions; as the text progresses, he becomes an icon observed through the glass of inscription, an enigma of frozen (ensphinxed) iconic power captured and then superseded by the virtual presence of the *"real"* Overman, a shadow that haunts and finally subverts him. Zarathustra becomes the shadow of his own shadow.

The course from the morning song with which Zarathustra's book opens to the revealed poetic power of the shadow song with which *Zarathustra* concludes is an extended parable of *étrangeté*, beginning in that most familiar Nietzschean mode: a cross-fertilization of image-oriented story/poem and parody of story-telling. Zarathustra's Foreword begins:

> When Zarathustra was thirty years old, he left his homeland and the lake of his homeland and went into the mountains. Here he enjoyed his spirit and his solitude and passed ten years without tiring of it. But finally his heart turned,—and one morning he rose with the dawn, stepped before the sun, and spoke to it thus:
> You great star! What would your happiness be, if you had not those for whom you shine![5]

The setting, the isolation, the physical/spiritual relationship, and Zarathustra's heavily framed voice all establish motifs to be developed in the autotelic narrative. An iconic Christ-figure parallel is introduced, of a figure "called" to bring enlightenment to humanity. The image of the man-god, part Crucified and part Dionysus, part dogmatist and part disrupter, part parable teller and part mythographer, focuses the autoaesthetic *agon* through which a Nietzschean being's spiritual manifestation goes.

Nietzsche introduces Zarathustra, in the first part of the Preface, as naive, exuberantly simple, yet unaware of his energy's simplicity. He is what Derrida would call pure supplementarity, the emblem of the dialectic of self-involvement: "Behold! I am sick of my wisdom, like the bee that has gathered too much honey, I need a hand outstretched for it." In his weighty virtuality, Zarathustra declares to the sun, "I must, like you, *go down*, as men to whom I will descend call it." Embracing his going-under, the emblem of his humanness, he verifies that "his heart" has indeed "turned";[6] out of his cave and into his story Zarathustra strives to become the *active* figure in his own narrative landscape, thinking that in his *untergehen* he will return to his *Heimat* (homeland), the world of man.[7] This abrogation of otherworldliness is itself "ensphinxed" by Zarathustra's closing declaration in the Prologue's mock-biblical metaphor: "Behold! This cup wants to be empty again, and Zarathustra wants to be man again." As if in response to this articulated desire, we are instantly told, "Thus began Zarathustra's going-under." The playful metaphor of the empty and full cup, and by extension of image superimposed on concept and concept on image, anticipates the multiple levels at which the text's *étrangeté* will operate: to be empty *again* is to be man *again*; to be full is *not* to be man.[8]

When Zarathustra comes down from his cave for the first time, his heart full to overflowing with the wisdom he must impart to the world of men, he is innocent of what he will discover as he confronts this energy and its dialogue with humanity and therefore with himself. Zarathustra's descent into the world of man, in which he confronts saint, disciples, and common humanity, is presented as a coming down from the language-less satisfaction of "his spirit and his solitude" and into a book/self. In announcing the Overman and revealing the will-to-power through which he must be delivered, Zarathustra gradually discovers the depth (in the sense of the abyss, not in the Platonic sense of knowledge) and distance of the eternal recurrence, about which he knew nothing when he began his descent. Thus is *Zarathustra* a *Künstlersroman*: in section after section of *Zarathustra*, in confrontation after confrontation with his own mankindness, the prophet batters away at the lessons of his own innocent and ignorant humanity, returning to the increasingly tenuous safety (though only we on the "outside" perceive this) of his animal and human companions and his cave, where he is less and less "safe," finally to be assaulted there by his "shadow."

In his first aesthetic confrontation, still most spiritually removed from man, at the edge of civilization on his way toward the marketplace at which articulated human life will be engaged, Zarathustra meets the hermit-"saint," the *last man* he saw on his way up the mountain ten years previously. Though the saint is blind, he notes the change that has occurred since he saw Zarathustra last. Thus we confront without delay, at the highest (human) spiritual level, our first unreliable witness: the change in Zarathustra is precisely, parabolically mis-defined as Zarathustra's having become a "child" (to be explained in the "Three Metamorphoses" of Book One, as the final phase of enlightenment or awakening). Nietzsche's lesson is complex here: the saint's blindness is a double irony, in that while, traditionally, blindness in a spiritual figure (Tiresias, the enlightened Oedipus) denotes deep insight, already an irony, *this* figure is both blind and naively blind. Zarathustra is not the "child" of spiritual awakening, though he contains that possibility within him, as do we all. But merely being the repository of the potential of spiritual elevation is not possessing it, whatever it might be. In the saint's mis-identification of Zarathustra we see that Nietzsche's spiritual order of descent from the mountain is heavily ironized and therefore inverted. Precisely because of the saint's spirituality, his inability to understand the nature of articulation and *étrangeté*, that is, because of his own *étrangeté* (which he also cannot see), he is the least likely among men to be able to see and describe Zarathustra "correctly."

Having been failed by the most likely, because the most "spiritual," candidate to provide accurate identification for the descending prophet (and we must note that this process of defining himself is Zarathustra's "message" to men, since what the prophet brings is the revelation of self-becoming, and therefore extraordinarily important to Zarathustra), he turns to his own (autoaesthetic) attempts to describe himself that occupy us and him for the rest of the book. His efforts meet, as we must expect them to, the same fate. Three key passages from *Thus Spoke Zarathustra*, one at the beginning, one in the middle, and one near the end, demonstrate this all-too-human but failed effort most clearly. In all three of the following scenes, Zarathustra is "ensphinxed" by Nietzsche to show an autoaesthetic mock spirituality at work.

ZARATHUSTRA AND THE TIGHTROPE WALKER

The parable of the tightrope walker is a masterpiece of metaphoric compactness and a remarkably disturbing set of autoaesthetic images that will produce innumerable echoes and shadows throughout Zarathustra's book. This initial attempt at articulating himself takes place in Zarathustra's first confrontation with the people in the market square of the first village through which he passes: "I teach you the Overman,"[9] he says, with all the confidence of the (un-ironic) spiritual mentor. But when he teaches the Overman—defined to the villagers as "something beyond themselves," the desired goal of perfection all species of creatures have striven for, this figure so ensphinxed as to be no more accessible to Zarathustra than to any other man—he too misconceives the Overman in his formulation and is forced to construct his gift to man, the message of the Overman, in the vague and elliptical metaphors he finds for this "here and beyond" relationship, striving fairly desperately for clarity.[10] Yet in this improvisation Zarathustra speaks truer than he knows. Fitting his lesson to the anticipated arrival of the highwire performer, he refers to man as "a rope, tied between beast and Overman,—a rope over an abyss."[11] Man is here neither beast *nor* Overman but between them, stretched not over the supporting *ground*, that safe plane of the earth, but over the vertiginous abyss, the *Abgrund* into which he will plummet and vanish should he relinquish *either* of these dialectical poles. Given that the earth is eradicated in Zarathustra's definition of the man-Overman relationship, one must see his declaration, that the Overman "*shall be* the meaning of the earth,"[12] in a different light. The "meaning of the earth," in the conventional (spiritual) way in which we think about that sort of wisdom, is itself thrown into the abyss. Indeed, the very idea of definition undergoes a transformation requisite for the beginning of an understanding not only of the Overman but of the man in which it "resides" (this understanding is what Nietzsche ironically calls wisdom). Fittingly, this tightrope metaphor leads to another metaphor: "But whoever is wisest among you, he too is but a conflict and cross between plant and ghost";[13] that is, this wisest person knows what even Zarathustra does not yet know—that he is a dialogue between the organic body and the *spiritual fiction*. Zarathustra's "clarification" of the Overman is a heap of metaphors because, like metaphor, the wisest man is simultaneously connective and generative, not *merely* disjunctive; he is a conflict of forces and pulls. As man "improves," he becomes more and more enmeshed in the *étrangeté* of metaphor itself, unable to separate himself from it, as we shall see more fully in chapter 7.

Appropriately, Nietzsche frames Zarathustra as not only teaching the Overman but himself engaging in the same multileveled game of self-designation. The people in the marketplace have stopped to hear Zarathustra only because of the rumored promise of a tightrope walker, an entertainer who, because he will also elevate the attention of the crowd, is schematically Zarathustra's equivalent but who will not entertain with thinking. The tightrope walker will act out in images the ironized message of the Overman, allowing the onlookers to forget their own lives, to subsume and sublimate themselves in the show they will see. The tightrope walker is himself an emblematic narrative of Zarathustra's earth-bound-ness: Zarathustra finds himself all too earthbound, literally and in terms of his transcendent message, when, after a delay, the tightrope walker finally steps from a high doorway (one to add to our growing collection) out onto the rope Zarathustra has now given a new, highly charged meaning. But then the crowd (herd), which has been utterly uninterested in Zarathustra's lesson and only mildly more so in the tightrope walker's performance, is itself *ensphinxed*, and the parable takes flight:

> Then something happened that made every mouth mute and every eye rigid. For meanwhile the tightrope walker had begun his act: he had stepped out of a small door and was moving over the rope, which was stretched between two towers and thus hung over the marketplace and the people. When he was precisely in the middle of his walk, the little door opened again, and a brightly dressed fellow who looked like a buffoon sprang out and followed the first one with quick steps. "Forward, lame-foot," cried his terrible voice, "forward, sloth, smuggler, pale-face! Or I'll tickle you with my heel! What are you doing here between towers? You belong in the tower, you ought to be locked up, you're blocking the way of a better man than you!"—And with each word he came nearer and nearer: but when he was still one step behind, the dreadful thing happened that made every mouth mute and every eye rigid:—he cried out like a devil and sprang over the man who was in his way. But this man, seeing his rival win, lost his head and the rope; he threw away his pole and fell faster than it did, a swirl of arms and legs, into the depths. The marketplace and the people were like a sea when a storm strikes: the crowd surged over and under one another, and most of all where the body would crash down."[14]

Thus Nietzsche establishes, in an extraordinarily powerful aesthetic narrative, the conditions by which we can begin on our *real* journey, with Zarathustra, toward the goal of self-overcoming.[15] The images through which he presents it here are physical (overcoming as a literal overleaping, danger, tension, contest), the fall from the wire an emblem of man's *necessary* going down, an emblematic self-search that can be completed only in the impossible combination of laughter and death. That Zarathustra does not immediately nor even eventually perceive the relationship between the tightrope-walker scenario and his own shows him not as a lesson for the Overman but as a demonstration *to the reader* of man's benightedness and the superhumanness of metaphoric, autoaesthetic power: like Beast and Overman, that power of evocation and man are always and necessarily separated by an unbridgeable gulf. Nietzsche's lesson here is turned outward. Though Zarathustra does not have eyes to see, *we* may begin to learn our first emergent autoaesthetic lesson from Zarathustra's own lack of insight.

But the price of the lesson is high: any "value of unorthodoxy" must also have its price. Dionysian life can only be learned about at the cost of life itself. The parable of the tightrope walker shows a performer challenged and finally *leapt over* by a mysterious stranger, a jester, this performer failing to maintain his balance in the face of this taunting attack, falling to the ground, dying; the performer learns, as he tells Zarathustra with his dying breaths, that "I lose nothing when I lose my life,"[16] that the "value" of striving is to have lived dangerously, to have turned aside from the straight and narrow and to have gone beyond the expected and the accepted, even if that means the inevitable *untergehen* of actual (physical or figurative) death.

This Heraclitan striving against the chimerical but immensely powerful limitations of the encultured world helps define the particular autoaesthetic over-reaching of Zarathustra as poet. A central aspect of this poetic over-reaching is Zarathustra's gradual *étrangeté* from the lesson he has only just begun to preach. Like Nietzsche, Zarathustra undergoes a metamorphosis as he stretches with the implications and ramifications of his strategic self-search. For Nietzsche, terms like "will-to-power" develop over time; Zarathustra too, in his evocation of such terms as "Overman" and "teach," transmutes slowly. For both, development is a matter of the acknowledgment of *falling short*. Nietzsche's handling of Zarathustra in and after this scene shows us the difference between him, as a poet, and Zarathustra, as a failed one: while Nietzsche grows further and further into his terminology, Zarathustra recedes from his, confused and frightened by the burden the interpretation of the tightrope walker's death is to him. Confronted by the weight of the complex story he now must tell, Zarathustra is ensphinxed, silent as he carries the corpse on his back. And the resolution of the tightrope walker's story is doubly ensphinxed. Zarathustra has put the body into the hollow of a tree to protect it from the wolves, and has slept. When he awakens, he has had a revelation of wisdom concerning not only the corpse but his own role in the world. "Companions, the creator seeks, not corpses, not herds and believers. Fellow creators, the creator seeks—those who write new values on new tablets" (Prologue 9). His resolve is that "never again shall I speak to the people: for the last time have I spoken to the dead. I shall join the creators, the harvesters, the celebrants: I shall show them the rainbow and all the steps to the overman." Just as Zarathustra has become heavy with the tightrope walker's weight, so shall the hearts of the "hermits," the "lonesome," and "whoever has ears for the unheard-of" become heavy with insight (which Zarathustra calls "my happiness").

Then, having claimed companionship with the tightrope walker, Zarathustra shifts his autoaesthetic frame to the jester who has killed the companion: "To my goal I will go—on my own way; over those who hesitate and lag behind I shall leap. Thus let my going be their going under." In this woven double imagery by which Zarathustra defines his task, he catches himself between the beast and the Overman yet again, at yet another level. The tightrope walker, as he was dying, called himself "not much more than a beast that has been taught to dance by blows and a few meager morsels";[17] and about the jester Nietzsche's last words are that "he uttered a devilish cry and jumped over the man who stood in his way,"[18] not to be heard of again. The jester vanishes *up* and out of the tightrope walker's story, a kind of momentary visitation of the Overman's (dark and disruptive) shadow.

Zarathustra's vital lesson in the story of the tightrope walker has to do with words' chimerical promise to "complete" us and make us self-substantial. The disruptive jester, in his critical relationship with the tightrope walker, shows the error of this notion. The bifurcation of man into beast and Overman, the one organic and the other fictional, is Nietzsche's autoaesthetic revolution, the power of *étrangeté*, seen in Zarathustra as the ultimate tension of lack and force.[19] Zarathustra's lessons from his own Prologue are long in coming: the images for this lack and force begin to show themselves in Book Two's appropriately titled "On Immaculate Perception," a poetic analysis of the slightly blasphemous transformation of the Immaculate Conception of Christ into the immaculate perception of autoaesthetic man, engaged in a subversive strategy to create a genealogy of the spiritual. For Nietzsche and the evolving Zarathustra, the immaculate conception of *étrangeté* is both genealogical and dangerous, transcendent of the physical but threatening. Considering the immaculate perception, Zarathustra is once again ensphinxed, caught between admiration and distrust:

But this shall be your curse, you who are immaculate, you pure perceivers, that you shall never give birth, even if you lie broad and pregnant on the horizon.

> Verily, you fill your mouth with noble words; and are we to believe that your heart is overflowing, you liars?
>
> But *my* words are small, despised, crooked words: gladly I pick up what falls under the table at your meals.[20]

In the inevitability of his falling short, that is, of his fall *in* and *into* poetic language and the embracing of "least is best," Zarathustra begins to walk *his* strait tightrope, inviting his own jester to appear and to overleap and topple him. The more he perceives the gap between the beast and the Overman, the more he eschews the overarching action necessary to transcend. His limiting response is an impetus toward the *less*, finally a tendency toward abstinence from his own language. This is the great implication of Zarathustra's going under and his eventual separation from the shadow of autoaesthetic narrative power. As Gadamer suggests, Zarathustra's speeches, which directly follow the tightrope walker, tend toward *silence*; in his "crisis of modernity"[21] he tends toward the final, breathless silence of writing and toward the power inherent in this silence. His voice leaves him with the realization that increased self-knowledge means acknowledged self-ignorance: the poet "is an artist who does not know himself. To know means simply to rediscover schemas that the artistic instinct has already cast over things."[22] Once again, Nietzsche's own autoaesthetic strategy is to shadow this Zarathustran ambivalence in the text itself, in which metaphor, as tightrope walker and jester, (over)leaps the conventional, awakening in us "the infinite carefulness of a 'great mistrust' that can return language to its proper course";[23] that so-called proper course is one in which metaphoricity, poetic condensation, the economy of fragmentation, and finally silence itself, the watermarks of *écriture*, are transmuted from abyss into an ironic *Abgrund*, a new kind of inverted or textual spirituality. This insight, in turn, transmutes Zarathustra into the attacker of conventional spirituality, with its essentialist rhetoric, who exhorts the reader to reject that conventional unity, which turns out to be "evil":

> Evil I call it, and misanthropic: all this teaching of the One and Full and Unmoved and Sated and Permanent!
>
> All the permanent—that is only a parable. And the poets lie too much.
>
> But of time and becoming the best parables should speak: they should be a praise and a justification of all impermanence.[24]

Zarathustra's inversion of the Goethean ideal is emblematic of Nietzsche's task throughout his writing.[25] In his increasingly estranged play with parable (*Gleichnis*), Zarathustra rehearses the message of the tensions of Dionysian proximity, which are the source of his "new" spirituality. A revised parabolic didacticism begins in the parable of the tightrope walker, in which Zarathustra, now a double-beast, roams the countryside with this weight of discovery, learning, and metaphor, divided into and forming the terms of an imagistic, *living* metaphor. His deadweight burden is an adumbration of his shadow. The effect is that Zarathustra creatively misunderstands Goethe's message about parable at the same time that he understands it, acknowledges it (by quoting it), and ironizes it. Zarathustra's complex instruction for successful earthly life is not only that both his and Goethe's formulations are true but that neither can be understood—we do not have ears to hear any more than did Faust's (nor Christ's) disciples; we, like Zarathustra, are ensphinxed. To understand Zarathustra, we must understand that he does not conceive of the Overman's will-to-power as *over* man, a crude imitation of the "real" will; the reign of the Overman is marked by removal (*étrange-té*) and concealment of/in parable: " 'Only where there are tombs are there resurrections.'—Thus sang Zarathustra."[26] Zarathustra is concealed within the text in order to be validated; or, to put it another way, he takes power. But this validity or power is finally not one of revelation, not of concealment per se but of its metaphoric declaration, will-to-power as metaphor.

The gathering revelation that *Zarathustra* is pushing the nature of philosophy closer and closer to something that is also not philosophy raises Nietzsche's most troubling question: In an autoaesthetic world, can such a thing as philosophy exist? For Nietzsche, *Zarathustra* is a manifestation of the "gay science," not "proper" philosophy.[27] Zarathustra's shadow leaves no doubt of this when he declares to Zarathustra that

> With you I unlearned faith in words and values and great names. When the devil sheds his skin does not his name fall off too? For that too is skin. The devil himself is perhaps—skin.[28]

Like Zarathustra, the devil here undergoes a transformation. At first he is *covered* by skin, then he is skin itself. It is as though he is working out of himself in a manifestation of *étrangeté*. One must keep carefully in mind here that Nietzsche's world, one of inversions, may place the devil in a different position than would the tradition out of which Nietzsche writes. In this passage, as Zarathustra throws off the devilish skin of dogmatic value-inscription, the Shadow becomes *true*, in the sense that he is at once the devil and free of the devil. This formulation of the Shadow itself, this designation for the "man" who has shed the devil, exists in a vital interaction with this new philosophy and is a metaphor for the process of *emergence* to a new understanding of the metaphoric nature of philosophy, since, for Nietzsche, philosophy, like religion, must always overcome its dogmatism (as well as the "subtexts" it gathers and imposes) in order to become itself.

ZARATHUSTRA AND THE GATE OF MOMENT

The development of Zarathustra's message manifests his redefined, elusive power to conceal and reveal, to tease and enlighten at once. The text shows the autoaesthetic abstraction (spirituality) through which Zarathustra goes to construct this message, most clearly demonstrated in the parable of the Gate of Moment.[29] At the fulcrum of Zarathustra's book, Nietzsche shows him wandering in high mountains, still struggling to overcome his human-ness, yet constantly pulled down, as he says, by "gravity" (*Schwere*, that is, by the beast of "historical" human life), which here takes the form of a highly metaphorized beast variously called "spirit," "gravity," "dwarf," and "mole," a protean (or Dionysian) metaphoric power that *itself* ranges (as do the aspirations of the philosopher, that metaphoric beast) from the pole of animal to that of god, from mole to spirit. The scene of Zarathustra's confrontation with the dwarf and its manifestations are genealogically de-scended from the tightrope walker. In Zarathustra's striving against the evertransmuting inertia (the ensphinxedness) of human activity, the philos-opher and the poet pool their autoaesthetic resources, committed to resolv-ing the puzzle of the self mathematically, chemically, and, finally, when these prove to be chimerical anyway, rhetorically.

To begin to understand the parable of the gate, we must first remember the primacy of appearance as a new spirituality and then take a circuitous route to it. We must remember that Zarathustra's appearance is also his profoundest identity; the images now, however, as we see them at work in *The Gay Science*, become overt appearance in a new way ("played on a new instrument," to use Nietzsche's autoaesthetic phrase) in the conclusion of Book Three's "On the Spirit of Gravity," as Zarathustra transmutes appear-ance into its active guise, declaring that "'This is *my* way; where is yours?'— Thus I answered those who asked me 'the way.' For *the* way—that does not exist. Thus spoke Zarathustra." This message, with all of its implied ques-tions, makes sense only as a kind of preparation-cocoon, foreshadowing Zarathustra's complex emergence into a new moral/spiritual contextualiza-tion of his project, which in turn has emerged in his declaration that "A tablet of the good hangs over every people. Behold, it is the tablet of their overcomings; behold, it is the voice of their will-to-power."[30] Two possible meanings of this last passage persist. In the first, Zarathustra has come to warn of the dogmatic repression under which man lives and by which he is controlled. In this interpretation, the good is not good but powerful, in the way that social conventions are good/powerful. In the other interpretation, Zarathustra is himself this voice, the "tablet of good," hanging in Damocle-sian fashion over the people and judging their ability to comprehend, both in what he says (in the way he is written) and in what he represents in the fiction that surrounds and creates him. In the text, the separate voices of these interpretations echo and shadow each other.

Zarathustra, as bearer of the "tablet of the good," standing either at the exact center of—or in such stark contrast to—that implied moral quality of

Socratic philosophy that establishes the chief criterion of ethical life for Plato and Aristotle, is everywhere apparent. By the time we have reached Part Three of *Zarathustra*, in which the parable of the Gate of Moment appears, however, he is revealed as himself not merely caught between interpretations, as was the tightrope walker, but among virtually endless interpretations. Although this idea may be a commonplace to anyone reading philosophy or literary theory today, it was not to Nietzsche nor to his day; Zarathustra's is a lesson in which he, like so many before him, *mis*understands his role. His synecdochic self-definition, however, concerns itself with the writing that must always be the prophet's announcement: "My hand is a fool's hand: beware, all tables and walls and whatever else still offer room for foolish frill or scribbling skill" ("On the Spirit of Gravity" 1). The "fool's hand" is the hand of the radically altered (human) poet, the "tables and walls" not only the surface or face on which he places his paper to write but that writing façade, the face of the paper itself, physical and metaphysical.[31] One can much more easily see, in this regard, Nietzsche's justification in referring to *Zarathustra* as "the greatest present that has ever been made" to the world,

> the highest book there is, the book that is truly characterized by the air of the heights—the whole fact of man lies *beneath* it at a tremendous distance—it is also the *deepest*, born out of the innermost wealth of truth, an inexhaustible well to which no pail descends without coming up again filled with gold and goodness. Here no "prophet" is speaking, none of those gruesome hybrids of sickness and will-to-power whom people call founders of religions. Above all, one must *hear* aright the tone that comes from this mouth . . . .[32]

Nietzsche claims here that in Zarathustra *no* prophet is speaking, that it is the "tone" (a word we have considered in its Nietzschean sense before) we must hear aright, and that Zarathustra (or rather Zarathustra's *performance articulation*) is not a hybrid but rather—always provisionally, of course—a self-declared *original*; his prophecy is one that declares itself exempt from conventional reading. He declares that his book has not been read when it has simply been read; "rather," Zarathustra tells us "one has then to begin its *exegesis*."[33] The implication is that the book is a kind of I.O.U., to be redeemed in a chimerical future of infinite readings. Many such declarations provide the grounding for Zarathustra's revitalized, re-spiritualized project for philosophy and literature, a project that has moved beyond what Nietzsche inherited as philosophy into an interdisciplinary realm encompassing psychology, anthropology, sociology, politics, literature, and, most of all, the tightrope of poetry.

To perceive the "vision of the loneliest,"[34] Zarathustra again climbs away from the world of men; "Striding silently over the mocking clatter of pebbles, crushing the rock that made it slip, my foot forced its way upward. Upward—defying the spirit that drew it downward toward the abyss, the spirit of gravity, my devil and archenemy."[35] Crowding back around us are images from Zarathustra's confrontation with the tightrope walker: the "clatter of pebbles" akin to the crowd in the marketplace, the slipping of the foot evoking the tightrope walker's slip, and the defying of the spirit of gravity (the jester, who is indeed the "devil," as he has been called earlier by the fallen performer, and indeed Zarathustra's archenemy). The conditions for a re-inscription of the parable are in place. But the image of the "dwarf" is even more ambivalent than that of the jester: here, the "devil" who urges Zarathustra upward toward the spiritual heights does so by dragging him down; it is the prophet's will, dialectically struggling with the dwarf, that propels him upward, whereas the tightrope walker's "will" was to succumb to the law of gravity. Zarathustra is a much more autoaesthetically powerful descendent of the tightrope walker. The dwarf sitting on Zarathustra ("half dwarf, half mole, lame, making lame, dripping lead into my ear, leaden thoughts into my brain") refers to Zarathustra as a "philosopher's stone," a pun on the alchemically magical substance that could effect transformations of material essence and on the ruminative weight of philosophy. "You threw yourself up so high," says the dwarf, "but every stone that is thrown must fall." The image here seems clear enough, defining Zarathustra as self-thrown into the high reaches of the sky, but subject still (like the tightrope walker) to the law of gravity. But the dwarf goes on: "Sentenced to yourself and to your own stoning—O Zarathustra, far indeed have you thrown the stone, but it will fall back on yourself." The image has altered significantly: the thrower remains behind and indeed becomes the victim of his throwing, as the stone he throws falls back and crushes him. The dwarf voices the chimerical transformation of autoaesthetic force, from whose perspective it is impossible to differentiate the doer and the deed, since both are fictions. Zarathustra throws himself and is thrown, falls and falls back on/to himself.

But the parable, with its evaluative strategy of suffering, takes a turn at this moment: "Then something happened that made me lighter, for the dwarf jumped from my shoulder, being curious; and he crouched on a stone before me. But there was a gateway just where we had stopped."[36] The virtual repetition here of the critical narrative moment in the story of the tightrope walker, but which relieves Zarathustra's heavy burden, reveals the book's loneliest *Hausthür*, the dialectical gate ("Behold this gateway, dwarf! It has two faces."), to which Zarathustra has come, carrying the dwarf to unheard-of heights. This gate, like the threshold in the epigraph of *The Gay Science* and the jester's door, is layered with autoaesthetic symbolism; unlike the others, this one describes a liminal *étrangeté* at the very boundary of the self. Nietzsche describes here, in the most economical and elliptical of terms, the human psyche itself, within which thresholds of time, consciousness, and Dionysian force occur. No longer is the dwarf the harasser of Zarathustra, but the pupil. The dwarf, as an overdetermined emblem of Dionysian forces that would drag Zarathustra down from the Apollinian heights, which at the same time are heights of misunderstanding, dangerously threatening the Dionysian creativity that "gravity" destroys, is no longer a nagging imp but has fallen silent in his "curiosity" at the image before him. Zarathustra instructs him in what he and we see before us:

> Behold this gateway, dwarf! It has two faces. Two paths meet here; no one yet has followed either to its end. This long lane stretches back for an eternity. And the long lane out there, that is another eternity. They contradict each other, these paths; the offend each other face; and it is here at this gateway that they come together. The name of the gateway is inscribed above: "Moment."[37]

The dense *prosopopoeia* of the gateway, with its two "faces" meeting and confronting each other at the airy archway, doorless but divided, shows some of the ways in which Nietzsche wants this image to work. Two of the faces contradicting each other here are Apollo and Dionysus, opposite force-clusters that form us all. In the end, the gateway symbolizes the polarizing force itself, the principle of *étrangeté* by which Zarathustra (like all of us, so incompletely) knows himself.

The gateway, a kind of ultimate *framing device*, also frames Zarathustra's discourse with the frequently transmuting dwarf, showing itself as an *evaluative* device. The Gate of Moment is the emblem of the threshold of consciousness (and unconsciousness) and, therefore, of the will-to-power. Autoaesthetic consciousness, including consciousness of the unconscious, however inaccessible it may be, and the articulation that empowers consciousness, frames a strategy of perpetual evaluation that is as eternal as the lanes stretching away from the gate, into the past and into the future. In this respect, the Gate of Moment, as the emblem of the eternal return to the autoaesthetic self (its most powerful meaning), is also an emblem of the way in which time itself is part of that evaluation. Again, Nietzsche is echoing and inverting a Goethean Romantic ideal: Faust's challenge to *his* devil is to find a moment he would want arrested forever, a moment so satisfying that it could suffice for an eternity. Nietzsche, too, desires such a moment, but the goal is not an arrest nor stasis of life but a perfectly pitched *force* that would sustain the Dionysian human in a positive suffering. This moment is possible only for the Overman, though lesser humans can glimpse its potentiality, and the Overman is a fiction. At his own final question in response to the gateway, "Must we not eternally return?" Zarathustra begins to speak more softly, sensing the implications of this multilayered *topos*, "for I was afraid of my own thoughts and the thoughts behind my thoughts"—at which point Zarathustra has been transported (or transmuted) again: "Where was the dwarf gone now? And the gateway? And the spider? And all the whispering? Was I dreaming, then? Was I waking up?" Zarathustra cannot be sure of any of this, even whether he is asleep or awake, since the parable he has "lived" is taking place at *some other level* of articulation. The increasingly distant narrative voice in *Zarathustra* confesses that his language is itself an exile, "born in the mountains," that in terms of the weighty parable that language has been a function of what, he calls

> verily, a wild wisdom—my great broad-winged longing! And often it swept me away and up and far, in the middle of my laughter; and I flew, quivering, an arrow, through sun-drunken delight, away into distant futures which no dream had yet seen, into hotter souths than artist ever dreamed of, where gods in their dances are ashamed of all clothes—to speak in parables and to limp and stammer like poets; and verily, I am ashamed that I must still be a poet.[38]

Zarathustra's poetics must be an autoaesthetic of desire,[39] whatever the implications, since that *longing* of which life consists is most ardently and clearly figured forth in the highly charged transference of this description itself, which mirrors the exile (*étrangeté*) of language away from conventional thought and interpretation.

The parable of the Gate of Moment, incomplete until one sees its frame in Zarathustra's autoaesthetic narrative, shows the articulated power of *étrangeté* at work *outside* of him. Behold the advent of the shadow.

ZARATHUSTRA('S) SHADOW

Understanding the transformative power to reveal will-to-power is the goal of all Zarathustra's, and Nietzsche's, interrogations, and its revelation is for Nietzsche an ironic spiritual apotheosis, a playful poetic art. Its redemptive if chimerical slippage, a perpetual self-reenergizing out of what seem to be depleted metaphors, is the gift of poetry to philosophic discourse, a gift unanticipated and often unwelcomed by philosophy, and contains Nietzsche's re-inscription not only of transformation but of trans-substantiation. The degree to which autoaesthetic awareness calls attention to its own need for interpretation and subversion marks that to which the poet *has overcome* the philosopher/prophet in the *going-under* of a Dionysian poetic consciousness.

One of the most significant aspects of this power of abrogation is the vitality with which it occurs. This vitality begins, as does all energy for Nietzsche, with a volcanic anti-dogmatism bounded only by the play of metaphor. Zarathustra plays obsessively with Persian and Christian liturgy, inverting and ironizing its iconography, combining iconoclasm with poetic

power and finally with a "confession" of power's abrogation in the knowledge that the poet is no more than an "ink-fish" (the autoaesthetic Christ/
Dionysus).[40] Indeed, this *process* of privileging and cancellation is one
through which Zarathustra goes as a matter of intellectual course and development:

> Alas, there are so many things between heaven and earth of which only
> the poets have dreamed.
> And especially *above* the heavens: for all gods are poets' parables,
> poets' prevarications. Verily, it always lifts us higher—specifically, to the
> realm of the clouds: upon these we place our motley bastards and call
> them gods and overmen. For they are just light enough for these chairs—
> all these gods and overmen. Ah, how weary I am of all the imperfection
> which must at all costs become event! Ah, how weary I am of poets.[41]

Zarathustra's weariness with *himself* comes about as a result of his own
inevitable failure to become icon, but also with his ineluctable entrapment in
the all-too-human desire to do so. Significantly, the power of his non-
position results from constant self-ironization; the play of *Dichter-Gleichnis*
and *Dichter-Schreibnis*, like the tightrope, determines Zarathustra's parabolic turn from both self-determination and self-cancellation. The moment
the energy of the poet becomes "event," the moment he is implicated in
writing,[42] he is implicated in the fallen world of humanity, which itself
conjures up the energy out of which his frustration (to which what he calls
"weariness" is an unavoidable reaction) is born.

But the more obvious spiritual iconoclasm out of which Zarathustra
builds his autoaesthetic edifice is matched by many other less obvious
permutations of that energy, always toward the goal of an autoaesthetic
assertion of power. He calls his words the "crooked," the remnants or
rejects from the great structure of (canonical) language he sees all around
him. Just as convention is his enemy, so is he its enemy (again, two confronting faces, though in provocatively Dionysian fashion his chief metaphor for
this antagonism comes not from the realm of abstract poetic rhetoric but
from *mastication* of a meager diet through what he will call, in his preface to
On the Genealogy of Morals, "rumination"); on its inverted trip away from
substantiality this figure of the enemy of human metamorphosis into and
then beyond poet/philosopher is given progressively a beastly, human, and
then extra-human form. It progresses from animal (eagle, serpent, dog,
spider, etc.) to the shadow itself.

I said that Nietzsche's transformative power is a parable of trans-
substantiation, and that this theme is present in *Zarathustra* from the beginning, always adumbrating the shadow with which it concludes. One of the
most interesting early avatars of the shadow, in Part One of *Zarathustra*, is

the chivalric and mythic "great dragon," the enervating force whose task is the destruction of the will,[43] but which is the first ancestor of Dionysian trans-substantiation. I want to spend a moment on this figure before (over)-leaping to the shadow.

The dragon, like the jester, is not merely nor simply an enemy but the emblem of *étrangeté*, which can be seen as a rewriting of trans-substantiation: Zarathustra goes to the "loneliest wilderness/desert" to seek out the final self-absorption, "his last Master: it will be hostile to him and to its last god, he will struggle for victory against the great dragon." Victory over the dragon would be victory over the repressive, blindered, and protective scales of dogma and thus of the concept of a unified and monological self. On each scale of the dogma-dragon is written "Thou shalt," a mocking inversion of the word and the constraining intent of Mosaic law, each a tombstone-like epitaph commemorating the death of creativity and the *protection* of *ressentiment* made into law and written on the "tablets" of the dragon's body: "Values thousands of years old shine on these scales," Zarathustra says. Zarathustra's struggle against the dragon, as if defying the austere repetition of the scales, is ensconced in a weltering succession of metaphors and symbols, which only come to rest when the atavistic Nietzschean lion ("I will") appears and confronts the dragon. But a struggle between dragon and lion does not occur; rather, the dragon, we discover, has somehow acted as the catalyst for the first great transformation about which Zarathustra must learn, that from the camel (herd-mentality, beast of burden) to the lion (freedom to create). In the lion's creation out of a confrontation with the dogma-dragon, Nietzsche tells us, we witness the first requisite for the creation of new autoaesthetic values:

> The creation of freedom for oneself for new creation—that is within the power of the lion. The creation of freedom for oneself and a sacred "No" even to duty—for that, my brothers, the lion is needed. To assume the right to new values—that is the most terrifying assumption for a reverent spirit that would bear much.[44]

The spiritualization of creativity reaches its apotheosis in this first transformation, which overleaps the parable of the tightrope walker. But the lion cannot *act* upon its created freedom. Only the child, the next metamorphosis, can do that. The child, Nietzsche tells us, is "innocence and forgetting, a new beginning, a game, a self-propelled wheel, the first movement, a sacred 'Yes.'" To take the power to free oneself for new creation, and then to act upon it "to create new values," this is the autoaesthetic ideal and the goal of all of Zarathustra's subsequent confrontations and adventures. Thus, at another level, Zarathustra's course from mountain-hermit to philosopher-poet begins in these "metamorphoses." The parable of the catalytic dragon is a new and truly transformative enlightenment, differentiating and melding powers together as an adumbration of the eventual union of Apollo and Dionysus in the shadow. Such a Nietzschean understanding "rends the drapes of night" and "weds dark and light," for "evil is necessary, necessary are the envy and mistrust and calumny among your virtues."[45] Within this context of trans-substantiation we are prepared to confront and understand the shadow.

In fact, it is the *"voice"* of his own shadow that formulates Zarathustra's final autoaesthetic self, in "The Shadow," the ninth section of Part Four, but we must remember that the advent of the shadow's *voice* into Zarathustra is not its first appearance. The shadow is a product of a gathering convocation of images from the previous three books, which are then transformed into and transcended by the pure voice of the insubstantial. The process begins with Zarathustra inscribing his own self-overcoming. He sits before his cave,

> but as he was sitting there, a stick in his hand, tracing his shadow on the ground, thinking—and verily, not about himself and his shadow—he was suddenly frightened, and he started: for beside his own shadow he saw another shadow. And as he looked around quickly and got up, behold, the soothsayer stood beside him—the same he had once fêted at his table, the proclaimer of the great weariness who taught "All is the same, nothing is worthwhile, the world is without meaning, knowledge strangles."[46]

Yet another jester on the tightrope walker's heels, the soothsayer/shadow, now changed from his former self, with "ashen lightning bolts" running over his face, is the harbinger of Zarathustra's failure and his successful transcendence. Zarathustra *identifies* his shadow by defining it, literally inscribing it in the dust. The image of transcendence comes out of Zarathustra's writing himself down and the subsequent doubling of the inscribed shadow in the doubling of Zarathustra, when the soothsayer, Zarathustra's *doppelgänger*, appears. The great weariness the shadow/soothsayer brings is a harbinger of Zarathustra's eternal return to the world of men, away from any transcendent spirituality, and of his necessary failure to transcend this round. The soothsayer is also the welcoming harbinger of the selflessness of *étrangeté*: "The soothsayer, who had noticed what went on in Zarathustra's soul, wiped his hand over his face as if he wanted to wipe it away, and Zarathustra did likewise." This wiping is the first autoaesthetic gesture, as Nietzsche tells us immediately: "And when both had thus silently composed and strengthened themselves, they shook hands as a sign that they wanted to recognize each other." In this fresh dialectical opening, Zarathustra is told by the soothsayer that he is to be borne away from his mountain on the rising sea of empathy for and with *other men*; that is, that his transcendent spirituality is to be supplanted by gregarious humanness, in the form of *pity*.

In the next sections, Zarathustra is systematically reabsorbed into the mock-spiritual human world of the figures gathered at his cave, who mime the Christian apotheosis but, as happens literally at the end of his book, leave Zarathustra behind. This confrontation with the *first* shadow shows the initial steps of separation Zarathustra takes from his aspirations to the Overman.

Like Nietzsche's writing, Zarathustra's shadow establishes the abyss between his existence as such and the *remainder* of pure appearance, without substance, at the key autoaesthetic moment in *Zarathustra*. The shadow[47] is the (dis)joining—the fold or articulation—between the world of the parable and that of history. It appears as a character in Zarathustra's story when he is at his most open and vulnerable, as he brandishes a stick and chases away an "affectionate beggar" from his cave in Part Four. No sooner has the "voluntary beggar," Zarathustra's link with the world of man, departed than this "new voice" is introduced: "But as soon as the voluntary beggar had run away and Zarathustra was alone again, he heard a new voice behind him, shouting, 'Stop, Zarathustra Wait! It is I, O Zarathustra, I, your shadow!'"[48] This is no longer the voice of a figure in the shadows, as it had been with the soothsayer a few sections before, but the purely metaphorical voice of Zarathustra's own double, his (narrative) voice, without him. Initially, on hearing this uncanny voice, Zarathustra is not ensphinxed. His reaction, as a *man*, is to run away, back to the corporeal world, "but he who was behind him followed him [as shadows will], so that soon there were three runners, one behind the other, first the voluntary beggar, then Zarathustra, and third and last his shadow." Here again, for the last (and "highest") time, Zarathustra is stretched between beast and Overman. The voice of the shadow, which here calls itself a "wanderer," thus finally collapsing together the two figures from "The Wanderer and His Shadow," recounts in a long monologue the iconoclastic lessons of *étrangeté* it has learned with Zarathustra: "With you I broke whatever my heart revered; I overthrew all boundary stones and images; I pursued the most dangerous wishes." But then the shadow delivers the gist of his lesson *back* to Zarathustra, in terms of overleaping and the energized shallowness of autoaesthetic identity: "With you I unlearned faith in words and values and great names. When the devil sheds his skin, does not his name fall off too? For that too is skin. The devil himself is perhaps—skin" ("The Shadow"). Wrapped up in the shadow's introduction are the lessons we have perceived in each of Zarathustra's stories—of tightrope walker, gateway, dragon, shadow.

This gate of moment is the conclusive one, at which the shadow acknowledged its "unlearned faith in words and values and great names"[49] and foreshadows its departure from Zarathustra, the final autoaesthetic act and the breaking out of *étrangeté*. He commences to do so with the great

Nietzschean/Zarathustran dictum "Nichts ist wahr, alles ist erlaubt [Nothing is true, all is permitted]," a realization that only when it lied did the shadow tell the truth, only when it surpassed the human did it begin to exist. But Zarathustra, in his final (concealed) rejection of the Overman, runs to the human beast instead:

> And now let me quickly run away from you again. Even now a shadow seems to lie over me. I want to run alone so that it may become bright around me again. For that, I shall still have to stay merrily on my legs a long time.[50]

Still seeking to lighten his way, to relieve himself of the weight of gravity whether it take the guise of tightrope walker, dwarf, or shadow, Zarathustra chooses the world of *étrangeté*, of self-estrangement, which is still merry and full of dancing. The yes-saying to suffering Zarathustra exhibits here is his final language-sin.

When the shadow spoke first, we had to ask what he (Zarathustra) had learned and what it (the shadow) was teaching. For all his exuberance, we see in response that Zarathustra is finally ensphinxed and that part of his ensphinxedness is clearly an ability not to learn but, rather, to be "fixed in his tablets." Zarathustra is, finally and ineluctably, caught in the conflictual oppositions of *étrangeté*—ensphinxed. He returns to his cave, ostensibly to retreat from the world of man, but he does not and cannot leave it and is quietly erased from his own narration, supplanted by the shadow.[51] In the section entitled "The Song of Melancholy," Zarathustra begins to vanish, displaced by a series of dithyrambic songs ("Only Fool! Only Poet!" with its "only screaming colorfully out of fools' masks, climbing around on mendacious word bridges") portraying the timelessness and heightened significance of the very "linguistic sin" Zarathustra commits as the shadow sings. The culminative song begins "Wilderness grows: woe unto him who harbors wildernesses!"; the wanderer-shadow, which pursues the going-across and the going-under of the autoaesthetic beyond Zarathustra, is itself *umsphinxt*, at once the metaphor and the concept on which Nietzsche bases his program for rewriting philosophy and art.

This ensphinxedness, announced by the shadow but lived by the man, is unlike that of the sphinx (Zarathustra) alone; indeed, unlike the condition of any *actual* man who has ever existed. Like Zarathustra, Nietzsche comes to announce, as Michel Haar says, "the coming of a new type of man,"[52] who is sphinx and man. But in what way can this man be seen as "modern" or, indeed, as man? Nietzsche/Zarathustra/shadow forces the reader to work actively and diligently for a satisfactory response. How can the reader "pass beyond" *this* metaphor of ensphinxedness to see it (since existence can only be seen from the perspective of *étrangeté*)? It speaks in parables,[53] seeming to turn away from direct explanation but in fact offering the most direct one possible (that is, the parable itself). The sphinx/shadow, who is caught inexorably outside of time, world, and word, makes Zarathustra a prisoner of a vastly overdetermined monument to the *writing in* of his own signification.

But the shadow, appropriately, plays even more roles than those of self-image and distance. Zarathustra is revealed in the shadow's ensphinxing as a function of the power he has declared as uniquely his own: that of the declarer of the will-to-power. For Nietzsche, autoaesthetic will-to-power is to be conceived in detachment from, indeed as the canceller of, both other and self. Zarathustra and his shadow, as manifestations of will-to-power, are at once self-conquering and self-defeating. This very detachment makes Zarathustra, like the sphinx, as Paul de Man claims, the "ruthless forgetting" not of speaking-as-being but of writing-as-becoming.[54] He is a function of sphinx-like isolation, but also of chimerical self-creation, doubting and cancelling himself, unable to gauge his place or his role in the world around him and therefore subject to the nausea, figuratively a kind of vertigo, he experiences as an inevitable result of this powerful ambivalence.[55] Man's inability to see his own nature, his striving for that which he is not and through which all is permitted, initiates both his significance and his benightedness, from which there is no possible extraction. Man, always his own double, persists in the folly of seeing himself as immediate, as Zarathustra has done at the advent of the shadow's narrative, and this is part of his and our radical myopia: "the blindness with which he throws himself into an action lightened of all previous experience captures the authentic spirit of modernity."[56] This blindness is a writerly self-cancellation which, more clearly in *Zarathustra* than anywhere else in Nietzsche, is the collapsing together of poetry and philosophy. Zarathustra, as his shadow says, abrogates traditional powers of conceptualization (seen as power "over") and acquires a new mode of force; he leaps outside the world of traditional man and becomes a "sinner" against tradition, by virtue of the very declaration he makes of himself. In acknowledging his "linguistic sin," crowding much into one word, and thereby becoming the shadow of the shadow of writing, Zarathustra is the spirit of the will-to-power's embodiment.

Nietzsche declares that "self" resides in its own abrogation into text. Writing is the place of the eternally recurring question. Each creates his own world in his image, Zarathustra tells us in "Upon the Blessed Isles," but that world is one of *Künstwerk*. His effort has been to be "the overcomer of the great nausea"[57] of humanness, but now, in reviewing his work, he begins to see that such nausea cannot be avoided:

I taught them all *my* art and strivings: to create and carry together into One what in man is fragment and riddle and dreadful accident—

—as creator, riddle-guesser and redeemer of chance, I taught them to work on the future and to redeem with their creation all that *has been*.

To redeem man's past and re-create all "it was," until the will says "Thus I willed it!"[58]

Like the prophet creating his own eschatology, the tyrant his own genealogy, or the human being its own history and spirituality, Zarathustra "redeems" his story by countermanding his own program: in declaring that it is now the "One" man strives for, Zarathustra overcomes overcoming. His last retreat to the cave of disciples, birds, and lions means, for Zarathustra, the abrogation of the Overman. The eternal recurrence, for him, is a falling back into an interpretation (a reinterpretation) of the past that *we* know was not "his."

It is, in the end, for this reason that the Overman is that "attempt at something which is no longer man" and why his book is for all and none. Even the highest man is a quantum unit, a step toward a chimerical goal. He must be spoken of in the end by and as his shadow; he must remain an ambivalent figure, an inverted symbol, leaving his cave to descend into the twentieth century and all subsequent ones, the spirit of the shadow.

6

◆

From Old Gold to I.O.U.s: Ike McCaslin's Debased Genealogical Coin

Alas, what are you, then, my written and
forged thoughts! . . . what are we able to forge?
Alas, always only what has begun to fade and
lose its fragrance. Alas, always only receding
and exhausted thunderstorms and old, yellowed
feelings.

—Nietzsche, *Beyond Good and Evil*, 296

To redeem those who lived in the past and to
recreate all "it was" into a "thus I willed it"—
that alone should I call redemption. . . . The will
cannot work backwards; and that he cannot
break time and time's covetousness, that is the
will's loneliest melancholy.

—*Thus Spoke Zarathustra*
(II. "On Redemption")

William Faulkner's thematics of language and validity may usefully be seen
in a dialogue with Nietzsche's conception of the forgery always lying behind
our ensphinxed language, the ironic yes-saying which revels in assertions
and demonstrations of the chimerical redemption of language. Nietzsche's
prosopopoeia of the "running down" inherent in language-feelings, in

136

Beyond Good and Evil, and in the weighing down of the will itself by time, in *Zarathustra,* with its implications for any satisfactory genealogy, is particularly applicable to Faulkner's meditation on genealogy in *The Bear.*[1] Faulknerian language, the richest and ripest of American Modernist prose, is at the same time caught in that spirited Zarathustran play of fullness and emptiness we have been exploring. Faulkner is particularly obsessed with the notion of a spirituality inhering in language but that he sees as a distillation of a spirituality *behind* language; which, as we have seen in the texts we have looked at here, "leaves language behind" as its mark or cipher. Like Nietzsche/Zarathustra, Faulkner/Ike carries a series of tablets and is caught within an enervating history that is itself an attempt at autoaesthetic power. Zarathustran language is clearly autumnal, and this does not show itself in Faulkner only in the withering irony of *The Bear.* Faulkner's irony is not Nietzsche's, in that while, for Nietzsche, the claim of *any* substantial truth is by definition ironized by language, though such claims cannot exist elsewhere and thus language always lives up to its promise, for Faulkner, language always fails to do so, detaching itself from the ineffable truths language always corrupts and alters, however diligently one works at making it "fit" (and no one works harder than Faulkner, whose "ear" and "hand" provide the reader with an uncanny combination of mimesis and artfulness).

As I Lay Dying's Addie Bundren, the most autumnal of Faulkner's central characters, best expresses Faulkner's attitude toward mock-spiritual language, ever rising toward some autoaesthetic apotheosis, shows Faulkner's volcanic ambivalence toward it, telling us that for all the eloquence and flight language offers, "words are no good";[2] indeed, "that words don't ever fit even what they are trying to say at," that they are "just a shape to fill a lack."[3] Addie's meditation on the ironic spirituality of language articulates the abyss between raw emotional experience ("doing") and interpretive linguistic frames, imprisoned in time, that must inevitably lead to the conclusion to which Nietzsche has already come in *The Will to Power*: "both the deed and the doer are fictions" because "spirit" is unavailable to us except as "something that thinks" (see the epigraph to this section, p. 113). In Addie Bundren's Faulknerian *schema,* this ironized fictionality takes the following eschatological form:

> I would think how words go straight up in a thin line, quick and harmless, and how terribly doing goes along the earth, clinging to it, so that after a while the two lines are too far apart for the same person to straddle from one to the other; and that sin and love and fear are just sounds that people who never sinned nor loved nor feared have for what they never had and cannot have until they forget the words.[4]

This is one of Faulkner's versions of the slippage of language we have been witnessing half-concealed at the center of the Modernist program. It is a very complex idea, simultaneously claiming that language is radically divorced from what Addie, Ike, and Faulkner see as reality, and that this very distance renders reality *less* powerful and language *more* so, in experiential terms. However much Faulkner's view of reality diverges from Nietzsche's, and we increasingly see the wide divergence between Nietzsche and the Modernist will, the idea of the forgetting that makes language powerful is a purely Nietzschean one does not find its most dramatic, and most Nietzschean, manifestation in Addie, for whom that forgetting never occurs and whose memory of the "gap over the lack" that language represents is always searingly present in her (narrated) thoughts and in her (after)life—and in the obsessively precise language that remains behind after her (literary) death, particularly in light of the fact that Addie's "literal" death is the catalyst for the opening, not the closing, of *As I Lay Dying.*

The Nietzschean element in Faulknerian will is pervasive even if subject to the complex, spiritualized surrogation of time and history. Patrick McGee points out that "memory is an open text because every interpretation is framed and limited by its historical moment and the disjunctive process of generation";[5] while Addie Bundren is a prime example of his sort of memory, the most strikingly forceful manifestation of this dilemma of language in Faulkner is to be found in Ike McCaslin, for whom language, particularly written language, represents a grounding which is simultaneously a conundrum in which he, like Zarathustra, is caught and one from which he cannot escape.

At first, the genealogical line from Nietzsche to Faulkner might seem at best dotted and speculative, at worst chimerical: Faulkner's familiar Modernist "truths of the heart" seem to find no comfortable place in the compass of Nietzsche's radical, exilic rhetoric. But John Irwin[6] has helped us to read Faulkner in a new way, to begin to forge a provocative Nietzschean link. Irwin urges us to see Nietzsche's chief effort as that of freeing man from *revenge* and working toward the self-overcoming Nietzsche sees as possible (only) in writing. Both of these efforts are genealogical in the Faulknerian sense, functions of man's dealing with his past, his "lineage," and his willful autoaesthetic efforts, and they are also genealogical in the Nietzschean sense, functions of the interrelationship and echoing of texts of the self. This play in Nietzsche, between time-as-historical event and text-as-power, formulated in the epigram from *Beyond Good and Evil* in such highly metaphorized fashion, is also the play of distance and difference: here the genealogy of Nietzsche and Faulkner interweave to form a powerful narrative force. For both Faulkner and Nietzsche, the idea of distance, and of the *différance* of both space (difference) and time (that autumnal deferral), is inherent in the idea of writing. In this way, the Nietzschean concept of loss, the abrogation of traditional genealogical power in that textual genealogy, allows us to see Faulknerian *loss* in a new way. For Nietzsche and Faulkner, self-conceptualization must always operate within this framework.[7]

In *The Bear*, which Faulkner includes in the highly spiritualized *Go Down, Moses*, this idea of loss must always exist in a dialogue with the self-inscription from which the so-called past and present are constructed. In the relationship between Ike McCaslin's legacy of gold and the promissory notes that he eventually discovers have replaced them, we can see Faulkner's play with this problematic theme: the ostensibly autoaesthetic (noble) person is reduced, literally, to an echo of "himself." Moreover, the medium (language) in which that potential human nobility is created, verified, checked, challenged, and asserted is that in which it is finally cancelled.

This is the dilemma in which Ike McCaslin is always caught: for him genealogy is, as Nietzsche's epigraphs suggest, an inevitable disjunction of thoughts and writing about past and present, the elevation of the legitimacy of the past and the illegitimacy of the present. This inversion of the unified life Addie Bundren has hoped for and been denied is inspired by *étrangeté*. The very sense of genealogical grounding, in the chronological recounting of events, is denied in *The Bear*. While in *Zarathustra* (and *As I Lay Dying*) the story is unfolded in order, as a series of repetitions that move forward even as they turn in place, in *The Bear* events are overlaid in such a way as to deny historical validity and to foreground the narrative complexity and power of the writer. As in so many of his other works, Faulkner employs the device of "exploded time" to augment narrative force; among the effects of this strategy are the diverse ones of greater manifested narrative power over time and diminished will, on the part of the central thematic characters, to affect time and history. The overall effect of Faulkner's exploded time in *The Bear* is to produce a swirling, vortextual *pastiche* of time in which the reader cannot find solid grounding and is constantly and provocatively frustrated. This temporal strategy is a central example of Faulkner's imitative form: his history-privileging and history-blasting are both focused in the atemporal telling of Ike's story. Ike does not understand, as Faulkner and Nietzsche do, that this disjunction is "unreal," that his despair and frustration result from the incommensurability of a text of the past juxtaposed with texts of a present that do not match: Ike's is a setting up of conditions for historical, redemptive self-completion and self-reification that must necessarily result in a radical failure to find an interpretation of the world and the self sufficient to ameliorate the "will's loneliest melancholy."

Among the dramatic complexities of *The Bear*, one of the most provocative to pursue, in light of Faulkner's own project for fiction and that of his characters in their own fictions, all within the larger framework of ironic Nietzschean interrogation, is that of the nature of the Zarathustran higher man and the way in which this posited "heroic" figure twists itself around what *seems* to be the formless, chthonic power of the woods,[8] but which turns out to be the highly shaped and honed power of the word. For Ike, the heroic hunt depicted (and which eternally returns) in the story is not merely for a bear but for the most symbolic of autoaesthetic bears, the bear that will make Ike real. Yet even in his fervid searching, Ike is caught in Addie Bundren's ambivalence of word and deed, and in Nietzschean *étrangeté*. Ike considers his autoaesthetic goal, the accomplishment of the heroic or noble person, to be able to "read the signs" of nature around him, to be the decipherer of the order that lies behind the enervation of puny human reason (and reasons). Ike's own reading of the signs is always a displacement into old and new tablets, on which the will must write. Significantly, in this Nietzschean respect, Ike enters Major de Spain's bear hunt not with the simple chronological rhetoric of a phrase like "when Ike was ten," but rather "on the day when he first wrote his age in two ciphers"[9]—from the outset of Ike's story, writing and the power of ledgers are central.

But I want to delay looking at the initiatory experience of the hunt in my own Faulknerian autoaesthetic, and rather examine some of the themes and later scenes by which we come to know Ike, whose whole story is framed in autoaesthetic terms by the mythic hunt and its spiritual quarry, which is not Old Ben but the *bare* Ike McCaslin. In this regard, in his initiation into the hunt, Ike is brought by his cousin McCaslin to the big camp in the woods "to earn for himself the name and state of hunter provided he in his turn were humble and enduring enough."[10] To earn the name and state of hunter: Ike's struggle is not simply genealogical but also nominal, always at play with the nature of the cipher. He must heroically and persistently struggle with symbolic bears and with language designations. In addition, this will only occur if he, "in his turn," is "humble and enduring enough." This humility is the more powerful in light of Nietzsche's claim that "man is no longer evil enough,"[11] that "not the corruption of man but the extent to which he has become tender and moralized is his curse." It is only by a return to the Dionysian, to our Old Ben-nature, that "beautiful men are again becoming possible" and that the "barbarian in each of us is affirmed."[12] Nietzsche's description of the last man, incapable of this Dionysian nature, is an apt accounting of Ike:

> Man, imprisoned in an iron cage of errors, became a caricature of man, sick, wretched, ill-disposed toward himself, full of hatred for the impulses of life, full of mistrust of all that is beautiful and happy in life, a walking picture of misery.[13]

Here we must remember Nietzsche's discussion of Napoléon and his greatness, as being *untier und Übertier*, beast and overbeast. Old Ben is indeed this dichotomous animal/spirit for Ike, though Ike himself, in his misunderstanding of Nietzschean genealogy and humility, can never achieve this self-overcoming. The information Ike is to receive on his hunt is a vital part of his legacy; indeed, the inception of the hunt is the beginning of the trial of Ike's self-telling and the beginning of *The Bear*. The conditions are clear yet only vaguely entabled, since Ike must learn to interpret, not *inherit*, the value of woods, the hunt, his past, and therefore himself. Ike himself experiences his arrival for the hunt as "the arrival of his own birth."[14]

A vital offshoot of this narrative birth and its misunderstanding of the bear's role is its concomitant schematic establishment of Sam Fathers as the *human* father figure that the nascent hero must emulate. The conditions of this inverted adoption seem clear: patience, humility, solitude, reverence, insight. These qualities, of course, are requisites for the hunt Ike will conduct not for the bear but for the Ike who can confront the bear, who can *tell and subsume* him. The mythos of the story is that of Ike's search for self not in the substantial woods but beyond the brittle lore of the woods, a search into the issue of self-conception to which he alone has access. The quest for the higher man, the self-overcoming for which Ike yearns—his heroism, as it is defined and employed in *The Bear*—is as chimerically elusive as Tennie's Jim. Ike's idea of the higher man is saturatedly genealogical: the heroic is intricately bound up with the concept of legacy, history, and time. As John Matthews points out,[15] legacy is always a coordination of possession and loss: legacy, like Ben, rises up *in order to* run down and to fade. Even beyond the mystical power of Sam Fathers, this genealogical mandate is fundamentally logocentric, to place this Derridean word in its place as a descendant of Nietzsche's ambivalent self-declaration and of a "theological presence" in written language.[16]

This logocentricity is, for Ike, a function of spiritual texts. Just as Zarathustra is named for the Persian seer, so Ike's biblical namesake, Isaac, the son of Abraham, the issue of God's mercy from the centenarian Abraham and his wife Sarah, is the father of the tribes and the legitimizer of the nation.[17] Isaac, in the biblical narrative, is the chosen one, to whom all riches and power shall go—the highest man. Abraham's Isaac has the heroic power of legitimacy written on his birth and his life, a divine mandate, as it were, derived directly from the *logos*. For Isaac *McCaslin*, therefore, in the many levels of self-crafting, as in lore of the woods and in the stories of the men with whom he learns the woods, the mythic note of validation is one of narrative genealogy and the play of history and time. As we have seen before, in Julien Sorel and Jude Fawley as well as in Zarathustra, this narrative eschatology receives further play in Ike's emulation of Christ, whose mythography captures Ike's own deepest desires. Within this framework, the tradition of the hunt as metaphor for life is "passed down" as part of a knowledge, vague and powerful, that will supposedly allow Ike to be a man.

Ike's own legacy from the "it was" of the past, modeled on this vague and powerful concept of legitimacy, is an even more specific convocation of written and forged thoughts than I have suggested. As Patrick McGee shows,

> Isaac's first attempt to find the bear and to face it down is a scene of reading. . . . After this first encounter with the bear, the division between wilderness and civilization begins to break down in the boy's mind although this only increases his will to maintain the division.[18]

For the palimpsest Faulkner calls Ike, one reading obscures but reveals another, which takes us toward the thematic core of Ike's story. His genealogical legitimacy is not only a function of the hunt metaphor; he has received a tantalizing, sealed burlap package from his Uncle Hubert Beauchamp, containing, purportedly, the gold which itself validifies that "greater" past, to be redeemed by Ike in some apocryphal future: in Ike's *present* world, gold is itself a function, an emblem, and a manifestation of the past—there is no *new* gold, so the package itself stands as a concrete symbol of a better prior time, a time of greater heroism and of the human character's real *summer* substance before its autumnal falling off. This spiritualization of purportedly legitimate goldness is a "mendacious word bridge," as Gary Lee Stonum points out: "The concept of value [in Faulkner] is common to the study of language and to the study of wealth,"[19] and since the thought of legacy is for Ike both a gold thought and a narrative thought, as the burlap package's transformation from the former into the latter in the end shows us, its "tinkling promise" of future wealth and past solidity is not merely a voiceless object projecting into Ike's life from a dark, other time, but already a *text* of that time, and of the chasm between that time and his. He describes it as "no pale sentence or paragraph scrawled in cringing fear of death by a weak and trembling hand as a last desperate sop flung at retribution, but a Legacy."[20] This "Legacy," in distancing Ike from his own physicality, confounds and reverses the fear of erasure/death Ike confronts, which frightens him just because it threatens always to truncate the bear hunt of which his life consists. Ike, like all Modernist heroes, seeks a legitimation beyond language, but always discovers it to be a "sentence or paragraph" inscribed at the gate-of-moment crossing of life and death, at the autoaesthetic moment. Ike wants a self-ratification beyond language, a self that will not be part of the ephemeral world of words, that can actually be legitimized. Uncle Hub's package, like Sam Fathers' ineffable wisdom, represents just such a possibility.

This substantial coin of the heroic past is set by Faulkner in contrast to its closely related but dialectical opposites: Ike's father's *very* ephemeral legacy, his ledgers. Even though the old books on the commissary shelves are what is left of the McCaslin plantation, even though Cass himself is vitally concerned with them, and even though they represent the *text* of his past in a way the burlap package does not and cannot, because of his obsession with that over-real, heroic legitimation beyond writing, Ike is made fundamentally uneasy by the dusty day-to-day business of the ledgers. The alternative heritage to that of Carothers McCaslin, a heritage of "blood" rather than "words," is stronger. And yet it is only in words that he finds an escape.[21] The shift of location, in Section 4 of *The Bear*, from the woods to the commissary, is a shift from experience to written history, from that reality Ike has tried to embrace to the texts out of which he must fashion chimerical experience and chimerical value. As for the "truth" of these ledgers, "the only truth Isaac can find in the ledgers is the truth he puts there,"[22] since the meaning of a text must always be a function of the reading subject, for whom the act of reading is an act not of discovery nor revelation but of generation. This self-generation is a textualizing of both civilization (the ledgers) and wilderness (the woods/bear): Ike establishes his own "line" in this blood claim, declaring that he is "married" to the woods,[23] that the woods are his wife and mistress.[24]

Further, as he claims to establish his own line based on the chimerical lore of the woods, he "inherits" the most important aspects of the woods as well: Old Ben and the legacy of Sam Fathers.[25] If Ben is a "phantom," which for the early part of the story he seems to be—larger than life and impossible to incarnate—then Sam Fathers is the incarnation of Ben's human antagonist, the amalgam of, ironically, *Ben's* possible human characteristics, truly the distillation of the natural father. Sam and Ben come to Ike from the inscribed dream of a better old world, in which understanding occurred between statuesque figures in such a way as to validate experience itself. Insofar as he is a manifestation of an old spiritualism and an old ritual, Sam embodies for Ike the fundamental dilemma of ritual itself: it is *civilized* and therefore detracts from nature, but it is also the link to the law of the land (as in the hunt itself) and therefore good. Ike's great trajectory is the translation of the rites of the beautiful and magnetic wilderness to the civilized ledgers of the tamed, "beautiful field" ("Beauchamp"). Sam's legacy to Ike, that of solitude, ancient wisdom, and silence, which Ike wants to believe is the more substantial, is "transcribed."[26]

Indeed, Ike's legacy from Uncle Hub, Uncle Buck, and grandfather, from Sam himself, is *not* one of silence but of a crowded heap of monological and dialogical texts from which Ike has no escape and which seem to want to crush him.[27] We see this clearly in the now-familiar theme of heavily ironized (literary) paternity on which Faulkner's genealogy is based. *The Bear* insists that the genetic and the genealogical links between biological father Theophilus McCaslin and Ike are weak, a mockery of that between Abraham and Isaac (Abraham is the model of the lover of God— Theophilus—and Ike's genealogical father-model, just as Isaac is Ike's ironic genealogical model): like Abraham, Buck is very old when Ike is born to Uncle Hub's sister, but unlike the story in Genesis 21, Ike is an afterthought, a piece of marginalia, not the final, ratifying chapter of the legitimizing book of Adam's line. Genetic linkage is not permitted to be the source of Ike's power but rather the genesis of his obsession with questioned and lost inheritance and heroism. The heroic past in which Ike believes is all in the telling, however much he is unable to accept or admit it. His self-dream and that of the world of the woods is clearly substantial only as an attempt at an autoaesthetic articulation. Ike's renunciation of his plantation, a gesture that heralds the end of genealogical legitimacy through the land, is also an "enunciation"[28] of his own personhood, the positing of a separate identity, however oxymoronic that might seem. It is an acknowledgment of the insoluble puzzle of self-validification beyond, Ike and Faulkner might say, the overwhelming weight of history and time.

But that renunciation is also not the sign of a world view that can produce any accurate of sufficient self-assessment, let alone an adequate sense of self. Ike and many who have read his story want greatly to make this autoaesthetic fervor into a comic (in the sense of "integrated" or "integrated") narrative; Ike would feel great satisfaction at the language of R. W. B. Lewis, who calls the story a "miracle of moral regeneration," in which Ike is "uniquely capable of reading the past correctly,"[29] but this view, although it correctly sees the thematic basis for the novel clearly, is as muddied as is Ike's. Ike's ceaseless reading of the past is anything but correct, at every level, and he knows it. While Zarathustra persistently denies his ghostly insubstantiality, Ike perceives his clearly: he is no more than a "shadow" of himself at age sixteen, through the first three sections of the novel, and then at eighteen in Section 5. As though picking up on the seeming reverie in which Zarathustra moves through his disjointed story, Ike "dreams" himself in Section 4 of *The Bear*, engaging in a shadow-narrated autoaesthetic self-fabrication by shooting ahead into his own future nearly sixty years and then returning to the 1880s, a radical disrupting of Ike's story designed to produce a "higher," narrative sense of the continuity from which a totalized self might be built. But only in the differentiating power of these narrative leaps is he constituted. The disrupted structure of the story itself, its exploding chronology, enables Ike to write his own "deed of property," which will finally allow him to try to appropriate, one might say with Nietzsche (and of course with Joyce) to forge, a sense of ownership of those words, if nothing else. Ike is increasingly concerned with the "consequences of the diverse organizations of experience" man adopts and invents—Ike's obsession is with the *design* of legitimacy.

Ike's dream of himself, overt in Section 4 but inherent in Faulkner's autumnal language and in the posture and plot of the rest of the story, is part of an heroic vision which embraces Old Ben and Sam Fathers, but in which the mock-heroic Ike is always "tainted" by being too "pure" to enter fully into the world of hunters, who are always, according to Ike, fully themselves. Ironically, his origins are tainted because they do not spring from the pureness of obscurity, as do those of Ben, Sam, the (Dionysian) fyce dog, and Boon Hogganbeck. Ike is imprisoned by his clear historical roots, just as Julien Sorel was. This "taint" of clarity that will not permit Ike to be *sui generis*, to exercise the power of autochthony, becomes clearer and clearer, and more clearly a power of *étrangeté*, as the dream of Ike develops.

Since Ike's power is that of the clarity of the past, and since that clarity is never in his aid but always an antagonist, an other, Ike can never come to terms with the fact that for him history itself is spiritualized. "History," as McGee points out, "wars with its counterpart—the myth of an original, uncorrupted nature, of a world without writing, without the markings of civilization, without the problematics of interpretation, without the conflicts of sexuality, without death."[30] These others come from a world beyond death (and therefore beyond life), a world of timeless story, while Ike comes from a world of objects, of lineage, of depleted power, and of his own deeply troubled awareness of the stories' ephemeral power. In a convoluted version of *ressentiment* Nietzsche ascribes to the last man, Ike always ascribes to others the power over the past and the self he so sorely lacks. Ike's "yes-saying," unlike the Dionysian one Zarathustra urges us to adopt, is a kind of empty catechism devoid of the spiritual energy that would make it viable; as for Nietzsche's last man, for Ike, tentatively inching along his insubstantial tightrope, every *other* is a typological reincarnation of the jester attempting to make him fall.

His empty yes-saying is most clearly depicted in the disastrous sexual relationship he has with his wife. In the intimate scenes in which we witness the physical unease he feels with his wife, we hear, as if in comment on the biblical Isaac, why his failed autoaesthetic embarrassment is so intense:

> *She already knows more than I with all the man-listening in camps where there was nothing to read ever even heard of. They are born already bored with what a boy approaches only at fourteen and fifteen with blundering and aghast trembling*: "I cant. Not ever. Remember": and still the steady and invincible hand and he said Yes and he thought, *She is lost. She was*

born lost. We were all born lost then he stopped thinking and even saying Yes, it was like nothing he had ever dreamed, let alone heard in mere man-talking.[31]

Ike's fraught sexuality, linked with his discovery of sex's reality as well as that of any genetic and genealogical lineage, cancels the story-telling faculty, permits only a lacuna in the text, adopting the word of Molly Bloom and of Nietzsche's (autumnal) Dionysus, "Yes," to stand for all the rest. The section concludes, lines later, with the wife's lonely and baleful admonition, "'And that's all. That's all from me. If this dont get you that son you talk about, it wont be mine': lying on her side, her back to the empty rented room, laughing and laughing"[32]—the section concludes without punctuation, with only the white space on the page to allow us to fill in Ike's reaction and our own. Although the scene is fully written prose, it has the effect of being an aphoristic condensation of a vital aspect of Ike. Sexuality, like Old Ben himself, is an "absent center."[33] Of course, just as Old Ben's death does not produce the insight Ike desires, neither does sex: unlike for Jude Fawley, the son Ike wants and of which the wife speaks does not appear.[34] The "empty renter room" in which Ike's sexual epiphany occurs is a symbol not of the powerful legacy of the history, nor of Ike's ability to overcome that history and reify himself, but of his dispossession. For Ike and his wife, the room is in lieu of the farm, a diminished symbol of the land-life Ike has experienced on the hunt, she has wanted, and to which Ike has been unable to commit himself. The room (an upper room, of course) is the emblem of denial. Ike cannot move from it to the farm, cannot allow even that fragment of legacy, always forcing himself to be the occupier of the borrowed space, the function of the text of his own displacement and denial of spirituality.

In fact, like the farm, Ike's wife is herself an emblem of ambivalent legitimacy: she is both validification and its denial. Dispossession from the land is, for Faulkner, a distancing but also a freeing from the sin of possession, which the land cannot tolerate.[35] The wife's tearful (Dionysian) laughter expresses the impossibility of Ike's decision to remain outside the world of flesh, even while making love, and to ensconce himself in the world of the man-talk he glimpses as cancelled by this physicality but of which he cannot really let go. For Ike to permit the legitimacy of the sexual encounter is to legitimize death itself, since it is to embrace life.[36] While it is true for Faulkner as for Nietzsche that acknowledgment of death is a dialectical opening, death is at the same time the end of discourse, and Ike cannot face it, just as Ike's mythic heroes do not. The historical, heroic world outside of Ike's rented rooms is one of the texts of transcendent truths obscured but elevated, for Ike, by the everydayness of life and death, by the physical. The death of the historically spiritualized body, certainly of Ben's, Lion's, and Sam's, is a fictional death, and one in which the ideal of the dead subject transcends the physical. This immortality of the heroic/fictive subject is a central aspect of Ike's heroism. His paradigms cannot die, but they can never be part of life. From these immortal subjects come a sense of super-time, outside of the diurnal round, which forms a fundamental and essential part of his linguistic self. Ike's world is a problematic, albeit necessary, fiction that sets him apart. Unlike other central figures in *Go Down, Moses* (notably Lucas and Rider), Ike cannot learn to live with his consciousness,[37] because, as we remember from the Nietzschean model at the beginning of this section (see page 113), he *is not* his consciousness. The bear hunt has taught Ike to "put down" his consciousness, just as he does his pocket watch, before Ben will permit himself to be seen; the systems and tools of Apollinian man must be rejected before the truth will appear. This fiction, felt deeply by Faulkner, is at the core of Ike's failed autoaesthetic tragedy.

As we have begun to see with Ike's wife, each of his relationships is not self-sufficient but part of a textual web of associations by which the autoaesthetic power of association can be asserted. Our sense that Ike's marriage, like Jude's, is still-born—that it could never *come to life*—is amplified in other relationships from earlier in the novel. Indeed, Ike's most important relationships are with graves—Sam's, Ben's (and thus Boon's), and Lion's. These graves are not crypts, in which the dead rest in the serene and reverent depths, the last resting places of the physical remains of their namesakes, but hallowed and active foci of Ike's heroic life of spiritualized history. When, eight years after his initiation into the hunt, at age eighteen, Ike has returned to the much-diminished forest and found his way (appropriately, by dead reckoning) to the knoll on which his spiritual progenitors lie, he makes a forceful and terse assertion: this place is

> no abode of the dead because there is no death, not Lion and not Sam: not held fast in earth but free in earth and not in earth but of earth, myriad yet undiffused of every myriad part . . . and being myriad, one: and Old Ben, too, Old Ben too.[38]

In Ike the heroic progenitors remain, perforce, eternally alive, free of the delineations that confound and confuse him.

But Ike is not one of these encrypted ancestral powers. Indeed, he is *ipso facto* barred from becoming such, any more than Zarathustra can become the Overman, since he is not and cannot be part of the lore of the woods but rather attempts to establish a valid life for himself by gathering together certain empowered sheets of self-inscription, an activity in which none of these others engages and which none could understand. Ike shows in his every strategic, autoaesthetic move, on his own terms for immortality, just how far he is from it. He has learned that while his heart may be the ultimate

arbiter of "value," his mind, the repository of his stories just as the mysterious burlap-wrapped package is the repository of his history, is precisely
what his heroes cancel in their "wisdom." Ike's mind, as the reliquary of the
various *epoi* of his collective story are articulated, is the location of whatever
imperfect sense of that valuation Ike may have. But the irony of Ike's
heroism, of course, is that it cannot be articulated: as Lacan articulates it, the
gap between *moi* and the *je*, between articulations of self and the
apochryphal and chimerical unification of those articulations, cannot be
closed. Whatever Ike may choose to do with time, whatever stylistic devices
he may select to demonstrate his freedom from the effacement of linearity
and of his own etiolated lineage, his new heritage is one not of the additive
power of lineage but merely of the accumulation of those disempowered
sheets and slips (in their own way, if not Freudian at least Lacanian slips) of
papers. One sees this in the very style of *The Bear*'s overwhelming Section 4,
in which Faulkner(/Zarathustra/shadow-narrator) transcends conventions
of narrative syntax and grammatical structure but in which, by contrast, Ike
chooses to construct himself of the detritus of narrative. In a gesture born of
faith in the outside world, of desperation in the face of his failure to achieve
self-discovery, he is caught in his own irony. In place of that legitimate self
which he seeks, Ike must write myriad fictive selves. Section 4 begins in just
this way, with the lineage of the unimaginable sentence fragment into which
all of Ike's background and all his obsessive troubles with it are stuffed. It is
an *accumulation* he must strive at the same time to encompass and deny:

4.

Then he was twenty-one. He could say it, himself and his cousin juxtaposed not against the wilderness but against the tamed land which was to
have been his heritage, the land which old Carothers McCaslin his grandfather had bought with white man's money from the wild men whose
grandfathers without guns hunted it, and tamed and ordered or believed
he had tamed and ordered it for the reason that the human beings he held
in bondage and in the power of life and death had removed the forest from
it and in their sweat scratched the surface of it to a depth of perhaps
fourteen inches in order to grow something out of it which had not been
there before and which could be translated back into the money he who
believed he had bought it had had to pay to get it and hold it and a
reasonable profit too: and for which reason old Carothers McCaslin,
knowing better, could raise his children, his descendants and heirs, to
believe the land was his to hold and bequeath since the strong and ruthless
man has a cynical foreknowledge of his own vanity and pride and strength
and a contempt for all his get: just as, knowing better, Major de Spain and
his fragment of that wilderness which was bigger and older than any
recorded deed: just as, knowing better, old Thomas Sutpen, from whom
Major de Spain had had his fragment for money; just as Ikkemotubbe, the

Chickasaw chief, from whom Thomas Sutpen had had the fragment for money or whatever it was, knew in his turn that not even a fragment of it had been his to relinquish or sell.[39]

This breathless inscription of the no-saying of human lineage and the displacement of validity by money will lead Ike, later in the section, to an ultimate and particular disenfranchisement, in the unwrapping of the burlap package. In the meantime, at the start of the section, Faulkner's overarching prose acts as an onomatopoeic deluge of heritage-language, the "begat"'s Ike cannot escape. Section 4 is Ike's *vouloir dire*; that is, it is his meaning, stated at the beginning of the crux of his story/history.

As he passes beyond linear time, attempting to delineate himself, Ike continuously questions his vision. In a seemingly balanced world of ledgers, the autoaesthetic Ike must interrogate and wherever possible understand the nature of the dialogues he has had with his genealogical forefathers, with Cass (as a concrete representation of them), and with himself. These investigations lead him to uncanny discoveries of the (concealed) Dionysian world beyond the ledgers. Discovering the solution to the "mystery" of Eunice's suicide, for example, seems at first enough to cause Ike to repudiate the spirituality of the old ledgers and of those who wrote and are written in them, recording the disappearance of Eunice's own grandson James Beauchamp, Tennie's Jim.[40] Ike's questioning of the vision has begun to take the form of making his own inscriptions in those hallowed ledgers, in an attempt to add his own voice to those he so reveres:

His own hand now, queerly enough resembling neither his father's nor his uncle's nor even McCaslin's, but like that of his grandfather's save for the spelling: *Vanished sometime on night of his twenty-first birthday Dec 29 1885. Traced by Isaac McCaslin to Jackson Tenn. and there lost. His third of legacy $1000.00 returned to McCaslin Edmonds Trustee this day Jan 12 1886* but not yet: that would be two years yet, and now his father's again.[41]

Ike closely analyzes his own writing as he makes the entry, and after having made it, emphasizes in that "but not yet" the way in which he does not and cannot ever disappear as Tennie's Jim has done but must always remain locked in the dilemmas of presence and legitimacy, writing "like his grandfather" except for the spelling. Ike can be more precise, but his "voices" are only the more tenacious for it. The precision of his own inscription stands now in direct juxtaposition to the inscriptions of his unheroic ancestors.

Ike's close self-analysis invites us to see what he writes in the ledger as some kind of necessary double, as John Irwin suggests, in just the way in which Uncle Buck and Uncle Buddy serve as doubles for each other and for Cass in the old ledgers, talking back and forth from a single consciousness but with different voices.[42] This self-questioning makes it inevitable that Ike should investigate the ways in which he interacts with the ghosts and echoes of others in the world. We have seen how Ike deals with some of his ancestors by directly textualizing them.

In addition, he uses two other strategies which, while still textualizations, take other forms. Ike operates a strategy of inclusion and one of exclusion: the former consists of fabricating a series of more overt *doubles* who are themselves inclusionary figures; the latter consists of excluded or sought-after *others*.[43] For Nietzsche, to take a slightly different tack, doubling is always a source of evaluation. This mode is more appropriate to Ike, since all of his strategies for dealing with the world, all of his fabrications of it, result from its complete re-evaluation.

Doubling and emulation, on the one hand, and objectification, on the other, must be distinguished here in terms of their employment in an autoaesthetic strategy. For example, although Ike emulates Sam, it is Boon with whom Ike is at least partially doubled and who provides Ike with a spectacular model of failed autoaesthetics. Despite Cleanth Brooks' argument that this doubling is of very limited scope,[44] Ike's careful set-up as Ben's potential killer, and then Boon's subsequent usurpation of the killing, must, I think, receive more than Brooks' passing scrutiny. Although Ike and Boon have been presented in the novel as in many ways opposites, the entire closing section of *The Bear* is a confrontation between Ike and Boon as doubled emblems of the lost wilderness over which they have agonized, in their own ways. Ike knows that Boon has killed Sam and cannot deal with it, that Old Ben's and Sam's deaths are Boon's curses since Boon cannot treat death as a fiction as Ike can. The deeds themselves will not permit Boon to so interpret the world: Ike is distanced from these mythic deaths by having been a non-participant in every sense but the narrative one. Though ignorant enough to be unaware of his importance to the heroic structure of the events around him, events which have shown him *capable of action*, Boon is essential to the dialectic of Ike's alienation from the heroic. *The Bear* concludes with a hysterical non-confrontation between Ike and Boon. In this final confrontation, the doubling consists of the narrator's presentation of Boon sitting on the ground before a lone tree which is crowded with squirrels, frantically lashing at the gun that lies in his lap. In this scene, as Ike's double, Boon is the "madman,"[45] now an outsider in a strange world, a symbol of *étrangeté*, whose tool (the gun with which Boon killed Sam Fathers, but which might equally be Ike's tool—writing) will not suffice to husband nor vanquish the wilderness, but who must hammer away at the now-ineffectual tool, unable to make it achieve its and his "proper" ends. Boon is seen by Ike as a double in the sense that neither, from his position, can achieve the desired relationship with the wilderness. Boon cannot command and overpower it, while Ike cannot become one with it. The doubling is particularly appropriate in that last scene of the novel, given Boon's manic (Dionysian) darkness: he responds to Ike, who has approached openly, with anonymous anger: "He didn't even look up to see who it was. Still hammering, he merely shouted back at the boy in a hoarse strangled voice: 'Get out of here! Dont touch them! Dont touch a one of them! They're mine!'"[46] Ike is left to assess the destructive message of this last mirror-text, a mock-possessive link with Ike's past and a final joke on the notion of "the hunt."

A less obvious but equally important model of the autoaesthetic double for Ike is Fonsiba's husband. He forms a sense of self that Ike finds even more difficult to face but which often comes to the surface in *The Bear*. Ike comes to Fonsiba's cabin, then sees the husband

> sitting in a rocking chair before the hearth, the man himself, reading—sitting there in the only chair in the house, before that miserable fire for which there was not wood sufficient to last twenty-four hours, in the same ministerial clothing in which he had entered the commissary five months ago,[47]

and wearing a pair of gold-rimmed spectacles that "did not even contain lenses, reading a book in the midst of that desolation," like Ike bound to the fantasy of alternative self-assessment, unreal and insubstantial. Ike sees and senses in him the unviability of this textual life. But the carpetbagger is himself free of his environment in a way Ike is not: Ike cannot leave his roots behind and go off to the city but must remain behind to dispense the (selfless) heritage for which he is responsible. Ike's judgment of the man is harsh indeed, concluding with the observation "and all over, permeant, clinging to the man's very clothing and exuding from his skin itself, that rank stink of baseness and imbecile delusion, that boundless rapacity and folly";[48] but it is not merely the spectral husband being judged but Ike himself, in his innocuous folly of self-pursuit. Ike is repudiated by his co-option in the double here as elsewhere.

The carpetbagger has been incapable of living in the world of rural Arkansas on the farm his father's participation in the Civil War earned him, just as Ike cannot live on *his* father's land; indeed, the carpetbagger can't "live" *anywhere*, since only his stack of books and his store-bought ideals sustain him; he is, in the same way as is Ike, truly dispossessed, manifesting the way in which Ike's fictions of altruism as a means of escape are themselves as inescapable as they are unsatisfactory.[49] Fonsiba's absent husband stands for the repudiation of Ike's heroism as much as Boon does. Here, the barriers of color and social power equate themselves with those of wealth and intelligence. When asked to bow to Ike's superior position, both in the McCaslin family and in the social system of the South, the husband replies:

"I acknowledge your authority only so far as you admit your responsibility toward her as a female member of the family of which you are the head. I don't ask your permission. I—" "That will do!" McCaslin said. But the stranger did not falter. It was neither as if he were ignoring McCaslin nor as if he had failed to hear him. It was as though he were making, not at all an excuse and not exactly a justification, but simply a statement which the situation absolutely required and demanded should be made in McCaslin's hearing whether McCaslin listened to it or not. It was as if he were talking to himself, for himself to hear the words spoken aloud. They faced one another, not close yet at slightly less than foils' distance, erect, their voices not raised, not impactive, just succinct.[50]

Ike's inability to tolerate the husband's response results from the very solidity of that response: the firm yet rebellious tone shows Ike the sort of pose he himself would like to strike but cannot. The ironies demonstrated in this disenfranchised man's words may be lost on Ike, but are not on the reader, who can suddenly see in them not only Ike's desired position but his link with the aristocratic (that is, narrative) McCaslin heritage. The husband's disappearance makes him one more catalyst for Ike's genealogical frustration.

The shadowy figure of Fonsiba's husband is a transitional figure for Ike, to be seen as substantial in *his* legacy to Ike—Fonsiba's new attitude of autonomy. When Ike takes Fonsiba's ironic portion of the McCaslin money-legacy to her, although he finds her destitute, she like Ike and his land is unwilling to use the money the family has offered her; when he questions her about how she will get by, Fonsiba's response to his insistent "'Fonsiba. Are you all right?'" is a quiet "'I'm free.'"[51] She is the legacy not of the McCaslin money connection but of the education and power of that shadowy, ghostly husband. Fonsiba presents Ike with a model of the monological power of self-creation. She is free, as is her husband, in a way that Ike is not. Ike's confrontation with Fonsiba, like so much else in *The Bear*, is cumulative and accrues its effect over *time* in the novel. Fonsiba and Ike are historical figures within the confines of *The Bear*. Only in its historical interpretation, in its aftershocks, does the event, here of Ike's meeting with Fonsiba, signify. Each of the significant confrontations Ike faces is akin to the gathering I.O.U.s he thinks are valid currency. For Ike, seeing Fonsiba becomes a constant reminder of all he is not and cannot be. In the case of Fonsiba, however, Ike knows right away that the meeting has had a lasting effect: after his confrontation with Fonsiba, Ike returns home, and we are told that "the old ledgers never came down from the shelf above the desk to which his father had returned them for the last time that day in 1869."[52] Since Ike knows nothing of freedom, his only defense against it is denial. He is harsh in his reaction to Fonsiba's reaction to his proffered legacy because he is unable to deal with his reflection in them.

The echo-effect of these doubles, as the creation of autoaesthetic discourse in and for Ike, the doubling of *self* to allow self-discourse, is the most autumnal strategy Ike manifests. The double is autumnal in the Nietzschean sense because it is always a function of self-reflection and self-interpretation, and an attempt at balance. When Nietzsche claims "I am a *doppelgänger!*" he means that the very process of self-reflection generates that un-canny distancing of *étrangeté*'s pervasive imbalance. This is clearest for Ike in the person of Cass. In Cass both emulation and doubling take place, since Cass is Ike's direct avatar in that he himself learned the lore and ways of the woods from Sam Fathers,[53] and Cass is dependent, too, on the ledgers of the past. For Cass, as for Ike, the ledgers are both physical and metaphysical. Faulkner makes the reader aware of a further doubling, both physical and metaphysical, in the relationship between Ike/Cass and Buck/Buddy, and again in terms of those historically overwhelming autoaesthetic documents, the ledgers. Both sets of doubles share an obsession with "accounting": for example, in Section 4, Ike and Cass assess the South's "taint" just as Uncle Buck and Uncle Buddy do, inadvertently, in the ledgers themselves. The ancestors' minute chronicle of the matter-of-factness of that taint is matched by its narration for Ike and Cass. Ike understands the notion of a "dialogue" as "writing hands," first one of the brothers' hands in a ledger and then the other's.[54] But as with his own dialogue with Cass, Ike considers these dialogues to be "metaphorical," a question of *leaving out*. Ike discovers that the ledgers, seemingly so exhaustively full, have in fact left out, effaced, or erased almost everything. The only things recorded there are not the heroic deeds of his glorious ancestors, and not even their sordid or heroic misdeeds, but merely (seemingly) the transactions within the com-missary; the rest is interpolation. All four men, it seems, share an inability to pass from history to any sense of valid, experiential reality. Even as Ike deciphers the ledgers, including finally the devastatingly succinct announce-ment of Carothers' fathering of *"Turl Son of Thucydus @ Eunice Tomy born Jun 1833 yr stars fell Fathers will,"*[55] the doubled taint and apocalyptic resignation of those last five words resonate in Ike. As we have seen, however, that resonance is a very problematic part of his narrative. Inter-pretation of this pivotal passage of the ledgers, which so undermines Ike and Cass's sense of legacy and taints the *epoi* of the McCaslin narrative past, is itself *left out*, the event of the illicit (Dionysian) birth announced so baldly that it must be faced, literally and figuratively, tangentially and between the lines. This interpretation Ike and Cass must make results for Ike in the same resolve as does Ike's confrontation with Fonsiba and her husband: after discovering the monstrous fact of Carothers McCaslin's sexual rela-tionship with his own black daughter, Ike "would never need look at the ledgers again nor did he; the yellowed pages in their fading and implacable succession were as much a part of his consciousness and would remain so forever, as the fact of his own nativity."[56] Here Ike echoes the autumnal Nietzsche of *Beyond Good and Evil*: the writing hand is withered by its separation from the life-spring of imagination.[57] Ike will not look again at the ledgers because his imagination is permitted to dwell only on the Dionysian crime of the ancestor. He is not allowed, by his own thoughts' intercession, to write or think further. In this way, Ike descends into the collective guilt of the McCaslin past. His doubles become infinite and infinitely narrative. Ike's relationship with Cass is precisely that of Ike and the ledgers themselves. The dialogue he has with man is a dialogue with the page. This distancing from any reality beyond the page is Ike's perception of life. Because of the complexities, the debasements, and the textualizations of this heritage, Ike has grown unable to see the world in any other way.

Doubling, on the other hand, provides a ready anchor for Ike. Appropriately, only beyond Cass and the ledgers, as it were, out in the woods where Ike feels that what he inscribes is a communion with ancestors other and more powerful than McCaslin with whom he has associated himself, do the deepest crises, as well as the first and most important debasements of the myth of heroic validity, occur. Just at this tendentious point of validification beyond discourse and self-determination in self-telling, however, Ike's world transfers from inclusionary (if highly problematic) doubles to antagonistic *others*. We have begun to see how Boon embodies something of this: he is both double and other, a direct rejection of the heroism to which Ike aspires, as Boon's shouts to Ike at the end of *The Bear* are a direct rejection of community. Like Ike's dialogue with legacy, his debasement can take the form of this juxtaposed alienation. In this respect, for Ike as for Zarathustra, animals are vital emblematic others and the *foci* of the other's theme of alienation. Ike's fyce dog, itself a kind of Dionysian shadow but capable of unbalancing the world (by helping to bring Ben down), is juxtaposed with (the Zarathustran/Dionysian) Lion, the (anti-)heroic opposite of the little spaniel. Sam Fathers himself misinterprets the ironic, doubled *étrangeté* of the two dogs, commenting that the fyce is "*almost* the dog to match Old Ben" but simply doesn't have the "stature." Compounding the linking of double and other, Ike's dog and Lion bear a clear resemblance to Ike and Boon. Lion (and Boon) can be quieted but never tamed. The "blank eyes" of Lion attest to this, as do the mad, blank eyes of Boon at the end of *The Bear*. The traditional view of Lion is that he represents a conclusion of the symbols of power in *The Bear*, that he is the manifestation of that chthonic power required to dominate the mythic Ben. But I would submit that in light of Ike's genealogical dilemma and its symbolism it is possible to see Lion quite differently. Even though a development of some kind, from the fyce to Lion, is required for the playing out of Old Ben's "last act," this huge, mysterious dog represents not an advance but a decline, a falling off. Lion is the epitome of self-reflexivity, a kind of mad self-creation that permits him to be no one's, to come from nowhere. In the context of Ike's "lessons," Lion is not the dog the little fyce is. Lion is pure, mad power, but without refinement, nuance, or judgment. Lion is introduced into *The Bear* as the phantom of an ultimate threat to the order, precise and necessary, of the hunt for Old Ben.

At his introduction into *The Bear*, Lion goes through the same Protean permutations as the Dionysian would require: he is thought to be a panther, then a bear himself, then a pack of wolves. Lion, despite the seeming clarity of his name, which is in fact a generic label for his fierceness and therefore, additionally, meaningless, is absolute (and therefore autoaesthetically useless) *étrangeté*. Indeed, he has less than no identity. He kills indiscriminately and leaves no trail;[58] the hounds will not hunt him. When Lion is finally captured, he still cannot be identified: Ike is part of the hunting party that traps this diabolically indeterminate beast:

> Peering between the logs, they saw an animal almost the color of a gun or pistol barrel, what little time they had to examine its color or shape. It was not crouched nor even standing. It was in motion, in the air, coming toward them—a heavy body crashing with tremendous force against the door so that the thick door jumped and clattered in its frame, the animal, whatever it was, hurling itself against the door again seemingly before it could have touched the floor and got a new purchase to spring from. . . . "What in hell's name is it?" Major de Spain said.[59]

What in hell's name, indeed. When de Spain learns from Sam that it is, unbelievably, a dog, his first order is to kill it, since it cannot be of any use and can only destroy. In terms of the lore of the woods and its place in Ike's legacy of reality and identity, it is a rich irony that Sam Fathers himself saves Lion and declares Lion to be Ben's dominator. But those qualities Ike has set out to learn at the beginning of *The Bear*, humility, patience, sensitivity, observation, and the rest, are not to be found in Lion. He would be the Goliath of dogs were he not devoid of *any* enculturation. Lion is pure, mechanical fury, linked with Boon in the way the fyce is linked with Ike. That Boon and Lion can bring Old Ben down is a source of awe to Ike. This is another source of the Nietzschean autumnal in Ike's story. The winding down of Ike's legacy includes the return to the rawest forces of Nature, re(in)stated in Boon and Lion. While appearing as pure, uncanny *étrangeté* to Ike, they are presented in a dialectic of otherness (not doubling) with Ike's textual refinement. Lion's otherness is that of Ike's wife's sexuality: throughout the entire section in which Ben is killed, not a moment's reflection from Ike interrupts the narrative. Ike is absent from the central scene of his own myth, as Douglas Canfield has clearly shown.[60] His only place in this part of *The Bear* is to stay in the woods rather than to return to school (a fitting choice). When Ike protects Boon against McCaslin's suggestion of having killed Sam, at the end of Section 3,[61] it is from the position of someone who has not assimilated and assessed the events of the past few days. Ike has been *removed* from such comment. Just as Faulkner's narrative presents only the raw sensory data with which to visualize Ben's death, so Ike represses its interpretation. Ben's killing is also the killing of Sam and the death of an order of the woods in which the wisdom of Sam Fathers is supplanted by the brute force of Boon and Lion. Though Ike defends Boon against McCaslin, trying to understand and assimilate the supremacy of Boon and Lion over Ben (and the tradition of Sam Fathers, whose funeral litter is behind them), the defense is a final funerary tribute: "Leave him alone!" he cried. "Goddamn it! Leave him alone!" In Ike's support of Boon against Cass, Ike acknowledges to his double the supremacy of the other and the relinquishing of the wisdom of the earth. Despite Ike's support of Boon, when he confronts McCaslin he confronts himself. Boon's "supremacy," as we shall see by the end of *The Bear*, denies legitimization but must be accepted.

Acceptance of Boon's "victory" over Ben, which at the same time cancels Cass's investigation into the story of Sam's death, thus leaving it unsolved (absent), must be seen as an acceptance of the autumnal, of a debasement, but also as another opportunity for the crowding around of history. This falling off is mirrored in the rest of the story as one of the destruction of the so-called natural habitat with which Ike associates the lessons of self-realization, although of course the rented rooms Ike will inhabit are no less "natural." At this juncture in the narrative, the centrality of the animal merges with the theme of nature and imitation of nature. Inanimate objects achieve animate status (or are *animated*, anthropomorphized). As the woods increasingly disappear before the whir of the sawmill trains, Ike presents us with a clear emblem of the falling off the coming of civilization will be, in terms of the heroic magnitude of the land and that dialogue with the niggardly hoarding of pennies and minimalist narrative information represented by the ledgers. Ike emulates Zarathustra here, showing us while he himself does not see that possession means loss. But it also means accumulation. Late in *The Bear*, as Ike approaches the woods in which he will soon confront Boon for the last time, he sees in the deforested distance the narrow-gauge train easing around a corner, resembling "a small dingy harmless snake vanishing into weeds."[62] No longer the symbol of the greatest wisdom, *this* serpent stands for the cancellation of the autoaesthetic dialectic Ike has had with his hoped-for autochthonous self in the old woods. Ike has "disappeared" into the remnant of the thick woods; "intuitively" coming across, he then symbolically walks across, the graves of

Sam, Lion, and the pawless Ben,[63] hearing the whisper of what he calls the "last admonition of Ash," one of Ike's first "shadow-figures" when he had gone out to the hunt for the first time years before. The old cook with the appropriately autumnal name had admonished Ike to beware of his "crawling feet,"[64] that is, to watch where he stepped—and he is doing so now. But in this voice of the old black cook is another voice—once again the Zarathustran voice of wisdom:

> Even as he froze himself, he seemed to hear Ash's parting admonition. He could even hear the voice as he froze, immobile, one foot just taking his weight, the toe of the other just lifted behind him not breathing, feeling again and as always the sharp shocking inrush from when Isaac McCaslin long yet was not, and so it was fear all right but not fright as he looked down at it. It had not coiled yet and the buzzer had not sounded either . . . less than his knee's length away, and old, the once-bright markings of its youth dulled now to monotone concordant too with the wilderness it crawled and lurked: the old one, and ancient and accursed about the earth . . . evocative of all knowledge and an old weariness and of pariahhood and of death.[65]

This confrontation with the edenic double, which is itself the paradigm of *étrangeté in* the double (Lucifer/Satan), the snake referred to only by the impersonal pronoun but then personified by Ike as "Chief," "Grandfather," results in the same words Sam has spoken to the phantom buck earlier in *Go Down, Moses*. Ike finds himself "speaking the old tongue which Sam had spoken that day without premeditation either,"[66] speaking to the emblem of Ike's confusion over the threat and the reward of self-inscription. This "fatal and solitary" thing, this "it" who judges Ike and allows him to pass, is juxtaposed with the train-snake of man's stupid, greedy threat and anti-wisdom. While Ike's lot is to be safe nowhere, he is safe wherever his stories, his "unpremeditated tongue," will hold. In his utterance, Ike creates the genealogical connection between buck and snake, the mythic and the knowable. Like the snake, Ike is a tainted descendant of that "Buck" of long ago, the "chief."

"Chief," the designation of genealogical and genetic power—the word itself of the "Fathers will"—is debased from buck to snake. Again, the edenic imagery of the forest guides the reader. As Lion had been the diabolical embodiment of illegitimate but dominant power, so the snake, as the symbol of illegitimacy and the temptation of disobedience, replaces the buck, the image of legitimate order, despite its ironic use elsewhere in the story as "Uncle Buck." And just as the word "chief" is debased from buck to snake, from heroic stance to diabolical and/or Zarathustran serpent, so is the heroic embodiment of "bear" debased in Ike's telling of the journey to the woods. Old Ben has been supplanted, as the logging train steams

infernally through the denuded forest remnant, by Ike's story of the
"middle-sized bear" so frightened of the sound of the train that it refuses to
come down from the tree into which it has climbed for a day and a half. Ike's
telling of this final story emphasizes an inability to participate, just as, in the
"original" story, the hunt for Ben, Ike misperceives (ironizes) Boon. "It
would not be Boon"[67] to kill Ben, Ike has declared wrongly, unable to read
the signs, since Boon is the innocent not capable of understanding nor
participating in the myth of which Ben (and Ike) is the center. But of course
Boon *is* capable of participating, as is Lion—as Ike is not, any more than
Ben's double, now treed—precisely because Ike tells stories and Boon does
not. In the end, Boon has brought Ben down not with his always useless gun
but with a knife,[68] an "old" tool, Boon on one side of Ben and Lion on the
other like a pastoral triptych, a *set* of ironic doubles. Boon, not Ike, has
inherited the now vanishing woods, according to the *correct* interpretation
of all the heroic tenets Ike has now learned. In his inarticulateness Boon has
earned it. Boon's last, mad call to Ike asserts not merely his possession of a
treeful of squirrels (what a debasement from Ben!—and again in the echo of
the Nietzschean, autumnal language of winding-down) but of the "nature"
of what is left of the old forest. Ike is fully disenfranchised, by Boon and by
the woods, a nameless, faceless intruder and interloper, for the triumphant
and tragic Boon a figure of *étrangeté*. In a final gesture of doubling, we see
Boon shouting at Ike the same message Ike has shouted at Cass before Sam's
litter, and it is a message of denial: "Get out of here! Dont touch them! Dont
touch a one of them!"[69] But then, Boon is able to conclude, as Ike never can,
"They're mine!"

The doubles Ike confronts are eclipsed only by images of *étrangeté* in *The
Bear*. The debasement of the wilderness and of Ike's ideas of heroic validification are made so problematic in *The Bear* by Ike's finding himself not
only in tangled doublings but in a state of anomie, an utter *étrangeté*, as
Arthur Kinney points out too.[70] Ike spends the first thirty-five pages of *The
Bear* as pronoun, remaining so until his name is mentioned indirectly in
dialogue. The reader, like Ike himself, must grow into a sense of his place in
those around him; he begins hazily and remains hazy, the "blanks" of his
selfhood only momentarily and occasionally filled in. He depends on others
for identity; equally, he depends on his own anonymity. But these "others"
so vital to Ike's self-definition are not the same as the doubles with whom we
have seen him in constant dialogue. Appropriately and ironically, the others
are those he cannot be like and those he most wants to be like.

The first is Sam Fathers. Sam seems to embody those *impure* origins, the
vague mixture of black, red, and white blood with which Ike must reconcile
if he is to have a sense of being *in* the legacy his grandfather has bequeathed
him. But Sam is too distant a father, already lost, too involved in his own

mythology; Ike can learn from him only as a stranger. More importantly, though Ike sees Sam as indeed a father (in part because that is his *name*), Sam's *language* is inadequate to account for a world beyond the snakes and bucks. Sam's *forgetting* of the conventions that civilize man, and his admonitions to Ike that he cannot be part of this world if he too cannot thus forget, attunes him to a wilderness unavailable to Ike, however much he might think he wants it. Ike's comment, like Fonsiba's, that Sam set him free is partially true,[71] but it is equally true that Sam's death frees Ike of another *absent* father at the same time as it removes the *other* in which Ike has tried to place himself.[72] Only at Sam's "funeral," as Ike and Boon sit guarding the funereal platform, does Ike assert himself as *verbal self* for the first time in the story. I have discussed this scene from another perspective, but from that of Ike's impossible identity it is important to look at the scene in its entirety, to see the *motivation* required to make Ike speak his lines of denial: "Did you kill him, Boon?" he said.

> Then Boon moved. He turned, he moved like he was still drunk and then for a moment blind too, one hand out as he blundered toward the big tree and seemed to stop walking before he reached the tree so that he plunged, fell toward it, flinging up both hands and catching himself against the tree and turning until his back was against it, backing with the tree's trunk his wild spent scoriated face and the tremendous heave and collapse of his chest, McCaslin following, facing him again, never once having moved his eyes from Boon's eyes. "Did you kill him, Boon?"
> "No!" Boon said. "No!"
> "Tell the truth," McCaslin said. "I would have done it if he had asked me to." Then the boy moved. He was between them, facing McCaslin; the water felt as if it had burst and sprung not from his eyes alone but from his whole face, like sweat.
> "Leave him alone!" he cried. "Goddamn it! Leave him alone!"[73]

The precision of the language in this passage, the photographic minuteness of description applied to Boon's agonized Dionysian movement, which then precipitates Ike's response, can only come through the narrative voice's adoption of Ike as the (weakly Apollinian) point-of-view character for the scene, deliberating over his responses, weighing with him the battle between the others, the strangers, he sees before him, all framed before the pyre of Sam Fathers himself. In the face of this confrontation of the antagonistic strangers, so well known to him in so many other respects, Ike himself becomes the *other* in the scene, not the arbiter, as might seem to be the case at first, but rather the protector of the truth about Sam's death, the concealer of the mythic end of the great hunter, whose finish must remain as enshrouded in mystery as his beginnings had been. Ike is, for the first time, protecting himself in this scene; he is defending his world view against the encroachment it suffers so often in the story, the advancement of civilization and brute force and unenlightened power. When Ike cries "leave him alone," one could well see him referring to Sam Fathers, not to Boon except in coincidental passing; by extension, one could see his reference as being to *himself*, since he and his world are the ones under attack. Following from this scene, Cass serves not only as a double for Ike but also as a kind of mirror-image of Ike's own otherness, by which Ike is distanced and through which Ike questions his legitimacy and its relationship to his genealogy. The substantial conversation between Ike and McCaslin in Section 4, to only a small segment of which is the reader party, reminds one of the curious monologic dialogues of Shreve and Quentin and *Absalom, Absalom!*, but with a difference. The dialectical voice, in *The Bear*, is not interchangeable in the same way—Cass and Ike disagree in a way Quentin and Shreve do not, but the disagreement is in a "devil's advocate" stance that shifts with Ike's impossible attempt to legitimize himself. Cass, the voice of the "new ledgers," can never fully provide the *other* Ike seeks, from which Ike must differentiate himself, partly because Cass is so caught up in the very things Ike has repudiated, partly because he is still only another "real" person telling his own stories, and though he is double *and* other, Cass (like Ike's fyce) nonetheless lacks the stature of the figures with whom Ike identifies in a mythic, narrative fashion.

It is perfectly appropriate, however ironic, that the two figures with whom Ike does identify in this central way, who do *not* lack the stature Cass does, are purely metaphorical, though they are strangely related to the "spirituality" of the woods. They are the *ur*-figures of the Father and the Son, God and Christ. The allusions to the Nietzschean view of the Crucified are particularly important here. For Nietzsche, the figure of Christ appears at precisely the focus of the problem of genealogy: Christ manifests the pure legitimacy of power, as the Son of God, and the absolute denial of that power in the parabolic *discourse* of which he consists, as I have suggested earlier. Of these two figures, Father and Son, that of Jesus, the son, is the more consanguineous for Ike because, while God is the lawgiver, the substantializer, he remains "only" immanent, in terms of lived reality, and thus aloof from the world, while Christ, in his *descent* and his corporeal reality and his literariness (the figure of spirit as metaphor), reveals the sort of no-saying Ike desires in a world from which he must remain distant and thereby untainted. "Human men," like Cass, try to "write down the heart's truth out of the heart's driving complexity,"[74] but what Ike needs, what he says Christ expresses, is simplicity, not complexity. Man is the "expression" of God for Ike, the epitome of what God "wanted to say." But since what God is saying in man is "too simple for man to write it," man persists in trying to write around and across that ultimate simplicity. In his own ledgers, man is condemned. The figure of the parable giver, Christ, allows Ike to imagine a dissent from this impossible elusiveness. But Ike's position becomes rigid and static even without his knowing it, even while Ike thinks he is "free," and the emulation he attempts is a failure. This most heroic of gestures, to emulate the Crucified, with all the complex implications this holds of being both in and out of life, of registering language as a central tool of understanding, of treating understanding as secondary to the energy of becoming, is literally more than Ike can comprehend. Ike's telling of himself, and of others in himself, is always a deferral of the "original" worth of the person or persona emulated: there is no Ike to capture except in parables.

And so all that remains is repudiation of history and of self. This takes the form of Ike's interpretation of life as increasing debasement, not simply the refusal to accept his patrimony but a rejection of legacy as unauthorized, without validity. This is to be Ike's attempt at liberty. He needs to be freed from the constraints of his past, which remains always a function of his presentational self: in his telling of it, his past *becomes* important.[75] Brooks says that Sam has *shown* Ike how to be free,[76] but Ike is never free. His ostensible freedom is bought at the price of a recognition of Sam's death. For Ike this is not a blood sacrifice, as we have seen, in that he cannot consider himself substantial enough to give something up. Ike tells us that he "repudiates immolation,"[77] but this only occurs in the context of his being "fatherless." We have seen that, if anything, Ike has far too many fathers, none of whom fulfill the role. Here is the foundation of the debased genealogical myth to which Ike must respond throughout the eighty years of his life. He is forced to admit that "no man is ever free and could not bear it if he were."[78] His desires mandate a repudiation of those who fail to meet his needs, and in this repudiation he debases not just them but himself and his quest as well.

Nowhere in *The Bear* is the self-loss from the debasement of the actions he and others commit more telling than in that one moment when the world tries to infuse his tarnished fictions with life, to draw him back into the world of patrimony and of blood. We have seen how he meets the offer his wife makes without knowing it: his only recourse is to define, to set boundaries and outlines, to deny the power of the sexual deed.

> He had moved, the hand shifting from his chest once more to his wrist, grasping it, the arm still lax and only the light increasing pressure of the fingers as though the arm and hand were a piece of wire cable with one looped end, only the hand tightening as he pulled against it. "No," he said. "No": and she was not looking at him still but not like the other but still the hand: "No, I tell you. I wont. I cant. Never": and still the hand and he said, for the last time, he tried to speak clearly.[79]

The wife, who extends herself to him as though she were herself a wilderness of dark forces, is "not like the other": she is like herself, and this is unacceptable to Ike. He "tries to speak clearly, but what he speaks to her is simply "I cant. Not ever. Remember." In the next instant, when he says "Yes," his message to her is "*We were all born lost.*" We remember. It is one of the bleakest moments in modern literature: the man desperate for life, fighting his way to the surface of the fictions in which he wants and needs to exist, confronting the impasse between what he can and cannot *do* and remain true to that struggle. Ike's inner forces and outer voices cannot be reconciled. The wife wants him, very justifiably and equally impossibly, to go in utterly the wrong direction. For Ike, to be lost and to be free are identical, faced here with the "simple" living force that Ike's wife, naked to him this once and never again, offers him.

Thus, for Ike, freedom and loss are always the same—they are invert faces of a spiritualized identity's coinage. Given the fact that freedom and loss are both creations of the fictions Ike fabricates of his life, which has been created for him by his insubstantial legacies, legacies of the debasement of discourse, it is an impossible dilemma. If freedom and loss are the same thing, and the only freedom available to him is the quasi-freedom of denial and etiolation, or of withdrawal and escape,[80] then that escape takes the form of a kind of a spiritualized death-in-life. And yet, ironically, this is, in the end, just what Ike desires. It is a lie, but at the same time, it is an enabling myth. For Nietzsche and for Faulkner, each in his own way, the ascetic urge, manifested here in Ike, is a coming to terms, literally, with the death wish.

Our picture of the world is always that which makes us seem most free, "i.e. in which our most powerful drive feels free to function."[81] As Sam Fathers has quit and died, so does Ike, though unlike Sam he continues to live on. The dialectical acceptances (his doublings) and rejections (his alienated others), that is, his distant, heroic stance, cannot come to the rescue. General Compson, who successfully straddles the worlds both of the woods and the city, has from the beginning appropriately divined in Ike something at work beyond Ike's static pose: "It looks like you just quit but I have watched you in the woods too much and I don't believe you just quit even if it does look damn like it."[82] Ike is alive, but in every respect he is impotent to become what or who he desires and to cancel the desires that stop him. The iconic nature of Ike's Christ-position cannot be reversed by any motion, since it is a fictive stance, caught in Ike's dilemma of self-definition. Since Ike's impotence—and his potency—come from the fictions he has made of his heritage, he cannot permit the violation of those fictions: he must maintain his distance. Ike commits a kind of suicide *into* myth, attempting to articulate himself like a figure in a story, at once mobile and forever static, inside the world and safely outside it, emblematic and vital. As a result, Ike is caught between action and inaction, doomed to repeat the same liturgy of the self, always in dialectic with the forces he has repudiated.

Having circled it all this time, we must look at Ike's debased coin, the keystone of Ike's genealogical edifice. Ike's crisis of valuation is epitomized in the long scene in Section 4 in which he reveals the vital physical trail-sign of his inheritance, in the enigmatic, burlap-wrapped package from Uncle Hub. In this package Ike has wrapped all the articulatable power of the tradition he finds pure, the *result* of the suffering and the knowledge his forebears have bequeathed to him. Faulkner takes nearly ten pages accounting for the opening of the package,[83] pages full of the weight of importance Ike attaches to the old, rattling package. The section begins in typical straightforward fashion but soon enough sounds the vital themes:

> There had been a legacy, from his Uncle Hubert Beauchamp, his god-father, that bluff burly childlike man from whom Uncle Buddy had won Tomey's Terrel's wife Tennie in the poker-game of 1859—"possible strait against three Treys in sight Not called"—; no pale sentence or paragraph scrawled in cringing fear of death by a weak and trembling hand as a last desperate sop flung backward at retribution, but a Legacy, a Thing, possessing weight to the hand and bulk to the eye and even audible: a silver cup filled with gold pieces and wrapped in burlap and sealed with his godfather's ring in the hot wax, which (intact still) even before his Uncle Hubert's death and long before his own majority, when it would be his, had become not only a legend but one of the family lares.[84]

The package does not *merely* represent, for Ike—it *is*. It contains solidity and validity, metaphorized and metamorphosed, Ike thinks, beyond the words Ike has used to manufacture these commodities all his life. The package is not merely a mummified remnant of a culture, without which Ike is lost, but a vital signifier of a culture and a world to which he does not have a key. Ike would go with his mother to "visit" the parcel, listening as he went to the endless stories of the great house and the great life that had been hers and which should have been his.

The ritual in which Ike is to open the package, forbidden until he is twenty-one, begins when he is ten, as McCaslin the iconoclast urges Ike to go ahead and *break faith* with the tradition of the package. Ike will not do it: indeed, the package is a shrine of Ike's *lares*. McCaslin brings out the "big iron key on the greasy cord"[85] to unlock the closet where the parcel is kept, Ike's "eyes saying Yes Yes Yes now." Cass says:

> "You are almost halfway now. You might as well open it": and he: "No. He said twenty-one": and he was twenty-one and McCaslin shifted the bright lamp to the center of the cleared dining-room table and set the parcel beside it and laid his open knife beside the parcel and stood back

with that expression of old grave intolerant and repudiating and he lifted it, the burlap lump.[86]

McCaslin's knife, like Boon's a reverent instrument for this ritual of valid-ification, hunting amid "the mazed intricacy of string, the knobby gouts of wax bearing his uncle's Beauchamp seal rattling onto the table's polished top and, standing amid the collapse of burlap folds, the unstained tin coffee-pot still brand new, the handful of copper coins and now he knew what had given them the muffled sound":

A collection of minutely-folded scraps of paper sufficient almost for a rat's nest, of good linen bond, of the crude ruling paper such as negroes use, of raggedly-torn ledger-pages and the margins of newspapers and once the paper label from a new pair of overalls, all dated and signed, beginning with the first one not six months after they had watched him seal the silver cup into the burlap on this same table in this same room by the light even of this same lamp almost twenty-one years ago:

I owe my Nephew Isaac Beauchamp McCaslin five (5) pieces Gold which I.O.U. constitutes My note of hand with Interest at 5 cent.

Hubert Fitz-Hubert Beauchamp
at Warwick 27 Nov 1867[87]

This is Ike's legacy, the paper on which the sentences lie that reveal that heroic tradition for which he hopes to be a "rat's nest' of false debts and associations, of worthless promises and fallen gods. The discussion of the validity of Ike's legacy descends instantly, with Cass, into a discussion of the "coppers" Ike has in his "fortune," but it has been his misfortune to see his symbolic structure turn from genuine gold to the yellowed scraps of paper he has been left. Ike has ostensibly hoped for a static, rooted identity, founded on the promise of the legitimacy of his heritage; in the paper scraps left behind the Beauchamp seal are revealed a fragmented discourse within a fiction of legitimacy.

Ike could choose, of course, to see this revelation as itself an agent of freedom. He is free from the curious legacy of the McCaslin heritage if he wishes to be. He could, after the discovery of the coffee pot, adopt the stance and the power of self-overcoming, as Nietzsche lays out the genealogical fiction of it in *Thus Spoke Zarathustra*. But Ike does not have this choice; as in *Zarathustra*, only (possibly) the (Nietzschean) narrator or reader can see it. The revelation of the fallen contents of the package fits into the pattern of revelations Ike experiences in *The Bear*. From the penetration of the woods to his entry into Fonsiba's house to the disemboweling of Lion to the mock intimacy of his marriage—to the coffee pot, Ike repeatedly experiences not freedom but insubstantiality. He cannot understand that the myths by which he lives *are their surfaces*, a constant juxtaposition of the static with the dynamic. But this misunderstanding, which will not permit him to overcome himself nor to see those others against whom and against which he gauges himself as parts of his autobiography, controls Ike and effectively shuts him down, as it does so many of Faulkner's "thinking" characters. The point at which static (as figuration) and active (as lived experience) cross is not *in* myth nor in heroism but in Ike's own discourse, in articulation of the mythic and the heroic. The real "truth of the heart" is that in Ike's discovery nothing is *lost*; legitimacy had never been present, had existed only in Ike's narratives. Ike is not and has never been "heroic," has never participated in the genuine validification of genealogy. He is a witness and never a "real" participant, not a mythic figure but a man who is condemned to see and talk about that seeing, trying desperately to order and control it. His *étrangeté* is derived from the mirror-image-filled monologue of which he constructs himself, out of the written records of which his past and his present consist. He must constantly *account for* the abyss he feels between his sense of himself and that which he can know or articulate about himself. In the end his story is the rich, dense story of the *writing hand*, not Ike's at all but a story in which Ike plays a character, just as Zarathustra is revealed as a character in a narrative much larger than himself. Ike's story is the best of talking, but it is an adequate articulation of his dilemma only insofar as articulation is always a deviation, a folding, a turning aside. His is what Arthur Kinney, in another context, calls an "unbearable desperation to realize a dream while acknowledging final defeat."[88] Kinney's pun on *The Bear* only serves to show how pervasive and powerful this borrowing and doubling of words can be: Ike's desperation is unbearable in the same way in which Zarathustra's friends at the Ass Festival are un-Zarathustra-able; both Ike and Zarathustra are unable to overcome themselves. Like Zarathustra, in order to "see," Ike must enter into a dialectic with—and still relinquish—civilization, but he is made up of an over-civilized sensibility that must accept its nature. Old Ben has "permitted" the sixteen-year-old Ike a vision of him only after the boy has become lost in the forest and vowed to *see*; when Ike relinquishes his (Apollinian) watch and compass, Ben appears. The "something" that occurs to Ike in this confrontation, and about which he talks the night before the hunt in which Ben will be killed and Ike matures, is the advent of the *loss* this vision of Ben produces. Like the shiny new coffeepot that is not a silver chalice, Old Ben is a bear, a thing, for better and for worse, not a myth. He too can be transmuted by man—by man's stories. Ben's life can be "found" by Boon's knife. Just as the ledgers are the record of an *un*heroic myth of the lost and chimerical past, just as the weight of their information curses Ike more than it blesses him, and just as Ben is finally a hunted and vanquished wild animal for Ike, so is the heroic coin of his patrimony transformed into the copper and paper, the tin and knotted string of Ike's story. It is no wonder that, as Faulkner projects Ike's history forward into a narrative version of the eternal return, Ike "at almost eighty would never be able to distinguish certainly between what he had seen and what had been told him."[89] In every sense, working within the economy of his own heroic standard, Ike is a *teller*, weighing and negotiating the coin of a value system in which he can only lament his own sense of loss.

Part Four

◆

STRATEGIC EMPOWERING

What then is truth? A movable host of metaphors, metonymies, and anthropomorphisms: in short, a sum of human relations which have been poetically and rhetorically intensified, transferred, and embellished, and which, after long usage, seem to a people to be fixed, canonical, and binding.

—"On Truth and Lies in a Nonmoral Sense" 84

"Beauty" is for the artist something outside all orders of rank, because in beauty opposites are tamed; the highest sign of power, namely the power over opposites; moreover, without tension;—that violence is no longer needed; that everything follows, obeys, so easily and so pleasantly—that is what delights the artist's will to power.

—*The Will to Power* 803

7

◆

Nietzsche beyond Good and Evil: Metaphor as Power

We have been exploring ways in which Nietzsche's dramatic notion of *étrangeté* has contributed to a strong nihilistic strain and helped formulate a hidden agenda of no-saying in Modernist literature, despite his admonitions that an understanding of the ensphinxedness to which we "last men" of the modern world are all subject, if such a thing as "subject" were to exist, leads rather to the joyous and emphatic Dionysian yes-saying, a triumph over opposites, with which Nietzsche's own books are punctuated. We must remember that *all* of Nietzsche's thought and writing contain an intended antidote to the pessimism he saw as being so antithetical to life itself. Nietzsche's writing is strong medicine for strong minds, for those with ears to hear through the din of modern life and the cacophonous clashings of so-called rational discourse in a world Nietzsche perceived as being desperately, negatively, ignorantly, and vitally irrational. His great question, "Have I been understood?," repeated throughout his great works, addresses this chasm between him and his/our age. Characters such as Ike McCaslin, trapped in their fixities, certainly have not understood. Nonetheless, Nietzsche persisted in his search for a way to make the *positive* understanding of the nature of the human dilemma accessible to us. In *Ecce Homo*, Nietzsche recalls his energetic but patient desire for understanding in both *Thus Spoke Zarathustra* and *Beyond Good and Evil*, a project in response to which only the true artists of seeing and hearing might rise up:

> . . . the slow search for those related to me, those who, prompted by strength, would offer me their hands *for annihilating*. From this moment forward all my writings are fish hooks: perhaps I know how to fish as well as anyone?—if nothing was caught, don't put the guilt on me. *The fish aren't there.*[1]

168

If we read this elaborate Nietzschean metaphor in light not of its ironic Christian context but of the evaluative process inherent in metaphor itself, it is almost impossible not to be attracted by this evanescent fishing lure, particularly as it relates to that cast out by Hillis Miller in his discussion of that most vital metaphor, the *Torweg* or Gate of Moment in *Zarathustra*, in the concluding chapter of Miller's *The Linguistic Moment*: that is, by the question—the lure and the mirage—of some kind of metaphoric ontological presence in autoaesthetic literary texts. For Miller, these heightened moments of self-evaluation are images and moments that "reflect on their own medium"[2] and therefore question both the potential presence of the self in general and their own autoaesthetic power in specific. I want to return to that genealogy of metaphoric power, at least to its most highly metaphorized embodiment in *Zarathustra* and its glosses, and to examine these self-creative, metaphoric "moments" further, to place the idea, the image, and primarily the *articulation* of Zarathustra's overabundant Gateway of Moment in a further development of a multiple context, of

1. Nietzschean spirituality as the power of transference, of
2. this passage from *Beyond Good and Evil*:
   Whatever is profound loves masks; what is most profound even hates image and parable. Might not nothing less than the *opposite* be the proper disguise for the shame of a god?[3]

and, to take a different tack from one we have been on, of

3. Lacan's re-reading of Freud, in light of the notable absence—indeed, the impossibility—of an adequate notion of self at the core of Lacanian theory; transference of a notion of nihilism or negation to one of *lack* as a psychoanalytic culmination of the Nietzschean autoaesthetic self-crisis.

I want to heap up an overabundant set of determinant frameworks in which to consider the very positive but troubling sense of power to be found in metaphoricity, which so centrally controls Nietzsche's concept of the self. The link needed to begin to gather these disparate forces into a concerted approach to Nietzschean metaphor, and particularly to metaphor as power, is to be found in Nietzsche's notion of the image. The Nietzschean image is fairly straightforwardly a manifestation of the Dionysian sensorium: the image precedes words and concepts,[4] and yet the image is itself troubling. The idea that the "most profound even hates image" ["allertiefsten Dinge haben sogar einen Hass auf Bild"] seems, at first, contradictory; it is a poetically compressed phrase in which almost every word has a life of its own—an elaborate, tropic *prosopopoeia*. Nietzsche treats these convolutions in even more complex fashion over the longer term, linking them to echoing passages throughout *Beyond Good and Evil*. The implications of the phrase "most profound even hates image" for evaluation of and in metaphor, and its devaluation of Platonic mimesis, seem to be involved in some obscure and evasive dialogue, for example, with their virtual echo near the conclusion of the book, in Section Nine's "What Is Noble?" which declares that

> the hermit does not believe that any philosopher—assuming that every philosopher was first of all a hermit—ever expressed his real and ultimate opinions in books: does one not write books precisely to conceal what one harbors? Indeed, he will doubt opinions, whether behind every one of his caves there is not, must not be, another deeper cave—a more comprehensive, stranger, richer world beyond the surface, an abysmally deep ground behind every ground, under every attempt to furnish "grounds." Every philosophy is a foreground philosophy—that is a hermit's judgment: "There is something arbitrary in his stopping *here* to look back and look around, in his not digging deeper *here* but laying his spade aside; there is also something suspicious about it." Every philosophy also *conceals* a philosophy; every opinion is also a hide-out, every word also a mask.[5]

The autoaesthetic activity that defines the (Nietzschean) ideal poet/ philosopher, by which the poet defines himself and the world, consists of a masking, even an intentional concealment, just as Lacan (through Freud) suggests that conscious life is a conscious concealment (repression and/or sublimation) of the Dionysian image-life of the unconscious. But in the Nietzschean context, are we to take *Nietzsche* to mean that this self-concealment of the philosopher is ironic? Nihilistic? Hermeneutic? Positive? That "behind" the hermit's philosophy is *another*? And what are we to take as "intentional"? Of what does intention consist in this context? And most importantly, how are we to see, to image forth and to schematize the "mask" of metaphor itself? In an artful life, what are the mechanisms of concealment and revelation? In this barrage of questions, a mere handful of the myriad questions one could pose to the Nietzsche of, say, *Zarathustra* and *Beyond Good and Evil* about the self, the conditions on which an answer might be forthcoming are themselves open to question. Is Nietzsche engaged in a retrograde and highly conservative motion, contrary to our expectations (if we assume him to be rejecting essentialism, substantiality, and conventional notions of essence)? Can we detect here the return of the mimetic, the substantial Platonic idea of art?[6] In the juxtaposition and articulation of these seemingly opposite assertions in Nietzsche, what *is* Nietzsche's message about the nature of the image, as it is constituted in the *étrangeté* of self-fashioning power?

Confronted by *Zarathustra*, and then by *Beyond Good and Evil* (which as Nietzsche claimed to Burckhardt and others says "the same thing," though "very differently," however we are to interpret *that*), two things strike the reader: first, the declarative power of those terms "good" and "evil," words over which so many lives have been lost and, second, the dynamic tension of those terms put together and then *propelled* by that initial but lingeringly disruptive "beyond." The tension of Nietzsche's Manichean juxtaposition[7] achieves a new dynamism and a new and indeterminate force through that *Jenseits*. One must not only ask what Nietzsche has in mind for "good" and "evil," in terms of self-determination, but even more importantly we must ask what one is to make of that "beyond." A careful look at Nietzsche's *Jenseits*—not as *the beyond* but as an analysis and critique of the use of the *word* "beyond" in this context—can help one understand more fully how to confront its relevance and "value," the way in which it relates to the conundrum of valuation and transcendence (that is, the "higher man"), as well as Nietzsche's solution to the conundrum of metaphor itself (a crossing that is not a crossing but that is *beyond* the higher man); finally, one can begin to understand the way in which metaphoric force *is* autoaesthetic power and the motif of *étrangeté* in the text and texture of human life.

The *beyond* of *Beyond Good and Evil* styles itself from its opening, ineluctably, as metaphor. *Jenseits* is a perfect Nietzschean "dangerous crossing," a mendacious word bridge. It is itself a function of *étrangeté*, a vector toward the other. It never appears nor disappears; like the Gate of Moment it has no signature, appears without appearing, has its effect, and never vanishes. Its image-effect is precisely that of Zarathustra's gateway taken at the furthest reach of its metaphoricity; it is an *étrangeté*, not a *dépassement*, vectored and empowered *both ways*. Thus the gateway is the inception and the overcoming of oppositions, as David Allison has pointed out in describing the power of *Beyond Good and Evil*: "The very threshold of metaphysics is to be found here, in the genesis of oppositions."[8] The nature of metaphoricity's "beyond" is, then, in the region of opposition, differentiation, and extension.[9]

To be *beyond good and evil*, then, in addition to being fundamentally oppositional, as is clearly and deceptively simply the case, is an extension or suspension of opposition, a difference of a difference. This suspension, or overcoming, of opposition in a kind of chaotic plenitude Nietzsche declares near the end of *Beyond Good and Evil*, in the "coda" to "What Is Noble?," is indeed made into a kind of manifesto of the higher man:

> To live with tremendous and proud composure; always beyond—. To have and not to have one's affects, one's pro and con, at will; to condescend to them, for a few hours; to *seat* oneself on them as on a horse, often as on an ass—for one must know how to make use of their stupidity as much as of their fire . . . .[10]

Nietzsche's Hamlet-like play of infinitives here, as well as the subtle play of the active and passive tone, particularly in light of the references to the Crucified that insinuatingly dot the passage—and to have all of it "at will," show the mendacious crossings Nietzsche travels to achieve the transparent selfness of metaphor. The stunning simplicity, what Nietzsche elsewhere calls the "shallowness," of this metaphoric will, sets up the conditions for the re-evaluation of the highest man, the word-artist.

Thus it is clear how the notion of value is revealed again as being a matter of truth only and redemptively as "a sum of human relations," beginning with the relations of the singular human to itself; that is, psychological rather than philosophical. Once again, we see how the great poet-philosopher is in fact an artist-psychologist. In turn, it is clear how Nietzsche's manifesto of concentrated metaphoric humanity provides a word bridge to that other great *Jenseits*, Freud's *Jenseits des Lustprinzips* (*Beyond the Pleasure Principle*), and its resultant interpretation by Lacan,[11] in which the pleasure principle's structural quiescence has *its* "pro and con," adjusting to the realities of the world in the yes-saying acceptance of *un*pleasure. Freud's *Jenseits*, not incidentally and in a fascinatingly related way, introduces his concept of the eternal return, repetition-compulsion, as a kind of evaluative drive to repeat fixed patterns of behavior or to revert to an earlier state—or, more to the point for Nietzsche's *Jenseits*, to metaphorize and so attempt to ensphinx or to "freeze" the idea of the self. For Freud, this metaphoric repetition is vital to pleasure and to a formulation of the self; even more importantly, in terms of Freud's debt to and repetition of Nietzsche, it is a dominant determiner of life's value, a measure in thought of its reality. As Lacan points out, "The whole history of Freud's discovery of repetition as function becomes clear only by pointing out in this way the relation between thought and the real,"[12] that is, between autoaesthetic process and historical annotation and denotation. But the powerful determination to which Lacan comes in his analysis of Freud is that this repetition, for Freud, was never and could never have been a re-presenting, a making-present-again of a past self. Lacan points out that its power is not that of "reproduction": "nothing can be grasped, destroyed, or burnt, except in a symbolic way, as one says *in effigie, in absentia*."[13] The power of the pleasure principle, beyond which the analyst (and the autoaesthetic self) persistently tries to go, is that it reminds and evokes but does not reproduce. Thus, the metaphoric power of the autoaesthetic operates like Derrida's *trace*, as a remainder that is also a supplement, but whose power derives from the problematic play of absence of a whole self. The implications for a full disclosure of the self in the language of transference/metaphor, or in any aesthetic, are obvious: Freud and Lacan concur with Nietzsche in his determination that *Jenseits* is always an absence we cannot bear, one which produces the most intense unpleasure, and thus one for which we compensate in the originary supplements of language and in art, which are thus compensatory conscious naturalizations and traces of the *Treib* toward the real at the "frontier," which Lacan represents as "a *ditch*, around which one can only play at jumping."[14] The autoaesthetic action of the poet/ philosopher, metaphorizing him or herself in self-inscription, is not just an approach to self-overcoming, but a *jouissance* in itself, an ultimate self-satisfaction. This is not a question of seeing the self as a story or play, in which one plays one of the characters (though this is of course possible, as Alexander Nehamas and Gary Shapiro have convincingly pointed out), but an elaborate metaphorization of the very idea of self, a translation of feelings, memory, and experience into the grammatological realm, based in Nietzsche's no less dramatic autoaesthetic sense.

Freud's *Jenseits*, like Nietzsche's, particularly in Lacan's formulation of it, is a manifestation of *étrangeté*.[15] For Freud and Lacan, the protean fullness of the unconscious, driven as it were by the libido, accounts for the "beyond"; for Nietzsche, any measure of that fullness is itself made a function of transference. As Eric Blondel has shown, a fundamental similarity exists between Freud's *beyond* as what he calls the "plasticity of the libido" and Nietzsche's, which is the transference of *metaphor*.[16]

What is one to make, then, of this displacement, the conundrum and cultural residue of a transcendence that clings to the "beyond" of *Beyond Good and Evil*? For surely it does so cling. The first step toward a satisfactory answer is that, for Nietzsche, transcendence is always rooted in dialectic. In the concluding section of *Beyond Good and Evil*, "What Is Noble?," he calls transcendence "the *Pathos of Distance*" itself, functioning at the level of order and rank. Anticipating Freud yet again, Nietzsche defines the making of *self*-metaphor as an emblem of enculturation, of "inner distances," what I have called articulation as a function of self-empowering. Noble transcendence for Nietzsche is

> the craving for an ever-new widening of distances within the soul itself, the development of ever-higher, rarer, more remote, further-stretching, more comprehensive states—in brief, simply the enhancement of the type "man," the continual "self-overcoming of man," to use a moral formula in a supra-moral sense.[17]

As always in Nietzsche, the juxtaposition of these appositives as quasi-equivalent serves only to point out their non-identity: "enhancement of the type 'man'" and "the continual 'self-overcoming of man'" are radically different varieties of evaluation. This is true at least in part because, as Nietzsche says three sections later, "The noble type of man experiences *itself* as determining values; . . . it is *value-creating*."[18] By experiencing itself, man creates values—the highest value is that self-experiencing, with its implicit chasms, abysses, and mountaintops.

In just this vein, and mirroring humankind's evaluative self-determination, *Beyond Good and Evil* culminates in that craggiest of poems from high mountains, in the rarified atmosphere above and beyond the pleasure principle and beyond the realm of even the highest man—the "Aftersong," in which the value-creation of the aspiring higher man demonstrates a raw solitariness that the autoaesthetic poet finds as unbearable as it is ineluctable.[19] The higher man always returns to a strange fiction of himself in the mode of inquiry, an eternal questioning. Thus *Beyond Good and Evil* fosters the Zarathustran dilemma: Can any evaluation of man, even higher man, be more than an insoluble puzzle of never-ending interpretation? How is a self fabricated out of the chimerical questions the writer poses about his own past, present, and future, which are themselves being eternally reworked?

When Nietzsche claims in "We Scholars" that philosophers are "dangerous question marks,"[20] echoing Zarathustra's very words, he hints at a response. In being "the bad conscience of their time," Nietzsche's famous formulation of the same section, the writer/philosopher no longer poses the question "Who is man?" but rather "How shall man be overcome?"[21] As the higher man is overcome, evaluation itself vanishes (—into *jouissance*, beyond the pleasure principle?). And yet the question as to how one might talk about this overcoming's actually *occurring* persists, in light of the metaphoric tension in and by which it exists: not only is this "beyond" hypothetical, provisional, apochryphal, or grammatological, but the purported goal, the *ur*-Zarathustra, is the most elevated—and celebrated— *failure* to respond to the autoaesthetic dilemma, as we have seen:

> He shall be greatest who can be loneliest, the most concealed, the most deviant, the human being beyond good and evil, the master of his virtues, he that is over-rich in will. Precisely this shall be called *greatness*: being capable of being as manifold as whole, as ample as full.[22]

This "manifoldness," "wholeness," "ampleness," and "fullness," were they really to inhere in the autoaesthetic poet, would deny him being—as well as any return to—"himself." A transformation, rather, takes place in light of the will's state of supersaturation, a transformation from philosopher to artist-philosopher, indeed, *away from man* as such and toward the image of man. It is just in this way that Lacan adapts Freud's structures to his own language. Lacan starts his essay, "The Function of Language in Psychoanalysis," with the statement that "such awe seizes man when he unveils the lineaments of his power that he turns away from it in the very action employed to lay its features bare."[23] According to Lacan, then, overwhelmed man turns to language in order to turn away not from a unified and whole self but from the "lineaments of power" unveiled by man in that very language: we know ourselves insofar as we do by turning into language that unveiled power whose origin in the metaphoric self we perceive only in that turn. Lacan, working through the Nietzschean model of differentiation, shows us as shifting from the undifferentiated absence to the always different self of transference and metaphor. In Lacan, these apocryphal designations are the well-known *je*, the chimerical unified self "beyond" metaphoricity that we can never "again" be but toward which we are always striving in our turning away, and the differentiated (and metaphoric) *moi* "of the subject which cannot be reassumed by the subject."[24] We see in Lacan's schema the vectors of metaphoric transference of the self, a Lacanian will-to-power. Nietzsche alludes to this transformative schema for the poet/artist in a passage of *The Will to Power* we have looked at briefly before, a passage eternally poised to return:

> One is an artist at the cost of regarding what all non-artists call "form" as *content*, as "the thing itself." To be sure, then one belongs in a topsy-turvy world: for henceforth content becomes something merely formal—our life included.[25]

"Form" is to be seen as "content" from the artist's perspective, the form of life included. Beyond the Platonic implications of this claim's evaluative status, it establishes the radical position that the world of nature (not just human nature) is anthropogenic, indeed, artist-created, that transcendence is inverted, re-defined "down" to man.

Nietzschean inversion, as we see it in *Zarathustra* and *Beyond Good and Evil*, in Lacan's paradigms, and in autoaesthetic works like Fowles' *Daniel Martin* that make central use of this schema, is that of human existence and the world "justified," then, *beyond* the higher man—beyond Zarathustra—beyond Nietzsche. What would characterize such a justification? What characterizes Nietzsche's "last great seekers," Napoléon, Goethe, Stendhal, Heine, Balzac, and a few others, and their more recent progeny? For the answers to these questions, we must return to Zarathustra: they are "ensphinxed," either by being idolized and idealized or turned into metaphoric "versions" of themselves. They undergo a *prosopopoeia* in which the image and the man become the object of *étrangeté*, as Nietzsche shows in this long passage from the appropriate genealogical section of *Beyond Good and Evil*:

> Literature dominated all of them up to their eyes and ears—they were the first artists steeped in world literature—and most of them were themselves writers, poets, mediators, and mixers of the arts and senses (as a musician, Wagner belongs among painters; as a poet, among musicians; as an artist in general, among actors); all of them were fanatics of *expression* "at any price"—I should stress Delacroix, who was most closely related to Wagner—all of them great discoverers in the realm of the sublime, also of the ugly and gruesome, and still greater discoverers concerning effects, display, and the art of display windows—all of them talents far beyond their genius—virtuosos through and through, with uncanny access to

everything that seduces, allures, compels, overthrows; born enemies of logic and straight lines, lusting after the foreign, the exotic, the tremendous, the crooked, the self-contradictory; as human beings, Tantaluses of the will, successful plebeians who knew themselves to be incapable, both in their lives and works, of a noble tempo, a *lento*—take Balzac, for example—unbridled workers, almost self-destroyers through work; antinomians and rebels against custom, ambitious and insatiable without balance and enjoyment . . . on the whole, an audaciously daring, magnificently violent type of higher human beings who soared, and tore others along, to the heights—it fell to them to first teach their century—and it is the century of the *crowd!*—the concept "higher man". . . .[26]

The figures Nietzsche brings to our attention here are products of their own literature, these "born enemies of logic and straight lines." They are not *historical* but *literary*, as we have seen in others, dominated by literature "up to their eyes and ears," "fanatics of *expression* 'at any price.'" In Nietzsche's necessary fiction of them, these Dionysian avatars understand art's "ontogenetic, that is, world-making significance," as Allan Megill calls it.[27] And they understand, as does Zarathustra, the Romantic nature of the metaphoric "drives," each expressing "its dissatisfaction with the present state of things," manifesting an eternal "Away from here!"[28] Nietzsche includes himself in this pantheon, as what Alexander Nehamas, in another context, calls "the last romantic."[29] But Nietzsche's emphatic self-constructive fiction counts him among the "first-born of the twentieth century," as he says in "Our Virtues," "with all our dangerous curiosity, our multiplicity and art of disguises, our mellow and, as it were, sweetened cruelty in spirit and senses."[30] One of the most important ways in which we are potentially beyond good and evil is that this "multiplicity and art of disguises," the amoral power of metaphor and its articulation, allows us a license to activate and engage our "dangerous curiosity" beyond *any* principle.

It is impossible to overestimate the radical nature of this overcoming. Nietzsche, not just as the "first Modernist"[31] nor, in his *Jenseits* as the last one, interrogates and subverts the most fundamental assumptions of Modernism in that he understands the implications, in language and in the psychology of self-fabrication, of overleaping even the higher man. This interrogation occurs in and through the self-constitutive power of transference. First, he defies any conventional evaluation and looks for our virtues "in our labyrinths,"[32] in the multiple in-folding of metaphor, as Sarah Kofman shows:

Beyond the Western philosophy inherited from Aristotle, as a disciple of Heraclitus, from whom he borrows the metaphor of the world as play, Nietzsche leaps the empty abyss, goes back, to rehearse Pre-Socratic philosophy; in the very *tableau* in which he outlines the Greeks, he reverses the opposition of the metaphor and the concept and the effacement, by the concept and in the concept, of metaphor.[33]

Only in the power of transference, as a function of *étrangeté*, can we overleap the empty abyss of powerlessness to seek to establish ourselves *jenseits von Gegenüberstehen*, beyond the opposition that produces orders of rank and *ressentiment*. In embracing difference, the artist is able to evoke what Nietzsche calls "beauty" (see the chapter's second epigraph again— *Will to Power* 803) in "taming" opposites while by no means eradicating them. This is the most vertiginous and dangerous balancing act imaginable.[34] But as Gilles Deleuze reminds us, we who are not the Overman only crudely know how to play: as we have seen in *Zarathustra*, even the higher man is unable to "cast the dice."[35] "We should not think of Nietzsche's Overman as simply a raiser of stakes: he differs in nature from man."[36] The model for this condition of agitation and contradiction, of crossing over, is not and cannot be human. In *Beyond Good and Evil*, Nietzsche alludes to this force in many ways, only in the coda to the ninth section, finally, referring by name to "Dionysus, that great ambiguous and attempter god."[37] This "attempter-god" has moved, since *The Birth of Tragedy*, from the simplicity of opposition to the ampleness of contradiction and metaphoric overfullness.[38] It is what Hillis Miller calls an "endless contradiction and a strangeness."[39]

But in *Beyond Good and Evil*, as in *Zarathustra*, a solution to the conundrum of transcendence occurs not in image, which is still for Nietzsche Socratic/Platonic, but in the crossing that does not cross. This force, as Michel Haar claims, awakens in us "the infinite carefulness of a 'great mistrust' that can never return language to its 'proper course.'"[40] This mistrust (and one only need think of the parable of the tightrope walker) "overleaps" the higher man and produces Nietzsche's "ostentatious exuberance of style."[41] Beyond good and evil, indeed, lies Nietzsche's metaphoric style; beyond knowledge lies metaphor; beyond truth lies metaphor (indeed, Blondel refers to falsehood as "the repetitive blockage of metaphor" by science, religion, morality).[42] *Jenseits* is part of the play of metaphoric crossing-over. Just as the Overman announced by Zarathustra is a *cross* between plant and ghost, between biology and textuality, and therefore textualized, he can be seen as a cross between writer and written, the quintessential autoaesthete.

For Nietzsche, as for Freud (and Lacan even more clearly) in a slightly different context, metaphor, as the articulation of *étrangeté*, is "the plastic principle that is no wider than what it conditions."[43] It is the basis of the science of psychoanalysis and the force of contemporary philosophy; it is the eternal ground of fiction and poetry. And it is the powerful—and positive—rejoinder to both God and Nihilism, as Nietzsche repeatedly points out, the only remedy for the fear of facing the Other.[44] The traditional hermeneutic view ("view" in its sense of *theoria*) of metaphor, terms juxtaposed in a tension of interconnected, fixed meaning, is cancelled in the Nietzschean text. Nietzschean metaphor is a phylogenic manifestation of language and human comprehension in which, out of the minutiae of articulation, the entire cosmos of interstitial possibilities of thought and language is generated; these possibilities, never fulfilled and yet always adumbrated in the self-reflexivity of language itself, as well as in its usage as autoaesthetic ground, show how Nietzsche wants us to see *Beyond Good and Evil* as the "Prelude to a Philosophy of the Future." Nietzsche's Prelude gives his writing an explosive succinctness that undercuts and derides the usual nihilistic idea of aphoristic fragmentation. The Nietzschean fragment, as in *Beyond Good and Evil*, is not merely a part nor an overspilling whole, not a reference nor a connection but an active connecting linkage to other links, always *en passant*: Nietzschean metaphoricity denies the traditional closed duplicity of meanings and gives the impression of playing *directly* with the elements of meaning, which at the same time resist and deny his play. Language becomes *his* interlocutor, as in the first section of the "coda" to the ninth section of *Beyond Good and Evil*, the last part of "What Is Noble," which takes up where the dialogue between Zarathustra (the wanderer) and his shadow concludes; it is itself a dialogue between the "Wanderer" and the figure of the writer. As we have seen adumbrated in the final dialogues in *Thus Spoke Zarathustra*, this section of *Beyond Good and Evil* shows the confrontation of the poet and his (fictional) character, the Overman. But interestingly, given the positive nature of autoaesthetics for Nietzsche, this echo of *Zarathustra* is now the no-saying obverse of *Zarathustra*:

> [The poet:] Wanderer, who are you? I see you walking on your way without scorn, without love, with unfathomable eyes; moist and sad like a sounding lead that has returned to the light, unsated, from every depth— what did it seek down there?—with a breast that does not sigh, with a lip that conceals its disgust, with a hand that now reaches only slowly: who are you? what have you done? Rest here: this spot is hospitable to all—recuperate! And whoever you may be: what do you like now? what do you need for recreation? Name it: whatever I have I offer you!
> [The Wanderer:] Recreation? Recreation? You *are* inquisitive! What are you saying! But give me, please—
> [The poet:] What? What? Say it!
> [The Wanderer:] Another mask! A second mask![45]

The metaphor of the mask becomes increasingly common near the conclusion of *Beyond Good and Evil*. The dialogue of world and fiction, of writer and metaphoricity itself is not only one of masking as we think of it, however, but a "semantic mirage," as Joseph Riddel has called it,[46] "generated by the play of heterogeneous signifiers which refuse to be commanded by any single element within (meaning) or without (author) the text." Image, for Nietzsche, is not a grounding but a constitutive mask over the force of metaphor, as the dream "masks" the unconscious.

We are led to this conclusion in a much more systematic way in *Beyond Good and Evil* than in *Zarathustra*: Nietzsche's *Jenseits*, like Freud's and Lacan's, is a constitutive and creative abyss between sign and meaning. An entirely new perspective on the *positive* in Nietzsche is to be had if one understands the anti-rational liberation offered by the metaphoric gap, the distance between terms out of which creative fabrication takes place. It is in the *étrangeté* of this void that the Overman can be glimpsed; indeed while in *Zarathustra* we thought the Overman played at the threshold of the abyss, in *Beyond Good and Evil* we learn that the Overman *is* this void. Once perceived, we see this repeatedly in Nietzsche, subjected to the primal *prosopopoeia* out of which metaphoricity becomes autoaesthetic, in the narrativity of the self. In fact, early on in *Beyond Good and Evil*, Nietzsche has prepared us for the confrontation of the Wanderer and the poet by asking,

> Why could the world, *the one that concerns us*—not be a fiction? And if somebody asked: "but to fiction surely belongs an author?"—could one not simply answer: *why?* Doesn't this "belongs" perhaps belong to the fiction, too? Is it not then permitted, with regard to the Subject, as well as to the Predicate and the Object, not to be a little ironic? Should philosophers not rise above faith in grammar? All due respect for governesses: but has the time not come for philosophy to renounce faith in governesses?[47]

There is no level, for Nietzsche, at which this constitutive fiction does not operate, very much including that of the grammar-"governess." In this passage, the typical Nietzschean attack on the subject is couched in a rich metaphoric image, acknowledging its own governing trope. The Nietzschean gambit is the removal of this word-play from the mimesis of representation, a freeing of the image, and of the trope, in a *world* of fiction in which, as he says, we "improvise," concluding that "we make up the major part of experience and can scarcely be forced *not* to contemplate some event as its 'inventors,'"[48] responding to experiential stimulus as its "inventors." The power of autoaesthetic metaphor's alterity is the "positive loss" of style as an element of signature or autobiography, a force that is generative but not measured in the imitative nor the imagistic. "*Measure* is alien to us," he says,[49]

Let us confess it; our titillation is the tickle of the infinite, the unmeasured. Like a rider on a forward-snorting horse we let go the reins for the Infinite, we modern men, we semi-barbarians—and arrive first at *our* bliss even where we are most—*in danger.*

Nietzsche employs many layerings over the metaphor, image on image, reversal on reversal, to achieve the effect of that dangerous affirmation of the autoaesthetic, in the metaphoric *transfer of energy* that Sarah Kofman simply declares to be "the basis of all human power of the sort in which Nietzsche is interested."[50] Just as the "voice" of the concluding pages of Joyce's *A Portrait of the Artist as a Young Man* becomes, simultaneously, indeterminately intimate and detached, personal and "purely textual," the voice of Joyce himself and that of D(a)edalus, the Hawk-like Man, and just as—as we are about to see, the narrative power of John Fowles' conclusion is a dangerous crossing into the autoaesthetic, so Nietzsche, at the end of *Beyond Good and Evil*, manifests this Dionysian indeterminacy, the power of metaphor itself, in his very discussion of it and its power. In the writers at whom we have looked briefly so far, this Dionysian indeterminacy has been a negative source, but from another point of view, as we shall see in Fowles' *Daniel Martin*, this indeterminacy is inverted again; one can conceive of no more subtle nor powerful autoaesthetic affirmation than this grammat(olog)ical reflection of the trope on itself.

Nietzsche's affirmation of subjectless self-construction reaches another apotheosis at the conclusion of *Beyond Good and Evil*. The *Nachgesang* ["Aftersong"] that concludes the book is Nietzsche's reprise of the Zarathustran theme of self-overcoming in the way I have laid it out here, not as self-loss but as the acknowledgment that the nature and any notion of "self" is always *topical*, a function of the *topos* of articulation and *étrangeté*. "Self" here, then, is not that of Zarathustra but Dionysus, the loneliest attempter-god, the manifestation and symbol of metaphor. "Am I another? Self-estranged?" ("Ein Andrer ward ich? Und mir selber fremd?") asks the text-voice. This echo, the multiplied self, in its high world of glacial reflections where all depths are a chimera,[51] is the quintessential Dionysian, measured out by *alogia*, the unmeasured or unproportioned which escapes form and determination. It is the world of what David Allison, echoing Nietzsche and Freud and melding them together (again) nicely, has called "proximate surfaces, of cathected intensities and forces."[52] This purely autoaesthetic world is a "beyond" that never arrives, as the Dionysus-voice articulates it in its last chorus:

> *This* song is done—longing's sweet cry
> Died in the mouth:
> A wizard did it, a timely friend,

A midday friend—no, ask not who he is—
At noon it was that one became two—

Now we celebrate, sure of victory,
The feast of feasts.
Friend Zarathustra came, the guest of guests!
Now the world laughs, the dreaded curtain tears,
The wedding of light and darkness has come . . . .

In light of the concluding sections of *Zarathustra* and of its development in *Beyond Good and Evil* (and throughout the rest of Nietzsche's writing), we see not the Overman but the power of transference, the metaphoric force, employed to show the *impasse* at which even the best of poet-thinkers must halt. Dionysus itself, so to speak, caught in verse, finds images for the celebration in which the *Übermensch* is celebrated. The Dionysus dithyrambs, Nietzsche's favorite products along with Zarathustra, show what they tell. If we have ears to hear it, this is Dionysus' song of disunion, nontranscendence, and autoaesthetic power: remembering that the first words of *Beyond Good and Evil* are "Suppose that truth were a woman— what?," we see the ironic employment of Goethe's Eternal-Feminine, transformed through the agency of Nietzsche's reconsideration of the feminine into circular metaphoric imagery, employed to show us how image—any image—resolves finally into the autoaesthetic power of metaphoric tension.[53]

8

◆

The *Je me manque* of John Fowles' *Daniel Martin*

The crisis consists precisely in the fact that the
old is dying and the new cannot be born; in this
interregnum a great variety of morbid symptoms
appears.

> —Antonio Gramsci, *Prison Notebooks*

The spirit is always somewhere else.

> —Jacques Lacan,
> *The Language of the Self*, 34

What is essential in art remains its perfection of
existence, its production of perfection and
plenitude; art is essentially *affirmation, blessing,
deification of existence*. . . . There is no such
thing as a pessimistic art—Art affirms.

> —Nietzsche, *Will to Power*, 821

Having reviewed the pessimism of Modernist responses to Nietzschean autoaesthetics in three works, I want to look at a sampling of another sort, since having ears to hear Nietzsche means listening to his passionate desire that strategies of self-creation be positive ones, even as understood in light of the dangerous thresholds of *étrangeté* we have been investigating. In the remaining literature I want to attend to, this positive force finds its way through webs of syntax to the surface of the text.

Here I want to work through the autoaesthetic aspects of Fowles' *Daniel Martin* to see how the will-to-power of articulation operates. Fowles' own epigraph for the novel, from Gramsci, which I have appropriated for my own (particularly in light of reading it through Lacan), initiates the displaced and shifting nature of Daniel Martin's novel as it slips from life to death and back again, from memory to desire, and all—miraculously—within an affirmative and strategically empowering strategy. Despite or because of its morbid symptoms, *Daniel Martin* demonstrates the redemptive, metaphoric empowering of Nietzschean autoaesthetics.

But in keeping with its theme of Nietzschean/parabolic reversals, in *Daniel Martin* we see how autoaesthetic empowering requires *both sides* of the dialectic of loss: to gain a powerful sense of metaphoric self is to relinquish the self to metaphor. Indeed, Fowles presents us, before the novel begins, in his epigraph from Gramsci, with a set of symptoms of the loss of self and the discovery of the autoaesthetic self. In the novel that follows, we witness the gradual emergence of a quite different perspective on the notion of the "morbid symptoms" that the apocryphal "essential self"'s undermining entails, particularly when that undermining is a function of the fluid development (the becoming) of the chimerical, fictional self. Writing the self, for Fowles/Martin, is a question of the shedding of metaphorical skins, including those of the writing surface, leaving behind the signs of a fictional presence that always points elsewhere. "The old is dying" and yet "the new cannot be born," but in the midst of this apparent dilemma, which is a crisis of both genealogy and power (as evidenced in Gramsci's word to describe the hiatus: "interregnum," between reigns, a clear adumbration and introduction of the theme of power), it is not signs of impending life that appear except through symptoms of morbidity. Dan is himself a hypothetically emergent fabrication of a series of fragments, what Lacan calls a *corps morcelé*[1] of a life sundered and then patched together in a fictional continuity. But for Daniel Martin, as for Ike McCaslin, this can never be never enough; Daniel Martin invents himself as the imaginary product of an impossible fiction.[2] Never does *Daniel Martin*, the novel, succeed in coming to rest: as in Nietzsche's texts, the spirit (and we might profit from thinking about the Lacanian notion of spirit, as expressed at the beginning of the chapter, in light of Jude Fawley's as well as Ike's) is always elsewhere, the "self" is always a lack evoked from the self-conscious retreat from what appear to be real surroundings and their substitution by fictions. The very self-conscious novel (literally) unfolds for us a man who reaches into an impossible past to derive a sense of an impossible future. He lives in his reveries in a world of ghosts, of whom he is not one but many. The novel manifests and represents the fundamental, energizing frustration of self-completion and of covering over that frustration, while at the same time confessing the gaps and losses among which Daniel Martin tries to construct himself in the very language in which those losses are constituted. Daniel Martin makes self-construction a question of power and of its denial, which is seen in his novel as yet another kind of power. His own articulation of this complex structure reminds the reader that, finally, Daniel Martin's self-reification places him in a deeply ironized position of hiatus: "Forbidding himself a real self reduced him to being a psychic investigator who began his inquiry by requesting a service of exorcism that, if it worked, would leave no ghost to inquire about."[3] Self-discovery is from the outset a conundrum; the process is, in Dan's own words, literally and literarily an expelling, a displacement of the self "out" into other (inscribed) versions of himself, and the discovery of reflections of that lost self in others, and finally in that most *other*, writing itself.[4]

The consequences of this displacement and fragmentation are far-reaching in terms of Daniel Martin's novel, which acts as a comment on narrative theory itself.[5] Lacanian narrative theory, as Robert Con Davis and others point out in *Lacan and Narration*, is generated in Freud's writings, particularly between 1900 and 1905, from *The Interpretation of Dreams* to *Jokes and Their Relation to the Unconscious*. According to Freud's own comments, much of this period's work owes a large debt to Nietzsche, though the Nietzschean influence, according to Freud, has been repressed. Freud's interest here is in the "sliding signifiers," of which dreams, indeed of which the entire "scene of writing," consist.[6] This narrative strategy, like Nietzsche's and Lacan's, demonstrates the fragmentation of which Daniel Martin constitutes himself, as "a sequence of opportunities for linguistic substitution and (re)combination."[7] In Lacanian as in Derridean narrativity, this substitution is ubiquitous and fundamental, so much so that the movement of narrative and the constitution of "subject" are made up of substitutions at its very foundation: there is nothing prior to substitution. This means that (re)combination is the grounding energy of the (lost) subject, which in Lacan's words "is a new trace to be interrogated in order to know what we mean when we speak of the subject of perception."[8] This eternal difference of the writing subject is Daniel Martin's constant confession. Derrida's declaration that "there is no presence before and outside semiological difference" might well lie behind Dan's autoaesthetic.[9] We know from the treatment Fowles gives to literary theory in *Mantissa* that for his own reasons (closely aligned to Dan's declared ones, and very Faulknerian in nature) he cannot allow the Derridean/Lacanian framework to install itself without a battle, and so Daniel Martin's book skirmishes at the edges of a direct confrontation with the issues that this *étrangeté* engenders. Denial by the "writing hand" serves only to bring the discussion into greater relevance, both for an interpretation of *Daniel Martin* and for its implications in contemporary literature and life.

For us to arrive at our positive autoaesthetic conclusion in *Daniel Martin*, we must take our own odyssey through a multilayered sense of loss. The effect of Daniel Martin's displacement and of his substitutions is the creation of a deeply problematic reality and a dialogue with being that makes reality if not impossible, at least, in Gramsci's word, morbid. Dan's elusive textualization produces a frustration with declaration and what he can know of reality that bursts through the surface of his monologue in typically but suitably tortured syntax again and again: "To hell with cultural fashion," Dan says, "to hell with elitist guilt; to hell with existential nausea; and above all, to hell with the imagined that does not say, not only in, but behind the images, the real."[10] What we do not realize at first is that this curse by Daniel Martin is actually a rallying cry for the trip to a certain kind of "hell"—of *étrangeté*. The suspension of the word "real" in the preceding passage, "the imagined that does not say, not only in, but behind the images, the real," is Dan's way of declaring the ambivalence of his program: it at once declares the narrator's power over the release, the utterance (and therefore the creation) of the salient word, and at the same time the suspension that same narrator, and therefore his reality, undergoes, his abrogation in the discovery that the imagined can ever only say the real.

Daniel Martin's emphatic barricades-language here mirrors precisely the Lacanian Imaginary order, though Dan purports to mean something quite different. To say the real in images is just what Lacan's Imaginary strives to do, though cannot, since the Imaginary, "like shadows, has no existence of its own," yet "its absence, in the light of life, cannot be conceived."[11] This Zarathustran echo is appropriate to the Imaginary, since the idea of the shadow is that of the resemblances of which the Imaginary order is composed. The relationality of the shadow to the so-called self (Lacan's *moi*) is the *topos* in which a chimerical coalescence of the signifier and signified occurs. But as Anthony Wilden points out, Lacan's Imaginary relationality is also a "lure" or "trap,"[12] in that it seems to promise a relationality which it contains *as chimerical* but does not report as such. "The imagined that says, not only in, but behind the images, the real," to torture Fowles' syntax further, is an impossible fiction contained in the Imaginary order. Daniel Martin spends his time searching for the Real—from a vantage point from which no such thing, as he searches for it, is possible.[13] In fact, in terms of Daniel Martin's traversal from the negative to the positive, the Lacanian Real remains, according to Lacan, "veiled by negative forms,"[14] and is not at all even a version of any "external reality" but the intersection of the complex forces of the Symbolic and Imaginary. In other words, for Lacan as for Nietzsche and Daniel Martin, any notion of the real must be measured against this dialectical empowering, as against Nietzsche's statement that "we have measured the value of the world according to categories *that refer to a purely fictitious world.*"[15] "To hell with existential nausea," indeed.

Increasingly through the course of the novel acknowledging the dual autoaesthetic strategy of *his* fictions of the real and the imaginary, Dan focuses his energy on what to him becomes teleologically of most value: a growing sense of what he posits as the real behind the image. His project is to define this reality and to establish its relation to perception, thought, and language. Ironically, the project is frustrated by the fact that Dan is a writer. Daniel Martin's own writing, within the novel, is at once a manifestation and a confession of his own impossibility—and the energetic denial of that impossibility. Though Dan has a passionate faith in his idea of the real behind the image, he is circumspect about his ability to distinguish himself from his characters, his cast of figures, even as he writes them. Unwittingly, Daniel Martin has created character as a manifestation of the *étrangeté* of Lacanian Imaginary, and therefore as a series of *autres*, as he shows in this remarkable passage:

> "I've spent most of my adult life learning how to use the least possible words, how to get scenes crisp. How you pack your meaning in between the lines. How you create other people. Always other people." He pauses again. "As If I'd been taken over by someone else. Years ago."[16]

This multiple transference of the self, in the progression from first to second to third person, is a mimetic confession of his own dilemma. In his self-exorcism, Dan's creating of other people is a process of "packing meaning in between the lines," as though the lines of words, like a prison's bars, rigidly permit no intercourse within, but only through them. The implication is that in the lines themselves meaning is insufficient, that the lines provide only a skeleton of meaning but cannot contain it; indeed, Daniel Martin's suggestion is that the lines themselves lie, in that they do not correspond to reality. This idea of truth and lies, introduced by Nietzsche in "On Truth and Lies in a Nonmoral Sense" but then amplified throughout his writing, not only makes liars of us all (and most particularly of the fiction writer) but will simply not permit us to be tellers of truth (we remember Ike McCaslin's condition in this regard). "The liar," Nietzsche says, is a person who uses the valid designations, the words, in order to make something which is unreal appear to be real."[17] These "valid designations" are the assignments of meaning we make for words that we have "forgotten" are in no way congruent with things—including memory.[18] Daniel Martin perceives, without knowing what to do with the perception, that his "lines" cannot be true, in the way he wants them to, cannot *contain meaning*. He is always writing words whose greatest vitality is their echoes or shadows, what lies "behind" them in his telling *double entendre*, any articulation performed by one (or another) of his characters, like his own, having been "taken over by someone else." He moves from first person, that of the writing hand, to second person, with its indeterminate singular and plural encompassing the listener in and out of the text, to third person ("He pauses again"). As we try to separate out his sense of himself and his own significance from this veil of self-determinations, we come to understand his own dilemma more fully. We are aided in this greater understanding by the writing character, this undetermined other, Lacan's *moi*, which prevents Daniel Martin's seeing, as it were, into the purported reality behind the imagery, which Dan always takes to be his real being, the *je*.[19] As his multiple persons indicate, Daniel Martin's distant self-images also constitute an eternally deferred self in his own language, reminding Dan of his lacks while permitting him only a kaleidoscopic sense of himself, fabricated entirely of fictional others in a fictional landscape.

Daniel Martin's job is to try persistently to constitute that fictional landscape, which accounts at least in part for the rich imagery and dense layers of inscription of which the novel consists. When Jenny suggests that he write his memoirs, saying "But you wish you could go home," Dan replies, "Not literally. Metaphorically."[20] The conditions of the following— and the preceding—lines and pages are established. Jenny acts for Dan as the jester to his tightrope walker, providing the impetus for the crossing of a Nietzschean threshold. She insists that he will be able to write his seemingly impossible memoirs, because "something will happen. Like a window opening. No, a door. Like a door in a wall."[21] You will, she says, be able to tell "your real history of you."[22] Though in the end it is ruinous of their relationship, Jenny's naiveté is largely responsible for Dan's being able to overcome the morbid symptoms of which he has constructed himself and which prevent him from committing himself to the self-telling without which the novel would (fictionally) not exist.

Daniel Martin's "beginning," however, does not occur in this conversation with Jenny, in which Dan first catalyzes it out of her energy. It begins, literally, with a *tour de force* that is pure story, an enabling myth permitting the opening of that door in the wall, called "The Harvest," an extended parenthetical prologue evoking Dan's emergent *stade du miroir*, a first self-awareness in others, an originary *étrangeté*.[23] While the Lacanian mirror-state occurs in infancy (six to eighteen months), in Dan('s novel) this autoaesthetic initiation (which is not possible without language, we must remember) is not chronological but what Bakhtin calls "chronotopic": it provides the unity of time and space out of which the novel Dan will write can come, giving the causal impression of initiating Dan's life because it begins his novel.[24] This empowering tale told by Daniel Martin of himself permits Dan access to memory, thus to time, and thus to a sense of the real that, though very different from what he had expected it to be, is nonetheless what it is. Dan does not have the strength of Bakhtin's convictions in this respect, however, being haunted by the suspicion of his words' emptiness, which he sees as a "fall" from the (Bakhtinian) world of identity of word and thing, of life and word. It is in just this sense that Lacan posits the Empty Word, "where the subject seems to be talking in vain about someone who, even if he were his spitting image, can never become one with the assumption of his desire."[25] Dan's loss of confidence in his and the real world's continuity is announced as an initial "falling out of" self-unity, an initiation into self-awareness in the other-self that shatters the spherical continuity from which Dan's now vitiated life has seemed to emanate. Dan's novel is constrained to begin with the chronotopic first chapter. This grounding chapter of Dan's past begins appropriately with an epigraph from George Seferis' poem "Mr. Stratis Thalassinos Describes a Man," a telescoping series of stories within stories which constitute a *mise en abîme* and in which several layers of narration tell of the purported continuity described by Seferis as a "flame" (of desire) that burns "behind" all forgotten events. This flame of desire is a Dionysian force for Daniel Martin. Throughout his novel, he will repeatedly assert that "I try to keep myself going with a flame," the desire for self-empowering, "because it does not change."

The harvest of the initial chapter, a reckoning of memory and of value(s), begins then with Seferis:

> But what's wrong with that man?
> All afternoon (yesterday the day before yesterday and
>   today) he's been sitting there staring at a flame
> he bumped into me at evening as he went downstairs
> he said to me:
> "the body dies the water clouds the soul
> hesitates
> and the wind forgets always forgets
> but the flame doesn't change."[26]

What is "wrong with that man" is that he is mesmerized by the image of the flame, and has not (cannot) transfer them into an *epoi*. Nonetheless, Seferis' Stratis Thalassinos goes on to tell him a story of lost love, of death, and of an attempt at constancy in life that set up the conditions under which he can tell his story (the Seferis epigraph's last line is "Then he told me the story of his life"). When we confront Seferis' poem, of course, we have as yet no idea of its significance for what we are reading; only with the aftersight of memory can we perceive its meaning as we read the rest of the novel between *these* lines. Dan, we discover, has rekindled his autoaesthetic flame with a protean series of tales that appear as disparate and murky images of his own emergence from a time before time. "The Harvest" is, among many other things, a wonder-filled evocation of Devon rurality, a Constable landscape with the energy of Rubens and the sad reality of detail of the Rembrandt to which Dan will return at novel's end. And the chapter is just this sort of "masterpiece," a set piece of narrative orchestration. As enabling myth, however, this evocation of idyllic Devon youth has as its function that it leaves *everything* to be desired but demonstrates the storyteller's most perspicuous energy. A nameless young boy who has not *come into his own*,[27] working in the fields, participates in the rituals of harvest, one of which is story-telling, in the voice of "the land itself," manifested as a transcription of the Lacanian Imaginary:

> The crackle of the stubble, the shock of the stood sheaves. The rattle of the reaper, the chatter of the mower blades, the windmill arms above them. Lewis' voice at the corners: hoy then, hoy'ee, Cap'n, back, back, back, whoy, whoy. Then the click of the tongue: jik-jik, the onward rattle and chain and chatter. Thistledown floats southward across the field, in a light air from the north, mounting, a thermal, new stars for the empyrean.[28]

The nameless boy's perceptions "at work" here, whose shadowy voice overcomes him as the passage mounts toward the "empyrean," labor at his narrative descriptions like a craftsman, showing his craft audaciously. His bravura description of life in the Devon fields at harvest time could only come about through the heat of the flame from his desired attachment to it. Indeed, all present in this pastoral scene "honor the field" in this autochthonous way:

> Everyone there knows how Babe came by the lurcher; it is a village joke, like his nickname. The Devil came to Thorncombe Woods one night to thank him for selling so much rotgut to all the Yanks back over the Camp; and brought him the lurcher as a present. But as they watch man and dog, they know he isn't there because he needs rabbits; he has every moonlit night and field for miles round for rabbits. But his is an ancient presence, and quasi-divine, of a time when men were hunters, not planters; he honors fields at cutting time.[29]

Dan, too, honors the field, by looking and describing its substantial reality within its social and narrative context. In these moments of his initiation, not to Self but to the *stade du miroir*, his effort consists of first trying to become (again, in his autoaesthetic) one with the earth. He has sat, "nursing his solitude, his terrible Oedipal secret; already at the crossroads every son must pass,"[30] aware now of his ineluctable separation from the "mother," earth. Desperately, like Jude Fawley sliding out onto his frozen pond, he embraces the earth, but he cannot return to it. So "he sits with his back to a beech-trunk, staring down through foliage at the field,"[31] viewing the world, for the first time, from outside it, in the *étrangeté* requisite to any self-articulation. Instantly (in the next sentence), as though the door in the wall has been opened, Dan slips into the stories that allow his perceptions to operate, stories of a written/fictive self he refers to as "without past or future, purged of tenses; collecting this day, pregnant with being. Unharvested, yet one with this land."[32] But this is nostalgia speaking: to be one with the earth and one with the self, to be "purged of tenses," one cannot be a storyteller. Dan's fear that he will die before "the other wheat was ripe" melts into this inescapable separation: a whole paragraph, which follows this last immediately, consists of the isolated statement, "Inscrutable innocent, already in exile." He plunges into the leaves, becomes a part, for a moment of the world of nature-fantasy; he reconstructs the mirror: "Down, half-masked by leaves. Point of view of the hidden bird." And then a disconcerting, instantaneous switch from third person to first—and then back to third, a mimetic confusion of substitutions, recombinations, and persons careening along as though they were psychic baggage:

> I feel in his pocket and bring out a clasp-knife; plunge the blade in the red earth to clean it. . . . He stands and turns and begins to carve his initials on the beech-tree. Deep incisions in the bark, peeling the gray skin away to the sappy green of the living stem.

Not only is Daniel Martin not without tenses; he is ranging across person and tense as though, in the first nanoseconds after the Big Bang, he were inventing them all and trying them out. Recombination has revealed itself as fragmentation: when he catalogues his possibilities, he must acknowledge this most elemental separateness and his own *différance*.

In this generative and culminative scene, Dan's confusion gives way to a first Nietzschean certitude, a "natural" self-signification metaphorized in the tree/tablet. Daniel writes himself as the "sappy green" of the "living stem," with all of its libidinous and Oedipal associations, peeling away the gray skin to find the life inside. And then his first writing of himself, as he comes into his own, carving "D.H.M." with his knife(/pen) in the tree next to which he is sitting above the field, his triumph of entering the *stade du miroir* merges with a lament: "Adieu, my boyhood and my dream." Daniel comments on his emergence from an oblivious self-unity into a greater awareness, at the same time confessing his nostalgic desire for a return to that unity, however false. As his "boyhood" disappears, so ends the "dream" of his inclusion and begins his separation and *étrangeté*. The Freudian/Lacanian juxtaposition of self-narrative and dream fuses. In perfect Derridean fashion, as a manifestation of the first morbid symptom of his now articulated life, he turns the living stem of inscription into a funerary monument: "D.H.M. And underneath: 21 Aug. 42." The tombstone of

Daniel Martin's ensconced (or interred) boyhood propels him into the novel we are reading, a novel of maturity, of search, and of loss. Dan's becomes in that moment a narrative of the eternal return to the regenerative power of fiction, which he places into a dialectic with a burningly animated, nostalgic inner life that Dan will always feel exists beyond fiction, however far he may feel from it.

But he has, of course, cancelled his undifferentiated identity: "Adieu, my boyhood and my dream." This culminative act is also an inception; the tombstone is also a birth certificate. When he inscribes himself, he takes up the challenge of articulation's power, which he has seen as an ancestral urging: "someone else" has been "operating" him; in "The Harvest," Dan reports the discovery that this ancestry and his authority are really his own teleological project. But as Derrida reminds us, teleology is always external, always other. No wonder the originary, authoritative scene itself, beneath the beech tree, is a confusion of persons. Dan expresses himself as part of and emerging from not the earth but a purportedly chthonic history, "purged of tenses" (this last word now revealed as a homonym referring to both tension and syntax), timeless (unharvested), weaving stories into a fabricated self. Otherness precedes and culminates in self-inscription. This initiation figuratively catalyzes the novel: *Daniel Martin* is Dan's extended carving of his initials, though he still cannot distinguish between "I" and "he."

The "sappy green" of which Dan composes himself is "real," as opposed to imaginary, for him, only at the distance of his metonymic structuration: symbolic or metaphoric links have turned to substitutions. But this is itself a morbid symptom; it introduces the novel's secondary Dionysian theme: death. Death is not merely a symbol for Dan, any more than is life. It is a concomitant presence, as it were, behind the events that imitate it. Death and life in this respect act in the same way as does Dan's absent self relative to that "someone else" who "acts" for Dan.

Just as in "The Harvest" Daniel Martin's novel is distilled from the visitation of death in the form of a Nazi Heinkel bomber, so in a chronotopic sense the novel's catalyst is the dying of Dan's college friend Anthony, who, correctly seeing himself as a father substitute,[33] is also a model of passivity (another way to translate Gramsci's "morbidity"), thus linking him not with Dan's father, a familiar though distant figure of aridity, but with Dan's spectral mother, dead when Dan was three, a "dim ghost" he "really cannot remember at all."[34] She and Dan's father are figures of an "unharvested" unity because of their common fictive distance, shown here as *overcoming* life and death, because though they seem to Dan to exist in the same narrative realm, one is alive and the other dead. Father, mother, and Anthony engage Dan in that dialectic of absence and presence that results in his ambivalence about himself. Anthony, from the beginning of their friendship, has, like Dan's spectral mother and father, been absent, enshrouded, content to live at a distance. The novel incorporates this dilemma from the beginning, as Dan in his California exile hears the telephone voice of his former wife Nell (knell, indeed), calling him back to England, to Oxford, to Jane, and to other previous and future Dans.[35] As Nell speaks, Dan is transported, hearing

> In his ear, distances.
> Then a voice; and unbelievably, as in a fiction, the door in
> the wall opens.[36]

The door, in Dan's elaborate fictions within a fiction, leads "back" to the stories he will tell; it is opened by Nell's report of Anthony's impending death, with its evocation of the death of Dan's marriage to Nell and of Jane's youth and his; finally, with the "primordial masochism," the death in language with which Dan struggles. Anthony's dying, in this respect as well as in the program Anthony himself lays out and which Dan is accomplishing in the scene in Palmyra (of revivifying Jane), permits Dan to begin writing his novel.

However, the important Anthony has never been the fleshly one but rather the *epos*-constituted one of Dan's narrative, the legendary Anthony of Dan's stories. "I mustn't make him too austere and unworldly,"[37] Dan says of Anthony, constructing him *for the reader* in the image of the father and acknowledging that he is making Anthony up, sculpting him in words as the *poietes*, at once the magical and the practical fabricator. Anthony is both *l'autre* and *l'Autre*, the created presence of exteriority Dan needs to fabricate his own sense of himself, and the figure of significant and radical otherness; as a detached ghost from a detached past, Anthony functions as pure language unto silence. Anthony talks, now, with Dan (and the reader is absent from this talk, in the novel's present and in its retrospect) as someone whose life is past, giving Dan power both *over* Anthony and *of* his own writing.

This fabricated purity becomes all the more complex when, shortly after his meeting with Dan, Anthony, who has shown himself to be alive in a way he has never been before (and shows Dan as being, relatively, moribund), commits suicide. Dan interprets Anthony's final, enigmatic, autoaesthetic act as the spoken act of hermeneutic power, an enigmatic sign in which life (and by extension death) has new value; it is a "message" to Dan that out of his (Anthony's) death a new life, not just for Jane (Anthony's requested project for Dan) but for Dan, too, is possible. In terms of Daniel Martin's narrative, Anthony's death story permits Dan to declare himself again available to an existence he has abrogated. He has two reactions to

Anthony's suicide: one is the "thunderbolt" of the death itself, the other his reaction to Anthony's wife (and Dan's first love) Jane and her own reaction. Baffled by how to deal with his first reaction, he can only analyze the latter. Dan seeks Jane out and, talking with her after such a long time, his reaction is that "out of nowhere the past was with us, former selves, almost uncannily, in a silence that was not like the other silences of that night, but an ancient remembered kind of silence."[38] Dan has reabsorbed Jane, as a listener (un-languaged), and this new stance propels him to his own strategic reaction: later, having just left Jane, Dan looks at himself in the little mirror in his room;[39] then, having gone to bed but not to sleep, reflects on himself in a return to the context of his familiar non-syntactical self, not only in first and third person but in both the singular and plural:

> Even the humblest of dialogue-fixers and life-inventors must have such moods, however inapt, however callously oblivious of other human suffering, to survive. They live not life, but other lives; drive not down the freeways of determined fact, but drift and scholar-gipsy through the landscapes of the hypothetical, through all the pasts and futures of each present. Only one of each can be what happened and what will happen, but to such men they are the least important. I create, I am: all the rest is dream, though concrete and executed. Perhaps what Dan always wanted of his looking-glasses was not his own face, but the way through them. This kind of mind is self-satisfied only in the sense that one must suppose God is self-satisfied—in an eternity of presents; in his potentiality, not his fulfillment. A perfect world would have no room for writers.[40]

This internal monologue is catalyzed by Anthony's death but by Jane's re-entry into Dan's life as well. The "opening to life" Anthony and Jane, in their opposite ways, have afforded Dan produces the secondary reaction of precipitating a reevaluation of his life, within the context of the dream. He has discovered through Anthony and Jane that he *can* go home again. The fact that his writing of life is called into question by these events, within which he is playing a role but over which he seems to have no control, accounts for the dissociation Dan feels in his self-constitution. Dan's commitment to Anthony has been in a sense to re-commit himself to an apprenticeship to life and to Jane, and this disconcerting reversal of his life causes Dan to *return* to his life as what Derrida calls, in discussing Freud's *Beyond the Pleasure Principle*, "his [own] household ghost," in a "tautoteleology" that "erodes" Dan into his own "other [*étranger*]."[41] Of the complex series of openings in the wall and to himself, through which Dan peers as the multilayered inception of his story unfolds, none is more subtle than the Eros/Thanatos effect of Anthony and Jane on the self-recounting Dan now (re)commences.

But we have seen already how Dan *must* interpret these potential wall openings: he must attempt to reify himself among and against the other(ed) voices surrounding him, and this always initiates Dan's sense not of life but of loss and *étrangeté*. We saw how, before he returns to Oxford, Jenny has noted his inability to substantiate himself. Jenny's role in Daniel Martin's autoaesthetic seems at first provisional or tangential, but as we focus on his revaluation in terms of articulation, Jenny moves nearer the center of Dan's project. In fact, since Jenny is part of Dan's "story," he includes a series of letters written by Jenny to Dan as "contributions" to the novel growing around her. That she can only write these letters because Daniel Martin is absent adds to the thematic vitality of her pieces. Her perspicacity is more candid than, and as poetic as, Dan's about himself. She sees and declares, in one of her letters, that his real mistress is "loss," but Jenny's conclusive (and accurate evaluation) of Dan occurs too early on for him. So he must manipulate Jenny's "honest" figure of autoaesthetic speech. Having allowed Jenny to "speak for herself," he then cancels her interpretation by casting it out into an appropriate autoaesthetic distance, refining her image in his belief that his (Faustian) mistresses are in fact parables of *étrangeté*: "His mistress was not loss," he says, "so much as that he expected the loss of all his mistresses, and in more or less direct proportion to his discovery of them."[42] The intricacies of this exchange, first Jenny through the post, then Dan to us "directly" (though both received by the reader through the *étrangeté* of the text), reveal *Daniel Martin*'s characteristic procedure: Jenny, by being subjective in her response to Dan, is refined into an edited distance. This telescopic zoom, like Jude Fawley's framing, is a mimesis of the novel itself, which is, according to Daniel Martin's own words, "written in two past tenses: the present perfect of the writer's mind, the concluded past of fictional convention."[43] But the "present perfect," already dripping with homonymic irony, is always subject to the abysses of articulation, and the "concluded past," equally problematic, is fiction. In the face of Jenny's urging that Dan write a/his novel, as opposed to the screenplays and stage scripts he has been producing, Dan is repeatedly confronted by moments in which "he suddenly saw the proposed novel as a pipe dream, one more yearning for the impossible."[44] This must not be misunderstood: Daniel Martin actively yearns for the impossible, mirrored in the enigma that only in the "silence of other voices" will he achieve any self-communion. His own voice is among those "other voices," but, confronted with the increasingly serious prospect of committing himself to the writing of a novel, he is ambivalent for purely autoaesthetic reasons, judging that "I've invented quite enough paper people without adding myself to the list," and adding, "anyway, libel. I couldn't make reality honest."[45] This joke of/on honesty is vital but, as he sees it, impossible.

Nostalgia is only another of those "silent voices," recalling Dan to the dilemma of solitariness and discovery. His cherished "sacred combe," to which he retreated at troubled times during his youth and which he distances from the reader by referring to it as *la bonne vaux*, in the archaic, distanced French of Restif de la Bretonne, can never regain its "reality," its purported edenic significance. The silent voices of the copse in Thorncombe, the hollow in the valley Dan identifies as his own, indeed, as the reflection of himself and his most secret desires, are of course fictions of pre-mirror-state voices of seamlessness, of

> a place outside the normal world, intensely private and enclosed, intensely green and fertile, numinous, haunted and haunting, dominated by a sense of magic that is also a sense of a mysterious yet profound parity in all existence. Of course it recurs again and again in literature and art, in one form or another.[46]

The mysterious and profound parity[47] in all existence, and not incidentally in the string of (Nietzschean) appositives with which Fowles/Martin describes it, occurs only on the Nietzschean surface of the text, in which "retreat" is a key word. The hidden place of the "true self," for Daniel a kind of literary unconscious known only in its fictions and always at the distance of desire, is nonetheless full of both the silence of voices and the voices of self-exploration. The chapter concludes with the italicized other(ed) voice of Daniel Martin the epigrammist: "*If life is largely made of retreats from reality, its relations must be of retreats from the imagined,*"[48] since it is imagination that the images recalling pre-linguistic unity inhabit. Fowles' patently Lacanian language here, of course, occurs within the framework of the symbolic nexus of the *bonne vaux*, thus gathering together all three registers of the Lacanian/Nietzschean self. To back away from the sense of solid reality is to retreat to the realm of the imaginary and the symbolic, though that retreat is itself a nostalgic self-loss, as Daniel Martin discovers in the novel.

Thus, "The Sacred Combe," as a chapter, reveals itself as an examination of the inception of the *reality* of Dan's novel as a convocation of his imaginary and symbolic voices, which, though presented in the surface narrative as both outer voices (other characters past and present) and inner ones (aspects of Dan himself, such as lover, child, etc., and then more directly autoaesthetically as script writer, playwright, and finally novelist), are all facets of the autoaesthetic focus of Dan's novel *itself*, which we are reading. His sense of retreat, now both a protective and nostalgic trip away from the harshness of mundanity and a receding into *différance* and its *étrangeté*, begins with the sacred combe but extends to writing itself: As Dan bluntly says when deciding to write the fictional story he has been molding: "I simply sensed a far greater capacity for retreat in fiction. In Robin Hood terms I saw it in a forest, after the thin copses of the filmscript."[49] The richness, density, and privacy of the novel attract him. His writing is revealed as self-protection, "his" displacement into the *étrangeté* of language in a system of transference and counter-transference.[50] Dan determines that language salves the *blessure* of the distanced and fragmented self, a process that becomes the distancing "blessing" that occurs when the image-oriented mirror-state gives way to the *écart* of word representation, leaving only its trace. To be able to say that "self is language," according to Derrida in *Glas*, is to be able to substitute one for the other, to allow that static (dis)order glued together by the copula, the "is," to produce an enduring sense of self. The self-mirroring of Daniel Martin's novel reflects the *écriture* of which the proper name, "Daniel Martin," forms the center. This center is the elusive Derridean archi-trace. For Daniel, this figure-of-figure is the collapsing together of phantom mother (about whom or which Derrida talks extensively in *Glas*), the enervated father, and the displacement of sexuality "out" into *le tracé*, that blank which is traced by words. The narrative that Daniel Martin recounts (and creates) is, for him, a substitution for the fiction of an absent grounding his text will never write except in the language of a symbolic desire.

And so, out of the sacred combe and his inscription of its protective distance, Daniel writes his novel. It proceeds, as I have begun to show, through a series of flashbacks, all of which demonstrate the chronotopic power of narrator over story and his control of the dispensing of information and image. Indeed, Dan says of himself, in light of his *étrangeté*, that he is of the race "that live in flashback, in the past and future."[51] Dan's manipulation of his material is thematic rather than practical, reflecting "his" own needs: his retreats are mirrored in the structure of the story itself. So-called "events" are repeatedly presented such that they cannot be judged until more and further information, presented later though often occurring before, is made available (this is Freud's narrative strategy in his case histories as well, as Lacan reminds us). Jenny's interpolated chapters, for example, operate in this way, without comment from Dan. He carefully orchestrates the reader's judgment of him in the midst of this palimpsestic heaping: his story is engineered to meet the double demands of covering his retreat and facilitating his provisional emergence.

In addition to this very problematic non-grounding in a resident time scale, Dan rehearses and reiterates the central thematic place of retreat in the novel. We have seen how the sacred combe acts as the fount of his energy of writing, similar to Jude Fawley's Marygreen well; just as, for Jude, that originary place is echoed or traced in other *topoi* of retreat (as, for example, the milestone on which Jude's initial writing occurs), so, as Dan's novel proceeds, we discover other places of retreat which offer their energy to his autoaesthetic search. The originary place is never a unitary one, any more than the mirror-state could be located specifically or singularly. Such a localizing is clearly impossible, a function of the fictions of hindsight and the hindsight of fiction. For Daniel Martin, the first of these surrogate retreats is Tsankawi, an ancient Indian ruin lost to time in the mountains of New Mexico, beloved of D. H. Lawrence, visited by Dan when a movie screenplay he had written was being shot, and to which he brings Jenny near the middle of the novel. It is a place "haunted by loss and mystery, by a sense of some magical relationship, glimpsed both in the art and what little is known of their inhabitants' way of life, between man and nature."[52] This mysterious quality, on which Dan ruminates at some length, comes about as a result of the site's transcending "all place and frontier,"[53] but Dan does not stop here: his description of *this* sacred place re-fabricates the *étrangeté* of Tsankawi as the avatar of that other sacred place-beyond-place, the womb-like combe, with an added luster:

> There was a sense in which it was a secret place, a literal retreat, an analogue of what had always obsessed my mind; but it also stood in triumphant opposition, and this was what finally, for me, distinguished Tsankawi from the other sites: in them there was a sadness, the vanished past, the cultural loss; but Tsankawi defeated time, all deaths. Its deserted silence was like a sustained high note, unconquerable.[54]

Indeed, the organizing idea of his novel comes to Dan in this place beyond time, precisely because of this quality of timelessness. The site is "something dense, interweaving, treating time as horizontal, like a skyline; not cramped, linear and progressive."[55] The defeat of death Dan feels Tsankawi offers is also, then, an offer to write beyond death, as Dan's novel (the one we are holding as we read this chapter) manifests.

Tantalizingly in terms of Daniel Martin's autoaesthetic doubles, the Tsankawi chapter is not a presentation of Dan but a test of Jenny. Dan brings her to the site so that he can check her reaction to it, test her sensitivity to the/his powerful fictional issues of spirit, evocation, and essence; only if she has *his* reaction, his reverence and sense of depth, is she somehow to be worthy—worth of *him*. Lest this appear the rawest and most sophomoric exercise in ego-centrism, we must quickly note that it is in fact the opposite. Tsankawi, in his prior visit to it, tested Dan and his life, gave him that magical sense of connection he so desperately needs and cannot find nor sustain. He uses it as a litmus to test an *other* because that test is an ongoing test of himself. Dan is disappointed by Jenny's reaction: she searches the ground for pottery shards to make into necklaces and earrings. *Most* disappointing. Dan reports an awareness of his unfairness in judging her as he does, but the judgment stands nonetheless, because in some deeper sense it is not at all unfair. Dan has shared a secret place with Jenny, who did not, it appears, come to it with him. She came instead to another place altogether, occupying the same space but with a completely different feeling and (lack of) power. Attached to the conclusion of the chapter, a curious and unique appendage in the novel, is a short section in Jenny's voice, a telling response to Dan's unuttered judgment. Her section, which reprimands him, in hindsight, for the trick he played on her, concludes with the admonition that he should have told her of the weight of the place for him. The point is that Jenny, like Dan, cannot believe in directness, relying on the scripted indirection of her missive. She writes him what she cannot say to him. *His* chapter concludes, again, in the silence of other voices.

Thorncombe itself, the country house Dan has bought in Devon, which is the beloved place/home of his youth, is the retreat epitomizing all the rest. As for Zarathustra before the gate, for Dan the return to Thorncombe is always a self-assessment and self-valuation, and at the same time a suspension of that judgment. Return is never the same, is always *différant*, as presented by Lacan as the underlying theme in "The Unconscious and Repetition," "the notion of cross-checking, the function of return."[56] Thorncombe is both Dan's desire and the fulfillment of his desire. For Dan, as for Lacan (and Freud), in the Nietzschean sense repetition is not reproduction: the life Dan has at Thorncombe is not the reinstitution of primal completeness but of perpetual self-reevaluation, always the same *and* different. Indeed, all of Daniel's surreptitious dialogues with the theme of chimerical self-unity begin not in the sacred combe nor in the *bonne vaux*; it is at Thorncombe that Dan begins to articulate, to confess, his separation from a protracted dream of mirror-state unity. This occurs because he has approached and defined what here might validly and not tritely be called his significant other: he discusses his idea of writing a novel with Jane. In some real sense, the novel has focused on this moment more than any other. Prior scenes have been preambles to this one, and in fact the conclusion of the book is no more nor less than a re-write of—an eternal return to—this scene between Dan and Jane.[57] Of course, all of the ingredients of a thick, rich Daniel Martin soup have converged on the room, embodied in the person of Jane and her eternal return into his life as its gauge and measure. He is, he says here, able to "see her better" than ever before, now, after Anthony's death, "not two miles" from the pulpit from which his father had preached. The initiation of the novel's writing and its shape, of course, are to be seen in the (eternal) re-initiation of the relationship with Jane, which is to be "tested," in the Tsankawi sense, by Dan's asking Jane to come to Egypt with him (the irony that this has been engineered by Anthony on his deathbed is enormously complex, is not lost on Dan, and should not be lost on the reader in terms of the Eros/Thanatos theme inherent in grammatology and its *étrangeté*). Fowles operates this multileveled test with a host of metaphoric overlappings, not missing an opportunity to engage Dan in the process of his emergence through the actual writing of the scene (and through writing Jane), as when, after having asked Jane to go with him on the Nile trip, Dan weightily informs us that he "returned to put a guard in front of the fire,"[58] the most reportorial of actions and the most perspicuously symbolic of Dan's persistence.

Jane, as the focus of true-self/love, offers Dan another, more complex sort of retreat. Though their story itself continues in an unbroken fashion from this point, as we shall see, something has altered after the fireplace scene. In the opening in the wall that Jenny has imaged forth and that Jane provides, Dan has glimpsed again the possibility of life affirmation that Jane offers,[59] and about which he is now determined to write in the novel we hold. When Nietzsche declares in the Preface to *The Gay Science* that "perhaps truth is a woman," he means it in just the metaphoric way that Dan does here. The world is reordered to the force of Dan's quickening self-sense. "In the Orchard of the Blessed," the chapter following "Thorncombe," begins with a Zarathustran image: "If Dan had launched a strange ship on impulse, he had behaved much more habitually in another matter. The truth was that he was falling very rapidly in love . . . ." The reader's expectations move in a single direction: toward Jane. But the sentence concludes ". . . with the idea of his novel."[60] The double theme of Dan's quickening love (for Jane, present but unreported) and his quickening novel (the same theme, in the end, and at the same time the "book-ends" of Dan's confession of *étrangeté*) merge in Jane, and Dan will never be able to separate them again. Ostensibly, "In the Orchard of the Blessed," another genealogical descendant and echo of the *bonne vaux*, is about the choice of a name for his protagonist, that is, how to go about forming the fictional self that would inhabit "his" novel. As he stands in his "forest," alone, he comes finally to the decision that will energize and guide the rest of the novel, which has formed what we have read for 400-plus pages already. Confronting the enigma of a Jane who is both herself and numerous others, as he can clearly see, he decides on the strategy of his own self-telling:

And then, in those most banal of circumstances, in the night, in his orchard, alone but not alone, he came to the most important decision of his life. It did not arrive—nor do most such decisions in reality—as light came on the road to Damascus, in one blinding certainty; but far more as a tentative hypothesis, a seed, a chink in a door; still to be doubted, neglected, forgotten through most of the future of these pages.[61]

To ensure that this most momentous of decisions remains neglected, Dan concludes this paragraph, "However, Dan wishes, for reasons of his own, to define it as it was to grow."[62] We are deprived of Dan's conclusion, "the most important decision of his life," in a strategic thematic of selfhood-in-suspense. Like a tightrope walker, Dan suspends his revelation to maintain power over it, to keep from having to articulate it (to keep it in the *bonne vaux* of his loving imagination, always a potentially perfect articulation), and to lead the reader into the true condition of its unfolding, which will follow. This is Dan's version of "honesty," and his ability to achieve it becomes the manifesto examined earlier, framed in Idealist language that, we are told, will "be defined as he grows"; that manifesto is framed as a kind of desirable curse on the potential nausea of autoaesthetic force: "To hell with cultural fashion; to hell with elitist guilt; to hell with existentialist nausea; and above all, to hell with the imagined that does not say, not only in, but behind the images, the real."[63] The suspension of that last and most important part of his "doctrine," the desire for suspension in grammar as well as in theme, in which Daniel Martin posits, behind not only language but images themselves, a reality that grounds and validifies them, at the same time validifies the imagination.

Remembering that, as a function of the imagination, the Lacanian Imaginary is the realm of perceptivity, which when combined with the Symbolic constructs the Real, the Imaginary is the invitation to this abysmal nausea, having no existence (for consciousness) but its absence, which, again, "cannot be conceived";[64] seemingly ironically, however, the Lacanian sense of self, the projection of self into image (Lacan's *moi*) is rooted in the Imaginary, so that it is in the Imaginary that the inception of the identification of subjectness occurs. In appropriate Nietzschean fashion, then, the subject is "built" out of materials that do not exist even for the purported subject, that do not inhabit the *topos* of the real.[65] Failure to recognize the indistinct boundaries between the imaginary realm and that of the real pervades *Daniel Martin*, as a continuous commentary on this cross-breeding and tightrope-walking. Dan himself begins to become cognizant of it as he builds toward the autoaesthetic acknowledgment of himself (in his novel); indeed, the build toward the self-empowering required to write the novel we hold as we read *Daniel Martin* consists chiefly of the increasing manifestation of this discourse, which will not break out into Fowles' rhetoric until the novel's last page. We have seen how, at the end of "In the Orchard of the Blessed," Dan has begun to foreshadow this overt manifestation, declaring his recognition of the radical difference between (and revaluation of the meaning of) the imaginary and the real. Dan insists there and for a long time on a "real" behind the images, whereas in fact the real is that which the Imaginary and the Symbolic *leave out*, that which is not accounted for by them. Since the Real is, therefore, as Dan claims, beyond language and beyond all the cultural determiners of which he wants to be free, it is unavailable to him. The "Real" is, therefore, for Daniel Martin as for Lacan, another name for the impossible, for what has not succumbed to the "ineliminable residue of articulation,"[66] and can have only the most frustrating relationship with Dan's novel.

But the Real must exist for Dan in order that the Imaginary, defined by him as the raw material of his experience, be able to ground the Symbolic, defined as articulation, and give it validity. That is, Dan chooses here at the inception of writing to eschew the imagined that "does not say, not only in, but behind the images, the real," thereby failing to recognize himself as a function of those articulations. Dan tries to ground himself again in this section of the novel as in the beginning, in the *ground* itself, making the edenic orchard at Thorncombe the chthonic source of valuation rising out of what he wants to think of as a pastless present, or a present that encompasses past, present, and future but which is revealed as one of those places at which Dan tries again to *retreat* into the Real.

Out of this project to fabricate the real, Daniel Martin makes his most decisive retreat: the trip to Egypt with Jane. Aware of the infinite complexities of this last chapter of the theme of retreat, Dan writes the journey as itself a series of layerings. If the journey to Palmyra heralds Dan's final commitment to Jane and their "story," the trip up the Nile is the final commitment to the writing of the story in which that other commitment will be articulated. The river trip is a story not of river travel but of the (Heraclitan) flow of stories, of the dynamic *epos* out of which Dan will amalgamate the motifs that have inductively gathered around him. Daniel Martin has, up to this point in the novel, been most deeply concerned with the achievement of a certain stasis of self, wanting his sense of himself to sit still and behave. On his and Jane's trip up the ancient Nile, Dan adds the final ingredient to his autoaesthetic force: a sense of the active flow out of which his self-writing must come. He has been employing the wrong self-metaphors to his self-conception, mistaking a desired autochthony for a more usefully dynamic self-narrative, a movement instead of a position (and self-empowering rather than self-identifying). Dan learns here to let himself be dislocated.

Dan, with Jane, meets an old (East) German professor, an expert on the river and its environs as on the Egyptians and their culture, who is also an expert storyteller. The catalytic raconteur, referred to only as "Herr Professor," whose claim about articulate artists since the Greeks is that they wish "to be remembered by name—like the ancient pharaohs," himself remains nameless, another manifestation of fictionality and of *étrangeté*. In his function in the novel, he has and needs no other name (we are reminded of *Daniel Martin* and his/its concern with the naming of the protagonist who is and is not Daniel Martin). Herr Professor "primes" Daniel for his movement into writing and frees him to write with a series of stories of "the river between," metaphorizing Dan's condition as he prepares to write. Within the framework of the history lessons they seem to be, the professor's stories collect the cultural, psychological, and metaphysical strands of Dan's developing strategies and galvanize them into a single theme, an enabling myth of the autoaesthetic writer that the emergent Dan actually calls, in fact, "dislocation,"[67] articulations artfully purporting to reveal what they invent and distance. The professor (of antiquities, of course) has always felt, he says, that the papyri he has studied have been a series of "screens I had put up to hide what I did not understand."[68] He has come to discover that "everything is a kind of screen if one wishes it so. An excuse for not understanding." Herr Professor recounts a river dispute between two tribes irresolvable because there is "never any peace among men, on either bank. Only in the river between."[69] Dan begins to understand the function of this narrative *étrangeté*, replying that the river between is "the one place we can't live." It is in that dislocation, in the atemporal pseudo-transcendence of the possible, that Dan begins to see his writing as occurring, where one is no longer "one's own self, a modern archaeologist,"[70] but rather where "one is the painting," not the noun but the participle.

In this realization, Dan perceives what he calls the screen-existence behind the "illusion of time." It is in this section that Dan's understanding of that relational tension of writing, the story-telling crossover that never achieves the desired effect of self-revelation, is deepened and secured. Egypt becomes, for Dan, more than ever before, a rich density of signs, a function of its ubiquitous hieroglyphs. He discovers the power of words not to capture but to fabricate feeling. This is both a great release from the pressure of self-seeking and a denial of release into the self. Only in this atemporal context does Dan begin to have a sense of the metaphoric reiteration of the voices of his past. As he watches Jane in a bazaar, he imagines, repeatedly, what it might feel like had they married, and had their life progressed as it would have done had they not separated. This imagined life merges with a written one with Jane, in a time without time:

> For days now he had been split internally if not outwardly, between a known past and an unknown future. That was where his disturbing feeling of not being his own master, of being a character in someone else's play, came from. The past wrote him.[71]

That past all around Dan and within him that is both imagination and memory, both "his own" and a cultural memory, becomes a more and more complex (Lacanian) palimpsest of other voices. His fear of the future and of what it holds comes out of Dan's anxiety of influence; he feels so strongly that he has and can have no clear sense of himself but is caught in the river between. Now, ironically, as these issues congeal and clarify, Dan becomes increasingly aware of that lack of unity, that distance from any self, that he ineluctably feels. And since the greater part of his and Jane's life is now overtly or covertly about feelings, this frustration becomes a major element in his self-formulations. His formula for truth is now identity between "saying" and "feeling" ("Lies: not really saying what one feels,")[72] but no longer can he claim that self-truth, such as it might now be, is the saying of that feeling. It is no longer so simple and schematic, and in its complexity his self-narrative causes a further dislocation/dissociation, in a kind of gap of desire:

> He suddenly saw the proposed novel as a pipe dream, one more yearning for the impossible.
> The terror of that task: that making of a world, alone, unguided, now mocking, like some distant mountain peak, mediocrity in his dressing-gown. He could never do it. Never mind that what he felt was felt by all novelists, all artists, at the beginning of creation—that indeed not feeling the terror was the worst possible augury for the enterprise; he could not do it. Above all he could not do it because his thoughts were metaphors.[73]

The dream of the novel is in and of the order of the Imaginary, accomplishable only in the silence of other voices. Dan has finally perceived what Fowles and we have known, that voices are other, and that the *écart* between his feeling, such as it is, and his articulation is unbridgeable. Dan feels that truth lies in silence,[74] not in the "other voices" he and Jane produce: all Dan hears now are "other voices,"[75] which disrupt his "reading" of Jane and eclipse his deepening reading of himself. Having all the ingredients for his book, except Jane, Dan is lost. The following scenes in the novel, nearly fifty pages, find Daniel in his diaspora, wandering through the desert of his thoughts with no anchor for his sense of dislocation. Dan's focused dialectical battle between feeling (confessed love, now) and saying (his novel, his and Jane's conversations, his thoughts) leaves him radically unrooted. In this journey through the wilderness, Dan reaches his most abject darkness, a fundamentally threatening, disempowered enervation.

But then the last incarnation of the door in the wall opens. It is at once physical—the door in the hotel room at "the end of the world"—and metaphysical—the opening to a series of new understandings of feeling, selfhood, and articulation. But even at the opening of this final enabling set of doorways (which, as we shall see, truly act as Gates of Moment), Dan's echoing "retreats" and their silent voices are manifold. Jane's physicality provides Dan with his ultimate one. When Jane asks why he has confessed secret thoughts to her about their past relationship, he replies that he has done it to "try to regain what I once did feel for you. When I had a whole being."[76] The reader knows that Dan did not then have a whole being, as

Dan later confesses: from the first moments of self-awareness Dan has been "lost," and yet the ingenuous *stories* of his completeness sufficed; now they will not. But Dan's fiction of the power of Jane's presence mandates that she then provided him with a sense of wholeness he has now lost and can regain only through her, the paradigmatic figure of *self-value* in whom writing (as the impetus and catalyst for Dan's) and feeling (as love-object)—both as functions of the river between of desire—coalesce.

Jane's ultimate value to Daniel Martin is that his novel treats her as a liaison to a revitalized past that might conceivably exist beyond or behind but at any rate outside the *epos* of which Dan is made. Jane is revealed as having been for Dan the reifier and therefore the bestower of life. She is the figure of power able to wrest Dan back from the abyss of *étrangeté*, once it is discovered. This is what he means by "love." Through his growing re-acquaintance with Jane, despite all the discussions of feeling and of feeling's dialogue with saying, Dan permits himself no interpretive definition of his feelings for her. Gradually, through their visit to Egypt, this retreat begins to alter as Jane is restored to her former (covert) role: she is at first the human emblem of the nostalgized ruins they pass, as they boat up the Nile and in Palmyra, but finally the emblem of the river between. This role alteration at first defines Jane as metaphorically among the substantial relics by which Dan identifies himself, and then increasingly as the metonymic force through which he increasingly sees himself as needing and being unable to achieve self-completion. In the former guise, Jane has been as much an artifact as those in stone around her, but Dan, so fervently convinced of Jane's revivifying power, has had to learn this slowly—in order to pass beyond it. Gradually, the monuments of Egyptian antiquity have themselves begun to darken until, at Abu Simbel, Dan has reviled them as poor, empty imitations of substantiality, as hollow as he himself. At his nadir, "end of the world" at Palmyra, Dan begins finally to separate the monuments around him from those "inside," increasingly polarizing what come to be his two sorts of relics, the physical and the metaphysical.

But then in the Palmyra hotel the door in the wall opens and Jane capitulates, shattering the distinction between physical and metaphysical retreat: she opens the door in the wall (of Dan's room) and comes to his bed. Her action, we and Dan feel, should erase the troubling distinctions that have plagued Dan. Anthony's Eros/Thanatos program should be complete, though no more for Jane than for Dan. Feeling (love and sex, Eros and Agape) and saying (the Thanatos of *l'autre*) should ostensibly no longer be the tendentious and romanticized halves of a potentially unified whole or should remain so only insofar as both feeling and saying are themselves parts of the latter. But this hope of substantiation transmutes into the positive *étrangeté* with which *Daniel Martin* concludes. In the damp hotel room in

Palmyra, in their first love-making in twenty-five years, Dan's dislocation is recapitulated in its apotheosized guise, in a series of incarnations. First, Jane is seen as a rejuvenating signifier:

> Suddenly, in that first naked contact, there was no time, no lost years, marriage, motherhood, but the original girl's body. He had an acute and poignant memory, re-experience, of what it had been like, once . . . the strange simplicity of it.[77]

This is the feeling for which Dan always searches. The (Dionysian) "simplicity" lies not in the tactile but in the transcendence of time. This constitutive sense, however, cannot hold; the body is of course not the "original girl's body" at all. And so, in a second phase of discovery, a page later:

> It did not take place as he had dreamed, did not reach that non-physical climax he wanted, fused melting of all further doubt. . . . It came to him, immediately afterward, when he was still lying half across her, that the failure could have been put in terms of grammatical person. It had happened in the third, when he had craved the first and second.[78]

Not only is Jane removed at this most intimate moment from second to third person; Dan himself suffers the same removal, not only in his reference to Jane's absence in language but in the frustration he feels with his own third person-ness. As rejuvenator, Jane bestows life on Dan; for Dan, this life is autoaesthetic and purely literary.

In his program to transcend this literization, to live a renewed life with Jane, Dan attempts to remove the veils of declaration from a hypothetical experience, to knock a hole in the wall of otherness Lacan tells us constitutes our discourse and from which we receive echoes of what seem to be ourselves and the reality of experience. But since to constitute any sense of self is ipso facto to create and enter a dialectic with otherness, again and again Dan's agonistic confrontation of death and life occurs: in Anthony's suicide Dan has tried to see its inversion, a mnemonic reinvigoration in death. But this must be, according to the Dan who responds to Anthony then, in an impossible place beyond language. Dan has never discovered the reason for Anthony's suicide, because this disclosure would cancel the veil between the dead Anthony, for whom all questions are answered, and the living Dan; cancelling the veil would cancel discourse. It is only in this ironic scene of Dan and Jane's reintegration that Dan's perception of Anthony's final gesture ripens into understanding.

Dan wants his novel's language to be what he might hope, in the great Modernist humanist tradition, to be trans-subjective, but is always finally (often painfully) aware of the displacement he undergoes in his own telling. He is aware that language is constitutive, but he is prevented by his own mode of self-analysis from reconciling himself to the fact that, like Seferis' poetic flame, language—and the reality he wants to make honest—are never and can never be at rest. It is in this interregnum that a great variety of morbid symptoms appears, to repeat Gramsci's words, but these symptoms remain a complex web of more or less depressing instances of *méconnais- sance* until Dan rediscovers (his love for) Jane. This love becomes the redemptive catalyst Dan needs to transform the morbid symptoms of a solipsistic autoaesthetics into the "affirmation, blessing, deification of exis- tence" to which Nietzsche refers.[79]

But we must—we are forced to—remember that one of Fowles' chief (Nietzschean) themes in *Daniel Martin* is suspense, both the suspense of the tightrope walker, whose life is always on the line, and that of the *raconteur*, for whom suspense is the dramatic lifeline of a story. Dan's relationship with Jane, suspended as they themselves are away from time and self, in that dark hotel room, is in their trip into the Middle Eastern desert, still not "working out," and they know it, again in terms of the compact of reality through which they are working, and within the context of which they are learning about love. In fact, Dan, in recording their malaise in this most intimate of troubles, echoes here precisely the "imagination/reality" passage in another context:

> We are saved from breeding relationships we cannot feed; but we are also prevented from breeding those we need. All pasts shall be coeval, a backworld uniformly not present, relegated to the status of so many family snapshots. The mode of recollection usurps the reality of the recalled. Images are inherently fascistic because they overstamp the truth, however dim and blurred, of the real past experience; as if, faced with ruins, we must turn architects, not archaeologists. The word is the most imprecise of signs.[80]

Dan is caught between where he *senses* he is and where he wants to be, in a discourse of desire revealing language's supplementary otherness but that is schematized as being composed of sense and sentence. He knows and has always known that language is the most meaning-full of signs, and yet that its power lies in its very discursive and relational, metaphoric imprecision; indeed, that "only a science-obsessed age could fail to comprehend that this [imprecision] is its great virtue, not its defect."[81] The growing sense of tragedy surrounding Dan and Jane in these late scenes is that Dan still consistently searches for that final, full word that will link his displaced, "true" past to a reinvigorated present and a potentially full future. He sees that he writes not only to make others, *les autres*, but to participate in that most powerful otherness of language itself, *l'Autre*, with its infinite poten- tial(s), and because he sees language as being not "*ex nihilo*, but out of pre-existent memory-stores and experience,"[82] to which he ascribes the status of an ineffable reality which he cannot leave alone, and which through his manipulations he must replace. Daniel Martin-the-writer is always "rearranging and inferring, even when he writes about what has never happened or even what will or can never happen."[83] His effort is to reorder the past, catalyzed in his rediscovery of *his* Jane, toward some future *verbe* he can never find in a future/potential world of loss and mutability. The gratuitous nature of the self's self-creation in the other is that *telos* is always deferred into a projected future; it is always a slipping into potentiality fabricated in a purely hypothetical time.

For Dan (but not the reader), the re-advent of Jane provides the rejuvenation of love that can catalyze creation. For us, serenely on the outside, this "love" is an acknowledgment of distance and of the gap between feeling and saying. The Herr Professor's admonition that in moments of transcendence one is no longer "painter nor self" but "painting," that is, the "river between" where "we cannot live," is the adumbration of a transference into writing. It is a vital manifestation of this distance that the seeming obligatory scene of Dan and Jane's decision to live and to make a life together is missing from Dan's novel about them.

But Dan has one final confrontation in which to see the mirror of his displacement, his *méconnaissance*. In *Daniel Martin* the affirming art-object transcends being gratuitous by subsuming and embodying, always at a distance, a sense of truth "beyond" it. Dan's most significant "othering" occurs in his making himself an *objet d'art*, which he reserves for the penultimate cluster of scenes in the novel. He does this, predictably, by finding the novel's last significant double in the silence of the voice emanating from the serene visage of a Rembrandt self-portrait. Having returned to England with Jane, having set up house together in Oxford,[84] Dan comes to London for a last meeting with the visiting Jenny that, embarrassing as it is, concludes "properly" but with a very uneasy sense. After this scene, Dan needs the substantiation of an oracular voice. He goes to visit a Hampstead art museum, a great house lined with visages from the past; the chapter, in fact, is appropriately entitled "Future Past," a declaration of the circularity time can have in self-inscription. The chapter begins with a perfectly circular paraphrastic (and oracular) inscription from Seferis:

> At the hour when one day ends and the next has not begun
> at the hour when time is suspended
> you must find the man who then and now, from the very beginning,
>   ruled your body
> you must look for him so that someone else at least
> will find him, after you are dead.[85]

The hour between days is also Gramsci's potential time of morbidity; indeed, for Dan a new time is beginning, the time of the present tense of the novel. In the art gallery Dan stands before a revered self-portrait by Rembrandt, a wonderfully rich autoaesthetic text at the crossroads of the imaginary (it is a complex image) and the real (a portrait before him on the wall, declaring—affirming—itself a work of art).

Before this "sad, proud old man," with "the entire knowledge of his own genius and of the inadequacy of genius before human reality," like the gray bark of the distant beech tree in his sacred combe, Dan confronts, mirrored in Rembrandt's image, his own impaired self-creation. Rembrandt's weathered and gentle face, within its highly self-conscious frame and in its highly self-conscious ambiance, further framed by the high Modernist ideals of portraiture, is Daniel Martin's final retreat, a most sacred combe in which for the first time he brings together all the elements of past, present, and future tenses he has gathered in the previous pages. Dan's confrontation with the Rembrandt is the apotheosis of Fowles' Modernist program: the portrait meets, is informed by, and informs the portrait, image to text, imaginary to real. None of the elements Daniel Martin has confronted on his journey to this ending would have permitted the novel to occur without this punctuation on the sentence of Dan. According to Dan/Fowles, the old man's face, "a date beneath a frame, a presentness beyond all time, fashion, language,"[86] embodies Dan's desire, but he (Daniel) cannot "reach beyond" language to that presence. While Rembrandt can seem to partake of the "wholeness of silence," in Dan's formulation the difference of language separates him from it. The very sentence in which Dan discovers and declares this manifests the un-presence of his own self-portrait, his own (now increasingly positive) self-lack; looking at the portrait, Dan declares that

> it spoke very directly, said all he had never managed to say and would never manage to say—even though, with the abruptness of that dash, he hardly thought this before he saw himself saying the thought to the woman who would be waiting for him on the platform at Oxford that evening.[87]

The self-referentiality of that vortextual dash, which has the effect of injecting the reader into Daniel Martin's text itself, validating and reifying it, and of propelling us away from the Rembrandt portrait, since in Fowles' text, with its spotlighted reference to punctuation, we are so patently in another medium, transforms the autoaesthetic process by which Dan has arrived at this completion of his project and himself. Dan is always suspended in that dash, the non-verbal copula, which is the perpetual river between, the place where "no man can live, and which is therefore at peace." The *corps morcelé* of Daniel Martin's disembodied figure, his reflection in prose, is always only suspended, never cancelled. It is written over with a false wholeness that must finally confess its writtenness. His fragmented self, which is not a self at all but a series of phrases taken from an apocryphal whole that has not and cannot pre-exist, exists, as Geoffrey Hartman declares, "in the verbal or symbolic" in contrast to "the nonverbal or imaginary."[88] Hartman's Lacanian formulation is, in fact, capitalizing on Derrida's discussion of "un Rembrandt déchiré" in *Glas*, the "torn up Rembrandt" *signature* Jean Genet dismembers as a function of control over and comment on the name. Here the name that is torn up is not that of integrated authority but of autoaesthetics, of insight and inherent feeling. Dan ascribes to that face behind Rembrandt's paint a romanticized knowledge that he cannot have, being able to interpret the hieroglyph in terms of his own *Weltanschauung*. Dan turns the old man's eyes into a *sentence*, a window on a sense of truth he postulates but lacks. To repeat the passage in a slightly wider context, again galvanized by that medial dash:

> The great picture seemed to denounce, almost to repel. Yet it lived, it was timeless, it spoke very directly, said all he had never managed to say and would never manage to say—even though, with the abruptness of that dash he had hardly thought this before he saw himself saying the thought to the woman who would be waiting for him on the platform at Oxford that evening.[89]

Dan's transition here between Rembrandt and Dan/Jane, which is purely grammatical, depicts the interpretive stance Dan will take of the portrait of his own life he is about to paint. Dan's own language becomes an autoaesthetic, self-referential, and awkward veil, "with the abruptness of that dash." This is Dan's most mimetic attempt to displace reality (here, paint) and words from their separate spheres. Yet, always aware of the metonymic nature of the art object he sees (and is writing as he sees), Dan can never go beyond his own "frame, fashion, and language." His inability to pass beyond his own framework for himself, and his concomitant inability to perceive these nets, endures; Dan fights for that unity of feeling and saying he can never achieve but which he desires to the very end. Standing before the Rembrandt portrait, Dan feels again that sense of "vertigo" he has felt in Egypt and discussed with the Professor: in that sense of timelessness and suspension, Dan feels Anthony's project come to fulfillment. Indeed, Dan reveals himself as living out Anthony's romantic dream of revivification, not for Jane alone but for Jane and Dan himself. Dan persists in seeing this vital impulse as a transcendence of saying, even of imaginative saying, a sublimation into the realm of "real" feeling beyond saying: it is, for him finally, "not a matter of skill, of knowledge, of intellect; of good luck or bad; but of choosing and learning to feel."[90] In his "marriage" with Jane he has achieved an understanding of the synthesis he has longed for. This has been Anthony's insight into Dan and Jane's incipient union:

> Dan began at last to detect it behind the surface of the painting; behind the sternness lay the declaration of the one true marriage in the mind mankind is allowed, the ultimate citadel of humanism. No true compassion without will, no true will without compassion.[91]

The seemingly bloodless Anthony has achieved his own autoaesthetic ideal in Dan and Jane. Dan has actively forged, to use Joyce's famous word for it, his own Modernist interpretation of the Dionysian fusion Nietzsche posits out of feeling and saying; and in perfect Nietzschean fashion, in the next two paragraphs (the novel's last two), we see that this fusion is an accruing, integral function of articulation, of the novel Dan has written and we have now almost finished reading.

Within the context of that novel, Dan is trying to discover who, in his own monologue, is speaking, and to whom, but until the very end his answer is always lost in the echoes of voices that remain indistinct. The quest for origin, for a lost "authentic" self, depends for its inception, as we have seen, on a *literary* sense of original loss and Dan's acknowledged discovery of difference and displacement. Self-knowledge has come to depend on a purported transcendence of *méconnaissance*: that Zarathustran/Dionysian fusion of will and compassion operates within the orbit of the novel Dan will write and has written. This is (and Dan knows it) a reversal of the hoped-for discovery of unity. Dan's acknowledgment of his novel's otherness and of his own fragmentation occurs in a series of reversals in the very sentences in which they are declared, in *Daniel Martin*'s final paragraph:

> That evening in Oxford, leaning beside Jane in her kitchen while she cooked supper for them, Dan told her with a suitable irony that at least he had found a last sentence for the novel he was never going to write. She laughed at such flagrant Irishry; which is perhaps why, in the end, and in the knowledge that Dan's novel can never be read, lies eternally in the future, his ill-concealed ghost has made that impossible last his own impossible first.[92]

Dan's play here with "last sentences," his own and his novels, with its implications of both the literary and the legal (in the sense of judgments— even judgments-unto-death), turns *Daniel Martin* back on itself—folds it and articulates it, in that the last sentence he has found to conclude his novel does not conclude it but is, rather, the novel's ("impossible") first sentence, the consummate judgment by which the entire novel has been set up, enigmatically, for judgment. According to Dan at the "end," the reader is thrown into the opening chapter again, and the novel itself becomes a kind of coda attached to its autoaesthetic reevaluation. This circularity of desire for a successful self-telling concludes itself in this real last sentence, the one with which the novel actually begins/concludes.

This "real" last sentence, almost unreadably convoluted, an initial and a final mimesis and a suspension of the closure with which it occurs, becomes the point at which the novel can begin, arranged by the "ill-concealed ghost" of Dan's "writing hand." The "impossible last sentence" of the novel Dan does write, which he has turned into the impossible first sentence of the novel we are holding, is

Whole sight; or all the rest is desolation.[93]

Dan lays out, at the beginning, what we can only understand at the end: Dan's dilemma of self-realization orbits that other, deeper dilemma of impossible self-articulation. Dan's irony is that whole sight is itself a powerful Modernist fiction. Dan claims that his novel can never be read, it must be re-read, but the "challenge" is to achieve a full reading of him and his world through that re-reading. This circularity has a distancing effect: Dan exits from his own novel in a kind of whimsical dance around a self-imposed, Manichean ultimatum his impossible first sentence poses, whole sight or desolation, his version of "whole sight" having led to a desolation only mitigated by the energy of its wonderful, rich irony and its powerful inscription.

His circuitous path through the labyrinth of his novel's language, a labyrinth he makes in that link of ending to beginning into a Moebius strip defiantly turning on itself, is a search for a self he comes to realize cannot be reached and has never existed and cannot exist. Desire, for Dan, especially desire for some final static identity, is an obscure and obscuring object. The apparatus behind Dan's reading of himself, like that behind this reading of his novel, is always in the process of being effaced. "Frame, fashion, and language" provide for Dan and for Fowles at once a catalytic intensity and a thematic series of veils. Dan's final announcement of the impossible novel's genesis, a hope-filled declaration, must be decoded by the reader in its other form: as a comment on the impossible nature of Dan's quest. Dan is caught in the vortex of the river between, in the dialectic of the grammatological Full Word, unable to say just who it is who speaks and writes. Finally, bemused, he turns the novel into its own imitation, a self-portrait of writing that is suspended in writing the written self.

Part Five

◆

DIALECTICAL GRAPHTINGS: TOWARD A PARAMODERN AUTOAESTHETIC

In brief, the development of language and the development of consciousness (*not* of reason but merely of the way reason enters consciousness) go hand in hand. Add to this that not only language serves as a bridge between human beings but also a mien, a pressure, a gesture. The emergence of our sense impressions into our consciousness, the ability to fix them and, as it were, exhibit them externally, increased proportionately with the need to communicate them to *others* by means of signs. The human being inventing signs is at the same time the human being who becomes ever more keenly conscious of himself.

—*The Gay Science* 354

The drive toward the formation of metaphors is the fundamental human drive, which one cannot for a moment dispense with in thought, for one would thereby dispense with man himself.

—"On Truth and Lies in a Nonmoral Sense" 88–89

9

◆

Opening the
Dialectics of Writing:
Heraclitus/Nietzsche

I set apart with high reverence the name of *Heraclitus*. When the rest of the philosopher-crowd rejected the evidence of the senses because these showed plurality and change, he rejected their evidence because they showed things as if they possessed duration and unity. Heraclitus too was unjust to the senses, which lie neither in the way the Eleatics believe nor as he believed—they do not lie at all. It is what we *make* of their evidence that first introduces a lie into it, for example the lie of unity, the lie of materiality, of substance, of duration.... Reason is the cause of our falsification of the evidence of the senses. In so far as the senses show becoming, passing away, change, they do not lie.... But Heraclitus will always be right in this, that being is an empty fiction. The "apparent" world is the only one: the "real" world has only been *lyingly added* ....
—*Twilight of the Idols*, "Reason in Philosophy," 2[1]

No treatment of the Modernism that Nietzsche critiqued and undermined so forcefully could ignore the facet of that program asserting the "lie" of contemporary (post-Socratic) philosophy and the highly dialectical literature it generates. Even when the Modernist agenda shows its more positive force, as in the remarkable concluding paragraph of *Daniel Martin*, the elliptical limitations of its always partial opening of the dialectics of writing frustrate it. The seemingly positive but elusively chimerical narrative assertion of Fowles' ending, placed in a Nietzschean context, though a quantum leap from the pessimistic Modernist framework we saw in the earlier works of literature we examined, is still a leap not into an abyss but across into another possible (para-)tradition already at work, an autoaesthetic *accompaniment* to Modernism adumbrated in Heraclitus and articulated by Nietzsche, a Paramodern[2] reorientation of the readerly and writerly within a

214

dialectic of self-assertion, self-dismissal, and self-interrogation. Fowles grafts onto his Modernist certitude, in the end, a Paramodern coda that throws into a different register everything that has preceded it. He charts a divergent, subversive (of Modernism) course for the novel we are reading, after we have read it, transforming any subsequent reading into a Paramodern one.

This, too, then, has been a book about avatars; one of Nietzsche's most important was Heraclitus, who showed him the way to the fuller meaning—and the richer danger—of Paramodern *étrangeté*. Nietzsche's conclusion cited above, from *Twilight of the Idols*, at the end of his writing life, demonstrates the centrality to his work not only of Heraclitus' understanding of what he called will-to-power but the adumbration in Heraclitus of autoaesthetic force juxtaposed against what would become the Western metaphysic. His tribute to Heraclitus, among the last of Nietzsche's references to the philosopher with whom he felt the closest kinship (except for his troubled kinship with Socrates), and with whom he compared himself throughout his life,[3] displays the reverent son contending with the original (absent), totemic father, and this is just how he saw his relationship with the Heraclitus who provided the impetus for Nietzsche's *Weltanschauung*: the driving of forces and the energy of inquiry propel Nietzsche into that "total instability of all reality" we have seen at work in *Daniel Martin*, through which, as *Zarathustra* argues, the Overman might appear. The world Heraclitus points toward is a dialectical, *fictional* one of drives and metaphors, manifesting itself as the working out of Dionysian process. This is how writing operates, Heraclitus shows Nietzsche: the plenteous dialectical chaos of his (of any) text discloses autoaesthetic paratexts. Nietzsche's self-reflexive project is to re-instill the rich Heraclitan dialectic in an enervated Positivist world: "Let us confess how utterly our modern world lacks the whole type of a Heraclitus, Plato, Empedocles, and whatever other names these royal and magnificent hermits of the spirit had."[4] Nietzsche reminds us about these hermits of the spirit in order to counteract Modernism's lies, to use his own strong word. From his condemnation of the "Modern"(/Modernist) world in *Beyond Good and Evil*, Nietzsche moves through and ostensibly beyond dialectic to the yes-saying of the *Genealogy of Morals*:

> From now on, man is *included* among the most unexpected and exciting lucky throws in the dice game of Heraclitus' "great child," be he called Zeus or chance; he gives rise to an interest, a tension, a hope, almost a certainty, as if with him something were announcing and preparing itself, as if man were not a goal but only a way, an episode, a bridge, a great promise.[5]

The Dionysian, Zarathustran "promise" of humankind, of the receptive and energetic "child," lies in that typical string of sliding appositives with which

Nietzsche articulates him/it. This is the chimerical promise of the textualized Overman, and the power of the self-constitutive fictions out of which the world (of experience) can be transformed. Nietzsche's initial "from now on," a manifesto for the Overman, is inspired by Heraclitus' "dice game" (we must remember it in terms of its Nietzschean dialectical treatment in Derrida's "Double Session" in *Dissemination*, let alone in his concept of the *pharmakon*[6]) and leads to the struggle between each of the terms by which man is "included" in this abysmal dialectic. The great Heraclitan *agon*, with its clashing of forces, is revealed as an overflowing of the realm of language. Jaspers summarizes this Heraclitan drive and its influence on Nietzsche thus:

> From beginning to end Heraclitus, as the philosopher of becoming, is *the* philosopher to Nietzsche. Never does he write anything derogatory of him. Even in his first account of the philosophy of Heraclitus [in *Philosophy in the Tragic Age of the Greeks*], he presents, in effect, his own conception of becoming and, therewith, of the strife of opposites that underlies the constant movement as well as his thoughts about necessity, justice, and the innocence of becoming.[7]

The (beyond) dialectics of Paramodernist writing opens up to Nietzsche in this immanent strife of opposites posited by Heraclitus, tailor-made by history for his dialectical role in that he is almost entirely fictional: no firmly known dates, no substantial writings other than in quoted and cited fragments referenced by other writers of antiquity. "He" is an originless, metonymical text, a para-philosopher, an articulation of the *étrangeté* forming the autoaesthetic Nietzsche's "artist thought."[8]

> Wisdom is one thing: to be skilled in true
> judgement, how all things are steered through
> all.[9]

> —Heraclitus

Despite the obvious irony, for Heraclitus as for Nietzsche, knowledge, wisdom, insight, and writing all began in exegesis; indeed, philosophy in the Heraclitan mode is itself exegesis. But this is highly complex. In Heraclitus' formulation of the basis of wisdom, one sees, from a distance, those sliding Nietzschean appositives as *two* things (thus potentially more) or, indeed, as *nothing*. The balance and poise of Heraclitus' mock-dogmatic formulation undermines itself *at the colon*, speaking double. Heraclitus adumbrates the program by which what Nietzsche calls modern thought will come about; all writing is writing after the colon.

This is not only grammatical; it is grammatological in its allusive slippage. Given Nietzsche's concern with *health* and the body, the physical analogy of this Heraclitan *colon* should not be lost. Writing is always a dialectic of expulsion and retention. The interrogation in which writing is produced is a follow-on to a process of consumption that, even if it is satisfying, must *organically* lead to expression.[10] This "writing after the colon," some of the implications of which Derrida discusses in *Writing and Difference*, also implies the spatial/physical order of writing, as well as the "order" of the sphere of physicality, from the sexual to the respiratory to the imaginative, by which literature and writing have traditionally metaphorized themselves. The colon is the articulation[11] of what is revealed as missing.

Heraclitus demonstrates this: taken literally, "wisdom is one thing" is nonsense; its copula of equivalency, "wisdom = one thing," is at once indeterminate and overdetermined.[12] Following the colon, Heraclitus' second "sentence" undercuts the problematic closure of the first even as it purports to act as its completion. One must first ask if this reversal is a *dénouement*, whether the qualification of the second clause enhances or cancels the difficulties encountered in the first.[13]

These inquiries invite another opening of the aphorism. Heraclitus here pretends to philosophy-as-science, by which one may "know" "things," yet, in appealing to the imagination, it collapses together science, art (poetry), and language in an adumbration of their cross-absorption in Nietzsche:

> A quantum of force is equivalent to a quantum of drive, will, effect— more, it is nothing other than precisely this very driving, willing, effecting, and only owing to the seduction of language (and of the fundamental errors of reason that are petrified in it) which conceives all effects as conditioned by something that causes effects, by a "subject," can it appear otherwise.[14]

Nietzsche follows Heraclitus' lead, locating science within language (within *logos*). And yet judgment continues, for Heraclitus and for Nietzsche, as a bastion[15] against disorder; the primacy of reason (and the tradition that privileges it) derives from a response to this fear of disorder, chance, unpredictability. Judgment—even Nietzschean evaluation—is a positive force for order, the first of the Socratic virtues (the second is that the only "sin" is ignorance; the corollary third virtue is that the virtuous man is a happy man). This impetus to the unity, truth, and goodness of knowledge is the Socratic counterattack against Heraclitan force, characterized by Nietzsche as a reverence for a love of "error, the mother of knowledge."[16] Science is thus a foil in the Heraclitan dialectic, seeming to embody or to demonstrate the ability to manifest knowledge as an answer to questions one poses about the world while sliding inevitably (as does Derrida at the conclusion of *Dissemination*, for example, and Nietzsche *passim*) into condensed poetic language: for Heraclitus, knowledge is only to be had in our search for it. In this Heraclitan definition of "science" is the root of Nietzsche's usage, as in

The Gay Science, where its meaning is ironized and multiple: for Nietzsche, as for Heraclitus, "science" and poetry are equally explanatory, a kind of Daedalian flight.

When Heraclitus declares that "war is the father of all things," his "war," like that of Nietzsche, is the persistent human activity of contest, striving, the working of *Eris*, the goddess of discord, as Nietzsche discusses it in "Homer's Contest," where victory and defeat are secondary to contest itself. Exegesis is, in this respect, as contest and paradox a wresting forth of that which the process of exegesis itself posits. This pseudo-extraction is the force behind the Hellenic notion of culture, metaphorized and made central to thought, as judgment.[17] Nietzsche, in his assessment of this Hellenic phenomenon, instructs us that

> the strife of the opposites gives birth to all that comes to be; the definite qualities which look permanent to us express but the momentary ascendency of one partner. But this by no means signifies the end of the war; the contest endures in all eternity. Everything that happens, happens in accordance with this strife.[18]

Indeed, as Nietzsche points out, every *thing* that happens, including the "thing" called wisdom, happens within the *agon* of *étrangeté*. This organic, progenitive image forms a cosmic vision of contest: Heraclitus' "War is the father of all things" becomes Nietzsche's "Strife is the perpetual food of the soul."[19] For Heraclitus, thoughts move in a world of purportedly free-standing but in fact deeply buttressed metaphor/metonymy.

The implications of Heraclitus' flux ("Nothing is still; all is flux") show us a way to account for the Modern and, in fact, the writerly "post-modern."[20] Writing itself serves up to the philosopher and the artist a response to its own inherently indeterminate act, in the same way as does Heraclitus' pronouncement: a necessary veil of solidity. The moment we ask the Nietzschean "What kind of statement is 'all in flux'?" we submit ourselves to the obliquity of the existence not only of a satisfactory response but of this very question's validity beyond its formulation, since, when it is substantiated in the power of entablature (when it is written), its problematic nature is enhanced simply because it is codified. For Nietzsche and his theoretical and literary progeny, the entire concept of *Weltanschauung* has been inverted, transposing itself into an inverted mirror of the world; that is, into metonymy. Heraclitus' "currency" for the "modern" conceptual world lies in this metaphoric indeterminacy: Heraclitus points us directly toward a questioning of the inclusionary, from Aristotle to Schopenhauer to Sartre to Derrida. But equally, Heraclitus seems to echo an engagement with language we see in Joyce, according to Beckett: as not *about* something; *it is that something itself*.[21] In this momentum, the equally problematic space of "modern philosophy" reveals itself as a revolutionary, even insurrectionary, phenomenon receiving its impetus from a new awareness of the power of discourse.

> The fairest order in the world is a heap of
> random sweepings.[22]

> —Heraclitus

Heraclitus' exegetical concern, which informs the rift Nietzsche brings to autoaesthetic interpretation, makes its appearance in this declaration of the conundrum of Paramodern exegetical order; the clause is a tightrope between the Modern and the autoaesthetic Paramodern. In the paradoxical context of order/randomness, the "judgment" declared in Fragment D41, with which we began, is revealed as being not nearly as simple, not as straightforward nor unified, as we might have thought—and as Heraclitus wants to insist. In the metonymic of "random sweepings" forming the heap of order, of which Beckett makes so much,[23] this discussion of the "fairest order" (*kosmos*) is itself the sweeping together of fragments as the Paramodern *telos* of exegesis. In true Paramodern fashion, that "fairest order/ *kosmos*" is a collapsing together of contemporary meanings (cosmos as best, universal world order) and of a meaning already archaic to Heraclitus's time but detectable here, *kosmos* as "adornment," an added attraction, an embellishment; that is, as used by Heraclitus, *kosmos* (as the Modernist ideal) is itself a supplement, a heap of random sweepings, among whose elements are preordination, fate, chance, and the (writing) hand of the sweeper.

Central among this aphorism's sweepings are the various disparate harmonics of *kosmos*.[24] A Paramodern/Modern harmonic focus in Heraclitus is the simpler historical/dialectical opposition between Heraclitus and Parmenides, expressly important to Nietzsche.[25] Heraclitus is Nietzsche's dark precursor, an originary (fictional) giant whose "style" (and this must be set aside in quotation marks, because we know nothing of Heraclitus's style, only the evidence of that small heap of strategically random sweepings) Nietzsche co-opts, and who is held up as polyphiloprogenitor. Thus, the Heraclitus/Parmenides "debate," seen in the formative historical framework of afterthought, engenders an autoaesthetic, metaphilosophical one at work in Heraclitus's metonymic first principles, which as Nietzsche points out are radically different from those of his philosophic ancestors and contemporaries. His championing of fire as primal substance is a case in point. The "primal element" discussion is a familiar part of early Greek philosophy, of course, as Nietzsche reminds us in *Philosophy in the Tragic Age of the Greeks*, but for Heraclitus the primal substance is not merely substantial fire but metaphoric fire; Heraclitus transforms Anaximander's primal element theory, according to Nietzsche, into a rising action toward the *Übermensch*:

"The period in which the world hurries toward the conflagration and dissolves into pure fire Heraclitus characterizes, with notable emphasis, as a desire, a want, or lack; the full consumption in fire he calls satiety."[26] In this instant of "satiety," Nietzsche goes on, the "world" transcends itself and is "seized by its need to create. Not hybris but the ever self-renewing impulse to play calls new worlds into being,"[27] and this play, an urge that "combines and joins and forms its structures regularly,"[28] leads directly to the Nietzschean (auto)aesthetic:

> Only aesthetic man can look thus at the world, a man who has experienced in artists and in the birth of art objects how the struggle of the many can yet carry rules and laws inherent in itself, how the artist stands contemplatively above and at the same time actively within his work, how necessity and random play, oppositional tension and harmony, must pair to create a work of art.[29]

Autoaesthetic man's primal nature, the urge toward an *artful* response to a lack, proceeds from his perception of the condition of flux in which the world *and the world of language* operate.[30] As inventor and manipulator of the power of "structure" to generate the conditions by which the world is textualized, Heraclitus is the originator of the rhetorical complement of dialectical opposition:

> The strife of opposites gives birth to all that comes-to-be; the definitive qualities which look permanent to us express but the momentary ascendency of one partner. But this by no means signifies the end of the war; the contest endures in all eternity. Everything that happens, happens in accordance with this strife.[31]

Heraclitus is the first not only to establish, but to establish *in order to question*, the autoaesthetic exegetical process and to engage in an exegesis of exegesis itself, that is, to identify exegesis as an artful self-attribution in articulation and *étrangeté*. For Heraclitus, fire is the primal element not in the way that water is for Anaximander; we might say that the Heraclitan world is *like* fire, perceived as always changing. That is, for Heraclitus, the *physis* of the world originates in the perception beyond metaphor of metonymic difference in the autoaesthetic beholder, in which the world's *logos* comes about through a ubiquitous transference (articulation) of desire or lack.[32] Heraclitus' "real" world, Nietzsche shows us, is in a way similar to the apocryphal register of the real in Lacan, "lyingly added" to the apparent one. Once established in Heraclitus, this autoaesthetic is pervasive: Jaspers' statement that all knowledge is a product of exegesis, that "there are no things in themselves and there is no absolute knowledge; the perspectivistic, illusory character belongs to existence,"[33] comes directly from the Heraclitan questioning of exegesis as the self-reflexive textualizing of experience.

Heraclitus' originality may point toward a Zarathustran solipsism, but not an isolated one; indeed, the Paramodern idea of originality as pervasive relationality finds its first articulation here. He writes within an already strong tradition; this is one of the most important aspects of his rebellious stance, which would not be possible without that context. Like Nietzsche, Heraclitus seeks that elusive philosophical grail of some final unification. When he says that "Wisdom is one thing," or that "Writing is one and the same," he expresses this *desire* for unity. He is pervasively concerned with the order of the universe and man's self-created place in it, as well as with problems of language, meaning, and communication. But as in Nietzsche, Heraclitus' inquiry into unity produces only difference and subversion. As Hans Vaihinger shows, Nietzsche links himself with Heraclitus (referring to the two of them as "we philosophers,"[34] to the exclusion of all others) with this autoaesthetic, articulated distinction:

> Parmenides said: "We do not think that which is not."—
> We at the other extreme say: "What can be thought must
>   certainly be a fiction."[35]

Not only does what Nietzsche treats as the Heraclitan *arche*-trace form a critique of philosophical "truth" preceding his own, from Thales, Pythagoras, Anaximander; further, he lays out the opening of a new narrative dialectic, based on perpetual difference. Thus, Anaximander's primal water *could not* be primal, because metaphorized it engenders stasis, not change; it signifies, for Heraclitus, a metaphoric principle of passivity not of perpetual action, and Heraclitus' world is fabricated of self-difference, divisibility, providing the relational tension required for existence.[36] For Heraclitus, thought is aimed like an arrow at explanation or explication and thus at exegesis and an ensuing judgment, not only of phenomena but of ethical relationships and of the implicit ideology in which they exist and operate. Yet here, too, Heraclitus stands apart from his historic peers while remaining in a Paramodern sense within his tradition, showing us a world of ideological tensions among paradigms of revaluation, in which those tensions do not cancel nor balance one another out but are re-energized by their juxtaposition.[37]

Yet, in the last aphorism above, Heraclitus can still be seen as part Paramodern, desiring to show that *true* self-knowledge must coincide with *kosmos* (world order) and, indeed, that *kosmos* and *logos* are identical. Although this initiates a radical re-reading of the nature of *logos*, and one that rendered him strategically peripheral to the soon-to-be-dominant hegemonic tradition,[38] Heraclitus consistently shows not unity but complementarity-in-difference. We have seen how what remains of his writing style, the fragment, contributes to this difference. This form itself is the precursor to an alternative philosophical and (auto)aesthetic tradition, introducing into mainstream philosophic discussion dialogue between style—one might even say condensed poetic style, since Nietzsche makes so much of Heraclitan terseness—and logical thought, making a connection between while assuming the separation of the so-called "substance" of thought and its formulation. Indeed, trying to capture Heraclitus' tension of rhetorical forces, this last is the sort of sentence that sometimes results. As a solipsist in a gregarious world, with no disciples or associates, with a deep scorn—born of proto-Nietzschean frustration—for the shallowness of the *demos*,[39] Heraclitus reinvents the *thought* of philosophy, perpetrating what is, for Nietzsche, "the equivalent of an earthquake," according to Georges Bataille, "robbing the earth of its stability." When Bataille declares that Nietzsche describes Heraclitus "in images that he used ten years later to describe the death of God, images of total yet brilliantly glorious fall,"[40] he shows another side of the Paramodern autoaesthetic, an inheritance of the fall from a Heraclitus who declares, in Fragment CXV, that "the mysteries current among men initiate them into impiety," that philosophic inquiry leads to an overturning of *doxa*, that "impiety" is the *natural* product of genuine inquiry.[41] Derrida's *pharmakia*[42] thus continues the Nietzschean discussion of a Heraclitan issue: articulation as the *topos* of *agon* as a reversal of dominant hegemonic usage. Plato's cautionary antidote (*pharmakon*) to Heraclitus, his assertion that writing is no more valuable as a remedy than as a poison, is re-reversed in Nietzsche, since interpretation and exegesis are themselves *pharmakia*, conveying while denying, instilling while removing.

Heraclitus' subtle *étrangeté* is revealed in his tacit dialogue with Parmenides. Their emblematic relationship is a prototype of Modernist/Paramodernist relationality, the ontological and epistemological groundwork for discussion of the nature of the self. For Heraclitus, the ontological opening is one of eternal recurrence, his "becoming," as Nietzsche will define it later; for Parmenides, Being, in what we would now call the Heideggerian sense, is *logos* itself.[43] According to Heidegger's interpretation of this relationship, as he discusses it in "Being and Thought" in the *Introduction to Metaphysics*, for Parmenides, being (*einai*) and thought (*noein*) are one. Man, according to Heidegger, is "deep in Being." Heidegger, appropriately for his own exegetical program, sees Parmenides as the advocate of existence as oneness is/of/with Being, while Heraclitus' world consists of flux, becoming, the denial of Being. Therefore, for Heidegger, Heraclitus' "error" is his misunderstanding of the world as flux, as ground, rather than the unity of Being. For Nietzsche's Heraclitus, what Heidegger attacks is to be applauded. What Heidegger does not and could not take into account (given his model of philosophy) is that, while Parmenides cannot perceive it, his theory that change cannot exist[44] is a product of *dialectical necessity*, articulated out of Heraclitus' perpetually disturbing rhetoric.

But this attempted murder can also be seen in light of Heraclitan complementarity. The passage with which this chapter begins, from *Twilight of the Idols*, responds directly to the autoaesthetic complementarity Nietzsche saw in Parmenides and Heraclitus: exegesis is not a question of one's *knowing* explanation or judgment, but an appropriation, an application and an attribution of meaning within a teleological strategy. Heraclitus thus pushes Parmenides to exegetical extremes as well as to the founding of a powerful (mainstream) philosophy: Parmenides' denial of the senses, and by extension of empirical and epistemological certitude, is a privileging of the insensible, the first claim in our tradition of the supremacy of thought over empirical evidence.[45] In his response to Heraclitus, Parmenides is "the first to exalt the intelligible at the expense of the sensible,"[45] to venerate thought: sense verification (which he calls "interference") is a part of the "pure illusion" of human interpretation.

Parmenides could not have pursued his own ideas without Heraclitus' challenge to *kosmos*; yet, from Heraclitus' viewpoint, Parmenides is not an opponent but an alternative voice, another in the heap of sweepings. Indeed, catalyzed by Heraclitus, Parmenides adds a vital autoaesthetic element to Heraclitan proto-grammatology: in refuting Heraclitan flux (and the implied centrality of metaphoric language), Parmenides reflects on the logic of words themselves, making his rhetoric the foundation of a theory that exists, as it were, only in its declaration. This is precisely the point Nietzsche makes as will-to-power transmutes from *The Birth of Tragedy* to *The Antichrist* and *Twilight of the Idols*: the opposing forces of Dionysus and Apollo collapse to form a single, unified *set* of oppositions, collapsed within the Dionysian, to indicate what Heraclitus calls "the counter-thrust" that, paradoxically, "brings together," such that "from tones at variance comes perfect attunement," since "all things come to pass through conflict."[47]

For Heraclitus as for Nietzsche, "perfect attunement" is possible only in the dialectical autoaesthetic of art's *étrangeté* within Parmenidean (read mainstream) culture. The poet owes a debt to the semantic tradition of unified opposition Heraclitus and Parmenides represent, as Richard Rorty points out, since the stasis of mainstream (Modernist) culture tinges poetry's Heraclitan metaphorics with what Rorty calls its "deliciously naughty thrill":[48] the poetic ironist owes far more to "the tradition of Western metaphysics than does the scientist. The scientific culture could survive a loss of faith in the tradition, but the literary culture might not."[49] The "naughty thrill" of the Paramodern begins in the alterity and play of Heraclitan flux within a Nietzschean context, as Rorty shows:

In the wake of Nietzsche's questioning of "the will to truth" and Heidegger's questioning of the "metaphysics of presence," a series of critics (notably Derrida) have been trying to do away with the notion of "referent" and saying things like "there is nothing outside the text." One could see this swelling chorus as auguring "the end of metaphysics"—as signalling the beginning of our liberation from the Parmenidean tradition. One could see Borges and Nabokov, Mallarmé and Valéry and Wallace Stevens, Derrida and Foucault, as guiding us out of the world of subject-and-object, word-and-meaning, language-and-world, and into a newer and better intellectual universe, undreamt of since the Greeks first made those fateful distinctions between *nomos* and *physis*, *episteme* and *poiesis*, which have haunted the West. But this would, I think, be a great mistake. It would be better to see these people as using the Parmenidean tradition as a dialectical foil, in whose absence they would have nothing to say.[50]

For Nietzsche or Derrida to claim their deconstructed world as a "newer and better intellectual universe" would be impossible, since, as Rorty rightly asserts, the Paramodern strategy, back to Heraclitus, is dialectical and interrogative (Nietzsche and Derrida amanuenses take note).

> The lord whose oracle is in Delphi neither
> declares nor conceals, but gives a sign.[51]
>
> —Heraclitus

As for the Delphic sign-giver, for Heraclitus, *ex-egeisthai* ("to lead or guide out") is inherently a comment on the very nature of dialectical interpretation, and thus on the act of guiding (as is *theoria* in its sense of "sending ambassadors to the oracle"). As our semiotic ambassadors, Heraclitus' fragments become the first great parables in Western literature, despite their inadvertent participation in the history of aphoristic style.[52] Containing in their play of form and content their own inversion, they are signs, as Heraclitus attests. The slippage of this semiotic *étrangeté* signals the auto-aesthetic *unknowable* which is simultaneously conceded and denied. Heraclitus' method of operation is "like that of the Delphic oracle."[53] Fragmentation in the Heraclitan sense is parable, neither uttering nor hiding but offering a semiotic alternative, a deviation.[54] As for his overhearers, "Not comprehending, they hear like the deaf. The saying is their witness: absent while present."[55] Men "hear like the deaf," that is, *ab-surd-ly*, literally out of the silence. Heraclitus' implication is that we do not "hear" at all but receive and translate signs referable only through indirection. Nietzsche's writing (re)constructs Heraclitan strategy. When Nietzsche "sets up an exegesis of the exegetical process itself,"[56] he acknowledges the Heraclitan economy of becoming.[57]

The Heraclitan Nietzsche comes to full expression in *Ecce Homo*'s analysis of *The Birth of Tragedy*, which in parabolic Nietzschean fashion he accomplishes by quoting lines from *Twilight of the Idols*:

> Saying Yes to life even in its strangest and hardest problems; the will to life rejoicing over its own inexhaustibility even in the sacrifice of its highest types—that is what I call Dionysian, that is what I understood as the bridge to the psychology of the tragic poet. . . . I have looked in vain for signs of it even among the *great* Greeks in philosophy, those of the two centuries *before* Socrates. I retained some doubt in the case of *Heraclitus*, in whose proximity I feel altogether warmer and better than anywhere else. The affirmation of passing away *and destroying*, which is the decisive feature of a Dionysian philosophy; saying Yes to opposition and war; *becoming*, along with a radical repudiation of the very concept of being—all this is clearly more closely related to me than anything else thought to date.[58]

The "warmth" of proximity to Heraclitus' metaphoric fire is a textual absorption of Heraclitus' *étrangeté*. In Nietzsche's metaphoric sublimation of "passing away" while eternally returning through the Gate of Moment, we see the most powerful becoming of autoaesthetics, transformed through *parabole* into a new kind of ironic god. Heraclitus has even foreshadowed this prior Crucified:

> God is day night, winter summer, war peace, satiety hunger,—*all the opposites, this is the meaning*—and undergoes alteration in the way that fire, when it is mixed with spices, is named according to the scent of each of them.[59]

"God" is the *étrangeté* of textuality itself; its power that of its style and grounding metaphoricity. Nietzsche shows that to read the signs of this *sophia* of *étrangeté* is to be wise indeed. *Etrangeté* is the unnamable; as Heraclitus put it in his Zarathustran way, "The wise is one alone, unwilling and willing to be spoken of by the name of Zeus."[60] The Nietzsche of *The Will to Power*, that is, the apocryphal Nietzsche of Elizabeth Förster-Nietzsche, is in the same position as Heraclitus in Diels' hands, but this textual *agon* contributes to Nietzsche's fascination with Heraclitan autoaesthetics, as he declares in "The Philosopher":

> The reason why *indeterminable* philosophizing retains some value, and for the most part a higher value than a scientific proposition, lies in the *aesthetic* value of such philosophizing, its beauty and sublimity . . . as a *work of art*. . . . In other words, the *aesthetic* consideration is decisive, not the pure *knowledge drive*. The poorly demonstrated philosophy of Heraclitus possesses far more artistic value than do all the propositions of Aristotle.[61]

Nietzsche found himself employing Heraclitus' aggressiveness to combat what Bataille calls his "happy yet somber receptiveness of life."[62] Nietzsche enlists Heraclitus to fan his rage against the introduction into a "tumultuous humanity" of "the principle, still weak, but bearing with it the quality of *immutability*, of the *GOOD*."[63] This is the genealogical link Nietzsche evokes when he calls Heraclitus "my ancestor,"[64] in *Genealogy of Morals*,[65] speaking only of himself and Heraclitus as "we philosophers." Heraclitus shows Nietzsche the meta-philosophical option, the very "darkness" Nietzsche so admires in Heraclitus, as in Section 24 of *The Birth of Tragedy*, admired for its disruptive, "primordial delight" in enigma.

Nietzsche carries this admiration even further into the open, as we have glimpsed, in *Twilight of the Idols*. The epigraph of this chapter, in which Nietzsche takes Heraclitus to task for his injustice to the senses, now appears in a different light, and needs to be reviewed:

> I set apart with high reverence the name of *Heraclitus*. When the rest of the philosopher crowd rejected the evidence of the senses because these showed plurality with change, he rejected their evidence because they showed things as if they possessed duration and unity. Heraclitus too was unjust to the senses, which lie neither in the way the Eleatics believe nor as he believed—they do not lie at all. It is what we *make* of their evidence that first introduces a lie into it, for example the lie of unity, the lie of materiality, of substance, of duration. . . . "Reason" is the cause of our falsification of the evidence of the senses. In so far as the senses show becoming, passing away, change, they do not lie. . . . But Heraclitus will always be right in this, that being is an empty fiction. The "apparent" world is the only one: the "real" world has only been *lyingly added*. . . .[66]

This dialectical force, the autoaesthetic drive of eternal becoming in Heraclitus, is for Nietzsche the most profound insight into the Greek soul[67] and the way toward the Overman: "What he saw, the teaching of *law in becoming* and of *play in necessity*, must be seen from now on in all eternity. He raised the curtain on this greatest of all dramas."[68] The drama of dialectical struggle and the inherently dialectical struggle of language to articulate that drama take the form of an aphoristic and dramatically autoaesthetic dialogue between "I" and "you" (Heraclitus/Parmenides):

> Against positivism, which halts of phenomena—"There are only *facts*"—I would say: No, facts is precisely what there is not, only interpretations. We cannot establish any fact "in itself": perhaps it is folly to want to do such a thing.
>
> "Everything is subjective," you say; but even this is interpretation. The "subject" is not something given, it is something added and invented and projected behind what is there.—Finally, is it necessary to posit an interpreter behind the interpretation? Even this is invention, hypothesis.
>
> Insofar as the word "knowledge" has any meaning, the world is know-

able; but it is *interpretable* otherwise, it has no meaning behind it, but countless meanings.—"Perspectivism."

It is our needs that interpret the world; our drives and their For and Against. Every drive is a kind of lust to rule; each one has its perspective that it would like to compel all other drives to accept as a form.[69]

This, then, is the thought that flows through and yet is lyingly added to all things, the opening of the dialectics of writing. Nietzsche treats Heraclitus as the "proud and lonely truth-finder,"[70] a Zarathustran *text* of autoaesthetic exegesis,[71] learning from Heraclitus and defining for the Paramodern how to reevaluate the dialectics of *étrangeté* in terms of an autoaesthetics of graphing and grafting beyond reason. Only when the artist of *sophia* perceives the Heraclitan tension of alterity in the grapheme, and in the unwritten and the unwritable self, does he become the lucky throw of the dice, the great promise that remains, eternally, a promise, a bridge, a literary episode.

10

◆

Dialectics of the Unwritten Self: Nietzsche/Joyce/ (Mallarmé/)Beckett

> The Phenomenon "artist" is still the most
> *transparent*:—to see through it to the *basic
> instincts of power*, nature, etc.!
> —*Will to Power*, 797

> One is an artist at the cost of regarding what
> non-artists call "form" as *content*, as "the issue
> itself." One then certainly belongs in an *inverted
> world*: thenceforth content is something merely
> formal,—our life included.
> —*Will to Power* 818

> Where now? Who now? When now?
> Unquestioning. I, say I.
> —Beckett, *The Unnamable*, 291

In allowing for the possibilities of transformation from a paradigm of self to one of self-in-language to one of self-as-language, across the metonymic Paramodern tightrope, Nietzsche's dialogue of concealment and revelation between artist-thought and the artist-role plays a central part in the interrogative autoaesthetic dynamic of power we have been exploring. We have seen how this power is accessible only through the coding, decoding, recoding, and (impossible) exegesis of Paramodern metaphorics that I have looked at through the Heraclitan "grapht" but which forms the basis of contemporary literary theory's *art* as well. The artist's semiotic "gamble," a game the artist (like the Paramodern philosopher) always profitably loses, itself becomes the ground for a transformation into the heavily ironic quest for meaningful redemption, by the autoaesthetic self, played in a parodic register.[1] Caught within the playful shifts of the Paramodern, this irony is deepened by the fact that finally, for Nietzsche, transference is the only power redemptive in its circularity. Thus, the transference of autoaesthetics is a dialectical *prosopopoeia* and a conundrum of originality; for Nietzsche: "*Originality.*—what is originality? *To see* something that has as yet no name, and hence cannot be mentioned, even if it is in our very eye."[2] Originality is to be seen—and notice again here in Nietzsche, for the millionth time, the ocular image and the specter of originality—outside the dialectics of autoaesthetic art, as we have seen them laid out by Heraclitus, Nietzsche, Derrida. Nietzsche shows that the metaphor-making animal needs to claim the originary power to name in order to visualize, thus to reify, thus to redeem. Paramodern power in Nietzsche is tautologically positive even though, caught within the dialectics of writing, what is not written cannot claim conventional reality. For the autoaesthetic philosopher, this is clearly demonstrable, and I have tried to go some distance toward showing it in the "originary" case of Heraclitus and Nietzsche above.

Indeed, such diverse and un-Nietzschean figures as Bradley and Peirce show a more-than-subtle Nietzschean influence in their formulations of the cognitive process, particularly in the devaluation of rational thought's teleological possibilities. This is also true of William James, and I have addressed elsewhere the particular case of Freud within the Nietzschean orbit.[3] Henry Staten's *Wittgenstein and Derrida* shows clearly (while suppressing the name of Nietzsche) how the Wittgenstein of the *Philosophical Investigations* reorients meaning itself along a Nietzschean axis; in the same convergent vein, Heidegger's voluminous "re-justification" of Nietzsche (like his lectures on Heraclitus) indicates another facet of the obsession with Paramodern Nietzschean issues that twentieth-century thinkers manifest; and of course, the orientation of such latter-day luminaries as Foucault, Lacan, and Derrida derive, as their own multiple acknowledgments demonstrate, from Nietzsche's autoaesthetic.

But to take Nietzsche at his word, an already complicated proposition, we must look further, beyond philosophy (even a gay philosophy) to the autoaesthetic of twentieth-century literary art. Nietzsche offers a reappraisal of the graphtings of the Paramodernist avant-garde, formed from the dialectics of the search for a new concept of identity in writing, and from the very power of that search as it works through the Nietzschean strategy of interrogation and reversal, in which the poet/philosopher emerges as the (always fictional) paradigm of the modern *littérateur*. For Nietzsche, this apochryphal figure, the "real" autoaesthetic poet, is one who can combine the volcanic sensitivity and feeling of Dionysus/Empedocles with the rational framework of an Apollo/Socrates. To neglect either is to fail, as Nietzsche shows in his investigations (in *Zarathustra* and *Genealogy of Morals*) of the ascetic priest and his antithesis, the "blond beast," and their relationship to the artist.

In this light, I want to look briefly at some of the affinities and inversions in the relationship between these Nietzschean strategies and those on which Joyce, as quintessential Modernist, builds his Modernist graphted word bridges, then to traverse another of those bridges via Mallarmé's "Un Coup de dés" with its literal word bridges, and finally to point toward a contemporary Paramodern autoaesthetic in Beckett.

A Portrait of the Artist as a Young Man focuses and renders programmatic Nietzsche's aesthetic questions in a way that even Joyce's great subsequent novels do not. If *Ulysses* and *Finnegans Wake* are the "mature" works by which Joyce is usually judged the founder of modern prose writing, *A Portrait* is the autoaesthetic, *darker* novel to be seen as heir to the Heraclitan genealogical foundations to which I have been referring. *A Portrait* is not only *not* an immature work; it is an intricately subtle and complex, direct and indirect engagement with Zarathustran *artistic maturity* and with the ironies of genealogy (both Stephen Dedalus' and Joyce's),[4] it is this irony, simultaneously concealed and revealed, that Joyce fabricates into a project in which the supreme (Nietzschean) artist/thinker rules a kingdom of illusory yet teleological revaluation, and which yet hovers on the brink of the Paramodern, unwilling to relinquish its high Modernist certitude even in the face of the fragmented Paramodern themes with which it engages.

Thus, the autoaesthetic writer operates within a crisis of power, in which Nietzsche's model of interrogation acts as a new valuation of time and space itself, through the poetic image, and a renovated privileging of the desire that posits a *program* of self-overcoming as the supreme human task. Richard Rorty's assessment of the Nietzschean opening, as being against that in which "we want to posit 'behind' the language of *a* time and *a* space, a matrix of 'reality's own language' in the *double*, the 'Noumenal Self'—the soul,"[5] declares the radical nature of the rift Nietzsche proposes. The tendency of language to exercise its power by manifesting some purportedly pre-linguistic reality is not merely Platonic nostalgia, however. "Over-reaching" is itself the foundation of the *inner* tensions we have seen at play in Nietzsche and which energize Joyce's prose. Such a program of literary self-overcoming is an impossible one, a "desire to wipe out whatever came earlier, in the hope of reaching at last a point that could be called a true present, a point of origin that marks a new departure."[6] Indeed, we have seen this apocryphal "true present" in each of the Modernist writers at whom we have glanced here. Nietzsche, on the other hand, as Rorty's evaluation shows, is presentless, suspended between a past and a future and, at the same time, trying to annihilate them. Nietzsche's dilemma is with the temporal *unheimlich*, located at the Gate of Moment itself, and with its mimetic crisis in language, in the face of the "impetus to inclusion" he sees (disastrously) in operation all around him, just as Joyce's dilemma is with his own version of an estranged, *unheimlich*, the crisis of exile (silence and cunning). This accounts for the shocking or troubling darkness of the images with which Nietzsche often jolts us,[7] and explains the dark luminosity of Joyce's self-superceding *suspensions*, the purely autoaesthetic epiphanies across which *A Portrait* is composed.

A constant crisis evaluation of the uncanny acts as its own mesmerizing entrapment, formulated by Derrida as one in which "fulfillment is summed up within desire; desire is (ahead of) fulfillment, which, still mimed, remains desire, *'without breaking the mirror.'*"[8] Desire's primacy as a condition, ipso facto, reads itself as that urge of the artist to achieve *Selbstaufhebung*, a condition that Nietzsche and Joyce consider and show to be both culminative and deeply problematic in more than its schematic Hegelian terminology. For Hegel, *Aufhebung* is subsumption or inclusion and disappearance-into-solution simultaneously, toward a synthesis of rational plenitude; for Nietzsche, "overcoming" is cancellation and uplifting in quite a different way: it is used in the same way Joyce revitalizes the concept of "epiphany." Nietzschean self-overcoming (and *Selbstaufhebung* suffers already a major loss in translation) is a function of the strategy of interrogation, of its inversion, and of irreconcilable oppositions that despite Hegel's desire can and must never be synthesized. Joyce's darkly positive and highly dialectical aesthetic vision in *A Portrait*, and subsequently in the two novels that follow, capitalizes emblematically on the Nietzschean opening of the dialectics of writing the unwritten self, never acquiescing in its disruptive program. In the end, Beckett's reply[9] to Joyce and to Modernism represents that other(ed) voice of the Paramodern, whose vestiges of humanistic warmth serve as encrypted reminders of Modernist hegemony caught nostalgically in a framework of strategic absence. Juxtaposed, particularly against the evidence of Mallarmé's "Un Coup de dés," Joyce and Beckett are the polar explorers of the Modernist/Paramodernist *glissage* Nietzsche articulates.

This is just how *A Portrait* opens.[10] Its thematic *agon* begins in the dialectical *étrangeté* of autoaesthetic narrativity itself, appropriately in a collapsed constellation of two voices, the father's and the emergent artist's: "Once upon a time and a very good time it was there was a moocow coming down along the road and this moocow that was coming down along the road met a nicens little boy named baby tuckoo. . . ."[11] The "double voice" here, read through Derrida's *The Ear of the Other* as the double voice of *étrangeté*, of the "uncanny ear,"[12] or as "the difference in the ear,"[13] is a sign of autoaesthetic transference symbolized by the literal transfer of narrative from father to son. Like so many Modernist heroes before him, Stephen Dedalus fledges himself from the *voice* of the father. Simon/Stephen's moocow story is also, of course, in terms of those other Modernist fathers, the Platonic birth of an Aristotelian catalogue of the senses, the sense of hearing to be followed immediately, through the liaison again of the father (voice to visage), by the sense of sight: "His father told him that story: his father looked at him through a glass: he had a hairy face." The novel's opening, a microcosmic synopsis, is itself synthesized in these two paragraphs.[14] The oddly metaphoric nature of Simon-God's telling straddles his sing-song lines so as to render us unable to avoid their tension of (physical) sense and articulation. Each word is itself a distillation of the dream of preordinate experience in the nascent autoaesthetic artist. Along with the opening of sense experience comes that of dialectical experience, and thus the advent of a sense of autoaesthetic power. The father "himself" is dispensable in Stephen's opening (or subsumable in other metaphoric fathers); his inscribed narrative voice is a quickening sign.

The development of the novel's initial section matures in schematic fashion.[15] The opening of Stephen's own *poetry*, however, is a further dialectical one, marking the advent of generic distinctions within the constellation of articulate will-to-power: sexuality, religion, society, tradition, language. In this respect, Stephen's mimetic introduction marks a series of leaps in progressive autoaesthetic power. We can actually watch this occur, through the second half of the aphoristically condensed introduction:

> The Vances lived in number seven. They had a different father and mother. They were Eileen's father and mother. When they were grown up he was going to marry Eileen. He hid under the table. His mother said:
> —O, Stephen will apologize.
> Dante said:

> —O, if not, the eagles will come and pull out his eyes.
> Pull out his eyes,
> Apologize,
> Apologize,
> Pull out his eyes.

> Apologize,
> Pull out his eyes.
> Pull out his eyes,
> Apologize.

This rippling expansion out (a powerful Modernist motif of lawful order and an image to be repeated many times in the novel) from the microcosm of the Dedalus flat into one containing the Vances shows us numerous fledgings, the most important of which is that of Eileen's introduction and the effect she has on Stephen's story. The play of sexual difference and the *étrangeté* of language marks Joyce's play with the requisite conditions for the inception of a Nietzschean poetics developed through the novel in each of the encounters Stephen has with E——— C———, with the prostitute at the conclusion of Chapter Two, and with the bird-girl on the beach at the conclusion of Chapter Four. Eileen Vance is their avatar, the supplanter of the mother, and the catalyst of autoaesthetic desire and poetics.

The progression from Stephen's hiding from Eileen to his neutralizing Dante's threat of damnation with his poem is one in which the valorization of *hiding* in a dialectic (and the actual dialogue of concealment and revelation) takes place. Confronted by evidence of ineluctable difference in the person of Eileen, "he hid under the table." Typically of Joyce, this sentence, a declarative grounding in the mundanity of diurnal experience itself, is written over something much darker and more fundamental. In *Zarathustra*'s "Seven Seals," with which Book Three concludes and which concerns itself with *nuptials*, Nietzsche introduces the manner in which Stephen's pun on "tables" can be read. Nietzsche's parable exclaims:

> If one breath came to me of the creative breath and the heavenly need, forced by chance to dance star-dances:
> If I laughed with the laughter of creative lightning, followed by the long thunder of the deed;
> If I played dice with the gods at the gods' table, the earth, until the earth shook and split and threw up flooding fire;
> For the earth is a god-table, and trembles with creative new words and gods' throws;
> Oh, how shall I not lust for eternity and after the nuptial ring of rings,—the ring of recurrence?
> Never yet have I found the woman from whom I wanted children, unless it is this woman, whom I love: for I love you, oh eternity!
> *For I love you, oh eternity!*

Nietzsche's sense of "table" here is precisely Joyce's: on the gods' table the world is written and, through the eternal recurrence (through self-interpretation and self-evaluation), underlies the revaluation of all values. Joyce's project is no less grand, despite his tiny, precious images. Stephen's confrontation with experience is itself entablature: *he* exercises the power of entabling, of *étrangeté*, to neutralize Dante's doxological threat to Eileen Vance. Here the Nietzschean bride becomes the provisional child-bride,[16] as the emblem of the poetic act's inception; that is, poetry emerges not from (a) birth but a marriage—it is not linear but dialectical.

For Joyce, then, power is the flow of dialectically concentrated textual forces, each "one in a series, to be revealed"; as for Nietzsche, the text of experience is an "inscription of forces, an invitation to unforeseen estrangements from the habitual,"[17] provisionally Modernist in Joyce, Paramodern in Nietzsche. Power over logic and habit is itself the opening of the uncanny text, the freeing of meaning-fabrication; as Peter Putz shows, for Nietzsche, "logical inconsistency . . . is not a sign of individual weakness" but "a principle of existence."[18] For Nietzsche as for Joyce, the fundamental poetic dialectic is one of will versus code.[19] But also, in this respect, Nietzschean genealogy when applied to the Joycean cosmos must allow a Modernist redemption without which Joyce cannot work. The Nietzschean dialectic points us toward what Jean-Michel Rey calls

> the impossibility of all stable, isolated signifiers, and thus the absence of all rigorous foundations of metaphysical truth . . . placed in the abyss by the unveiling of its arbitrary character in the system of metaphysical signifiers.[20]

In Nietzsche, truth is literally voided (we must remember that the "last pope" desires to become Zarathustra's disciple, even to make him a "new god," in the face of the absence of any other). For Nietzsche, self-overcoming occurs in *l'espace de l'après coup*, to use Jean-Michel Rey's Mallarméan formulation, and thus "in a space where origin is by necessity absent."[21] Privileging of the code's presence, as in Joyce, is always a repression of that other necessary absence. We begin to see how Nietzsche overcomes Joyce's redemptive language, which, though semi-detached from experience, still posits the artist's presence at its center, like the god of the creation.

We can see Joyce's struggle with Paramodern dialectics as it forges Stephen Dedalus' character out of Stephen Hero's. The Odyssean project Joyce laid out in the earlier, lost novel, and then condenses for *A Portrait*, contains the *donné* or lodestone (already split, however) of language imagery, on which Joyce/Stephen's transcendent language is based. The truly creative poet, according to Stephen Daedalus (whose name in that earlier work had not yet allowed the alpha to fall and be lost), is indeed dialectical, "a mediator . . . gifted with twin faculties, a selective and a reproductive,"[22] and this dialectic is infused with the vitality of poetic graphting. The selective and reproductive faculties, the former objective, empirical, Apollinian, the latter subjective, dream-oriented, Dionysian, must coincide perfectly in the perfect artist: a

> perfect coincidence of the two artistic faculties Stephen called poetry and he imagined the domain of an art to be cone-shaped. The term "literature" now seemed to him a term of contempt and he used it to designate the vast middle region which lies between apex and base, between poetry and the chaos of unremembered writing.[23]

This passage sets up the emblem and the conditions for the entire flight of apotheosized language in *A Portrait* and then into *Ulysses* and the *Wake*.

Stephen Daedalus constructs an un-ironized tightrope for the poet to walk, then stretches it *vertically*, recapitulating the Platonic order of forms, with an unreachable poetic perfection at its apex. Joyce's conditions for writing are those of Neoclassical Modernism itself, unalloyed and unchanged, whose very image or model in *Stephen Hero* is a nostalgic, emblematic, and regressive net in which Joyce/Stephen will be caught, no matter how innovative his linguistic experimentation. To manifest a perfect "reproductive" (mimetic) faculty, the poet must rise past the rank "chaos" of "unremembered writing," unworthy of the true poet, into "literature," which operates according to that archaic model.

In other words, Stephen Daedalus' program as he wants to manifest it shows no trace of the *étrangeté* with which Nietzsche approaches the artist's role, although certain kinds of irony are buried powerfully within it. What *can* be seen in the conic emblem of poetic aspiration is an adumbration of upward spiraling flight infusing the artist's project in *A Portrait*, transmuted into the metaphor of magical Daedalian flight: to "fly by" the nets of "nation, church, family." This "double-voiced" definition of poetic flight, to *fly past* those traps and to *be guided* by them, simultaneously to defeat and to be defeated by nets Stephen Daedalus associates with "unremembered writing," is indeed dialectical but is not Paramodern since, for Joyce, the magical artist, however invisible he may become, is still a powerful presence in his model. In Stephen Daedalus/Dedalus, this double voice is not the parodic one of the Nietzschean Paramodern but one of Modernist ambivalence, depicting the aspiring but always frustrated poet. Nietzsche possesses, so to speak, as Joyce does not, "knowledge of the impossibility of knowing," which "precedes the act of consciousness that tries to reach it."[24] For Nietzsche, humanness is inextricably caught in the *étrangeté* of an "infinite regression" resulting from a "prospective hypothesis" of a provisional future and a chimerical "reality that belongs to the past,"[25] while, for Joyce, such a regression is not infinite but firmly lodged in the interaction in the poetic double voice of the selective and the reproductive faculties, both Apollinian.

This tendentious upward spiral becomes the circularity of the *return* of Daedalian flight in *Ulysses*, Bloom's return to his home, Stephen's to his own through the June dawn, the return of language to its "unremembered" and lushly chaotic self-consciousness in Molly, and the final return of that affirmation with which she concludes, "Yes I said yes I will Yes." All of these returns are located solidly in character(s) whose self-formulation is richly human; the inherent *étrangeté* of language itself, the ultimate net by which they fly, is a separate issue. The development of *Ulysses'* affirmation into the circular sentence of *Finnegans Wake* is even clearer: the entire novel takes place within the period of the sentence, merging all experience and all language into a perpetual moment in which "riverrun, past Eve and Adam's, from swerve of shore to bend of bay, brings us by a commodious vicus of recirculation back to Howth Castle and Environs"; the very first word of *Finnegans Wake*'s circularity cannot be identified as noun or imperative verb form.[26] And yet this infinitely extended periodicity of the impossible world-sentence is still a significant step from the circular book at the heart of Borges' Library of Babel: the pervasive presence of the dreaming man/woman HCE/ALP is precisely the forged conscience of the race, the culmination of the Modernist Dedalean program as laid out at the conclusion of *A Portrait*, caught exuberantly in the final, eternal net of language.

Joyce privileges an aesthetics of this eternal moment from the first inscriptions of those epiphanies he recorded in his notebooks, which conclude each *Dubliners* story and each *Portrait* chapter. This Modernist transformation of the eternal return is what Joyce means by epiphany, the "poetic silence" Stephen's quasi-poetry aspires to but can never capture, the return to the sensorium and the mimetic imagination, the substantiation but separation of the inchoate poet.[27] Chapter One's conclusion, after Stephen asserts his (ocular) presence in the highly encoded world of Clongowes Wood, is just such a heightening:

> The fellows were practising long shies and bowing lobs and slow twisters. In the soft grey silence he could hear the bump of the balls: and from here and from there through the quiet air the sound of the cricket bats: pick, pack, pock, puck: like drops of water in a fountain falling softly in the brimming bowl.[28]

Each of the five chapter endings of *A Portrait*, like the stories in *Dubliners*, poetically rises through metaphoric exchange in a repeated recapitulation of the Aristotelian sensorium, in a series of steps leading toward the fledging of the poet. Progressively and schematically, Stephen must go through, first, a detachment from authority, then a sexual awakening, then a (false) epiphany in orthodoxy, then a poetic awakening as he perceives the difference between literature and poetry, and, finally, a transformation into the writing artist capable of producing that. At the end of Chapter One, as we have just seen, the conditions for Stephen's first-step epiphany have been fulfilled: "He was alone. He was happy and free."[29] But Stephen's aloneness, like his freedom, is dialogic. Stephen is *not* alone *except* within the context of the program he strives to learn, not free except as tightly restricted poet. What Stephen remains ignorant of, though it is only the thinnest membrane away, is not the aloof will-to-power of physical aloneness but his metaphysical aloofness, inscribed—entabled—in his rigid program of autoaesthetic discovery.[30]

Even more ironically, from the point of view of the frustration of any crossing into the Paramodern, Joyce uses the writing of the past, like the epiphany, in a very similar way to Nietzsche's: as a surface from which to propel himself.[31] This can be seen in each chapter-ending of *A Portrait*, in two important ways. The first is at the written surface of the novel. Each epiphany seems to achieve some sort of "conclusive unity," propelling Stephen forward out of an old sense of identity and toward a new, fuller and more poetic one that is, however, not only transcended in the following chapter but undermined and cancelled in a strategy that forces the reader to reassess the very *memory* of those seemingly satisfying conclusions, as *we too* spiral upward through the privileged literary realm. Chapter One's inclusive and powerful assertion of self-identity, in which Stephen feels "happy, alone, and free" as a result of his visit with Father Conmee, is painfully cancelled by Simon Dedalus' many-layered laughter in a conspiracy of father figures, reporting Conmee's narrative of Stephen's pandying and epiphanic self-assertion: "Father Dolan and I had a great laugh over it. *You better mind yourself, Father Dolan, said I, or young Dedalus will send you up for twice nine*. We had a famous laugh together over it. Ha! Ha! Ha!"[32] The jabs of the reported laughter, as sharp as the blow of a pandy-bat, work to adapt and even reverse our memory of Stephen's "pick, pack, pock, puck," the seemingly triumphant autoaesthetic conclusion of Chapter One, this reversal acting as an agent of propulsion into each subsequent chapter.

The same reversal occurs in the transition from Chapter Two to Three, as Stephen's first encounter with the imaginative liberation of sexuality becomes an obsession with sin. Chapter Two has concluded with the *overabundance* of the senses, in which Stephen, alone with a prostitute for the first time, succumbs to sexuality:

> He closed his eyes, surrendering himself to her, body and mind, conscious of nothing in the world but the dark pressure of her softly parting lips. They pressed upon his brain as upon his lips as though they were the vehicle of a vague speech: and between them he felt an unknown and timid pressure, darker than the swoon of sin, softer than sound or odour."[33]

This Aristotelian catalogue of the newly awakening senses, ripe with poetic hyperbole, in which the lips of the prostitute "press upon his brain" with "a vague speech," becomes in Chapter Three the catalogue of the deadly sins, the preamble for the famous retreat during which Stephen will vomit in disgust at his own sexual degradation. In the beginning of Chapter Three, Stephen reconsiders Shelley's poetic fragment on the companionless moon, and suddenly the stars begin to "crumble" and "fall," like Stephen himself. Stephen is reading in his "scribbler," and the "dull light on the page" becomes "his own soul going forth to experience, unfolding itself sin by sin, spreading abroad the balefire of its burning stars and folding back upon itself, fading slowly, quenching its own lights and fires. They were quenched:

and the cold darkness filled chaos."[34] So much, in the sixteen-year-old Stephen, for poetic enlightenment. This subversive, Modernist failure of the autoaesthetic process is recapitulated with each chapter transition: Chapter Three's religious indoctrination turns into Chapter Four's dogmatic automatonism, which is transmuted in Chapter Four into a provisional, epiphanic theory of art; this in turn transmutes in Chapter Five into a pedantic dilettantism ascending into the poetic (Daedalian) flight with which the novel ends.[35]

We glimpse a Nietzschean genealogy, a kind of Paramodern tendentiousness, in Joyce. The conditions set up in *A Portrait*, though solidly Modernist in their claim for a substantial, unironic language-value, establish a transmuting vision of a world in dialectical play, with negation and subversion, with knowing and with knowing that one does not know. This "final" implication of the will-to-power and the eternal return of articulation, inherent in writing itself, captures the writer and the reader in a condition of desire in which Zarathustra is the progenitor and which exposes both Nietzsche's and Joyce's Romantic roots. Richard Rorty claims that after Nietzsche, "it is simply no longer 'useful' to make a distinction between 'discovery' and 'creation,'"[36] since the "present" that would have distinguished between "that which matters supremely and the completely insignificant" is cancelled in the play between the Modern and the Paramodern toward which Joyce points.[37] Starting in the epiphany, the significant is identified as what is *left out*. In this we can recognize a potential liaison with the Paramodern Nietzschean style; *A Portrait* serves as a possible bridge (which will in the end only be a pier) across what Jean-Michel Rey ironically calls the "Nietzschean position," which

> decodes in the metaphysical text itself the procedures that constitute it around an absence,—that of the signifier. The text is put on stage, pluralized, subsumed in an operation of *Darstellung* by which the different implicated contradictions inherent within it reveal themselves.[38]

At the advent of the Paramodern artist-thought, the autoaesthetic nature of the text is that it is inherently theatrically self-questioning, an abyss over which the Zarathustran tightrope is stretched.[39] Joyce explores just this quality of exilic writing; Chapter Two is particularly full of this thematic, as the development of sexual awareness and of literary distance occur side by side. Stephen Dedalus' (unwritten) poem to Emma Clery is a good case in point. After his hallucinatory encounter with her on the tramcar, Stephen attempts to write his experience, but the writing, which Hugh Kenner calls a "Trojan horse by which the universe gets into the mind,"[40] permits him only the most interesting fantasies of connection and of history, all of which seem fragmented, ironic, and at a tremendous distance. It is not the experience of having confronted Emma that energizes Stephen but a kind of troubled Modernist Wordsworthism, whose tranquility is constantly in danger of being displaced into self-reflexive *angst*. Because of its highly energized quality of suspension between the doctrinaire framework of Modernist poise and parodic Paramodern distance, the passage is worth quoting in full:

> The next day he sat at his table in the bare upper room for many hours. Before him lay a new pen, a new bottle of ink and a new emerald exercise. From force of habit he had written at the top of the first page the initial letters of the jesuit motto: A.M.D.G.[41] On the first line of the page appeared the title of the verses he was going to write: To E——— C———. He knew it was right to begin so for he had seen similar titles in the collected poems of Lord Byron. When he had written this title and drawn an ornamental line underneath he fell into a daydream and began to draw diagrams on the cover of the book. He saw himself sitting at his table in Bray the morning after the discussion at the Christmas dinnertable, trying to write a poem about Parnell on the back of one of his father's second moiety notices. But his brain had then refused to grapple with the theme and, desisting, he had covered the page with the names and addresses of certain of his classmates:
>
>   Roderick Kickham
>   John Lawton
>   Anthony MacSwiney
>   Simon Moonan
>
> Now it seemed as if he would fail again but, by dint of brooding on the incident, he thought himself into confidence. During this process all these elements which he deemed common and insignificant fell out of the scene. There remained no trace of the tram itself nor of the trammen nor of the horses: nor did he and she appear vividly. The verses told only of the night and the balmy breeze and the maiden lustre of the moon. Some undefined sorrow was hidden in the hearts of the protagonists as they stood in silence beneath the leafless trees and when the moment of farewell had come the kiss, which had been withheld by one, was given by both. After this the letters L.D.S.[42] were written at the foot of the page and having hidden the book, he went into his mother's room and gazed at his face for a long time in the mirror of her dressingtable.[43]

Remembering Jude Fawley's mirror-gazing and all that it entails, particularly in light of the autoaesthetic *stade du miroir* we have examined elsewhere, Stephen's enervation as a poet is vital here. The scene's admixture of religion (the bare upper room and the heavy Jesuit atmosphere), literary history (Byron), his own literary past (the link to the post-Christmas-dinner failure to write), sexuality (the kiss and at the mother's dressingtable mirror)—these and other central themes of the novel must be juxtaposed with the fact that Stephen *does* write in this scene, though what he writes is hazy and uninformative ("the verses told only of the night") and, most importantly, not recorded in *A Portrait*. The reader receives only a vaguely narrated synopsis of this most important piece of developmental writing. We are given distant, objective narration and denied Stephen's verses.

More importantly, the experience of writing only serves to make the autoaesthetic Stephen question his own identity (the narration, like the dressingtable mirror, is another concealing table). Clearly, the world only exists through the mediation of language,[44] here displaced into the writing narrator. That last long passage, like virtually all of *A Portrait*, is a revelation of Stephen's struggle against autoaesthetic discomfort. Joyce gives us a dialectical glimpse of what we know to be an inherent Paramodern displacement in language itself, without taking the radical Nietzschean step of addressing, as Rorty says, "what our lives would be like if we had no hope of what Nietzsche called 'metaphysical comfort.'"[45] That very metaphysical comfort is, of course, a fundamental part of Modernism. To the end, Stephen persists in dreaming those fictional dreams of potentially unironic transcendence, only but always a step from Nietzsche: the set of images in the preceding passage has followed those of Zarathustra's "going under," but not the Paramodern displacement of the shadow, precisely. The Daedalaen poet's transcendence is his own disappearance *parmi l'herbe*.[46] The ironic inversion that informs the Modernist avant-garde itself becomes an ironic structural device "behind" the strategies of questioning Nietzsche initiates and which is developed so forcefully in contemporary theory. For Derrida, for example, the "space of framing" is now a topologically assignable "aperture-effect," so that nothing, as Derrida says in his discussion of Mallarmé in "The Double Session," will have taken place but the place[47] of the estranged text. This is precisely what we see in "Un Coup de dés," as Mallarmé tells us directly in the poem. Kenner draws attention to this Mallarméan connection in discussing Joyce, though in a significant (Modernist) way misunderstanding the Nietzschean link between them:

> The implications of the printed page, where words look just the same no matter who wrote them and their location in space . . . is what assigns them status. These implications had been noticed by Mallarmé in France but by no one, so far as I know, in the English-speaking world. . . . Joyce alone seems to have understood from the first what it can mean to be writing for print.[48]

While it is true that Joyce and Mallarmé share a common and growing interest in the nature of the *étrangeté* of the printed word (this is itself a function of a particularly Nietzschean *étrangeté*, I would suggest), for

Mallarmé, this printed word is not infused with Joyce's metaphor of artist-thought. For the Mallarmé of "Un Coup de dés," and not for Joyce, the written word is itself the constellation on which the cosmos is constructed, displacing the all-powerful, all-seeing, but invisible artist, who like the God of the creation pares his fingernails with the *stylo* or the printer's tool.

Once textuality goes beyond Modernist metaphorics to the Paramodern, that is, once it becomes a function of a disruptive transference (*transfert*, not *renvoi*), the nature of ontology itself is rewritten; at this point, the renovated autoaesthetic power of writing, the Mallarméan/Derridean hymen, must be located between Joyce and Mallarmé along the Nietzschean tightrope. It will no longer be possible to suppress Mallarmé's Paramodern *last step* here (as Eliot was able to do, for example), as we move through the latter parts of *A Portrait of the Artist*. Questions about writing, self, and ontology, according to Foucault, have become inevitable "when, with Nietzsche . . . thought was brought back, and violently so, towards language itself, towards its unique and difficult being."[49] In its most aggressive return to language, Derridean *différance*, a membrane or "hymen" (Mallarmé's word) siting the "confusion between the present and the nonpresent" that "produces the effect of a medium (a medium as element enveloping both terms at once; a medium located between the two terms)"[50] posits the penultimate step toward the Paramodern displacement, over the Joycean edge. The *terms* "present" and "nonpresent," in their difference, create the space for the *term* "hymen"; here is also the meeting place—the hymen—of ontology and language:

> The very motif of dialectics, which marks the beginning and end of philosophy, however that motif might be determined and despite the resources it entertains within philosophy against philosophy, is doubtless what Mallarmé has marked with his syntax at the point of its sterility, or rather, at the point that will soon, provisionally, analogically, be called undecidable.[51]

The hymen, then, which Derrida appropriates from Mallarmé's *Mimique*, is undecidable. For Nietzsche and the Mallarmé of *Mimique* and "Un Coup de dés," though not for Joyce, man lives in that undecidable *topos*, rewritten in Joyce, however provisionally, as *logos*, beginning for Stephen in his first poetry ("Pull out his eyes! Apologize!") and clearly manifested in the *étrangeté* in which, starting in Chapter Two, Stephen "confesses" the sin of being attracted to Emma, but becomes aware that his confession is a veil rather than a revelation of self, that "behind" his words are others in the entablature of whose pages he can "live."

And the life Stephen carves out for himself by the final chapter of *A Portrait* is prompted by the gathering, textualized of *étrangeté*, he perceives in the critical scene in which he purports to detach himself from convention. This begins with Stephen's facing the issue of his problematic "calling," a key issue for the Modernist/Paramodern schism. Stephen has been called by God to the priesthood, he is told by the director of his college, and is encouraged to follow it. As he enters the director's office, prepared to listen to the explanation of the special honor such a calling represents—to be chosen from the many by God to serve—Stephen perceives in the director's lifeless face another mirrored, life-and-death crisis of identity, again at the edge of the Paramodern but still *not there*:

> The director stood in the embrasure of the window, his back to the light, leaning an elbow on the brown crossblind and, as he spoke and smiled, slowly dangling and looping the cord of the other blind. Stephen stood before him, following for a moment with his eyes the waning of the long summer daylight above the roofs or the slow deft movements of the priestly fingers. The priest's face was in total shadow but the waning daylight from behind him touched the deeply grooved temples and the curves of the skull.[52]

Instead of taking the last step *past* the substance of the "artist," Stephen juxtaposes here the dead, cloistered world of dogmatic stasis and selfless "devotion" with the living world of the senses, framed in the dark window, the world of "waning daylight." The cadaverous, cold hand of the priest is only one of the nets Stephen must fly by; the *last* net, his own sensory and imaginative cosmos and the sense of substantiality—of subjecthood—it gives him, is far more subtle. Indeed, Stephen does not escape them, but powerfully flies by them.

When Stephen leaves the director's office, however, moments later, he has glimpsed the terms of his own Modernist *étrangeté*, a life-and-death issue in which dogmatic tradition is juxtaposed with the life of the (metaphor of the) imaginative mind, so as to redefine and perpetually conceal the issue of the *hymen* from Stephen:

> As he descended the steps the impression which effaced his troubled selfcommunion was that of a mirthless mask reflecting a sunken day from the threshold of the college. The shadow, then, of the life of the college passed gravely over his consciousness. It was a grave and ordered and passionless life that awaited him, a life without material cares. . . . At once from every part of his being unrest began to irradiate. A feverish quickening of his pulses followed and a din of meaningless words drove his reasoned thoughts hither and thither confusedly. His lungs dilated and sank as if he were inhaling a warm moist unsustaining air and he smelt again the warm moist air which hung in the bath in Clongowes above the sluggish turfcoloured water.[53]

Stephen's "choice" here is determined by the "drive" of corporeal, sensory life and manifests itself as a tumult of senses and metaphors. The "din of meaningless words," an aesthetic transposition of the "chaos of unremembered writing," that washes over him is still liturgical and dogmatic; in his compulsion to choose between one sort of literary dogma (religious) and another (aesthetic), Stephen confronts the images of *himself* in one guise and in another. He realizes that he must transpose his "calling" from a dead liturgical medium to the living one of a felt, experienced artist-thought. He sees his task as the reinvigoration of the senses, and will "adopt" language as the medium of his mimetic urge, painting word-pictures which portray his metaphysic. Fittingly, he begins with his own name:

> The Reverend Stephen Dedalus, S.J.
>   His name in that new life leaped into characters before his eyes and to it there followed a mental sensation of an undefined face or colour of a face. The colour faded and became strong like a changing glow of pallid red brick. Was it the raw reddish glow he had so often seen on wintry mornings on the shaven gills of the priests? The face was eyeless and sourfavoured and devout, shot with pink tinges of suffocated anger.[54]

Looking again in his own *Modernist* autoaesthetic mirror, Stephen's own deathmask is convincing evidence of his need to *write* another portrait of himself (which he is doing as we read it). His determination to live and to write, to be the poet, is a direct translation from the dead language he is already in the process of remaking, only fleetingly and vaguely aware of the Zarathustran implications for language *via* a suspended Mallarméan throw of the semiotic dice:

> He would fall. He had not yet fallen but he would fall silently, in an instant. Not to fall was too hard, too hard: and he felt the silent lapse of his soul, as it would be at some instant to come, falling, falling but not yet fallen, still unfallen but about to fall.[55]

In the "silent lapse of the soul" Joyce opens the Paramodern Gate of Moment, for an instant, an instant *to come*, falling but not yet fallen, suspended in the diacritical void. Joyce's interpretation of the fall into a commitment to art is one in which the "world" *is* the metaphoric interpretation of the senses: the world exists only insofar as it is interpreted by the presence of the poet. Thus, Stephen's commitment, his "impossible last sentence," to recall Fowles, is toward the Beckettian silence of an always *unwritten* autoaesthetic self that anticipates "its potential and its glow of association from its appearance on the page."[56]

Having glimpsed and retreated from the Paramodern fall, Stephen walks, at the end of Chapter Four of *A Portrait*, toward the Bull, the site of the sensory and syntactical shipwreck Stephen is about to begin, ruminating on his decision to "fall" into an autoaesthetic art, and reevaluating his life in

terms of that appearance on a page. At this pivotal moment, in this rumination Stephen produces his Great Code for Modernist autoaesthetic creation,
written out of *Stephen Hero* and incorporating its conic and Platonic design,
combining them with the physicality of the poetic sensorium, then infusing
the admixture with the magic of language, in the central passage of the novel:

> —A day of dappled seaborne clouds.
> The phrase and the day and the scene harmonized in a chord. Words.
> Was it their colours? He allowed them to glow and fade, hue after hue:
> sunrise gold, the russet and green of apple orchards, azure of waves, the
> greyfringed fleece of clouds. No, it was not their colours: it was the poise
> and balance of the period itself. Did he then love the rhythmic rise and fall
> of words better than their associations of legend and colour? Or was it
> that, being as weak of sight as he was shy of mind, he drew less pleasure
> from the reflection of the glowing sensible world through the prism of a
> language manycoloured and richly storied than from the contemplation of
> an inner world of individual emotions mirrored perfectly in a lucid supple
> periodic prose?[57]

Stephen has now seriously begun to articulate a world of a particular,
well-defined value, which lies in its "periodicity." The inner reversals in this
passage ("No, it was not their colours," after such an intricate description of
colors, etc.), the mimetic formulation of the "poise and balance of the period
itself," and the convolutions of the final sentence, with *its* poise and complicated balance, propel him off into a redefined Modernist mimetic in a
validated world of the *littérateur*.

Since writing is to be the outward sign of his identity, Stephen turns his
self-narration again to his name, which has from the beginning of the novel
been of strange fascination to him as a symbol (more than a sign) of his
nature. "Dedalus," the mis-written echo of the "great artificer," who
through unknown and unwritable arts changes the laws of nature, Daedalus
the forger, has been transformed:

> Now, as never before, his strange name seemed to him a prophecy. So
> timeless seemed the grey warm air, so fluid and impersonal his own mood,
> that all ages were as one to him. A moment before the ghost of the ancient
> kingdom of the Danes had looked forth through the vesture of the
> hazewrapped city. Now, at the name of the fabulous artificer, he seemed
> to hear the noise of dim waves and to see a winged form flying above the
> waves and slowly climbing the air. What did it mean? Was it a quaint
> device opening a page of some medieval book of prophesies and symbols,
> a hawklike man flying sunward above the sea, a prophecy of the end he
> had been born to serve and had been following through the mists of
> childhood and boyhood, a symbol of the artist forging anew in his
> workshop out of the sluggish matter of the earth a new soaring impalpable
> imperishable being?[58]

Stephen's project is nearly formed. He will go on to recreate the anonymous girl on the beach in the *language* of "the strange light of some new world."[59] His *étrangeté* consists of the poetic discovery of this strange light, a light he creates out of his own experience and its interaction with words; world existence becomes, and turns into, poetry.

Stephen immediately finds a perfect canvas on which to paint the evidence of his renovated art, infused with the "heavenly light" of poetic cadence. The swoon of his soul in the presence of the bird-girl, virgin (/Virgin) and lover, the Eternal Feminine and the mysterious ibis-figure of creativity, all transform into an epiphany of inclusion and order in which the Jesuitical has been supplanted by the aesthetic, just as Zarathustra is supplanted by the voice of his shadow. Remaining tantalizingly only a step from the Zarathustran shadow, Stephen awakens from the slumber of centuries *into* the eternal recurrence of metaphoric language, which, however breathless it may seem, is infused with the poet's living breath:

> His eyelids trembled as if they felt the vast cyclic movement of the earth and her watchers, trembled as if they felt the strange light of some new world. His soul was swooning into some new world, fantastic, dim, uncertain as under sea, traversed by cloudy shapes and beings.[60]

The conclusion of Chapter Four is akin, in terms of its *lightness*[61] and the euphoria of its upward-spiralling language, to the "Penelope" chapter of *Ulysses* (and by extension to the single, upwardly spiralling sentence of *Finnegans Wake*).[62]

In *A Portrait*, however, this epiphany concludes the *penultimate* chapter. Here, Joyce shows us what looks like a gesture—a frustrated bridge— toward the Paramodern that neither *Ulysses* nor the *Wake* take, a gesture toward a darker, more Nietzschean vision. In the concluding pages of *A Portrait*, Joyce seems to allow other voices (though never "othered" ones) to have the last word. This potential displacement is assiduously laid into the novel's last chapter, in which the tendentious "suppleness" of Stephen's imagined poetic prose has turned to the stiffness of numbers. The poetry he wants to write, which we want him to write, turns into arcane, esoteric debates with priests and undergraduate friends, his vague villanelle, and a gathering silence. Joyce warns us in Chapter Five to be wary of the nets of narrative convention. Here again, *A Portrait* is analogous to *Zarathustra*. In Joyce's portrait, as in Fowles', Nietzsche's strategy of supplanting Zarathustra with the Dionysian shadow is accomplished by allowing *person* to slip. Joyce is not nearly so subtle with this device as was Fowles, however, charting a gradual slide from third person to first through the course of the chapter as a whole. Instead of instituting a coy and energizing play with Paramodern *étrangeté*, as Fowles does, Joyce protects his exilic notion of presence by weaning himself from any view of the centrality of language codes themselves, respecting the inherent and dangerous *étrangeté* of language as another fearful pitfall to be avoided. In his confrontation with the unwritten self, Stephen Dedalus shrinks further from any Paramodern *étrangeté* toward his own inward substance, which he concerts even as he detaches himself from the "automatic values" of words:

> He found himself glancing from one casual word to another on his right or left in stolid wonder that they had been so silently emptied of instantaneous sense until every mean shop legend bound his mind like the words of a spell and his soul shrivelled up, sighing with age as he walked on in a lane among heaps of dead language.[63]

Stephen's "fall" is brought on by his own dwarf, a gravity that prevents its soaring, as the fulsome Modernist peers across the hymen of autoaesthetic *étrangeté* at the Paramodern poet: "His own consciousness of language was ebbing from his brain and trickling into the very words themselves" (179).[64] This ebbing is a powerful image, of course, of a new and *différant* kind of death; Stephen's language again has brushed against the Paramodern and recoils, becoming a dialectical tool of rebellion within the paradigm of Modernist self-substantiation, but not of disruption. "The violent or luxurious language in which Stephen escaped from the cold silence of intellectual revolt"[65] is a further transformation of the bird-girl and the hawk-man.

We must not forget, however powerful it may be, that behind Stephen Dedalus' "self"-protective Thomistic stiffness, the Joycean artist-project takes place in the same terms as those in Derrida's treatment of Nietzsche: sexuality, self-determinacy, ontological questioning, rebellion, indeterminacy.[66] But the project is rejected in Joyce, whose soul, like Stephen's, "frets"[67] in the shadow of language's hegemony: "My signature," he declares, "is of no account,"[68] relative to his sense of self. I would contend that Stephen is throughout Chapter Five trying to come to terms with his *étrangeté*, veiling them in exile and cunning. Despite strong evidence apparently to the contrary, Stephen is the most *heimlich* of poets: he attempts to fuse (forge) the literary into the metaphysical to produce a sense of spiritual overcoming that is absolutely never a self-overcoming. He overcomes obstacles on the way to himself—not as Dedalus the character but as Dedalus the writer (of *Portrait*)—as he expands his envelope of energy outward, to the personless essence of writerly presence "behind" *Ulysses* and the omni-human, super-writerly presence behind the *Wake*.

What Joyce/Stephen misses along his trajectory is that, acknowledging that he cannot feel at home in language, he cannot find meaning elsewhere; he is caught in the hymen/river between. He reconceives and re-entables this as a genealogical dilemma:

—My ancestors threw off their language and took another, Stephen said. They allowed a handful of foreigners to subject them. Do you fancy I am going to pay in my own life and person debts they made?[69]

Yet he cannot permit the tyranny of history, particularly Irish history, to subjugate and cancel him, even though he must work in a so-called foreign language (English, though neither Joyce nor Stephen knew Gaelic) that he must try to transcend: "When the soul of a man is born in this country there are nets flung at it to hold it back from flight. . . . I shall try to fly by those nets."[70] But to fly by those nets Stephen must devise a program of effacement and escape. Derived from Aquinas, that system (a formative version of which has resulted in Stephen's only overt poetry, his dogged villanelle) has ironically resulted in Stephen's *fall*, through torrid and tortured poetic images, wet dreams, arcane history. Anticipated implementation of that archaic system begins near the end of the novel in another—his penultimate—confrontation with his name, the charged signature in which he collapses non-meaning and all meaning, and by which he gauges his art. Once again, the name/signature reveals that fear of self-loss that characterizes Stephen's autoaesthetic fall:

> The colonnade above him made him think vaguely of an ancient temple and the ashplant on which he leaned wearily of the curved stick of an augur. A sense of fear of the unknown moved in the heart of his weariness, a fear of symbols and portents, of the hawklike man whose name he bore, soaring out of his captivity on osierwoven wings, of Thoth, the god of writers, writing with the reed upon a tablet and bearing on his narrow ibis head the cusped moon.[71]

The figure of Stephen's fear here, the monstrous figure of Thoth, Daedalus' equivalent in Egyptian mythology, god of learning, invention, magic, and messenger to the gods, is also the judge of the dead.[72] Thoth is the ultimate Zarathustran jester and *hymen*, poised between life and death, a paradigmatic emblem of the meeting of Modern and Paramodern writing. Thoth, caught between (having gone part-way through a transformation that never completes itself), has attached to his ibis head the image we first saw hovering over the hallucinatory sea at the end of Chapter Four, then, too, the ruler of the poetic scene, the cusped moon partly buried in the lucid evening waters. Here, the cusped moon is part of Thoth's judgmental regalia. Stephen is in the end awed by and afraid of the hawklike man toward whom he has striven.

Stephen reasserts his substantial poetic presence by transmuting Nietzschean *étrangeté* into his own physical exile. His doubly ironic effacement does not begin in the first-person final section of *A Portrait* but earlier, in the concluding sections of the conventional novel that precedes it. By the time Stephen actually falls into the first person, he is hardly more than a series of fragments anyway.[73] Stephen spends Chapter Five untying dialectical knots, the last being with his friend Cranly, in whose last words Stephen shows again his fear of autoaesthetic cancellation as loss of self:

—Alone, quite alone. You have no fear of that. And you know what that word means? Not only to be separate from all others but to have not even one friend.

I will take the risk, said Stephen.

—And not to have any one person, Cranly said, who would be more than a friend, more even than the noblest and truest friend a man ever had.

His words seemed to have struck some deep chord in his own nature. Had he spoken of himself, of himself as he was or wished to be? Stephen watched his face for some moments in silence. A cold sadness was there. He had spoken of himself, of his own loneliness which he feared.

—Of whom are you speaking? Stephen asked at length.

Cranly did not answer.[74]

This last piece of "conventional" narration, before the advent of the final diary section of the novel, is saturated with Stephen's recognized and unrecognized autoaesthetic dilemmas. It reads, at first, like another launching of the Paramodern. Not only does Stephen profess to desire the loneliness he perceives to be the corollary of his decision to exile himself, but he shifts the narrative from his own loneliness to Cranly's, as though the perspective of the receding Stephen were suddenly to be seen from elsewhere. Stephen's parallax view, his parting narrative comment, is a final interrogation of self.

This parallax view is followed by an even more dramatic demonstration of greater parallactic power, in the shift to first person that serves to mask the narrator. What might appear to be an ironic internalizing is in fact a final, apocalyptic attempt at transcending the dialectic of presence and absence in an ascent into the metaphoric apex of the cone of literature, into a rarified realm in which the associative force of exilic voices alone remains:

16 April: Away! Away!

The spell of arms and voices: the white arms of roads, their promise of close embraces and the black arms of tall ships that stand against the moon, their tale of distant nations. They are held out to say: We are alone. Come. And the voices say with them: We are your kinsmen. And the air is thick with their company as they call to me, their kinsman, making ready to go, shaking the wings of their exultant and terrible youth.[75]

Only the imprecations to the Father and the Mother, as grounds of the metaphoric self, remain to be entabled. The "kinsmen" with whose voices the air is thick are thinkers and poets whose "exultant and terrible youth" is that naiveté of which Nietzsche makes so much in Zarathustra, the childishness of the writerly imagination that does not comprehend the Paramodern. These voices and their calls to Stephen are his last forgeries.

Stephen's relationship to the voices of kindred artists[76] is a function of *Gleichnis*, in the sense not only of reflection and comparison (transference) but of a parable of the unwritten self, a slipping away of self-meaning that cannot be fathomed and does not rest. But it remains always a step away from its Paramodern transmutation, for which, as Philippe Sollers points out, "no longer is this parabolic opening the transcription of meaning," as it is in Joyce,

> but the virtually spontaneous upheaval of the written surface; no longer is it the recording and comprehension of a previous word, but an active inscription in the process of forging its own course . . . but nonpersonal literally in a world based on a dice throw: "*tout ce passe, par raccourci, en hypothèse; on évite le récit* [everything occurs, in short, hypothetically; one avoids the narrative]."[77]

Whereas, for Joyce, autoaesthetic exile consists of "bookish fragments,"[78] the Paramodern reversals Nietzsche adumbrates operate within another economy altogether, defined at the conclusion of *The Gay Science* that anticipates the Mallarméan shipwreck (remember the mast tops visible from the Martello tower at the opening of *Ulysses*):

> *On the question of being understandable.*—One does not only wish to be understood when one writes; one wishes just as surely *not* to be understood. . . . I approach deep problems like cold baths: quickly into them and quickly out again. That one does not get to the depths that way, not deep enough down, is the superstition of those afraid of the water, the enemies of cold water; they speak without experience.[79]

For Nietzsche, the economy of Paramodern exchange opens beyond the aphorism to a remade poetic consciousness. Nietzsche's metonymy anticipates and flies by Joyce's metaphorized view of experience as itself a critique of what Sollers calls "the symbolism of the book (of the end of the book and its absence) and of writing,"[80] leading to a grammatological cosmos in which the *abîme* is the fullness of the white space of the page, a critique completely absent in Joyce,[81] for whom the impossible *abîme* of the page is a fall back to turmoil, prior even to "the chaos of unremembered writing." Only in the perpetually chimerical *perfected text* (Nietzsche's *Revaluation of All Values*, Mallarmé's *Livre*) does the textual purportedly become a form of what de Man calls "perpetual writing, always at the beginning."[82]

> We must bend our independent minds, page by page. . . . Then, in the tiniest and most scattered stopping points upon the page, when the lines of chance have been vanquished word by word, the blanks unfailingly return; before, they were gratuitous; now they are essential; and now at last

it is clear that nothing lies beyond; now silence is genuine and just.

It is a virgin space, face to face with the lucidity of our watching vision, divided of itself, in solitude, into halves of whiteness; and each of these is lawful bride at the wedding of the idea.

—Stéphane Mallarmé, "Mystery in Literature," 694

The essay from which this passage comes, and which appeared in *La Révue Blanche* in 1896 (at the same time, roughly, as "Un Coup de dés"'s composition), shows clearly how Mallarmé's orientation evolved away from Symbolism, from his schematic concern with *precise* orientation of symbolic image, through a hidden world of substance, and toward the Nietzschean world in which articulation is the residence, but not the residue, of "substance." We must also realize how far this passage is from the Joycean cosmos. The power of *étrangeté* in (printed) writing, increasingly strong in Mallarmé at the end of his writing life, is an echo of the conclusion of *Zarathustra*'s Part Three, "The Seven Seals (Or the Yes- and Amen-Song)," whose refrain is *"I love you, O eternity!"* The eternity Zarathustra loves and embraces in this section is the frenetic one of the evaluative eternal recurrence, which Nietzsche layers heavily with metaphor. *Zarathustra*'s narrative, remembering Goethe, anthropomorphoses this metaphoric figure into the *woman* who stands for the desire to experience the eternal recurrence. Nietzsche does so, at the conclusion of each of the seven "seals," in a procreative image and one of marriage:

> Oh how should I not lust after eternity and after the nuptial ring of rings, the ring of recurrence?
>
> Never yet have I found the woman from whom I wanted children, unless it be this woman whom I love: for I love you, O eternity.
>
> *For I love you, O eternity!*[83]

In precisely the same way, Mallarmé, in "Un Coup de dés," gathers his images together beyond bird-girls and the cusped moon into a "constellation," "cold from neglect and disuse," out of which the fold of autoaesthetic articulation might provisionally come. The extraordinary tension of Mallarmé's poem (see Supplement), when placed in constellation with the uneasy tension of Nietzsche's desire, reflects on that particular Joycean tension in which the poet "weds" experience with articulation *in order to* lie in that "virgin space," subsumed word by word, page by page in the unwritten exercise of the will-to-power, revealed not as a power over the page nor *from* it but rather as a function of *étrangeté*, a dialectical power derived from the page itself. Like Joyce, Mallarmé privileges this free, independent, willful, and highly metaphorized dialectic, as well as the (re)unification of *word and silence*; unlike Joyce, Mallarmé inscribes the grounding conditions of his dialectics in the fold of articulation, without the poet:

A throw of the dice/never/ even indeed when cast in circumstances
  eternal/ at the depth of a shipwreck/
Be/that/the Abyss/
blanched/stretched/raging/sloping/
glides desperately/ on wing/ of its own/ beforehand fallen back unable to trim the flight . . . .

So begins another "perpetual writing, always at the beginning," Mallarmé's "Un Coup de dés,"[84] written, as can be seen in the Supplement, below, out of the originary fold (of the book), a pure articulation. The poem is the prescient reply to Joyce of the fold (*repli*) of the unwritten self, which I want briefly to stretch across the Paramodern abyss to Beckett's autoaesthetic. In "Un Coup de dés," Joycean fullness, the *rempli* of the text, is entirely avoided in favor of *étrangeté*. Mallarmé has set us up for this radical disruption, modelling the fourth section of his earlier *Igitur*, entitled "The Dice Throw in the Tomb," on the catastrophic confrontation of the "Absolute" with the "absurd," as a parable of the Modern/Paramodern confrontation we have been exploring. Igitur is the (transitional) explorer of the unknown, who essays the "dark womb of the unconscious"[85] and who, like Beckett, in the end goes beyond this wonderfully fecund Modernist image to discover the elemental, subjectless writing of "Un Coup de dés." The Daedalaen flight of the Modernist poet takes a radically altered autoaesthetic direction in Mallarmé's post-Symbolist formulation, requiring the "elocutionary disappearance of the poet, who yields place to the words."[86] Mallarmé's transition to the Paramodern begins in Igitur's ultimate *étrangeté* (silence/death). Standing in his own tomb, holding the book of spells that contains his genealogical past, Igitur closes the book and "lies down on the ashes of his ancestors."[87] Mallarmé then tells us that Igitur "feels in himself, thanks to the absurd, the existence of the Absolute," that he "has only forgotten human speech within the book of spells, and the thought in the luminary one announcing this negation of chance, the other clarifying the dream where it has arrived." Once we can unravel his language, on which Mallarmé (like Joyce) expects us to stop and take time, we see that in the confrontation of the Absolute with the absurd, his version of poetry and the chaos of unremembered writing, Igitur reveals the radically dialectical nature of all autoaesthetic value, beyond speech and the "spells" of self-definition. Igitur (Latin "therefore" or "consequently") is *igitur*, a name for the impetus of exploring the very displacement that cancels him as he discovers it.

This is the irresolvable dialectical dilemma of "Un Coup de dés," whose interrogation pours out of the very fold of the page on which it appears (I have marked the page-fold with a vertical line):

AS IF

an insinuation | simple
in the silence | wrapped with irony
| or
| the mystery
| impulsive
| howled out
in some near | whirlwind of hilarity and horror
hovers | around the abyss
| without scattering on it
| nor fleeing
| and cradles in it the virgin sign
| AS IF

The dialectical abyss (*hymen*) is as unwritable as it is undeniable in writing, and extends along both the vertical and horizontal axes. The fold in the center of the text will not permit us to forget the theatricality of the book itself nor the disparate "orders" of reality we confront in "page" and "word." Both confront the nature and idea of the self, suspended between the repetitions of mimetic irony with which the passage is framed; the page is indeed "as if."

Mallarmé carries his simulation and dissimulation further. The white of the page has been declared the mimetic equivalent of the white foam above the shipwreck of writing, and over it is poised the pen (*plume*),[88] which, when it falls (onto/into the paper/water) produces—nothing but the writing of the unwritten self, the *topos* of writing:

| Falls
| the pen
| rhythmic suspension of calamity
| to bury itself
| in the original froth
| lately from which his delirium surged to a peak
| faded
| by the identical neutrality of the abyss

NOTHING . . .|

| WILL HAVE TAKEN PLACE
| BUT THE PLACE

"EXCEPT . . . PERHAPS . . . ." Mallarmé goes on, "A CONSTELLA-TION . . . on some vacant and superior surface . . . at some last point that consecrates it." This *last point* is itself the final fall of the pen, the period *itself*, the "dissemination in the folds of the hymen."[89] This allusion to the rich sexuality of the multiple dialectical exchanges of paper, pen, ink, and sign transports us into the Dionysian realm of primordial forces fused and juxtaposed with the structure and syntax of writing—that is, to the condition of the (Lacanian) unconscious as a language and structure, the problematic collapsing together of the corporeal and lexical self, perpetually unwritten.

In suspense between the seemingly chaotic, raw forces of physical and metaphysical *necessity* and the signs by which we manifest them, Mallarmé investigates the "Master" who searches for the "unique Number that cannot // be an other" and, simultaneously, "Spirit/to fling it/into the tempest"; if this impossible juxtaposition can be achieved, the poem asserts, then "the veil of illusion" will falter, will fall, WILL ABOLISH, madness." For Mallarmé, the fall occurs in and into the fold, where all veils of illusion are broken," in these parts/of the void/in which all reality is dissolved"—"EXCEPT" that the constellation, writing itself, persists. Mallarmé concludes "Un Coup de dés" with a mockingly mimetic throw of the dice of words across the page and the interpretive consequences of their coming to rest:

> waking
>   doubting
>   rolling
>   shining and brooding
>   before halting
>   at some last point that consecrates it
>   All Thought Emits a Throw of the Dice

The final dice-throw comes to rest on an interpretive certitude that is itself an autoaesthetic tightrope, perpetually unresting in its self-referential strategy. The conclusion of Derrida's discussion of Mallarmé acknowledges this chimerical closure, in terms of the die by which it occurs:

Each of the six sides still has a chance although the outcome is predetermined and recognized after the fact as such. It is a game of chance that follows the genetic program. The die is limited to surfaces. Abandoning all depth, each of the surfaces is also, once the die is cast [*après coup*], the whole of it. The crisis of literature takes place when nothing takes place but the place, in the instance where no one is there to know.

No one—knowing—before the throw—which undoes it (him) in its outcome—which of the six—(die falling).[90]

Derrida's own strategy for the *étrangeté* of writing, here an exegesis of "Un Coup de dés," in which cross-reference and chance interaction of the "facets" or "sides" of the printer's cube is informed and infused by Mallarmé's *repli*, accounts in Derrida's text for the reinscribed Joycean fall ("[die falling]"). Pervasively, in "Un Coup de dés," one recognizes the interrogation of hegemonic language. All the traditional codes of syntax, person, and metaphoric convergence are questioned and undermined. The words seem at times to have been spewed out of some language-jet, like Jarry's famous Painting Machine, onto the wall of the page. At the same time, the seeming chaos of pages from which words seem to drip evolves into a series of layered sentences, discernible typefaces depicting various layers of discourse, references to arcane and esoteric disciplines, Symbolist images, and the simple but impossibly complex assertion that a throw of the dice will never abolish chance. This layered complexity, compounded by the physical treatment of the page and the interactive interpretive necessities any reader must bring to the poem, points up Mallarmé's Paramodern strategies and the introduction into *this* dialectic of the real possibility of the unwritten and unwritable self.

Am I as much as . . .
—Samuel Beckett, "Play"

Informed by Derrida's reading of Mallarmé, we can see the Nietzschean Paramodern as being in constant dialogue with dominant hegemonic literary encoding. Nietzschean Paramodernism is avowedly elitist, separating itself from the "literature" with which it interacts and on which it parodically feeds. With the receipt of the Nobel Prize for Literature in 1969, Samuel Beckett moved one step toward the legitimization of what must always remain illegitimate. Even the so-called action of the falling die is thrown into question in Beckett's elemental writing. But Beckett's version of the falling die is pervasively autoaesthetic and perpetually evaluative. The play of the interrogative and the declarative, of the writing of first person and the imperative *voice* chimerically "behind" it, opens Beckett's most dramatically Paramodern work, his novel *The Unnamable*, and grounds its explorations, gathering together in what *Endgame*'s Clov calls "the impossible heap," the themes of articulation and *étrangeté* for which Nietzsche has prepared us. Nowhere more clearly than in Beckett does the autoaesthetic conundrum find a focus. This opening forms the present chapter's last epigram: "Where now? Who now? When now? Unquestioning. I, say I."[91] As though re-reading the opening of Joyce's *A Portrait*, with *its* catalogue of covert questions, and then the entire interrogative strategy of "Un coup de dés,"

Beckett places the questions of articulation and *étrangeté* back into the context of the articulated self.

Beckett's inquiry into the Cartesian dyad, and therefore into the privileging of reason, past which Nietzsche shows us we must fly, goes to the heart of this Paramodern disturbance, which we can watch develop over the course of Beckett's work. In his first novel, *Murphy*, Beckett's "unredeemed split self" is only a metaphoric step from schizophrenia.[92] This is how Beckett reports Murphy's process of transcendence out of and into himself: "Slowly he felt better, astir in his mind, in the freedom of that light and dark that did not clash, nor alternate, nor fade nor lighten except to their communion."[93] But as the novel reaches its climax, Beckett transmutes Murphy's attempt at transcending a Cartesian hegemony of the *cogito* by taking the synaesthetic Paramodern turn. "The gas went on in the w.c., excellent gas, superfine chaos,"[94] the narrator continues, and Murphy is literally incinerated by his own meta-literal interrogation. Murphy's hallucinatory confusion shows his Surrealist and Symbolist roots, in an investigation of dreamstates (and with Beckett's own translations of André Breton's and Paul Eluard's Surrealist writing exercises imitating the language of pathological mental states;[95] his state or non-state is not merely one of disorder but of the interrogation of order and disorder—a true synaesthesia in which, as Beckett's subsequent works will explore, *all* referentiality is interrogated. Beckett's protagonists and narrators are obsessed with the Paramodern crisis of subject and object, which culminates in the non-character of the Unnamable, who labors unsuccessfully to identify himself in a Postmodern dialectic with Cartesian Modernism, and thus with Stephen Dedalus. Each sentence of *The Unnamable*'s relentless interrogation of subjectivity is supersaturated with synaesthetic concern:

> I have done nothing, unless what I am doing now is something, and nothing could give me greater satisfaction. For if I could hear such a music at such a time, I mean while floundering through a ponderous chronicle of moribunds in their courses, moving, clashing, writhing or fallen in short-lived swoons, with how much more reason should I not hear it now, when supposedly I am burdened with myself alone. But this is thinking again. . . . Would it not be better if I were simply to keep on saying bababababa, for example, while waiting to ascertain the true function of this venerable organ.[96]

The migration within the convocation of grammars upon which we rely to interpret experience determines "this venerable organ." The Paramodern crisis is again shown as evaluative, a confusion of "incommensurable vocabularies"[97] of signification, in which the ultimately non-referential character of grammar confirms Plato's worst fears and the *jouissance* of the text. We have seen how Mallarmé's later poetics consisted of suppressing the author in the interests of writing;[98] for Derrida, the grounding notion of grammatology is that culture is detaching itself from its basis in language per se and attaching itself to writing; this is a migration, in effect, "behind" ideas, a meta-migration. Hence, the growing primacy of silence and of what I have called elsewhere the "elemental" in Beckett's art. Grammatology always behaves "as-if," without becoming what it seems to claim to be, built on an abrupt disappointment of our expectations of meaning (related to the Surrealist "jolt"); textuality is "a tissue of quotations."[99]

Beckett's pursuit of these Paramodern themes (within the context we have built in Mallarmé) is legend; the pervasive interrogation of the self in his major works has been pointed out with regularity for the last twenty years. The monstrosity of Godot's absence from his own play, the persistently troubling imagery of *Endgame*, the progressive tightening of the Paramodern noose in the novel trilogy all gather as evidence of the Paramodern turn. I want to turn away from those grosser (and finer) examples to the enigmatic conclusion of Beckett's short play entitled "Play," "Am I as much as . . . ," which will serve here as the parable at the heart of a conclusive interrogation into the eternal return of the self in the Paramodern. In the play, the line "Am I as much as . . ." is spoken, then repeated, then re-repeated, by a mud-caked head protruding from a kind of burial urn, set between two other heads similarly entombed, only their heads showing, only their mouths moving. The three look virtually identical, though it turns out that two of them are women. They dramatically depict various levels of the interactive self: the dilemma of storytelling and repetition, a love triangle, the play of the human voice across language, the search for the self through memory, the purported rising of the voice from the purportedly dead page. And their complex play is a distillation of a search strategy toward an impossible articulation of the collective and individual self, from the play's affirmative opening (a unison "Yes") to its self-reflective and theatrical conclusion:

M: And now, that you are . . . mere eye. Just looking. At my face. On and off.
(*Spot from M to W1.*)

W1: Weary of playing with me. Get off me. Yes.
(*Spot from W1 to M.*)

M: Looking for something. In my face. Some truth. In my eyes. Not even.
(*Spot from M to W2. Laugh as before from W2 cut short as spot from her to M.*)

M: Mere eye. No mind. Opening and shutting on me. Am I as much—
(*Spot off M. Blackout. Three seconds. Spot on M.*)

M: Am I as much as . . . being seen?

. . . .

(*Repeat play exactly.*)[100]

Under the scrutiny of that second person "mere eye," that most telling homonym in English, a punning reference back to any hope of a first person, Beckett's protagonist asks the ubiquitous autoaesthetic question: What is the measure by which "I" am, and am to be seen? In that great *abecedarium culturæ*, the cultural eye opening and shutting on the repeated (and here staged) performance of an action claiming a certain status (am *I* as much as?), Beckett encapsulates as though outside of time (in "Play" the characters are actually dead) the emergence of the Paramodern self, distilled down to its most fundamental visual and oral constituents: characters who are themselves relics of antiquity, contained in vessels or vessels themselves from which their story is spewed, victimized by the theatrical attention to which they must respond. Moreover, Beckett's central character in the play, M, echoed by the two characters who flank him, is a distillation of the Nietzschean search for self. In light of Beckett's play, we must remember Nietzsche's warning that we should not concern ourselves with a *self* but with a subject; once attention shifts to the subject-nature of the self, however, "only a fiction" remains: the ego of which one speaks when censuring egoism no longer exists. It is our "bad habit," Nietzsche tells us, to "take a mnemonic, an abbreviative formula, to be an entity"; for example,

> the little word "I." To make a kind of perspective in seeing the cause of seeing: that was what happened in the invention of the "subject," the "I."[101]

Relentlessly interrogating the subject leads to the reinscription of the self across Mallarmé's falling dice, and to a questioning of the meaning and value of the self-theatricality W1 represents in "Play," as she herself says:

> And that all is falling, all fallen, from the beginning, on empty air. Nothing being asked at all. No one asking me for anything at all.[102]

Beckett posits the autoaesthetic self as a theatricalized interrogative dialectic, in which words make demands of each other, bracketed within the enculturated demands of other words that are not and could not be "judges" but are, rather, as M tells us, "Mere eye. No mind. Opening and shutting on me." Offering a hint at a dialectic of the unwritten self, Beckett takes up Mallarmé's effacement across the hymen into the *repli*, theatricalizing the very nature of the self so that the self, now the *word* "me," is just what the mere eye opens and shuts on, creating and extinguishing it. The question "Am I as much as . . . ," followed by its codicil, ". . . being seen?," like Zarathustra's jester knocks the self-performer from the tightrope into the vortex of the Paramodern, never to return to the certitude of Joycean balance again, whether it be the balance of the period itself, as in *A Portrait*, or even the seeming imbalance of the decentered world of *Finnegans Wake*.[103]

As happens in "Play," the Paramodern question, once asked in this theatrical way, must be seen not as circular but as merely tautological. Derrida has pointed out that the great conundrum of enculturated (that is, theatricalized) man is that the theatricalized post-Nietzschean self, like all notions of the theatrical, is born out of its own disappearance; Beckett shows us this subjectless state at its most critical. The Paramodern view of the self, indeed, as presented by Beckett, is as chimerical as its surface of inscription. Unwritten and unwritable, self in the Paramodern register "cannot be focused nor written. We cannot *know* a self; we can only *betray* a self."[104] The Absolute Identity that has grounded the Western speculative and aesthetic tradition from Parmenides to the present, and which is undermined by Heraclitus, Nietzsche, Derrida, and the Paramodern, is a theatrical evocation at play with the limits and needs of human thought, following directly from the curious impossibility of "self-reflection." Our drive or need for a sense of self creates that self, always (whether Paramodern or not) struggling to free itself from the "tyranny of the Gestalt."[105] Only with Nietzsche does the (auto)aesthetic *topos* of the artist take the final Paramodern step of claiming that the *étrangeté* infusing the subjective world corresponds to the "true dimensions of the self."

But even this is already undermined. We have seen what Nietzsche does with the "subjective world." This leads us to the lament of loss or the acknowledgment of new possibilities, however elemental they may seem. Both strategies can be found in Beckett, as in other of the best contemporary playwrights, such as Handke and Müller, whose work, along with Beckett's, reveals Modernism's fears of the theatricalization of art as not only well-founded but inevitable. The text of art is not an image nor a line of words releasing a single "theological meaning" but a "multi-dimensional space in which a variety of writings, none of them original, blend and clash."[106] All evaluation becomes an orchestration of migratory ideas; I am thinking here of Peter Handke's "The Prophesy," which has no plot, no conflict, no characters, no setting, no dialogue, only a monotone of spoken poetry, or Heiner Müller's *Hamletmachine*, in which Hamlet decides that he wants out of the script into which he has been written and must confront the question of one's extraction from the "script" of historical roles and pre-formed psychology; or of Beckett's later novels and radio plays or of Anselm Kiefer's quasi-historical art.

Thus, the betrayal of the self in the words and images in which we search for whatever we conceive it to be is only a "devaluation" or "disintegration" if one *expects* that language can incorporate the self, embody subjectivity, and transmit it to the "mere eye" of the reader/viewer, within the context of the multiple frustration of conventional self-analysis. Only from the othered stance of anticipated linguistic integration do Beckett and other seminal modern artists, here including such seemingly non-literary artists as Kiefer, Beuys, Cage, and others, show "decay" in their interrogation of the self. In fact, Beckett, along with a growing number of other artists concerned with a Paramodern autoaesthetic, has found a new way to utter Nietzsche's "Yes!": "I know now," says Beckett's M, "all that was just . . . play." The pun on the word "just," the allusion that all of life is a play of the elusive self, encapsulates Beckett's re-interrogation of the self. And in his next line, he repeats in new words the question of my title: "All this, when will all this have been . . . just play?" The play that continues in Beckett, and which *must not be permitted to stop*, is that very search itself, whether for Godot, for Hamm's "Me, to play . . . ," or for the end of the story, the truth of the self:

> W1: Is it that I do not tell the truth, is that it, that some day somehow I may tell the truth at last and then no more light at last, for the truth?

If the self were told, it would not "be" the self. The truth of the self is its play. In its re-investigation of the modes and strategies of the historical *kultur*-game, from Greece to the present day, Paramodern literature "repeats play exactly," simultaneously writing and erasing the self.

The privileging of writing as manifested in Nietzsche and Joyce begins to reveal itself as a kind of translation, not from a foreign language but into an unknown one. We must un-learn to read it, as the writer has attempted to un-learn to write it; the answers to the questions of the text are always other questions; the very notion of intelligibility is consistently under threat. To read the Paramodern text, we must learn to see language as Nietzsche sees it: as a (non)entity "radically different from himself."[107] For Joyce, the struggle is to reach out to that language, with all of its inversions and sparsity. The *telos* is to write only what signifies; but what signifies is that which cannot be interpreted but for which we go on striving, falling back, striving again, listening across the chasm. As Nietzsche tells us, in his poem called "Interpretation,"

> I put myself out, thus putting myself in:
> I cannot be my own interpreter.
> But whoever ascends to his own proper way,
> Carries my image too toward the radiant Light.[108]

The propriety of the "proper" way by which this chimerical first-person poet's narrative is framed is grounded in the dialectical differences of the Paramodern. Nietzsche's *étrangeté* from any narrative, in a Modernist sense, shows the way to a Paramodern autoaesthetic strategy whose Light is, at the same time, the dark, exilic strategy *toward* which Joyce works but which, going further, illumines the elemental graphtings in which both Mallarmé's and Beckett's art operates. They lead us to the dialectics of the unwritten and inconceivable self, whose autoaesthetic power, grounded in *étrangeté*, produces a series of lessons in interpreting the chimerical *written* self; indeed, *on évite le récit.*

Supplement

◆

A THROW OF THE DICE WILL NEVER ABOLISH CHANCE

Stéphane Mallarmé

Translation by Stephen Barker

A THROW OF THE DICE

NEVER

EVEN INDEED WHEN CAST IN CIRCUMSTANCES
ETERNAL

AT THE DEPTH OF A SHIPWRECK

BE
    that

        the Abyss

blanched
    weathered
        raging

            sloping
              glides desperately

                    on wing

                its own
                    be-

forehand fallen back unable to trim the flight
and skimming the whitecaps
cutting flush with the foam

deep inside summarizes

the shadow hidden in the deep by this alternative sail

thus to adapt
to the span

its gaping depths considered as the hull

of a ship

listed from side to side

THE MASTER

risen up
    inferring

        from this conflagration

          that there

        as one threatens
      the unique Number that cannot

            hesitates
         corpse by the arm
rather
   than to play
     as hoary fanatic
       the part
     in the name of waves
              one

      shipwreck that

beyond the old calculations
where the maneuver with age forgotten

long ago he gripped the helm

at his feet
from the unanimous horizon

prepares itself
tosses and tangles
with the fist that would grasp it
a destiny and the winds

be an other

Spirit
to fling it
into the tempest
to mend the division and to pass on proud

cut off from the secret it keeps

invades the chief
flows from subdued beard

straight from the man

shipless
no matter
where vain

ancestrally not to open the hand

                      clenched

             beyond the useless head

    legacy in dispersion

           to someone

                ambiguous

        the ulterior immemorial demon

having

      from cancelled regions

              induced

the old one toward this supreme conjunction with probability

                 this one

                   his puerile shade

caressed and polished and finished and washed

          broken in by the wave and escaped

      from the hard bones lost between the planks

        born

          of a romp

the sea by the old man tempting or the old man against the sea

     idle chance

                            Betrothals

of which

     the veil of illusion reanimated their haunting memory

     like the ghost of a gesture

           will falter

           will fall

              madness

WILL ABOLISH

AS IF

An insinuation
in the silence

in some near

hovers

simple

wrapped with irony
                    or
                the mystery
                        impulsive
                                    howled out

whirlwind of hilarity and horror

around the abyss
                without scattering on it
                                    nor fleeing
                and cradles in it the virgin sign

                                        AS IF

lonely frantic pen

except

that meets or grazes it a midnight toque
and fixes
in velvet crumpled by a dark laugh

this stiff whiteness

ridiculous

standing out against the sky
too much
not to mark
scantily
whoever

bitter prince of the reef

dons it like the heroic
irresistible but contained
by his small virile reason

in a flash

anxious

       expiatory and pubescent

                 mute

          The clear and lordly egret
            on the invisible brow
        glitters
         then shadows
         a delicate gloomy stature
         in her siren twisting

        with impatient final scales

            laugh

                    that

                            IF

of vertigo

upright
        time
            to slap

forked
            a rock
        false manor
                    suddenly
                        evaporated in mist

                        which imposed
                            a limit on infinity

IT WAS
  stellar issue

IT WOULD BE
worse
                    no
              more nor less
                indifferently but as much

THE NUMBER

WERE IT TO EXIST
other than as a scattered hallucination of agony

WERE IT TO BEGIN AND END
sprung up as denial and ending when apprehended
at last
by some profusion rarely spread
WERE IT TO COUNT

evidence of the sum however small
WERE IT TO ILLUMINE

CHANCE

Falls
the pen
rhythmic suspension of calamity
to bury itself
in the original froth
lately from which his delirium surged to a peak
faded
by the identical neutrality of the abyss

NOTHING

    of the memorable crisis
     or might have
         the event

come about of itself in view of all results worthless
                              human

                    WILL HAVE TAKEN PLACE
                    A trite loftiness pours out absence

                         BUT THE PLACE
any submerged swashing as if to disperse the empty act
                         abruptly which except
              by its lie
                              would have grounded
                         perdition

in these parts
                   of the void
                         in which all reality is dissolved

EXCEPT
    at the heights
        PERHAPS
            so far as one place

fuses with the beyond

                                    outside of interest
                                  for its part signalled
                                          in general
by such obliquity through such declivity
                                          of fires

       toward
             what should be
                        the Septentrion or North

                                A CONSTELLATION

                       cold from neglect and disuse
                              not so much
                              that it does not enumerate
                      on some vacant and superior surface
                          the next shock
                                        sidereally
                   of a final count in formation

waking
           doubting
                rolling
                     shining and brooding

                          before halting
              at some last point that consecrates it

              All Thought Emits a Throw of the Dice

UN COUP DE DÉS

JAMAIS

QUAND BIEN MÊME LANCÉ DANS DES
CIRCONSTANCES ÉTERNELLES

DU FOND D'UN NAUFRAGE

SOIT

   que

       l'Abîme

blanchi

   étale

     furieux

          sous une inclinaison

            plane désespérément

                  d'aile

                la sienne

                    par

avance retombée d'un mal à dresser le vol
et couvrant les jaillissements
coupant au ras les bonds

très à l'intérieur résume

l'ombre enfouie dans la profondeur par cette voile alternative

jusqu'adapter
à l'envergure

sa béante profondeur en tant que la coque

d'un bâtiment

penché de l'un ou l'autre bord

LE MAÎTRE

surgi
    inférant

        de cette conflagration

           que se

        comme on menace
l'unique Nombre qui ne peut pas

           hésite
         cadavre par le bras

plutôt
    que de jouer
      en maniaque chenu
        la partie
       au nom des flots
           un

      naufrage cela

                hors d'anciens calculs
            où la manœuvre avec l'âge oubliée

                    jadis il empoignait la barre

à ses pieds
            de l'horizon unanime

prépare
        s'agite et mêle
            au poing qui l'étreindrait
un destin et les vents

être un autre

                Esprit
                    pour le jeter
                            dans la tempête
                        en reployer la division et passer fier

écarté du secret qu'il détient

envahit le chef
coule en barbe soumise

direct de l'homme

            sans nef
                n'importe
                        où vaine

ancestralement à n'ouvrir pas la main
                              crispée
                    par delà l'inutile tête

        legs en la disparition

                         à quelqu'un
                                    ambigu

              l'ultérieur démon immémorial

ayant
        de contrées nulles
                        induit
le vieillard vers cette conjonction suprême avec la probabilité

                              celui
                                    son ombre puérile
caressée et polie et rendue et lavée
                        assouplie par la vague et soustraite
              aux durs os perdus entre les ais

                              né
                              d'un ébat
la mer par l'aïeul tentant ou l'aïeul contre la mer
                    une chance oiseuse

                                                  Fiançailles
dont
        le voile d'illusion rejailli leur hantise
        ainsi que le fantôme d'un geste

                        chancellera
                        s'affalera

                              folie

N'ABOLIRA

COMME SI

> *Une insinuation*
> *au silence*

> *dans quelque proche*

> *voltige*

simple

enroulée avec ironie
                    ou
                        le mystère
                                    précipité
                                            hurlé

tourbillon d'hilarité et d'horreur

autour du gouffre
                    sans le joncher
                                ni fuir

                    et en berce le vierge indice

                                            COMME SI

plume solitaire éperdue

sauf

que la rencontre ou l'effleure une toque de minuit
et immobilise
au velours chiffonné par un esclaffement sombre

cette blancheur rigide

dérisoire

en opposition au ciel
trop
pour ne pas marquer
exigüment
quiconque

prince amer de l'écueil

s'en coiffe comme de l'héroïque
irrésistible mais contenu
par sa petite raison virile
en foudre

soucieux

        expiatoire et pubère

                muet

        La lucide et seigneuriale aigrette
           au front invisible
      scintille
          puis ombrage
    une stature mignonne ténébreuse
      en sa torsion de sirène

    par d'impatientes squames ultimes

rire

    que

       SI

de vertige

debout
  le temps
    de souffleter

bifurquées
    un roc
   faux manoir
      tout de suite
        évaporé en brumes
       qui imposa
        une borne à l'infini

C'ÉTAIT

issu stellaire

CE SERAIT

   pire

      non

          davantage ni moins

               indifféremment mais autant

LE NOMBRE

EXISTÂT-IL
autrement qu'hallucination éparse d'agonie

COMMENÇÂT-IL ET CESSÂT-IL
sourdant que nié et clos quand apparu
enfin
par quelque profusion répandue en rareté
SE CHIFFRÂT-IL

évidence de la somme pour peu qu'une
ILLUMINÂT-IL

LE HASARD

Choit
la plume
rythmique suspens du sinistre
s'ensevelir
aux écumes originelles
naguères d'où sursauta son délire jusqu'à une cime
flétrie
par la neutralité identique du gouffre

RIEN

de la mémorable crise
ou se fût
l'événement

accompli en vue de tout résultat nul

humain

N'AURA EU LIEU
une élévation ordinaire verse l'absence

QUE LE LIEU
inférieur clapotis quelconque comme pour disperser l'acte vide
abruptement qui sinon
par son mensonge
eût fondé
la perdition

dans ces parages
du vague
en quoi toute réalité se dissout

EXCEPTÉ

    à l'altitude

        PEUT-ÊTRE

            aussi loin qu'un endroit

fusionne avec au delà

   hors l'intérêt
   quant à lui signalé
       en général
selon telle obliquité par telle déclivité
       de feux

  vers
   ce doit être
    le Septentrion aussi Nord

      UNE CONSTELLATION

   froide d'oubli et de désuétude
      pas tant
     qu'elle n'énumère
    sur quelque surface vacante et supérieure
      le heurt successif
        sidéralement
    d'un compte total en formation

veillant

  doutant

    roulant

     brillant et méditant

       avant de s'arrêter
     à quelque point dernier qui le sacre

    Toute Pensée émet un Coup de Dés

Notes

INTRODUCTION

1. Although *Apollinisch* is usually translated "Apollonian," I have throughout the book adopted Kaufmann's, Brinton's, Morgan's, and others' spelling, convinced by Kaufmann's simple statement in his notes to *The Birth of Tragedy* that "after all, Nietzsche did not say *Apollonisch*" (*Basic Writings* 9).
2. Nietzsche, *The Will to Power*, 481.
3. Nietzsche, *The Will to Power*, 796.
4. Images of birth pervade Nietzsche's writing from the title of his first book to the pervasive references to the Christ, the object of virgin birth with whom Nietzsche was fascinated throughout and particularly near the end of his writing life; both *Ecce Homo* and *The Antichrist*, his last two works, parodically treat the issue of birth and autoaesthetics. Among the strongest image-clusters in Nietzsche's writing, Zarathustra's repeated emergence from and retreat to his womb/cave takes on birth metaphors, as in *The Gay Science*'s section in which Nietzsche refers to the death of God for the first time:

   > *New struggles.*—After Buddha was dead, his shadow was still shown for centuries in a cave—a tremendous, gruesome shadow. God is dead; but given the way of men, there may still be caves for thousands of years in which his shadow will be shown.—And we—we still have to vanquish his shadow, too. (108)

   This particular sense of birth, which folds across numerous metaphorizations, comes from Nietzsche's cornucopic Greek sense of *chaos* as the rich *utopos* from which all birth occurs,

   > in the sense not of a lack of necessity but of a lack of order, arrangement, form, beauty, wisdom, and whatever other names there are for our aesthetic anthropomorphisms. . . . The whole musical box repeats eternally its tune which may never be called a melody. (109)

   The convocation of forces Nietzsche here designates as the autoaesthetic, those "aesthetic anthropomorphisms," are stretched in *this* book, like the image of the Overman, between Julien Sorel's difficult birth and the one to which Didi and Gogo refer in *Waiting for Godot*, "astride a grave." This is the sense in which Zarathustra calls his soul, and might well have called his *book*, the "umbilical cord of time" (3.14).
5. This duplicitous tendency, a dialectic of unity and disunity, takes many

nineteenth- and twentieth-century forms, starting with Nietzsche's designation in *The Birth of Tragedy* of the Dionysian and the Apollinian. One of the most useful, in addition to Derrida's designation of the *différance*, by which temporal and psychological difference is neologized, and Lacan's distinction between the *je* (an impossible self-sameness) and the *moi* (the designated or displaced self to which—but not to whom—we always refer in self-reference), is the *en-soi* and *pour-soi* of Jean-Paul Sartre, for whom the objective and the subjective self-sense achieve interact in very complex ways. I will refer to these four models throughout the book. Obviously, Nietzsche, Sartre, Lacan, and Derrida "mean" very different things by their designations of schism, of *étrangeté*, differences with which I will deal as the discussion ensues. Suffice it to say that I will try to indicate in the following how the *tendency* to see this differentiation and distancing, including that of the "body" of the text and that of the notes, is not a simplistically Cartesian one but has to do with complex autoaesthetic issues articulated and given life (another corporeal, though autoaesthetically metaphorical image) by Nietzsche. The Nietzschean foreshadowing of the "paratext," so richly developed by Derrida's *parergonia* and myriad formulations by other contemporary theorists and writers, pared to its familiar form, manifests a consistently disruptive force.

6. Nietzsche, *The Will to Power*, 800.
7. Ibid.
8. For Nietzsche the only good student is the one who kills the teacher; my version of killing Nietzsche is to translate his trinity of grounding terms into another trinity, based on his and engaged in the same combinative and combative tensions, to

   1. show how Nietzsche's terms can be seen to work, and
   2. open and explore a strategy for interpreting contemporary texts that find *their* grounding assumptions in Nietzsche's.

   The trinity of terms announced in my title, placed in a Nietzschean context and fleshed out in chapter 1, begin throughout the remaining chapters to weave a fabric out of Nietzsche's own texts, other texts he considered seminal to his own strategic redefinitions, and those subsequent texts (like Derrida's) which possess and acknowledge their own force as Nietzschean.

9. I do not mean to suggest that Nietzsche merely re-named and re-orchestrated High Modernist concepts of cosmic organization, nor that Nietzsche's central terms, Overman, Eternal Return, and will-to-power, are equivalent in any way to them. I do mean to suggest that, once again, Nietzsche is at play with the dogma of surrounding culture and with its very strategic structurations.

10. Throughout the section of *The Will to Power* entitled "The Will to Power as Art," Nietzsche explores this aesthetic of self-creation, the origin of his notion of autoaesthetics, when coupled or harmonized with its linguistic corollary, at its most elementary level. In this nonmoral or extramoral sense, any aesthetic of beauty and ugliness is "relative to our most fundamental values of preservation" (*Will to Power* 804). "It is senseless to want to posit anything as beautiful or ugly apart from this," Nietzsche goes on:

    > *The* beautiful exists just as little as does *the* good, or *the* true. In every case it is a question of the conditions of preservation of a certain type of man: thus the *herd man* will experience the value feeling of the beautiful in the presence of different things than will the *exceptional* or over-man,

were he to exist (which as we shall see he does not—except as a work of art).
Once the very existence of these concepts as anything other than tentative is
undermined, revealed as "shortsighted but persuasive" (*Will to Power* 804),
Nietzsche can go on to show that what we call the "form" of art is merely the
content of a formal structure we have defined or that has been defined for us,
"—our life included" (*Will to Power* 818).

One must remember that although the Enlightenment was decidedly this-
worldly, its standards and terms were solidly aligned with Judeo-Christian
tradition. If the Enlightenment view of progress is anti-Christian, in that it posits
the possibility of change through enlightened application of reason to the world
around us and the denial of transcendence and personal immortality, it nonetheless solidly maintains the metaphysical superstructure on which those "eternals"
have been built. Nietzsche's revolution of "the word" reveals past difference as
past similarity, in light of *his* differentiation.

11. Nehamas, 7. Nehamas sets the tone for much that follows here, in such statements as that on the last page of the book: "His passion for self-reference
combines with his urge for self-fashioning to make him the first modernist at the
same time that he is the last romantic" (234).

Gary Shapiro begins where Nehamas concludes: with the assertion that a
significant number of Nietzsche's texts are built on narrative rather than philosophical strategies and that, more importantly,

the narrative forms of these works (and I use the plural advisedly) have much
to do with Nietzsche's articulation of history, his presentation of the thoughts
of will to power, eternal recurrence, and the *Übermensch* ("man beyond"),
and with his representation of his own life. (8)

Shapiro is as interested in the *failure* of Nietzsche's strategic concerns to create a
self as he is in their success (or their vitality), which takes him one step further
than Nehamas, as in this comment on *Ecce Homo*:

Nietzsche is a *Döppelganger*, a double constituted by a play of oppositions;
since there is no external point from which that play can be controlled it tells
the story of how one becomes what one is not just as much as it tells the story
promised by its subtitle "how one becomes what one is." (30)

12. Rickels, "Introduction," *Looking After Nietzsche*, viii.
13. Derrida, "Interpreting Signatures," 16.
14. Rickels, "Introduction," *Looking After Nietzsche*, ix.
15. Rickels, "Introduction," *Looking After Nietzsche*, xxxiii.
16. Breazeale, "Introduction," *Philosophy and Truth: Selections from Nietzsche's
Notebooks of the Early 1870's*, 148.
17. Nietzsche, "On Truth and Lies in a Nonmoral Sense," 85.
18. David Allison, using the same gustatory image Nietzsche so often employs,
explains that

the Nietzschean text becomes something to be ingested, digested, transformed, and transfigured, and together with it, the reader. Such a text becomes
inseminated by the reader and disseminated through the reader, just as the
reader inevitably undergoes this exchange with the world. (xxiv–xxv)

The imagery here, digestive and tactile, in appropriately Nietzschean fashion
metaphorizes the notion of birth into one of consumption and "dissemination,"
both relations to but permutations of birth.

19. This term has become virtually anathema to clear discussion of theoretical issues.

See Andreas Huyssen's seventh footnote to Chapter Nine of his *After the Great Divide* (Bloomington, Indiana: Indiana University Press, 1986) for some salient thoughts on the word and its reverberations. In typically Nietzschean fashion, Huyssen, who uses the word "postmodernism" assertively in his overall title, in this note declares that he will not "define and delimit the term 'postmodernism' conceptually" (234), but that it will

> variously refer to American art movements from pop to performance, to recent experimentalism in dance, theater and fiction, and to certain avantgardist trends in literary criticism from the work of Leslie Fiedler and Susan Sontag in the 1960s to the more recent appropriation of French cultural theory by American critics who may or may not call themselves postmodernists. (234)

Throughout the following chapters, *j'éviterai le récit* of the "postmodern," since this is not a discussion of the "Modern" and the "Postmodern," an almost entirely specious discussion, but of thematic and theoretical genealogies and their strategic methods of operation. Although the many definitions of the postmodern are *all* heavily loaded with ideological and strategic forces, and a discussion of them is always stimulating, I am interested in something else here.

I modify the keyword in my title, "autoaesthetics," with the added enigma of "postmodern" because I want to point toward the undermining of essentialist Modernism in Nietzsche's autoaesthetic project, not because I want to link it to any particular Postmodernism, of which there are of course many. In some sense this volume is the prolegomena to an apocryphal future volume in which Nietzsche's autoaesthetic strategy is applied to the acknowledged "Postmodern" writers who themselves subvert essentialist Modernism (would this be Post-Postmodernism?), but this spiral could in the end occupy a whole wing of Borges' library.

20. Ackroyd, *Notes for a New Culture*, 145.
21. Ibid.
22. Ibid., 26.
23. Ibid., 145.

CHAPTER 1. NIETZSCHE'S TRINITY OF TERMS AND MINE

1. The Dionysian Man is a central part of Nietzsche's thought, without which the central terms on which I want to dwell in this chapter have little or no meaning, and certainly cannot be understood remotely as Nietzsche lays them out in his writings. The Western philosophic tradition, as a hegemonic phenomenon, had been, up to Nietzsche, obsessed by the idea of the Apollinian, the reasoned, controlled, harmonic figure first clearly articulated by Socrates and then Plato. Nietzsche, of course, attempts throughout his work to convince us that this obsession is just that, a blinding liability through which we have become a crippled culture. Nietzsche is also aware that in reminding us about the Dionysian Man he is risking all the acknowledged advantages of the ordered teleological structure on which the Apollinian Man rests. At the same time, Nietzsche is willing to take the risk, since being re-acquainted with Dionysus is potentially to be *whole* (or wholly potential) again. Many contemporary accounts of Nietzsche explore the nature of the Dionysian; an interesting recent treatment is that of Jacob Golomb in his *Nietzsche's Enticing Psychology of Power* (1987), in which

he nicely and succinctly sums up the relative merits of the two psychological "positions":

> The Apollonian pattern constructs artistic representations and fictions for the sake of life, functioning as the source of the various kinds of metaphysical comfort. Reliance on this comfort suggests the existence of an untiring will-to-life, but nonetheless a will-to-life which requires certain metaphysical supports if it is to maintain its course. But in this resides an insurmountable difficulty: as a fictive psychological pattern, which builds masks and illusion, it is continuously imperilled, and may be condemned to collapse if penetrated by an intuition of the tragic absurdity of existence. Then "the danger to . . . will is greatest" (*Birth of Tragedy* 7) and, in consequence, the danger to *life*. We see, therefore, that the second kind of psychological pattern—the Dionysian serving the Dionysian intuition, and performing the unmasking—is the more powerful of the two and fulfills a greater and more long-range function toward life-intensification. The man who adopts the Dionysian psychological pattern is "the Dionysian man," who "now sees everywhere only the horror or absurdity of existence." (50–51)

For Nietzsche, each of us must face something like the Manichean choice of one or the other of these "patterns" of behavior, though of course Nietzsche teaches (at least initially) that our lives are composed of elements of both a greater or lesser degree. Since the Dionysian, as conceived by Nietzsche, relates closely to the unconscious as it was soon to be conceived and developed by Freud, references to that link and to the traits of the unconscious that defy self-analysis must be discussed relative to the Dionysian and the self, particularly as an aesthetic strategy for self-declaration and power.

2. This is only the first of a string of what we would call Freudian terms one must use in assessing Nietzsche, chiefly because of the remarkable similarity between the (prior) thought of Nietzsche and its subsequent translation by Freud into many of the fundamentals of psychoanalysis. In several chapters to come, most notably 3 and 8, I will make some of those (Freud-Nietzsche) connections. Since the relationship between the two was downplayed so vehemently by Freud, I will also sublimate it, referring to its salient points in subliminal form (endnotes). This does not mean that the psychological connection or the psychoanalytic systematization of this connection is not vitally important to both Nietzsche and Freud—it is; what it means is that underlying *all* of the following is an awareness of both the vitally Nietzschean aspect of psychoanalytic thought and the repression Nietzsche suffered at Freud's hands.

   In a broader sense, the Nietzsche/Freud connection receives a remarkably different treatment in the sections of Derrida's *Post Card*, in which he speculates on links between Freud and the roots out of which he grew; Nietzsche figures prominently among them, as they must for Derrida.

3. The theoretical constructs of works like Arthur Kroker and David Cook's *The Postmodern Scene* make claims to being post-Nietzschean, in that a quite different aesthetic struggle is articulated there, within what they call the Postmodern world. Though that particular book is full of quite amazing insights (and some far-out, indefensible ones—for example that Saint Augustine is the first so-called Postmodern Man), the "post-Nietzschean" there is a poetics of excess oriented by media and powerlessness—a quite nihilistic vision—Nietzsche would condemn. Likewise, the politics of theory, particularly in the post-Poststructuralist discourses of ideology theory (Marxist, gender-oriented, "colonial," and other-

wise) and the so-called "New Historicism," both of which claim a post-Nietzschean status, has strongly desired to see itself in another arena than that articulated by Nietzsche. My contention is that these claims are invalid: though it is possible to view the world through theoretical eyes that diverge from Nietzsche's, his "position" still offers a remarkably rich avenue of inquiry that often asks the same questions in other forms or places certain questions (most notably that of the self and the meaning of human existence) in a primary position. Indeed, much of Nietzsche's project is to rearrange this interrogative structure, to privilege certain questions and de-privilege others, which is no more nor less than what all theoretical or philosophic discourses do. In this way, as in so many others, Nietzsche is in but re-makes the "mainstream."

4. This "pairing" of the declarative and the interrogative, of assertion and the undermining of assertion, might indeed be a very adequate working definition of the Dionysian as Nietzsche sees it and employs it in his philosophy. Every statement consists, fundamentally, of its own negation, reversal, and subversion. Every subversion has immanent within it its assertive "side," ready to confuse even the Nietzschean skeptic who would make claims such as "all statements are really questions." Among the most disturbing aspects of Nietzsche's mature philosophy, to the enculturated reader, is this slippage between opposites, caught in a kind of atomic tension the forces of which operate "below" any discourse. Of course, the metaphysical claim I am here making for a "fundamental force" must itself be shattered, if its principle is to hold. This is a great dilemma of writing or even thinking about Nietzsche—one is always thinking numerous things at once. This Dionysian synaesthesia gives birth to the chimerical self, simultaneously denying and privileging it.

5. Miller, "The Disarticulation of the Self in Nietzsche," 247.

6. Ibid., 249.

7. Ibid., 253.

8. Comments like this one of Deleuze's show how remarkably close Nietzsche came to a theory of the unconscious, which is nonetheless thoroughly adumbrated in his writing. We must remember, and will look more closely later at, that remarkable note of 1887:

> Toward a characterization of *"modernity."*—Overabundant development of intermediary forms; atrophy of types; traditions break off, schools; the overlordship of the instincts (prepared philosophically: the unconscious *worth more*) after the will power, the willing of end *and* means, has been weakened. (*Will to Power* 74)

Emergence from an unconscious that is worth more is a condition of the self in the modern age, without doubt; in fact, phrase by phrase one could see this reflection on modernity as prophetic. Certainly, it is a foreshadowing of the power of the unconscious vis-à-vis the immanent self.

Although Deleuze goes on to develop the idea of the unconscious in other contexts and other frameworks, the Dionysian word-system on which Nietzsche builds his sense of the unconscious grounds Deleuze as well, even in a work seemingly as distant from it as *Anti-Oedipus*, in which Deleuze (and Guattari) declare(s) that "the sole thing that is divine is the nature of an energy of disjunction" (13), purely Nietzschean language. Such phraseology, and numerous other points of contact with Nietzsche's Dionysus-word, are to be found throughout this work and Deleuze's others.

9. I argue elsewhere for Nietzsche's presence at the birth of so-called "postmodern irony," with his sense of the subjectless; see my "disorder of the lights perhaps an illusion" in *Open Letter* (Spring 1991). The chimerical self, the terms in which that self is so problematically presented (and absented), and the way in which those terms confound themselves and each other are treated in the essay.

10. One must remember his distinction between Jesus and Christ, between the radical dissenter and the eschatological judge. The former is, for Nietzsche, a figure of disenfranchisement and alienation, though of wisdom; the latter is an iconic figure of dogmatic oppression. For a full treatment of this theme, see *The Antichrist*. Walter Kaufmann also treats this theme (in *Nietzsche: Philosopher, Psychologist, Antichrist*), though he does not follow out many of its implications. Jesus/Christ is the perfect figure, for Nietzsche, of the dilemma of inclusion and exclusion: he is a figure of pure metaphor.

11. Gilles Deleuze develops this idea most clearly in *Nietzsche and Philosophy*. In his description of Nietzsche's philosophy, Deleuze begins with the body, which he says, for Nietzsche, is "a plurality of forces" (39). Deleuze takes the radical view that the "medium" for these forces is nonexistent, that

> there is no quantity of reality, all reality is already quantity of force. There are nothing but quantities of force in mutual "relations of tension" (VP II 373/WP 635). Every force is related to others and it either obeys or commands. What defines a body is this relation between dominant and dominated forces. Every relationship of force constitutes a body. (39–40)

Deleuze's suggestion is that the relationship of forces *is* the body of the self.

12. Of course, Girard's triangulation is heavily influenced by the Nietzschean "rift," as Girard himself acknowledges. He comments on the connection between Nietzsche and Dostoevsky, and on Nietzsche and Valéry, as "the supreme temptation . . . murmured in the ears of twentieth-century men" (274)—the temptation to see *autonomy* as a function of man's desire to *empower* himself through the "worship of his own nothingness" (275). Girard regards this "transcendence" as the fundamental human *askesis*, a *praxis* of displacement. Girard, however, goes on to posit man's desire for death—a version of the death-wish—in Nietzsche's program, a desire which fits his (Girard's) program better than Nietzsche's.

Without doubt, the Girardian triangulation and the Nietzschean one intersect and overlap in many ways. Girard's structure, self/other/sublimated object of desire, has harmonic resonances with my terms and Nietzsche's, though Girard uses his in a more schematic (one might even say simplistic) way, as follows:

self/power = will-to-power = self

étrangeté = *Übermensch* = other

articulation = Eternal Return = sublimated object of desire

13. As in Freud's idea of sublimation, "object-libido" that displaces sexual gratification, what Freud describes in "On Narcissism" as "deflection." See also "Three Contributions to the Theory of Sex," both in the *Collected Papers*.

14. As in so many things, Nietzsche here takes his cue from Heraclitus, whose primal element, fire, is not primal because it is a generative object (like water, for example) but because it is a metaphor for the continuous *force* of change, his word for displacement.

15. This movement is the transference about which I shall say much more later,

particularly in reference to *Beyond Good and Evil* and *Zarathustra*. In the relative terms I am using here, transference is the "faith" that links the three "positions"—the key terms—on which Nietzsche builds. That faith is the metaphorical power itself, revealed and manifested in tropic language.

16. In his notes, which became *The Will to Power*, Nietzsche sees his philosophy, the *best* of German philosophy, as returning to "allen jeden grundsatzlichen Formen der Weltauslegung wieder, welche der griechische Geist . . .—wir werden von Tag zu Tag *griechischer* [all those fundamental forms of world interpretation devised by the Greek spirit . . .—we are growing more *Greek* by the day]" (*Will to Power* 419). In the text, this is a direct reference to Nietzsche's relationship with Heraclitus.

17. Haar, "Nietzsche and Metaphysical Language," 11.

18. Ibid., emphasis added.

19. Ibid.

20. See Derrida's *Positions* (42), where Derrida refers to this interval as "this biface or biphase . . . of bifurcated writing," a writing to which he refers as "dislodged and dislodging" and finally, to complete the Nietzschean association, as provoking the "overturning of the hierarchy" (42).

21. On the subject of Elisabeth's midwifery of Nietzsche's work and of her own remarkable relation to it, see Laurence Rickels' comments in his "Friedrich Nichte," collected in his *Looking After Nietzsche*, particularly 152–156.

22. A concept—indeed, a word—not invented by Nietzsche but, as Walter Kaufmann points out, by Lucian, in the second century A.D. Lucian's *hyperanthropos* comes into German in the seventeenth century in the writing of Heinrich Müller, and then is used by Herder, by Jean Paul, and then appropriately by Goethe himself in a poem (*Zueignung*) and in *Faust* (I 490), where Faust is called the *Übermensch* who can control spirits (Kaufmann 266). Nietzsche characteristically gives the term new meaning, particularly in that most *Übermenschische* of texts, *Thus Spoke Zarathustra*.

23. Lingis, "Difference in the Eternal Recurrence of the Same," 90.

24. Danto, *Nietzsche as Philosopher*, 201–202.

25. See Kaufmann, *Nietzsche: Philosopher, Psychologist, Antichrist* (274–286) for a capsule review of the origins of this concept in Nietzsche.

26. Kaufmann discusses the Heine connection in the Introduction to his translation of *The Gay Science* (15–21) very interestingly, though without any note of the use of transference I want to attach to it. Kaufmann understandably begins with Nietzsche's struggle against nihilism, with the question of *weight* ("What is it that still has weight?"), and with the terrifying need to ascribe and inscribe a positive value to life. That is, Kaufmann correctly discusses the question of the Eternal Return, which he calls the "Eternal Recurrence" (not quite the same thing, at a metaphorical or atemporal level) as an aesthetic and ethico-moral one—"weight" in the sense of "importance."

27. Kaufmann, *Nietzsche*, 276.

28. See particularly the discussion of *copula* and of metaphor in *Margins of Philosophy* ("The Supplement of Copula: Philosophy before Linguistics," 175–207, and "White Mythology: Metaphor in the Text of Philosophy," 207–273). This discussion begins in the sections on "supplement" in *Of Grammatology*, 141–165.

29. In Nietzschean terms, the passage is even more resonant in Derrida's French:

> La question de l'appareil vocal est donc secondaire dans le problème du langage. Une certaine définition de ce qu'on appèlle *langage articulé* pourrait confirmer cette idée. En latin, *articulus* signifie "membre, partie, subdivision dans une suite de choses"; . . . En s'attachant à cette seconde définition, on pourrait dire que *ce n'est pas le langage parlé qui est naturel à l'homme*, mais la faculté de constituer une langue, c'est-à-dire un système de signes distincts correspondant à des idées distinctes. (96)

30. Spivak, "Introduction," *Of Grammatology*, xxviii.
31. See Derrida's discussion of "The Hinge" ("La Brisure"), based on a letter from Roger Laporte, in *Grammatology*, 65–73.

    In addition, Derrida has very provocative things to say about the relation of Nietzsche's self-declaration and the Eternal Return, as manifested in *Ecce Homo*, in the "Otobiographies" section of *The Ear of the Other* (1–39); for example:

    > Forcing himself to say who he is, he goes against his natural *habitus* that prompts him to dissimulate behind masks. You know, of course, that Nietzsche constantly affirms the value of dissimulation. Life is dissimulation. In saying *"ich bin der und der,"* he seems to be going against the instinct of dissimulation. This might lead us to believe that, *on the one hand*, his contract goes against his nature: it is by doing violence to himself that he promises to honor a pledge in the name of the name, in his name and in the name of the other. *On the other hand*, however, this auto-presentative exhibition of the *"ich bin der und der"* could well be still a ruse of dissimulation. (10)

    Derrida goes on to explore the nature of the connection between the name and the work of Nietzsche, in the context of the dissimulative property of writing.

    Of course, Derrida explores the Nietzschean connection to *différance* elsewhere, widely.
32. Nietzsche, *The Gay Science*, Preface, 7.
33. Haar, "Nietzsche and Metaphysical Language," 6.
34. Hollingdale, *Nietzsche: The Man and His Philosophy*, 90–93.
35. Nietzsche, *Philosophy in the Tragic Age of the Greeks*, 5.
36. There is, so far as I know, no evidence that Nietzsche had read or knew of Christopher Marlowe's *Doctor Faustus*. Had he known of the Elizabethan Englishman, or of this particular telling of the Faust story, Nietzsche would have realized that he had found another of those kindred spirits he infrequently happened upon throughout his life. In *Faustus*, the doctor's dilemma is not one of the spiritual versus the worldly, as in Goethe and others, but in autoaesthetics, in Faustus' case manifesting itself as the (impossible) apotheosis of art (poetry) and dogma (religion); in the end, Faustus is consumed by the dogma from which he cannot escape. Marlowe's hell-mouth is indeed a metaphoric language-grinder, swallowing transgressors who cannot recant (interesting word) their anti-dogmatic heresy. In this respect, as in a number of others, Marlowe is a proto-Nietzschean figure; Faustus, an avatar of the Zarathustran dilemma and of the Derridean fold.
37. One must remember that *On the Genealogy of Morals* was written to "explain" *Beyond Good and Evil*, which was written to "explain" *Thus Spoke Zarathustra*. The three essays of the *Genealogy* conclude, at the end of the book, with one of Nietzsche's strongest statements about the will's power of the play of denial and assent:

    > We can no longer conceal from ourselves *what* is expressed by all that willing which has taken its direction from the ascetic ideal: this hatred of the human,

and even more of the animal, and more still of the material, this horror of the senses, of reason itself, this fear of happiness and beauty, this longing to get away from all appearance, change, becoming, death, wishing, from longing itself—all this means—let us dare to grasp it—a *will* to *nothingness*, an aversion to life, a rebellion against the most fundamental presuppositions of life; but it is and remains a *will!* . . . And, to repeat in conclusion what I said at the beginning: man would rather will *nothingness* than *not* will. . . . (*On the Genealogy of Morals* III, 28)

38. This dilemma is much like the one Freud lays out so dramatically in *Civilization and Its Discontents*, in which the suppressions of innovation—the victory of the Apollinian over the Dionysian, form the *kultur* which forms the individual—and against which the individual perpetually struggles for selfhood.

39. Nietzsche, *Ecce Homo*, "The Birth of Tragedy," 3.

40. See the following chapter on *Thus Spoke Zarathustra*; see also the first and last chapters of Hillis Miller's *The Linguistic Moment*.

41. This evaluative aspect of the Eternal Return owes a great debt to Goethe, particularly in the second part of *Faust*, in which Faust searches the ethereal realm for the ideal moment beyond the physical, the moment at which he would demand of Mephistopheles that time cease and the present conditions last forever. For Goethe, that moment is bound up with a different concept of the eternal, of metaphysics, and indeed of physics, than Nietzsche's.

Ways in which the Eternal Return interacts with Heraclitan flux are made even more complicated as a result of the influence of Goethe's Faust: the Heraclitan/Parmenidean schism rises again in Goethe and Nietzsche. The only solution to this polarity is irony, on the part of both Goethe and Nietzsche—but, in terms of a grounding in eternal verities, that irony is a kind of devil's advocacy in Goethe, while in Nietzsche it is at the heart of all assertion. While Faust emphasizes the stasis of that apotheosis at the end of the Romantic agony, Nietzsche emphasizes the activity of the eternal round. Finally, for Goethe, articulation is a tool of (moral) definition and identity; for Nietzsche it is an eternal stimulus to restive, energetic, and (amoral) action.

42. As I am articulating it here, Nietzsche's Overman is a genderless and nonorganic construction of forces; as he shows in *Zarathustra*, even naming it is ironic.

43. Two texts stand behind this term as used; Nietzsche himself does not use the French. Sarah Kofman uses it in her *Nietzsche et la métaphore*. In his *L'Etrangeté du texte*, Claude Levèsque develops the theme extensively in the chapters "L'Etrangeté du texte," "Entre écriture et lecture," and "L'Inscription du dialogue." I want to maintain, by my use of the French, the sense in which Camus uses *étrangeté* in *L'Etranger*, with its sense of distance, alienation, floating, and veiled significance.

44. *Aufheben*, a common word in German, introduces the active double gesture: it literally means to "pick up," to "overcome," but secondary meanings include both "to cancel" and "to preserve," thus introducing the motif of reversal and of contending forces, as in metaphor, into the discussion. Kaufmann reviews this in an interesting and useful note to II,10 of *Genealogy of Morals*.

45. This is Alexander Nehamas' point in *Nietzsche: Life as Literature*, though Nehamas wants to take the slightly different tack of seeing Nietzsche *narratizing* his life, making it into an enabling fiction, and thereby achieving something like the distance I suggest here, though in the end his assertion, after much stunning preparation, seems anticlimactic.

46. This is what Sarah Kofman means when she states, in her fine *Nietzsche et la métaphore*, that

> le retour au texte va de pair avec l'exigence d'une nouvelle écriture philosophique. En philologie rigoureux, afin de dissiper les séductions métaphysiques et les contresens des interprétations fallacieuses, Nietzsche, stratégiquement, se fait poète: il multiplie les métaphores, répète les métaphores traditionelles en les accolante à des métaphores moins usuelles ou encore les pousse jusqu'a leurs dernières conséquences pour voir jusqu'ou elles peuvent mêner [the return to the text is on a par with the exigency of a new philosophic writing. In rigorous philology, after the dissipation of metaphysical seductions and the errors of false interpretations, Nietzsche, strategically, makes himself a poet: he multiplies metaphors, repeats traditional metaphors and links them with unusual ones or else extends them to their final consequences to see where they will lead]. (149)

    To see "where they [metaphors] will lead," itself a fascinating idea for the inception of a "poetic mode" of thought, is to see—and to reproduce—the *étrangeté* of writing.

47. Beckett has made a meal of this "nothing more need be said"—the culminative silence, like a permanent hiatus. See chapter 10.

48. See Leopold Flam's "Solitude et 'etrangement' de Nietzsche dans la pensée de Heidegger," in *Nietzsche aujourd'hui*, 1 (395–427), for a discussion of the way in which a Heideggerian interpretation of *étrangeté* brings its possibility into the world. One could see Heidegger's project vis-à-vis Nietzsche as one of the emergence into the world of the Overman and his power of language.

49. Ronse 9. Ronse goes on to suggest that this path led Derrida back through Nietzsche to Freud and then to Heidegger; Derrida politely suggests that he was indeed "moving along lines that would be more Nietzschean than Heideggerean" (10), and indeed, Derrida is concerned in his *critique* of Heidegger to adumbrate his Nietzschean position, which is corroborated by Richard Rorty in *Consequences of Pragmatism* (particularly in his Introduction and in Chapter Six, "Philosophy as a Kind of Writing: An Essay on Derrida" [90–110]).

50. In *Beyond Nihilism: Nietzsche without Masks*, 38–57.

51. Shutte, *Beyond Nihilism: Nietzsche without Masks*, 46–47.

52. Nietzsche, "On Truth and Lies in a Nonmoral Sense," 1.

53. Nietzsche, *On the Genealogy of Morals* I, 13.

54. A very provocative discussion of this distinction is made by Gary B. Thom in his *The Human Nature of Social Discontent: Alienation, Anomie, Ambivalence* (Totowa, New Jersey: Rowman and Allanheld, 1984), particularly in Nietzsche's idea of anomie relative to the unconcious and the social function of self-fashioning.

55. It even contains the *étrangeté* of the *unheimlich*, which abides but is what Nietzsche would call "abysmal": *étrangeté* as *unheimlich* reintroduces the element of the "unnatural," the unconnected and detached, but not necessarily the *other*: the *unheimlich* is always a powerful occult (and occulting) force precisely because it is concealed, not because it is "outside."

56. Levèsque's French leaves no doubt as to the connection I want to make here:

> Cette pensée du dehors serait essentiellement une pensée de la limite et de la transgression de la limite, une pensée à la limite de la pensée. Plus affirmative que négative, elle irait jusqu'à l'excès de l'affirmation, excédant toute négation et toute affirmation. . . . Pensée de l'*étrangeté* non negative. (86)

57. Levèsque, *L'Etrangeté du texte*, 91.
58. Ibid.
59. Ibid., 92.
60. It is this placelessness that prompts Levèsque to link Freud's *unheimlich*, as the fear of castration, to Blanchot's *Neutre*, to Nietzsche's "lexical ambivalence" in the eternal return, and to Derrida's *différance*. This is what Levèsque calls, in the last words of the chapter, "le texte: le mouvement d'écrire dans sa neutralité [the text: the movement of writing in its neutrality]" (111).
61. After *The History of Sexuality* (1976), Foucault turned his attention from sex to "techniques of the self," investigating what technologies of the self were before the Christian era. Foucault discovered, he says, that pagan "ethics" were not rules for the austere exercise of power, but "techniques of the self." His interview with Paul Rabinow and Hubert Dreyfus, in 1983, published originally in *Michel Foucault: Beyond Structuralism and Hermeneutics* and collected in *The Foucault Reader*, attests to this Nietzschean and autoaesthetic discovery. Foucault's sense of self here, though, remains less complex than Nietzsche's, and less a function of self-constitutive discourse than I am suggesting here.
62. White, "Michel Foucault," 84.
63. This very language demonstrates the link between Nietzsche and such writers as Mallarmé and Joyce, and with Derrida. To claim a force "beyond" desire is, of course, also a metaphor, that is, a formulation of and by the *Übermensch*.
64. Lingis, "Difference in the Eternal Recurrence of the Same," 38.
65. Ibid., 40.
66. In Kaufmann's translation, this word is "flown," indicating the double meaning Nietzsche intends: the lake flows off, but it also flies off, rising higher and higher, defying gravity.
67. Nietzsche, *The Gay Science*, 285.
68. Nietzsche, *Beyond Good and Evil*, "On the Prejudices of Philosophers," 22.
69. For a fascinating discussion of this detachment, which is also for Nietzsche a *dépassement*, that is, for another perspective on the issue of *étrangeté*, see Philippe Lacoue-Labarthe's essay "La Dissimulation: Nietzsche, la question de l'art et la 'littérature,'" in *Nietzsche aujourd'hui: 2. Passion* (Paris: Union générale d'éditions, 1973).

CHAPTER 2. *LA MÉTAPHYSIQUE DU SOI*: JULIEN SOREL'S ECHOING VOICES

1. A note on translation: I have used the Norton Critical Edition of *Red and Black* for translated passages, uniformly; on occasion I have left the French in the text for the sake of comparison. Translations of secondary material, when not indicated, are mine.
2. In one of those wonderful crossings on which Nietzsche relies so heavily, this is a grounding epigram of both Nietzsche and Stendhal. It appears in Stendhal, italicized, in the Garnier-Flammarion edition, as a thought of Julien's; and it appears without reference to Stendhal in Section 263 of *Beyond Good and Evil*, in the following context:

    Différence engendre haine: the baseness of some people suddenly spurts up like dirty water when some holy vessel, some precious thing from a locked shrine, some book with the marks of a great destiny, is carried past; and on the other hand there is a reflex of silence, a hesitation of the eye, a cessation of all gestures that express how a soul *feels* the proximity of the most venerable.

This is certainly commentary on Julien Sorel, whether Nietzsche acknowledges it in his text or not, and sets the stage for a consideration of *Le Rouge et le noir*.

3. In this light it is particularly interesting that no manuscript exists for *Red and Black*. Only one edition of it appeared during Stendhal's lifetime, in 1831, and the later editions, supervised by Stendhal's friend and literary executor Romain Colomb, and then those (four) edited by Henri Martineau, all contain editorial alterations. Before his death, Stendhal made notes and "improvements" in the margins of a copy of the first edition; the two editions supervised by Colomb contain numerous alterations, presumably authorized by Stendhal. Later editors made changes as well, for their own reasons. All this is complicated by the fact that Stendhal's marginalia in his copy of the 1831 edition do not necessarily indicate desired changes in the text but often simply respond to the narrative with general commentary and other seemingly unrelated material. In other words, Stendhal's own notes do not make a good case for alteration of the first edition. The Martineau edition of 1960 lists all the variants in footnotes.

In other words, as is often the case, in *Red and Black* we have a text that floats away from its historical grounding in a welter of voices, all of which have a significant impact on our reception of Julien—as a mirror of his own reception of himself.

4. "The Disarticulation of the Self in Nietzsche," 260.

5. Nietzsche, *The Will to Power*, 481.

6. Stendhal, *Red and Black*, 5.

7. Ibid., 12.

8. Ibid.

9. Ibid., 13.

10. The book is the *Mémorial de Sainte-Hélène* by Emanuel Las Casas, himself a martyr to lost causes and to the chivalric rhetoric of which *Red and Black* gives such rich attention. Las Casas had come to France immediately following the Revolution, joining Napoléon just in time to accompany him into exile—the central *hegira* of Julien's narrative history. While in exile with the Emperor, Las Casas had written the "long and richly rhetorical *Mémorial*, which is a keystone of the Napoleonic legend" (*Red and Black* 13, note 5). Again, the richly allegorical layering of voices in *Red and Black* shows itself.

Loss of the book causes Julien's dark, Dionysian eyes to "glance sadly aside" (13), that is, to change their nature in response to his loss of that *other* father, who is not Napoléon but the image of the Emperor in las Casas's narrative of him.

11. The Dedalean aspects of the changing of nature effected by Julien's father should not be lost on us. Although the man is a brute, incapable of what Nietzsche would call nobility, his vocation is in its own way magical, loaded with transformative power. He takes a substance and renders it into another, making it not just useful but *consumable*. In a darkly allegorical way, Julien's genetic father is a kind of protean *poietes*, recapitulating in his work the entire history of civilization (including writing and the autoaesthetic force).

The town in which Sorel lives, Verrières, which in French is "stained-glass windows," exhibits something of that same ironic cross-fertilization. Julien is represented as coming *up* out of the humanity that has preceded him, through images and doctrines, toward *himself*. The fact that "young Sorel" is "the carpenter's son" raises further connections between him and the protean Dionysus/Crucified that we will see exemplified in the novel.

12. The importance of Napoléon to Julien can only be matched by his importance to Nietzsche, for whom the French emperor occupies a place in the highest pantheon of Problematic People, along with Socrates and Goethe. Nietzsche's account of Napoléon's rise (and fall) is so apt to Julien's sense of self that several passages from Nietzsche must be included here. In the penultimate part of the First Essay of the *Genealogy of Morals*, after describing the *ressentiment* of the French Revolution. Out of the triumph of the unheroic, Nietzsche says,

> There occurred the most tremendous, the most unexpected thing: the ideal of antiquity itself stepped *incarnate* and in unheard-of spendor before the eyes and conscience of mankind . . . . Like a last signpost to the *other* path [as opposed to the debased one of *ressentiment*], Napoléon appeared, the most isolated and late-born man there has even [*sic*] been, and in him the problem of the *noble ideal as such* made flesh—one might well ponder *what* kind of problem it is: Napoléon, this synthesis of the *inhuman* and the *superhuman* [*Unmensch und Übermensch*]. (16)

Napoléon is for Nietzsche the emblem of the contemporary Zarathustra, the beast *and* the Overman conjoined. This is not to say that Nietzsche uniformly approves of Napoléon; later in *The Will to Power*, he declares that Napoléon was "corrupted by the *means* he had to employ and lost *noblesse* of character" (1026). This only goes to show how complex Nietzsche's thought on Napoléon was (see Kaufmann's *Nietzsche*, Chapter 11, for a fuller discussion of this fundamental relationship).

13. Ibid., 149.

14. The power of the gaze has become one of the central hegemonic images of twentieth-century thought. See Lacan and even Richard on the power of the gaze, in addition to Sartre. Richard also discusses the power of the night to mask the gaze and, thereby, acting as an "envelope," to protect Julien's dreams (52–54).

15. Hoog, "Le 'role' de Julien," 134.

16. Stendhal, *Red and Black*, 279.

17. This is a possible, partial explanation of the much-commented-on title of the novel not heretofore suggested: the life of the "old" valor (*rouge*) and the "new" hypocrisy (*noir*) juxtaposed, since the past is more live and vital than the present; also of the old, stale, dead memories (*noir*) placed beside the new life of the sensations (*rouge*), as Julien would formulate his program. Still, the title remains properly enigmatic and paradoxical, like Julien and his "message."

18. Richard, *Stendhal et Flaubert*, 69.

19. Stendhal, *Red and Black*, 295.

20. Crouzet, "Introduction," *Le Rouge et le noir*, 24.

21. Brooks, *The Novel of Worldliness*, 228.

22. In the very language one employs to describe this activity, the quest-rhetoric is evident. At no level can Julien avoid its programmatic, linguistic nature, and therefore its being doomed, just as was, one might say in retrospect, the program of his mentor, Napoleon.

23. Sartre, *Being and Nothingness*, 263.

24. Hoog, "Le 'role' de Julien," 132.
25. Hoog comments on this declaration that it "works well when the role is played by someone else" (132).
26. Stendhal, *Red and Black*, 19.
27. Ibid., 15. This reference to the holy book of Islam is not gratuitous nor ironic, except in the Nietzschean sense. Stendhal wants to give a sense of religious fervor to Julien's autoaesthetic, but not to put it into the context of Christian dogma, particularly in a story in which Christian dogma plays such a central part. That is, Stendhal distances Julien's creed from us, while still maintaining its power, by referring to it as a "Koran." It is equally true that for a good French Catholic, as for all in the West, the Koran represents the central document of a *pagan* creed, one that subverts and opposes our own. Thus, Stendhal is able to accomplish his own *étrangeté* through the use of this title, which consists not of the Koran itself, of course, but of a different sort of pagan creed—one of literature and of that most Nietzschean quality, style. Robert Adams, in his notes to the text of *Red and Black*, furthers this quasi-religious theme in Julien:

> The Koran, used to suggest a pagan creed. Stendhal himself used to sharpen his style for the *Rouge* by reading the Code Napoléon. His admirations for the laconic precision of an army bulletin, for the psychological subtlety and truth-at-the-expense-of-meanness of Rousseau, and for the noble resignation of Las Cases' *Mémorial*, make up for Julien a literary trinity. (15–16)

There is of course a Nietzschean mockery of his own reference in Adams' terms, particularly "trinity." For Stendhal, the style of Julien's rebellion is paramount.
28. Ibid., 16.
29. This scene is provocatively interrupted by the flashback to Julien's contrition at revealing himself in conversation: he talks about Napoléon, after which he straps his arm painfully to his chest for *two months* to remind himself to maintain his distance. He places himself in the famous pose of the ideal leader to mock *himself*: only a painful reminder of his own insignificance can provide the lesson that he must conceal the texts that constitute him or they will be appropriated by the world.
30. Ibid., 20.
31. Ibid.
32. Ibid.
33. Stendhal repeatedly juxtaposes the possibilities of a symbolic interpretation of red and black in Julien's wake. As in the visionary church scene with Jenrel, in his first meetings with Mme. de Rênal Julien fights between the staid and austere role he ought to be playing (the black) and the visceral, passionate autoaesthetic nature he cannot suppress (the red). The church scene has shown us this juxtaposition *literally*, as a paradigmatic first instance of the salient dialogue, but once introduced it never recedes.
34. Ibid., 110.
35. Giraud, *The Unheroic Hero in the Novels of Stendhal, Balzac, and Flaubert*, 72.
36. Ibid., 218.
37. Ibid., 170.
38. Crouzet, "Introduction: Lacan and Narration," 26.
39. Ibid.
40. Hoog, "Le 'role' de Julien," 141.

41. Stendhal, *Red and Black*, 30.
42. I will return repeatedly to this scene, which focuses a good part of the novel. Mme. de Rênal's hand is to be seen in many different ways here. It is a function of social convention (kissing the hand); it is a synecdoche (winning someone's hand); it is a manifestation of the difference between the world views of the two (Julien's hypocritical ambition and literal textuality, Mme. de Rênal's romanticism). The scene is played out many times in various forms in the novel, as the emblem of duty, ambition, power, and deceit, in aid of the autoaesthetic force.
43. Ibid., 44.
44. Ibid., 65.
45. One must recall here Nietzsche's occasional claim to be the descendant of Polish noblemen; what would he have done with Jarry's characterization of Poland as "no place" in *Ubu Roi*, a localizing that precisely jibes with Julien's own about himself, as the son of no one?
46. Starobinsky, "Truth in Masquerade," 117.
47. Stendhal, *Red and Black*, 25.
48. Ibid., 37.
49. Ibid., 139.
50. Ibid., 42.
51. Richard, *Stendhal et Flaubert*, 69.
52. Richard, "Knowing," 486.
53. This sparrow-hawk is transmuted into an "eagle," the Napoleonic symbol, in Adams' Norton translation, a metamorphosis that, in light of the Napoleonic theme of supremacy and the sub-theme of Dedalean "hawk-like" power is most provocative. A hawk is not an eagle; in Stendhal's complex and precise allegorical imagery, it is important that the spied bird is not an eagle, since Julien remains distant from the Napoleonic throughout his story, however much he may try to assimilate it.
54. Stendhal, *Red and Black*, 50–51.
55. Ibid., 478.
56. This clause might well be Julien's motto. In Stendhal's French, it reads, "en vérité, l'homme a deux êtres en lui" (479); it is translated in the Norton Critical Edition in a weaker form: "It's really true, he thought, man does have two spirits within him" (390). Following this thought, in a dialogue with himself, Julien asks, "Qui diable songeait à cette réflexion maligne? [Who the devil thought up that malicious expression?]" (390). The dialogues of spirit and devil continue throughout for Julien, something in the way those of the Dionysian and Apollinian do for Nietzsche.
57. Ibid., 391.
58. Ibid.
59. Ibid., 395.
60. Tenenbaum, *The Problematic Self*, 50.
61. Richard, *Stendhal et Flaubert*, 128.
62. Stendhal, *Red and Black*, 474.
63. Poulet, "Stendhal and Time," 472.
64. Stendhal, *Red and Black*, 52–53.
65. Ibid., Part I, Chapter 19.
66. Ibid., 481.
67. Ibid., 346.
68. Ibid., Part II, Chapter 34.

69. Ibid., 359.
70. Ibid., 361.
71. Ibid., Part II, Chapter 33.
72. Ibid., 354.
73. Ibid., 220.
74. Martineau, "The Ending of *Red and Black*," 451–452.
75. Ibid., 473.
76. Prévost, "Stendhal's Creativity," 459.
77. Stendhal, *Red and Black*, 18.
78. Tenenbaum, *The Problematic Self*, 53.
79. Auerbach, "In the Hotel de La Môle," 446.
80. Stendhal, *Red and Black*, 42.
81. Ibid., 263.
82. Ibid., 241.
83. See Lacan, *passim*, and Richard on the power of the gaze, in addition to Sartre. Richard also discusses the power of the (Dionysian) night to mask the gaze and, thereby, acting as an "envelope," to protect Julien's dreams (52–54).
84. Ibid., 329.
85. Ibid.
86. Sartre, *Being and Nothingness*, 265.
87. Stendhal, *Red and Black*, 338.
88. Ibid., 339.
89. Ibid., 260.
90. Crouzet, "Introduction," *Le Rouge et le noir*, 26.
91. Richard, *Stendhal et Flaubert*, 47.
92. Ibid., 49.
93. Crouzet, "Introduction," *Le Rouge et le noir*, 27.
94. Girard, *Deceit, Desire, and the Novel: Self and Other in Literary Structure*, 506.
95. Sartre, *Being and Nothingness*, 562.
96. Richard, *Stendhal et Flaubert*, 64.
97. Stendhal, *Red and Black*, Part I, Chapter 16.
98. Ibid., 115.
99. Ibid., 348.
100. Crouzet, "Introduction," *Le Rouge et le noir*, 28.
101. Sartre, *Being and Nothingness*, 263.
102. Sonenfeld, "Romantisme ou ironie: les épigraphes de 'Rouge et Noir,'" 149.
103. Stendhal, *Red and Black*, 408.
104. Ibid.
105. Ibid.
106. Ibid., 65.
107. Ibid., 408.
108. Ibid.
109. Ibid., 407.
110. Ibid.
111. Ibid.
112. Ibid., 400.

CHAPTER 3. THE MIRROR AND THE DAGGER: NIETZSCHE AND THE DANGER OF ART

1. Art, for Nietzsche, is a function of the general creativity of the human. The closest twentieth-century aesthetics has come to the Nietzschean art I want to look at here is related to Jean Cocteau's seemingly much more frivolous idea that the artist, as *poietes*, is a kind of dabbler concealing his or her expertise, and that whatever he or she fabricates through that faculty of creativity is art. This may include the traditional arts such as music, sculpture, painting, dance, drama, etc., but it may and should also explore infinite new forms of art—indeed, the bursting of formal structures is a central part of Nietzschean art. Central to Nietzsche's art concept is the notion of the art-poet as the inscriber of the human world on the world-in-general. For Nietzsche, this means a centrality of words for the art world. Thus, the poet as we mean "poet" today, the writer, is a central aesthetic image to Nietzsche. In his own fascination with poetic style, in his dithyrambs and interspersed poetry, we see the autoaesthetic Nietzsche, but so do we in his music. It is only when that aesthetic impulse, that force of creation, is channelled into the last-man ends of *this world*, the mundane and anxiety-ridden ends of the unperceptive creator, that aesthetics is perverted. Like so much of twentieth-century art and art theory, the most significant problem with Nietzsche's idea of art is evaluative—How are we to establish a set of criteria by which we can know what art is and how it is working? This question has been rehearsed, without adequate response, since Nietzsche's time. Art for art's sake, avant-garde art, fringe art, and minority art of all kinds fit into Nietzsche's notion of art.

    Of course, to be concerned about establishing a set of criteria by which we can know and identify art, let alone "good" art, is to be a Kantian moralist; that is, to be a Master at whom Nietzsche would and does laugh.

2. In traditional views of art, the artwork and the artist interrelate in one of four ways: mimetically, pragmatically, objectively, or expressively. Each of these methodologies (and not, as is usually thought, just the mimetic) envisions art as a kind of mirror. The mimetic theory sees the work as mirroring the world or imitating the universe; the pragmatic theory concerns a need or value of the audience/viewer/listener; the expressive theory mirrors feelings, moods, states of inner experience within the artist him or herself; and the objective theory mirrors the art object as self-sufficient. In each of these traditional modes of aesthetic relationship, the mind is a kind of lamp illuminating the art object and being illuminated by it, so that the interaction between enhances the "value" of both.

3. Nietzsche's German is difficult to translate, particularly in these short and pithy parables—and particularly when they are intended for epigraphs to whole books, a function Nietzsche takes very seriously. As the epigraph to *The Gay Science*, with its multiplied and parabolic word usages, this short poem is as enigmatic as any Nietzsche produced. I include the German here, by way of full disclosure.

> Ich wohne in meinem eignen Haus,
> Hab Niemandem nie nichts nachgemacht
> Und—lachte noch jeden Meister aus,
> Der nicht sich selber ausgelacht.
> Ueber meiner Hausthür.

4. Nietzsche, *The Will to Power*, 469.
5. Ibid., 818.
6. Nehamas, *Nietzsche: Life as Literature*, 3.
7. Nehamas, whose work on Nietzsche is very important and provocative, like so many other philosophers writing about Nietzsche, must arrange him within his own worldview, that of the well-trained and holistic thinker. This is not to say that we do not all do this, but philosophers are particularly prone to this categorizing. Indeed, at the conclusion of his Introduction, Nehamas sets out his project in the following way:

> Nietzsche is an author, a public figure, and all his writings are relevant to his interpretation. The importance we attach to any part of his work cannot depend on general principles about which is essentially primary and which necessarily follows. The importance of each text depends on the specific contribution that text makes to our construction of a coherent and understandable whole. (10)

The "coherent and understandable whole" Nehamas wants us to be able to construct of Nietzsche's work must in the end be as chimerical as the self Nietzsche works toward positing. In terms of the place and power of art, Nietzsche is elliptical and evasive (he is an artist).

8. Schacht points out, in his "Nietzsche's Second Thoughts about Art," that although Nietzsche's ardent defense of art's centrality in human life cooled as his work progressed, Nietzsche continued to devote a central place to it. In *The Will to Power*, Nietzsche points out that "art for art's sake" should be subordinated to the great "aim of enhancing life" (298), but as Schacht correctly points out this means that art makes life possible. As the Dionysian principle evolved through Nietzsche's writing, so did the place and role of art. Schacht points out that art, like life, is always "a good deal less than it might be," and so receives the same critique as does (failed) human life.

Art's role in *becoming*, also mentioned by Schacht, is a bridge to the autoaesthetic. Nietzsche's linking of the artist to the "actor" (see *The Gay Science* 361), who is permitted to be false with a good conscience, provides the opening to the *identity* of artistry and life. Art is "a form of activity in which engagement rather than observation is primary. And this means that it is above all upon the artist that attention should be centered, even if not exclusively" (Schacht 245). Schacht's contention, that the central role of art in Nietzsche's philosophy of life is under-considered, is one of the catalysts of this book. My contention, that art, like life, is finally strategically autoaesthetic, derives from Nietzsche's ubiquitous comments on art and life.

The idea of art as a "sign and signature" echoes through Derrida's notion of the signature, from "Signature Event Context" and the dense issue of absence and presence at the scene of the signature in "SEC" and *The Post Card*, as well as throughout many of his other pieces. One could argue that Derrida's style is itself, in this Nietzschean way, a signature of the absence and presence of the artist—the artist and craftsman Derrida, who is *déjà* in his writing style (see the discussion of *déjà* in *The Post Card* and in Alan Bass' glossary on it and its relation to *Derrida, Jacques*, precisely in the context of Socrates, Plato, and the Apollinian art of writing that Socrates—ironically—purports to be doing in the famous post card).

9. Nietzsche's preoccupation with the nihilism that results from the enervation of

man's forces (particularly artistic forces) became greater for him. It is in this view of nihilism that the heart of Postmodernism, seen from a Nietzschean perspective, lies. (For a most effervescent discussion of this issue, see Kroker and Cook's *The Postmodern Scene*, New York: St. Martin's Press, 1986.) As though in anticipation of the Postmodern, Nietzsche's concern at the outset of *The Will to Power* is with the nihilistic impulse, centrally in its relation to art. Book One of *The Will to Power*, "European Nihilism," concludes after 134 sections with this precaution: "The *multiple ambiguity* of the world is a question of *strength* that sees all things in the *perspective of its growth*. Moral-Christian value judgements as slaves' rebellion and slaves' mendacity (against the aristocratic values of the *ancient* world). How far does art reach down into the essence of strength?" (134).

The ambiguity of this very statement, as Nietzsche is pointing out, hinges on the issue of the strength of art; the multiple ambiguity of which the world consists is composed precisely of the levels of mirroring and incision that art *reveals* to us. In this light, Nietzsche's final question in the first book of *The Will to Power* is a central one for the responsibility of art, and its willfulness. Art's power to "reach down" is the great enigma of human life.

10. Breazeale, "Introduction," *Philosophy and Truth: Selections from Nietzsche's Notebooks of the Early 1870's*, xi.
11. Although it is convenient and useful to make this distinction—Nietzsche does, repeatedly—one must remember that these terms, and the forces they represent, are mutually exclusive only in some simplistic and schematic way. Art contains knowledge, just as knowledge contains art. The *production* of art is heavily infused with the cognitive processes, just as rational/logical thought is infused with imagination and art. My distinction here must, over the course of time, evolve in the same way as did the Dionysian in Nietzsche: in the end, the seemingly opposite principles of thought and creativity merge in the autoaesthetic force. Nonetheless, they remain teleologically *polar* tensions even when they are harnessed together in aid of self-fabrication.
12. Here lies the beginning of the problem of nomenclature: to say that one may "know life" through art is already to have applied the Socratic/Platonic/Aristotelian principle of known subject to it, and thus to utterly miss it. Language, in a tradition basing itself so fundamentally on such ideas of value, is constrained to recapitulate its own blindness and rigidity, as Nietzsche well knew. Hence, his concentration on poetic, parabolic language and its inherent, desired warpage.
13. Nietzsche, *Twilight of the Idols*, 20.
14. Nietzsche, *Ecce Homo*, 10.
15. Nietzsche, *The Antichrist*, 11.
16. Ibid., Foreword.
17. Adorno, *Aesthetic Theory*, 76.
18. Nietzsche, *Beyond Good and Evil*, 225.
19. Nietzsche, *The Will to Power*, 842.
20. Nietzsche, *Twilight of the Idols*, 19.
21. Nietzsche, *The Will to Power*, 814. Nietzsche's mimesis is thus not Aristotle's at all but something quite different. Gone is the referent in the physical or metaphysical realm, for Nietzsche. Mimesis occurs as the imitation of a state, or rather a state of flux, a condition of activity in which that set of forces of which life consists is eternally at work. Art mirrors this state-which-is-not-a-state. An

understanding of the oxymoronic nature of such terms as "state of flux" and "condition of activity," is necessary to a sufficient sense of Nietzsche's use of mimesis.

22. Deleuze, *Nietzsche and Philosophy*, 103.
23. de Man, *Allegories of Reading*, 114.
24. Kaufmann, "Preface," note 8, *The Gay Science*.
25. Think here of Heidegger's statements in *The Origin of the Work of Art* of the nature of truth, including the particularly Nietzschean statement that "Truth is untruth insofar as there belongs to it the reservoir of the not-yet-revealed, the un-uncovered in the sense of concealment" (180). Although, as always, Heidegger is hinting at an immanence Nietzsche would eschew, the idea of truth as untruth is quite close to the Nietzschean idea of truth in falsehood.
26. Nietzsche, *The Gay Science*, 4.
27. This is just the way in which Derrida refers to writing in calling it a "dangerous supplement," and, from a different perspective, it is what Adorno means, historically, when he says that "works of art become what they are by negating their origin" (4): art is *étrangeté*, a disjunctive principle.
28. Adorno, *Aesthetic Theory*, 74.
29. Deleuze, *Nietzsche as Philosopher*, 102.
30. This short passage in itself might be the basis of an entire Nietzschean aesthetic, as demonstrated by Hardy in *Jude the Obscure*, in which the worthiness to suffer, within the framework of self-reflection, is Jude's obsession. For Jude, the dagger is a chisel, which also invades its medium, controlling and enframing it, creating its dialectic strength.
31. Recognition of the artist, as an exceptional man, occurs through the suffering of art, as Nietzsche states in *The Will to Power*: "It is exceptional states that condition the artist—all of them profoundly related to and interlaced with morbid phenomena" (811). The texture of this condition is formed by the irony of the next sentence in the text: "—so it seems impossible to be an artist and not to be sick." Discussion of this phenomenon of sickness in art is to follow.
32. Nietzsche, *The Will to Power*, 804.
33. *The Case of Wagner* 74. This washing-out is appropriate to Hardy's treatment of Jude, who seems to fade away as his novel proceeds, just as Julien Sorel's voice fades from the pages of *Le Rouge et le noir* and Julien's *person* itself vanishes, leaving only his head.
34. The most extensive use of the word occurs in *The Antichrist*, in which "sick" is the continual designation for the priest.
35. The "states" of creativity exhibited by the artist, according to Nietzsche, require 1) "intoxication," 2) "an extreme sharpness of certain senses, so they understand a quite different sign language—and create one—the condition that seems to be a part of many nervous disorders," and 3) "the compulsion to imitate," from "within," so that "a kind of deafness and blindness towards the external world" results in which "the realm of admitted stimuli is sharply defined," as by the dagger thrusts of the sensorium (see *The Will to Power* 811). Nietzsche characterizes these states in Section 811, with the sort of double consideration of sickness and health Jude (and all the protagonists of the novels considered here) displays:

> It is exceptional states that condition the artist—all of them profoundly related to and interlaced with morbid phenomena—so it seems impossible to be an artist and not be sick.

This view of the polar dilemma of the artist adumbrates both Freud's and Jung's view of the artist/poet as inherently unbalanced; in terms of the theme of modernity I am investigating here, Nietzsche concludes Section 811 with the following admonition:

> It is to the honor of an artist if he is unable to be a critic—otherwise he is half and half, he is "modern."

The words of Didi and Gogo echo again (the worst insult they can hurl at each other is to accuse the other of being a "critic") across the issue of the modern.

36. Sickness and ugliness have a particularly interesting relationship in Nietzsche. In terms of aesthetic judgment, Nietzsche completes his re-definition of the aim of aesthetics by declaring,

> How is the ugliness of the world possible?—I took the will to beauty, to persist in like forms, for a temporary means of preservation and recuperation: fundamentally, however, the eternally creative appeared to me to be, as the eternal compulsion to destroy, associated with pain. The ugly is the form things assume when we view them with the will to implant a meaning, a new meaning, into what has become meaningless. (*The Will to Power* 416).

Though one must read the concluding statement of the preceding many times and meditate on it to appreciate its disruptive, salutary, and mimetic value, it describes the dialectical—even political—nature of Nietzsche's revolution. In it one can perceive the bombshells of early twentieth-century art and the confusion in the art of our own time, including much of the imagery in the novels treated here.

37. Nietzsche, *The Will to Power*, 1049.
38. Hayman, *Nietzsche: A Critical Life*, 353.
39. Nietzsche, *The Will to Power*, 1052.
40. I cite the entire passage in the supplement to show how Nietzsche juxtaposes Dionysus, the *pharmakon* and the *sparagmos*, with "the god on the cross." Here Nietzsche's imagery becomes uncannily Hardyesque: art is "left behind" and encrypted by the artist as a testament to his struggles.
41. Nietzsche, *The Will to Power*, 617.
42. Ibid., 822.
43. Ibid., 417.
44. Ibid., 415.
45. Ibid., 415, 801.
46. This singularity is just what Jude Frawley desires and cannot achieve. He is not able to undo his critical weaknesses and achieve the strength of the Dionysian man, nor is he able to eschew the artistry by which he perceives himself in the world. Being unable to do either, Jude languishes in the middle, pulled in both directions.
47. One must remember that, for Nietzsche, art is *neither* Apollo nor Dionysus exclusively, that by his later writings "Dionysus" has become the marriage of *both* principles as articulated in *The Birth of Tragedy*. In this condition of desire and of latent meaning, art is born:

> The man in this condition transforms things until they mirror his power— until they are reflections of his perfection. This compulsion to transform into the perfect is—art. (*Twilight of the Idols* 9)

Thus art *is* exceptional man in a state of intoxication, interpreting that state and leaving, *in his wake*, works of art.

48. The fable is the ultimate Nietzschean incarnation of *amor fati* and the frustration of ratiocination. Not only does Nietzsche introduce us to the "narrative logic" by which the artist works; he also thereby shows us the specifics of suffering.

49. Paul de Man's characterization of Nietzsche's metaphoricity captures beautifully what is at work in art:

> The idea of individuation of the human subject as a privileged viewpoint is a mere metaphor by means of which man protects himself from his insignificance by forcing his own interpretation of the world upon the entire universe, substituting a human-centered set of meanings that is reassuring to his vanity for a set of meanings that reduces him to being a mere transitory accident in the cosmic order. The metaphorical substitution is aberrant but no human self could come into being without this error. Faced with the truth of its nonexistence, the self would be consumed as an insect is consumed by the flame that attracts it." (*Allegories of Reading* 111)

De Man here "resorts" to metaphor, imitating Nietzsche, in rewriting the parable at the beginning of "On Truth and Lies in a Nonmoral Sense." The point de Man is accentuating is that only through the strategic metaphorization of the world in art can man "come into being."

50. de Man, *Allegories of Reading*, 115.

51. Nietzsche, *Twilight of the Idols*, 10.

52. In just the way in which Dionysus itself becomes the overcoming of opposites without cancelling opposition, preserving and maintaining the *agon* of *étrangeté* without producing dysfunctioning.

53. Nietzsche, *The Will to Power*, 803.

54. *The Birth of Tragedy* is indeed about the relation of distress and art, as Nietzsche declares in *The Will to Power* (463). In terms of Nietzsche's being "understood" in his autoaesthetic force, aphorism 463 in *The Will to Power* is interesting. Its short text lays out Nietzsche's theoretical forebears, as follows:

> My precursors: Schopenhauer; to what extent I deepened pessimism and by devising its extremest antithesis first really experienced it,
> Then: the ideal artists, that after-product of the Napoleonic movement.
> Then: the higher Europeans, predecessors of the great politics.
> Then: the Greeks and their origins.

In Kaufmann's translation this footnote occurs, appended to the conclusion of the section:

> The MS goes on: "In *The Birth of Tragedy* I gave hints concerning the relation of 'distress' and 'art'; personal education of the philosopher in solitude. The Dionysian."
> Schlecta not only omits these lines, following the example of all previous editors; he also omits the second paragraph—in which, incidentally, the MS has "Napol." instead of "Napoleonic."

In *Birth of Tragedy*, distress results from awareness of drives and of their terror, from which tragedy is fabricated. No doubt the early editors and Schlecta—and Kaufmann in his own way, who only restores the passage in a subordinating footnote—edited the passage, like so many others, in the interests of streamlining, but the intent and the content of the passage is of course completely changed by their omission. The missing paragraph puts what remains in the published version of the passage in a completely different framework, one of "distress" and "art" rather than a mixture of philosophy and politics. The missing framework is one of autoaesthetics.

55. Nietzsche, *The Gay Science*, 76.
56. This transliteration of the poem is a rendering of Nietzsche's German, which is not always well-served by Kaufmann's translations. The original goes as follows:

> "Kein Pfad mehr! Abgrund rings und Totenstille!"—
> So wolltest du's! Vom Pfade wich dein Wille!
> Nun, Wandrer, gilt's! Nun blicke kalt und klar!
> Verloren bist du, glaubst du—an Gefahr.

The artist-will is expressed here in terms of the balance of audacity and care the artist is always exercising by virtue of art's nature. "You asked for it—now you've gotten it" points to the artist-will and its power of self-framing. Leaving the path, straying from the known and recognized always lands one in the abyss, recognition of which is the acknowledgment of danger.

Kaufmann's translation, which takes some liberties and, as so often with his poetic translations, I think, weakens the effect of the poem to translate what he can of the rhyme, is:

> "No more path! Abyss encircling and deadly still!"—
> You willed it! Left the path by your own will!
> Now, wanderer, you have it! Now look coldly and clearly!
> You are lost, if you believe—in danger.

57. Nietzsche, *The Will to Power*, 1039.
58. The danger of art is that it emanates from within but resonates out into the world of others. Danger is a fearful emotional state, in which the artist is always working, but it is also the threat that the attitude and work of the artist offers to the rest of the world. Within the artist, both artist and layman exist side by side; in this condition, the artist feels both selves simultaneously—another instance of *étrangeté*. Nietzsche discusses this double danger in sexual terms, as the giving (masculine) and taking (feminine) of artistic energy forming the human whole: the "antagonism" between the "gifts" of the artist and the layman "are not only natural but desirable":

> The perspectives of these two states are opposite: to demand of the artist that he should practice the perspective of the audience (of the critic—) means to demand that he should impoverish himself and his creative power—It is the same here as with the difference between the sexes: one ought not to demand of the artist, who gives, that he should become a woman—that he should receive.
> Our aesthetics hitherto has been a woman's aesthetics to the extent that only the receivers of art have formulated their experience of "what is beautiful?" In all philosophy hitherto the artist is lacking—. (811)

The artist in each of us must remain distant from and antagonistic toward that critic in him or her who must receive. The artist, for Nietzsche, is pure cornucopic giving, an outpouring of Dionysian energy. Of course, as Nietzsche shows in *The Gay Science* quoted above, the complexity of the artist is the great strength and mystery of human being, the autoaesthetics of artistry the great subject of human life.

59. Ibid., 811.
60. Schacht, "Nietzsche's Second Thoughts about Art," 232.

61. de Man, *Allegories of Reading*, 118.
62. Paul de Man's characterization of this condition, and its difficulty, is articulated in *Allegories of Reading*:

> If we read Nietzsche with the rhetorical awareness provided by his own theory of rhetoric, we find that the general structure of his work resembles the endlessly repeated gesture of the artist "who does not learn from experience and always again falls in the same trap." (118)

De Man concludes his own chapter on the "Rhetoric of Tropes," which centers on Nietzsche, with the remark that "What seems to be most difficult to admit is that this allegory of errors is the very model of philosophical rigor" (118), which brings Nietzsche's around again to the philosopher.

CHAPTER 4. JUDE THE *CAMERA OBSCURA*

1. Hardy, *Jude the Obscure*, xxii.
2. Miller, *Distance and Desire*, 222. This is not the Tess of the d'Urbervilles, of course, but a *name* with which Hardy was fascinated. The "tone poem" Miller analyzes is one that combines a kind of dirge with the almost jaunty meter of a limerick, in extended form. The poem itself is an exercise in ambivalence about character and about the attitude one (including the author) ought to have about character.
3. Jude's sense of the image is of arrest. His desire to make life behave formulates itself in powerful efforts to make it *stop*, and this is how the image works for Jude. Rather than be a function of the imagination, Jude's pictorial sense—and it extends to concepts of world-order for him, reduces all of life to a still-life that can be pondered and pored over though never, of course, "understood." In this respect as in so many others, Jude takes up our Nietzschean themes and inverts them, removing the life from them rather than infusing them. It is as though Jude is in the right context with completely the wrong language: he is "modern" in the way Nietzsche means it, and will suffer for it.
4. *Jude the Obscure*, 203. In this sense, the novel goes well beyond the "causes" for which it was *célèbre*; seen in this Dionysian way, the novel is not "about" the marriage question, social convention, academic detachment, or rural village life, though it concerns itself with all these themes; *below* these issues, as it were, is the much more vital issue of artistic appearances.
5. In this context, Jude and Nietzsche are again similar. Wonderful reminders of Nietzsche's skirmishes with photographers remain: Nietzsche as a youthful and pensive student, as a young saber-carrying soldier, etc. Of course, even more interesting from the point of view of framing is the fact that the image we have of Nietzsche, the thoughtful and hawklike man with the walrus mustache, is a complete fabrication of his sister Elizabeth, who took Nietzsche to the photographer numerous times after his mind was gone, and literally posed him for the camera. Nietzsche was not present, only "Nietzsche."
6. Hardy, *Jude the Obscure*, 247–248. We remember that Jude has made his journey to Christminster because of a photograph of Sue he has seen at Aunt Drusilla's, though Jude has textualized himself differently here: the image of Sue is a catalyst for Jude's seeking out the palpable person beyond the graven image, leading Jude on toward her in a way that his own image does not for him.

7. Hardy is, of course, positively medieval in his choice of names. Jude's name is so over-wrought that it virtually vanishes beneath its own weight of avatars; Sue's name, "Bridehead," is a very un-ironic play on the redemptive nature of love. The fact that Hardy, Jude, and Sue cannot engineer a more satisfactory outcome for their moral tale is indicative of the ways in which conventional redemption *would* sour in the presence of an amoral Dionysian redemption, if they were able to perceive and act on it.

   Other names, including Jude's and Sue's, will receive further treatment further on.

8. Hardy, *Jude the Obscure*, 246–47.

9. Ibid., 248.

10. This framelessness of the Dionysian state is referred to often by Nietzsche. The version of this state that both elevates and confounds Jude is characterized in *The Will to Power* as follows:

   > The states in which we infuse a transfiguration and fullness into things and poetize about them until they reflect back our fullness and joy in life: sexuality; intoxication; feasting; spring; victory over an enemy, mockery; bravado; cruelty; the ecstacy [*sic*] of religious feeling. *Three* elements principally: *sexuality, intoxication, cruelty*—all belonging to the oldest *festal joys* of mankind, all also preponderate in the early "artist." (801)

   Thus, Nietzsche points out several sections later (804), our artist-selves transform into the festal in an effort of self-preservation; Dionysus rises up and dominates when the "understanding" has had too strong a voice (or chorus of voices, as with Jude, Julien, Ike, etc.).

11. Nietzsche, *The Will to Power*, 37.

12. The opening words of Kurt Leidecker's Introduction to *Nietzsche's Unpublished Letters* (Philosophical Library, 1959) refer to this Manichean dilemma, characterized by Nietzsche in the same section of *The Will to Power* (37) as one in which "opposites" enervate the world until "all one has left are the values that pass judgement—nothing else," thus: "Because the beauty of the overman came to him as a shadow Nietzsche asked no longer for the gods. Instead he felt creatively impelled toward men" (1). We will excavate the nature of the Overman as shadow at length in the next chapter; here, suffice it to say that the passing of judgement, equivalent in Nietzsche to no-saying, is the particular domain of the nihilistic and spiritual; a running subtext through Ike McCaslin's chapter (6) will show how these two protagonists relate in terms of Nietzschean spirituality and its ironies.

13. Hardy, *Jude the Obscure*, 294.

14. Ibid.

15. But as if parodying the idea of any autoaesthetic originality, Sue herself has retextualized Shelley: she has misquoted from Shelley's poem. The first two lines she quotes are lines 190–191 from the "Epipsychidion," the last two are the earlier lines, 21–22. She has inverted the order to form her own poem, her own self-design. Had she not inverted the order and continued to quote from the earlier section of the poem, moreover, she would have had to cite lines depicting the great emptiness of which she and Jude, like Shelley, are so afraid. The earlier section of the poem proceeds in this fashion:

   > Seraph of Heaven! too gentle to be human,
   > Veiling beneath that radiant form of Woman

> All that is insupportable in thee
> Of light, and love, and immortality!
> Sweet benediction in the eternal Curse!
> Veiled Glory of this lampless Universe!

Had Jude—or Sue—known the Shelley in question, they would have seen how their rejection of a love with an *earthly* grounding articulates the "lampless Universe," with what Nietzsche calls Shelley's "social pessimism of the anarchist" (*Will to Power* 1020), which he calls in the same section a "phenomenon of decay and sickness":

> To give excessive weight to moral values or to fictions of the "beyond" or to social distress or to suffering in general: every such exaggeration of a narrow viewpoint is in itself already a sign of sickness.

It is in contradistinction to this pessimistic no-saying that Nietzsche proposes the only positive no-saying possible:

> What must not be confused with all this: pleasure in saying No and doing No out of a tremendous strength and tension derived from saying Yes. . . . a form of bravery that opposes the terrible; a sympathetic feeling for the terrible and questionable because one is, among other things, terrible and questionable: the *Dionysian* in will, spirit, taste.

This is the autoaesthetic power *par excellence*, but Jude and Sue do not begin to perceive it; rather, they pursue its inverse.

16. Ibid.; emphasis added.
17. The relation here to Joyce's epiphanies is clear; both desire a still moment that, like Shelley's still fading coal, will, while it fades, resonate in the receiver as a kind of living presence or eternal being. The desire for this resonant image is a hallmark of Modernist aesthetics; all of the writers (except possibly [late] Mallarmé and certainly Beckett) and central characters discussed in this book believe deeply in it but are caught, one and all, in the Nietzschean subversion of this verity and its textualization. Only Beckett, of the writers treated centrally here, makes a strategic point of that subversion. Beckett and Peter Handke are the chief proponents—along with the French New Novelists and some other contemporaries like Robert Pinget, in addition to a good deal of current theory—of that strategic subversion in contemporary fiction writing.
18. Hornback, *The Metaphor of Chance*, 135.
19. Miller, *Distance and Desire*, 184.
20. The novel opens here because it is the first time in Jude's young life in which he has felt that abysmal *étrangeté* as a direct experience, however much he may realize, in the scene, that he has always had a dormant version of it but has been too young to realize it consciously. When Phillotson leaves the village, *Jude's* autoaesthetic dialectic is set in motion.

   The Marygreen well is, in a larger sense, the world's great *camera obscura*, the tube of light reflected from the well to Jude's eye, a great camera lens focusing and distilling the light of the world. Because it is a reflection, of course, the view in the well is a photographic inversion. The image of the well, in Jude's use of it early and later in the novel, is a perfect focus for the autoaesthetic vision of the *camera obscura* through which Jude is always looking.
21. Hardy, *Jude the Obscure*, 5.

22. Miller, *The Form of Victorian Fiction*, 61.
23. Hardy, *Jude the Obscure*, 26.
24. It is interesting to note here that in Hardy's manuscript version of this passage, the word "space" is crossed out and "time" inserted in its place. Hardy's decision to make Jude a man at the center of his *time* instead of *space* is very telling in light of the autoaesthetic he is about to unfold, for at least two reasons. First, Jude is *not* at the center of his space but is always afloat in the web of shifting frames of which he fabricates himself. Since time entails such a different metaphysic and aesthetic, Jude can be seen as at the "center of his time" without being located in any particular time. Second, as the passage proceeds, Hardy actively obscures the aesthetic sense he wishes us to have of Jude by his change of keyword: to be "at the center of your time, and not at a point in its circumference," particularly in light of the numerous spatial/ocular images in the remainder of the passage, is to be caught between space and time, jarringly de-framed or put out of the frame. The word change is indicative of Hardy's desire to displace Jude, and is a central strategy of that displacement.
25. Hardy, *Jude the Obscure*, 15.
26. Jude's problematic manipulation of frames is in many ways like those of later *Bildungsroman* heroes such as Stephen Dedalus, Antoine Roquentin, and the protagonists of Thomas Mann. Like theirs, Jude's program is the completion of consciousness in the manipulation of forms; unlike theirs, his involves his disappearance into the forms, not their manipulation. This is a vital distinction, in that Jude's passivity in the face of his ardent frame-creation contains even greater irony than the projects of those other heroes and anti-heroes.
27. Hardy, *Jude the Obscure*, 25.
28. Ibid., 6.
29. As is the case for Julien Sorel, even the Marygreen village church, purportedly a symbol of stability and stasis, is not "original" but new, "unfamiliar to English eyes" (6), erected on "a new piece of ground by a certain obliterator of historic records who had run down from London and back in a day." But Hardy goes further than Stendhal in this regard. The "obliterated graves" in the old/new churchyard in Marygreen are now "commemorated by eighteen-penny cast-iron crosses warranted to last five years" (7), and the attitudes behind those crass memorials are even more worrying in terms of substantial identity. Not only has the cemetery been transmuted into a new order, so has the countryside itself, in its physical appearance and its underlying themes. Tillage in Mary-green, "like new corduroy," deprives the country "of all its history beyond that of the few recent months, though to every sod and stone there really attached associations enough and to spare—echoes of songs from ancient harvest-days; of spoken words, and of sturdy deeds" (10). The (metaphysical) "history" is *there*, we are told (by a narrator sympathetic to Jude's sense of loss), immanent, though Jude has not been and cannot now be "educated" to it. Only Aunt Drusilla can remember the old songs the sods and stones seem to contain hidden within them, and now even she sees them as dimmed and fading; the old Roman road, a vital link to a substantial past, is "neglected and overgrown," hardly visible.

    Hardy would have been interested in and heartened by the architectural commentary of the current Prince of Wales, whose feelings about American, Postmodern, "poorly scaled," and "anonymous new" buildings are certainly descendants of Hardy's own views.

30. Ibid., 8.
31. Later, speaking of his child, Jude exercises an autoaesthetic power over his own roots:

> The beggarly question of parentage—what is it, after all? What does it matter . . . whether a child is yours or not? All the little ones of our time are collectively the children of us adults of the time, and entitled to our general care. That excessive regard of parents for their own children, and their dislike of other people's is, like class-feeling, patriotism, save-your-soulism, and other virtues, a mean exclusiveness at bottom. (330)

Though Jude speaks here of his offspring, he is clearly speaking about himself, too, fabricating a communal social fabric to use, like new corduroy, to cover the old abyss. It doesn't work for Jude any more than it does for Little Father Time.

32. Nietzsche, *The Birth of Tragedy*, 137.
33. Ibid.
34. The first images of *A Portrait of the Artist as a Young Man*, in which the naming-power (father/author) tells the story of the moocow, and so launches Stephen Dedalus, Baby Tuckoo, into his poetic life, cannot but come to mind here. The High Modernist desire for a gratifying and well-told story of origin is pervasive in each of the novels treated here.
35. Hardy, *Jude the Obscure*, 27.
36. Ibid., 31.
37. Ibid.
38. Ibid., 32.
39. Ibid., 233.
40. Said, *Beginnings*, 158. Nietzsche is quite clear about the metaphysical nature of hunger:

> In regard to all aesthetic values, I now employ this fundamental distinction: I ask in each individual case "has hunger or superabundance become creative here?" At first sight, another distinction might seem more plausible—it is far more obvious—namely the distinction whether the desire for rigidity, eternity, "*being*," has been the cause of celebration, or rather the desire for destruction, for chance, for *becoming*.
>
> The desire for destruction, change, becoming *can* be the expression of an overfull power pregnant with the future (my term for this, as is known, is the word "Dionysian"). . . . (*The Will to Power* 846)

The other kind of hunger, that of "eternalization," Nietzsche continues, can be "blissful," as Jude had hoped, but it is more often

> the tyrannical will of a great sufferer who would like to forge what is most personal, individual, and narrow—most idiosyncratic—in his suffering, into a binding law and compulsion, taking revenge on all things, as it were, by impressing, forcing, and branding into them his image, the image of his torture.

This sort of artful suffering is a precise definition of Jude's art and life, the "romantic pessimism in its most expressive form" Nietzsche wants us to overcome.

41. Hardy, *Jude the Obscure*, 86.
42. Ibid., 85.
43. Ibid.

44. Near the end of the novel, Hardy has Jude come to this marker, of course, in his directionless and delirious wanderings, to "catch his death." Lying at the foot of the marker, which becomes the beginning and the end, the alpha and the omega, Jude shows the inscription to be the memorial for his lost "original intention," which is itself no more than that—not an accomplishment but an intention, and a lost one. Jude frames himself in terms of the journey out from this marker, but the frame is extremely problematic, in that Jude *does* venture "thither" but at the same time does not, returning to the marker as though he is still in the black box in which he started. Jude's journey out becomes in this moment as ironic as that of Zarathustra, who *goes down* from and returns to his cave, none the wiser for the journey but, like Jude, more disillusioned. The dialectic of learning always takes place between intention and the "evil star" that intervenes. Again, the passage in *Jude* must remind the reader of the opening paragraph of "On Truth and Lies in a Nonmoral Sense," in which a cosmological figure for learning is also the grounding metaphorical text.

45. The obviousness and pervasiveness of the biblical imagery should not persuade us that because of these qualities it is unimportant. The eschatological framework within which Jude operates is a central one, of vital importance to many other of his perspectives—indeed, as vital as Nietzsche's appropriation of "the language of the enemy" (Christianity). Jude's "progress" from the "village mother" (Marygreen, Aunt Drusilla, the well, the pond, etc.) to the "urban father" (Christminster, rational inquiry, etc.) is the appropriate one; one need only think of the New Jerusalem, from the *Faerie Queene* to Joyce's *Portrait* to the songs English schoolboys still sing, to sense its power.

   Unexplored in Hardy and only suggested here is the Freudian imagery inherent in this exchange (wells to spires, etc.), but which could certainly be explored as central to Hardy's Dionysian schematics.

46. Ibid., 24.

47. His treatment of Old Father Time shows that Hardy does not mean to imply a greater, more sophisticated sense of self, nor a greater wisdom by "growing older," but rather a growing world-weariness—what Nietzsche calls pessimism. Hardy himself seems to have manifested this cumulative pessimism, which was both a social and a psychological phenomenon. His protagonists in general follow his lead here; nowhere in Hardy, however, does this pessimism take a more weighty, even tragic, form than in *Jude*, as each of the central characters succumbs to the great weight of pessimism. In the next chapter, as we explore *Zarathustra*, with its portrayal of the "gravity" that brings us *all* down, we must remember Hardy's greatest weight, the solitude and despair of Jude, Sue, and particularly of Old Father Time, in this Nietzschean light.

48. Millgate, *Thomas Hardy: His Career as a Novelist*, 334.

49. Significantly, in terms of the dense biblical framework in which Jude, Marygreen, and Christminster are located, immediately after calling Christminster the city of light and declaring that "the tree of knowledge grows there," Jude seems to forget that this three is the mark of benighted mortality, not of divine enlightenment, and to gloss over it as a cause of suffering—the tree of knowledge is the root of all our troubles, from the Christian point of view. Nietzsche declares that this sense of "troubles" is exactly that *ressentiment* that Christianity cannot stand, a sense of self that overpowers guilt, which religion cannot tolerate because such a power would disarm its own power. Jude himself, because of his overlapping frames, is ambivalent about such a metaphorical tree,

and uses it in this instance as a marker for that ambivalence: it is at once desirable as a source of knowledge and dangerous as the source of hubristic suffering. Nonetheless, in this first extension beyond childhood, Jude becomes aware of the problem of place and time in terms of the figuration of suffering.

It is in this light that Jude considers Christminster a "holy" city. Offering a prayer allows him to see it, he thinks, or to believe he sees it in the distance, as he declares: "It was Christminster, unquestionably; either directly seen or miraged, in the peculiar atmosphere" (20). Of course, the atmosphere is Jude's perspectival one, his aesthetic atmosphere, in which immediately, "like extinguished candles," "the vague city became veiled in mist." From within the *camera obscura*, Jude can only make out the "chimaera" of the city, never the thing-in-itself, any more than he can recognize something he can call himself.

50. Hardy, *Jude the Obscure*, 46.
51. The epigraph for *Jude the Obscure*, from the Book of Esdras in the Apochrypha, establishes this theme indelibly and not at all obscurely:

> Yea, many there be that have run out of their wits for women, and become servants for their sakes. Many also have perished, have erred, and sinned, for women. . . . O ye men, how can it be but women should be strong, seeing they do thus?

Jude is indeed "run out of his wits" for both Arabella and Sue, "redeemed" only by his artful incorporation of them into his life, as art. This sublimation of woman into art is, of course, utterly invisible and absolutely unsatisfying to Jude.

52. Ibid., 70.
53. Ibid., 49.
54. This theme of rebellion has ambivalent and interesting consequences in the novel, as both Jude and Sue rejoin their "right" partners, both with disastrous consequences. Readers of *Jude* who claim, as some feminist critics have, that Sue and Jude's attitude toward marriage is, at base, purely a rebellion against social restrictions, need to spend some time re-reading the novel's conclusion.
55. Hardy, *Jude the Obscure*, 41.
56. Ibid., 294.
57. Ibid., 43.
58. Ibid., 44.
59. Ibid., 53.
60. Ibid., 47.
61. Nietzsche, *Zarathustra*, I,9.
62. Ibid., Prologue 10.
63. Ibid.
64. Hardy, *Jude the Obscure*, 42.
65. In keeping with his complex iconography, Hardy indicates that Arabella does something similar as well, as a secondary effect behind the primary one I have mentioned. Even in Jude's physical lust for her, he must acknowledge his "other side," the very *idea* he has of her, which remains outside of Arabella, something other than the woman herself—and in some ways of more importance to Jude. "His idea of her was the thing of most consequence, not Arabella herself" (65), Jude declares. Her sensuality, and his in response to her, is detached from her physicality and becomes itself an idea, displaced from the flesh. After his first long afternoon with Arabella, during which Jude was going

to read the New Testament, he returns to his room; it has become a map of loss and neglect:

When he got back to the house his aunt had gone to bed, and a general consciousness of his neglect seemed written on the face of all things confronting him. He went upstairs without a light, and the dim interior of his room accosted him with sad inquiry. There lay his book open, just as he had left it, and the capital letters on the title-page regarded him with fixed reproach in the grey starlight, like the unclosed eye of a dead man:

'Η ΚΑΙΝΗ ΔΙΑΘΗΚΗ (53)

Hardy's telling *prosopopoeia* here, the painting of intention across the face of all that confronts Jude, is focused on the dead eye of the New Testament, which stares at him with its accusatory dead stare, killed by his libido.

66. Hardy, *Jude the Obscure*, 98.
67. Ibid., 98.
68. Ibid., 276.
69. Ibid., 165.
70. Ibid., 105.
71. Ibid., 247.
72. Ibid., 139.
73. Ibid., 147.
74. Ibid., 233.
75. Ibid., 243.
76. It is as though Little Father Time has been born, like Athena, whole out of Jude's fears and dilemmas. Hardy has written, in Father Time, a character with an almost Kafkaesque or surreal quality about him. The weight of the world lies on Father Time in a wholly unrealistic way, preventing the character from being read as real. He is a schematic character whose dark outline underlies Jude's and contributes to our deepening sense of dread for Jude, who, in his unsuccessful autoaesthetic efforts, treats Father Time as a kind of omen of disasters to come.

   One might say that Father Time is an emblem or symbol of the failure of a successful autoaesthetic strategy, an allegorical figure who floats through the story, never able to relieve himself of his greatest weight. In this respect, Father Time exemplifies the Dionysian dilemma of action: he is able to act only when he perceives the hopelessness of his dilemma, and then his action is crazily hyperbolic. Father Time is an emblem of the cancellation of balance and rationality, in favor of a perpetual Dionysian disruption that can end only in death. The way Father Time is described by Hardy (see quotation below in text) cements this view.
77. Hardy, *Jude the Obscure*, 332.
78. Ibid., 235.
79. Ibid., 396.
80. Ibid., 406.
81. In this, Father Time's action instructs Sue, who adopts a new set of Commandments: "You shan't learn, you shan't labour, you shan't love" (407).
82. Nietzsche, *The Will to Power*, 2.
83. Ibid., 80.
84. Nietzsche, *Human, All-too-Human*, 122.
85. Hardy, *Jude the Obscure*, 405.

86. Said, *Beginnings*, 138.
87. Father Time becomes the solipsistic precursor of the officer in Kafka's *Penal Colony*, whose execution machine inscribes on condemned men the charge against them and, in the same phrase or clause, their illuminating final instruction.
88. Hardy, *Jude the Obscure*, 10.
89. Ibid., 11.
90. Nietzsche, *The Birth of Tragedy*, 9.
91. Hornback, *The Metaphor of Chance*, 131.
92. Derrida, "The Supplement of Copula," *Textual Strategies*, 83.
93. Hardy, *Jude the Obscure*, 390.
94. Ibid., 137.
95. Ibid., 393–394.
96. Ibid., 409.
97. Ibid.
98. Ibid., 82.
99. As is so often the case in *Jude*, the sexual imagery of the parent and the child is not very well concealed: the son moves to the center of the pond, which sags under his weight, but he cannot penetrate it. One could construe Jude's actions as deriving from one or two objectives: he is attempting to reawaken his mother, symbolically, or beckoning to her to take him back to her. He seems to be attempting to join (with) her, to go beyond all the stories he has heard and make some direct contact with a different reality from the one(s) in which he generally lives. His jumping on the ice is at once an acknowledgment of (impossible) frames and an attempt at piercing and breaking them. At once he adheres to and violates the texts, though the surface of the pond remains intact. Rather than to be able to go down to join her, Jude remains above, curious and doubtful of his own "dignity" (self). The episode on the ice is, in fact, Jude's last attempt at autochthonous existence and at finding this kind of mortally dangerous link to his so-called natural roots.
100. Ibid., 92.
101. Ibid., 98.
102. Ibid., 92.
103. The fact that Oxford is so transparently disguised in Christminster, as is often the case with Hardy's novels, is another interesting autoaesthetic strategy. In becoming Christminster ("Christ's large church), Oxford becomes the seat of self-adherent fictions that refer to the historical world but alter and thematize it.
104. Nietzsche, *The Birth of Tragedy*, 9.
105. Submerged here is Jude's occupation, which hardly deserves mention in terms of his suffering life, but which is vital to his autoaesthetic. As a restorer of stones and an artist in stone, Jude is heir to the most archaic ideas and forms of autoaesthetic self-recuperation. He produces, with his hands, the "texts" out of which he and others can facilitate their own self-fabrication, whether successful or not.
106. Hardy, *Jude the Obscure*, 98.
107. Ibid., 469.
108. Miller, *Thomas Hardy: Distance and Desire*, 235–236.
109. Hardy, *Jude the Obscure*, 203.
110. Hornback, *The Metaphor of Chance*, 136.
111. Miller, *Distance and Desire*, 236.
112. Hardy, *Jude the Obscure*, 484.

113. Ibid., 464.
114. Ibid., 484.
115. Ibid., 472.
116. Ibid.
117. Millgate, *Thomas Hardy*, 411.
118. Ibid., 334.
119. Ibid., 328.
120. Jude's illusions of that were destroyed on a previous Remembrance Day, as he watched a horse being kicked at the gate of the city, a scene derived not only from that other great novel of the autoaesthetic of pain, *Crime and Punishment*, but also, for us, from the text of Nietzsche's life, in those last few moments of sanity in January 1889, when Nietzsche, too, seeing the scene Jude witnesses at the gate, took his last step into unreachable difference and pure appearance.
121. Hardy, *Jude the Obscure*, 474.
122. Miller, *Distance and Desire*, 214.
123. Hardy, *Jude the Obscure*, 475.
124. Ibid., 33.
125. Ibid., ix.
126. Nietzsche, *On the Genealogy of Morals*, 149.
127. Miller, *Distance and Desire*, 6.
128. Ibid., 221.

CHAPTER 5. ZARATHUSTRA AS THE SHADOW OF THE SHADOW: PHILOSOPHY/POETRY/POWER

1. —u m s p h i n x t. dass ich in Ein Wort
    Viel Gefühle stopfe:
    (Vergebe mir Gott
    Diese Sprach-Sünde!)

    A note on translation and text: for the text of *Zarathustra* I have relied on *Nietzsche Werke: Kritische Gesamtausgabe* (KGW), ed. Giorgio Colli and Mazzino Montinari, Sechste Abteilung, Erster Band (Berlin: de Gruyter, 1968). I refer to this edition parenthetically, by named and numbered sections, as is usual, rather than by page number. I have consulted Hollingdale's translations occasionally but have relied on Kaufmann's more standard American English translations, except where he changes the terse paragraphic form Nietzsche employs and where he "simplifies" punctuation or makes enigmatic passages more "available" to the reader, or when his own imagination or poetic sense permits him to stray further from Nietzsche than I wish to go, in all of which cases I have interpolated my own translation.

2. The idea of the alternate name is very appropriate to Nietzsche's sense of self; that he employs the so-called Zoroaster's "proper" name rather than the version derived from Greek transliteration and given to the historical Zarathustra's religion is telling from an ironic and historic point of view, since Nietzsche's story of Zarathustra is a synchronic and mythic fiction designed to be, and to remain, true and at the same time to defy any limiting truth-claim or localization.

    About the historical Zarathustra very little is known; it is thought that he lived *either* in the tenth or ninth century B.C. or in the sixth or fifth. He might have lived in eastern Iran or in northwest Iran. Traditional accounts of Zarathustra's life have him the son of a pagan priest, who, at the age of thirty, had some sort of strong religious experience (an angel took him to meet the Great Spirit, Ahura-Mazda), out of which he vowed to "purify" religion. He and his faith, worked out in great detail and fervently followed over a large part of the Middle East for centuries, had a great influence on Greek religion and Greek thought (he is thought to have been a contemporary of Thales; see Ruhi Muhsen Afnan's *Zoroaster's Influence on Greek Thought*, Philosophical Library, 1965, for exhaustive documentation and analysis of this influence). Zarathustra's religious doctrines apparently had a strong influence on Heraclitus; I will look further at this in chapter 9.

Zoroastrian links to Nietzsche's ironic sense of religious conversion *away* from traditional doctrinality and dogma—as well as to Faulkner's much more straightforward treatment of Ike McCaslin as a displaced Zarathustra—are readily apparent and closely linked in the Nietzschean tradition, on only the most cursory reading of these two texts, though their affinity is at first not obvious.

3. The four stages:

  1. early period, associated with Zarathustra himself
  2. period in which Zoroastrianism was the official religion of the Persian Empire under Darius (late sixth and early seventh century B.C.)
  3. renewal of influence after a decline due to monarchic changes (third century B.C. to sixth century A.D.)
  4. submersion in Islam, except for "Parsi" ("Persians") in India and elsewhere

Each of these stages is a greater and greater watering down of Zarathustra's teaching, a more powerful interaction of the religion with surrounding cults and dogmas, and a consequent greater and greater loss of its original distinction. As Zoroastrianism became more and more popular, more and more enculturated as it were, it also lost its identity.

4. This displacement of the *voice* of Zarathustra, which mocks the subject, occurs more and more frequently throughout Book Four; finally, Zarathustra disappears from his own story, only to reappear in the concluding section, "Das Zeichen [The Sign]" as the center of a parody of biblical prophets—he is truly *ensphinxed*.

5. Nietzsche, *Zarathustra*, Prologue 1.

6. An even better translation of *verwandelt*, in this context, would be "transformed."

7. The fact that Zarathustra's autobiography leads him to a cyclic return to his homeland (back to what he thinks is "himself") is a particularly powerful example of the fold of narrative articulation, discussed in Chapter One, as the Eternal Return. Potentially, the four books of *Zarathustra* represent four instances of a never-ending chain of returns through which Zarathustra measures himself and the world around and below him; it is an emblematic example of that reevaluation of all values to which Nietzsche devoted his writing life, directly and indirectly. Of course, as *Nietzschean* articulation, in its ensphinxedness it misses Zarathustra as much as it misses Nietzsche.

The potentially eternal return of Zarathustra to his cave is a parody of the ever-upward spiral of spirituality one sees in steeples, minarets, renderings of the

Tower of Babel, and in such artworks as Bach's "Musical Offering," whose key signature rises through the scale as it repeats its fugal round. Unlike Bach's offering, which is dedicated to the greater glory of the God, Nietzsche's offering is to the greater glory of the "spiritualized" autoaesthetic self as self-narrator.

8. Since *untergehen* also means "to decline," the moment Zarathustra chooses to be in the world he begins his fall away from the fruitless solitude of his cave but also from any proximity to the Overman. The spirit of gravity, which will play such an important part in Book Three, is operating from the first words of the Prologue.

9. Nietzsche, *Zarathustra*, Prologue 3.

10. For a thorough and rich discussion of the *topos* of the Overman, see Bernd Magnus' "Overman: An Attitude or an Ideal?" in *The Great Year of Zarathustra (1881–1981)*, ed. David Goicoechea (New York: University Press of America, 1983), 142–165.

11. Nietzsche, *Zarathustra*, Prologue 4.

12. Preface 3. See J. Daniel Breazeale's "The Meaning of the Earth" in *The Great Year of Zarathustra*, 113–141, in which Breazeale develops the idea of the Overman as the value-creating force, and hence the meaning of the earth, *der Sinne der Erde*. In his discussion of the *instrumentality* of values, Breazeale suggests also the utility of metaphor for life in *the* metaphor of the meaning of the earth. Breazeale correctly asserts in his conclusion that it is impossible for philosophy to continue in the same way after *Zarathustra*'s critique of value.

Thus, the wisest man is himself *ensphinxed*: the word Nietzsche uses for this generative connectedness is *Zwitter*, which means "crossed" or "connected" in the way that an hermaphrodite is crossed, a mingling of distinct and separate genres. Nietzsche strives to maintain the "connectedness" of the higher man to the earth, and to the physical humanity of man through *Zarathustra*, by maintaining—and ironizing—his sexual nature.

13. Nietzsche, *Zarathustra*, Prologue 3.

14. Nietzsche, *Zarathustra*, Prologue 6.

15. See Otto Manthey-Zorn's *Dionysus: The Tragedy of Nietzsche*, particularly the chapter on *Zarathustra* (82–107), for interesting comment on the nature of Zarathustra's wisdom and learning and the Dionysian nature of self-overcoming.

16. Nietzsche, *Zarathustra*, Preface 6. I have explored elsewhere ("Recovering the *Néant*: Language and the Unconscious in Beckett," *Psychiatry and the Humanities*, 1990) the nature of that nothing one loses in dying. Taken in the way Beckett, and I think Nietzsche, mean it, the nothing is the most valuable thing one can lose: it is the unconscious self, the Dionysian *Übermensch*, whose rage to live and to experience *is* human life. Seen thus, the nothing lost by the tightrope walker in dying is enormous.

17. Nietzsche, *Zarathustra*, Prologue 6.

18. Ibid.

19. This bifurcation is a central tenet of Modernist art of all genres. See Peter Ackroyd's *Notes for a New Culture* for a penetrating and very convincing portrait of Nietzsche's influence on Modernism, an account different from that presented by many others. Although a general influence of Nietzsche on Modernism is acknowledged, as, for example, by Sanford Schwartz and others, far too little is made of the fundamental power Nietzsche exercised over the thought and art of the time.

20. Nietzsche, "On Immaculate Perception," II, 15.

21. Gadamer, "The Drama of Zarathustra," 351.
22. Haar, "Nietzsche and Metaphysical Language," 27.
23. Ibid., 35.
24. Nietzsche, "Upon the Blessed Isles," II, 2.
25. In this passage, Zarathustra shows his own shadow-existence, playing the jester to Goethe's tightrope walker. He constructs himself out of quotations that *are* his mentors, derived from his experience of *étrangeté*: his mantric repetition of "all permanent—is a mere parable" is an inverted and ironic derivation of Goethe's last chorus, in which Goethe's mantra-like, repeated refrain, "all that is destructible is but a parable," serves the prophet of acknowledged and desired, articulated distance rather than desired Romantic fusion. Nietzsche reverses and ironizes Goethe's conclusion to *Faust*, thus reopening consideration of parable, spirituality, and narrative itself.
26. Nietzsche, "The Tomb Song," II, 11.
27. That is, philosophy without art: *Wissenschaft* that is not *fröhliche*.
28. Nietzsche, "The Shadow," IV, 9.
29. Nietzsche, "The Vision and the Riddle," III, 2.
30. Nietzsche, "On the Thousand and One Goals," I, 15.
31. Again, see Peter Ackroyd, *Notes for a New Culture* (London: Vision Press, 1976). Ackroyd's comments on this aspect of Nietzsche have just this impetus, particularly in his chapters "The Emergence of Modernism" (11–26), where Ackroyd quotes Zarathustra's assertion that "all existence is a kind of speech," and "The Uses of Language" (47–65), in which he links Nietzsche to Joyce through Nietzsche's "invasive irony" (56). It goes without saying that Poststructuralist and deconstructive theory (from Foucault and Derrida to Lacan, Lyotard, and Lacoue-Labarthe) rest in large part on this interpretation of Nietzsche, who remains a fragrant figure (sensed but not always seen) behind and in all contemporary theoretical discourse.

   In terms of a possible Modernist take on Nietzsche, it is most provocative to see that the Zarathustran (and un-Nietzschean) Heidegger makes his project, in "Who Is Nietzsche's Zarathustra?" a programmatic re-privileging of a static, Parmenidean being. Heidegger does what Zarathustra accuses poets of doing in Book Two's "On Poets": he "muddies the waters to make them appear deep," formulating a religious experience from the text's inversions. But this reintegration will not hold: the "subversion" of all that a Heidegger would do with his text, to use Michel Haar's word (5–6)—even that he would do in seeming imitation of Zarathustra, is the key to Zarathustra's (cancelled) self-textualization.
32. Nietzsche, "Preface," *Ecce Homo*, 4.
33. Nietzsche, "Preface," *On the Genealogy of Morals*, 8.
34. III, 2 "The Vision and the Riddle," 2. The following section contains a close analysis of the single section from Part Three of *Zarathustra* referred to here— the section in which Zarathustra confronts the Gate of Moment. For economy's sake, and not to become maddeningly redundant, citations in this section refer only to the subsection within that particular chapter.
35. Nietzsche, "On the Vision and the Riddle," III, 1.
36. Ibid., 2.
37. Ibid.
38. Nietzsche, "On Old and New Tablets," III, 12, 2.
39. A belated word here on Nietzschean poetics. Taking Zarathustra up his moun-

tain to the Gate of Moment, Nietzsche is able to go beyond and to overcome the separation of the philosophical and the poetic, and thus to produce the dawn of the Overman's shadow. *Zarathustra*, Gadamer asserts, "is not only a successful poem but a product of genius of a thinker" (347); it is, as a book, so seemingly difficult to understand (according to Gadamer, it is particularly difficult for philosophers and Germans) precisely because it is "a work belonging by half to poetry" (Gadamer 349). But this is not an unmixed strength in terms of Nietzsche's desire to be *understood*. Zarathustran poetics dictate that he will not let *his écriture* rest on its nor on any established ground, but shakes that ground with its own message. This is the context in which Nietzsche, in his virtual rewriting of German idiom and more generally of customary phraseology (what Kaufmann calls Nietzsche's "monadologicality"), and Zarathustra's narrator—this is by Part Three the only way in which one can refer to the narrative voice in *Zarathustra*—call his language an "exile," "born in the mountains." The relationship between poet as seeker and wanderer, and truth as "stopping place" at which wandering is arrested, in the Goethean sense, is the fundamentally problematic mirage Zarathustra will never be able to reach:

> "Suitor of truth?" they mocked me; "you?"
> No! Only poet!
> An animal, cunning, preying, prowling,
> That must lie,
> That must knowingly, willingly lie:
> Lusting for prey,
> Colorfully masked,
> A mask for itself,
> Prey for itself—
> *This*, the suitor of truth?
> Only speaking colorfully
> Only screaming colorfully out of fools' masks,
> Climbing around on mendacious word bridges,
> On colorful rainbows,
> Between false heavens
> And false earths,
> Roaming, hovering—
> *Only* fool! *Only* poet!'

The *arch* of Zarathustra's parabolic poetry, his "word bridges," joins with the poet/philosopher's ironic project of self-discovery, always simultaneously frustratedly or satisfyingly truncated. These bridges, according to Zarathustra, are always "mendacious" (an echo of "On Truth and Lies in a Nonmoral Sense"), and because of their lying nature they can only "scream colorfully out of fools' masks," "between false heavens and false earths." The poet is a fictionalizing beast who must lie—in order to *be*—not only because in lying he tells the truth but because he seems to claim that he does so in a "deeper" or more fundamental sense than the philosopher. In this denial of the desired metaphor of self-depth, we perceive the most powerful meaning of self-overcoming, as Hollingdale hints:

One has misunderstood Nietzsche completely unless one realizes that he visualized the overcoming of *self* as the most difficult of all tasks, as well as the most desirable; that he considered the will-to-power as the only drive alive in man.... The men he admired most were those whose will-to-power was strong but sublimated into creativity. (154)

Zarathustra is the paradigm of these sublimated, creative men, but he also personifies the *process* through which these best of men strive to transcend their "beastly" natures in autoaesthetic force. Here Nietzsche returns to his philological roots, calling on the Greek sense of the *poietes*, the maker, fabricator of identity in creative action. Zarathustra is the figure of the thinking poet's displaced nature; he is everything and nothing, "all and none." "[Nietzsche's] foregrounding of the artistic as the philosophical, or the birth of philosophy out of the spirit of art—and perhaps its return there" (72), is the influence Geoffrey Hartman sees as Nietzsche's gift to modern thought. Zarathustra's poetic insight rests on the fact that art privileges appearance, seen here as a dialectic between what is revealed and what is (dialectically) concealed. As poetry plays with fragmentation, with the nature of the hidden and revealed, and with language as discourse of surface and reflection, it is the highest manifestation of the autoaesthetic art, whose power is to have the will to reveal will-to-power.

40. Remember Kaufmann's discussion of Nietzsche's repudiation of Christ (as against Jesus) in his *Nietzsche: Philosopher/Psychologist/Antichrist* (New York: Meridian Books, 1956), Part IV, Chapter 12 (288–333), in which he makes of the former an icon, of the latter a subversive rebel. This distinction might very well be followed up in terms of self-representation, as for the way the Jesus of the Gnostic Gospels and the Book of Thomas differs from the canonical, iconic Jesus Christ of the formative Church that Matthew, Luke, Paul, and a few others made of him. Another time.

41. Nietzsche, "On Poets," II, 17.

42. In autoaesthetic terms, this moment of writing has heavy links to the Gate of Moment, with its interfacing vectors. To Derrida's grammatology, the moment of writing means "the moment of thinking" or "the moment he thinks," which of course, as Derrida points out, does not solve our problems of articulation but transports them to the realm of *étrangeté*.

43. Nietzsche, "On the Three Metamorphoses," I, 1.

44. Ibid.

45. Nietzsche, "On Enjoying and Suffering the Passions," I, 5. Indeed, the most deific of men falls short: even "Dante is, compared with Zarathustra, *merely a believer* and not one who first *creates* truth" (6, emphasis added). This release, this overcoming, results from the fact that "one must still have chaos in oneself to be able to give birth to a dancing star" (Foreword 5): the unorthodoxy and value of Zarathustra's Hellenic chaos, with its plenitude and potential, is to be discovered in this vitalized animation.

46. Nietzsche, "The Cry of Distress," IV, 2.

47. The shadow is itself directly *fore*shadowed in Nietzsche's "The Wanderer and His Shadow" (1880), and is, like so much in Nietzsche, a quotation of a quotation.

48. Nietzsche, "The Shadow," IV, 9.

49. Nietzsche's German is very tight and apt here:

Mit dir verlernte ich den Glauben an Worte und Werte und grosse Namen.

Wenn der Teufel sich häutet, fällt da nicht auch sein Name ab? Der ist nämlich auch Haut. Der Teufel selber ist vielleicht—Haut.

The introduction here of the creative Nietzschean forgetting (*verlernte*) by which we can come to have Dionysian power beyond intellectual memory, as well as the more obvious references to the value of appearance itself, fits into the textual nature of Nietzschean autoaesthetics precisely and brings *Zarathustra* on track for its mock-transcendent conclusion.

50. Ibid.
51. A useful commentary on this surrogation occurs in W. D. Williams' "Nietzsche's Masks," in *Nietzsche: Imagery and Thought*, ed. Malcolm Pasley (London: Methuen, 1978), 83–104.
52. Haar, "Nietzsche and Metaphysical Language," 24.
53. See Tracy B. Strong, *Friedrich Nietzsche and the Politics of Transfiguration* (Berkeley: University of California Press, 1975), for a connection between "The Ass Festival" as parody of eucharist and Zarathustra as parody of Overman. The dramatically rich metaphoricity of the Ass Festival section of Part Four is so obviously an ironic comment on the spirituality Nietzsche is ironizing that I have hardly mentioned it here. My contention is that the allegorical significance of the Ass Festival can best be understood in terms of the Gate of Moment and the Shadow, so I have spent time on them instead. By the time of the Ass Festival, so near the end of *Zarathustra*, reference to any conventional spirituality is radically undermined. Seen in this way, the Ass Festival is a fairly straightforward parody of the Mass *and* of Christ with his followers, which *untergehe* into Dionysian chaos, demonstrating the way in which the Dionysian underlies *all* ritual, however "spiritualized" it may declare itself.
54. de Man, *Blindness and Insight*, 147.
55. The voluntary beggar has established the terms for this distancing. To become himself, the beggar has said, man would not forget nor "get rid of his melancholy—his great melancholy; but today that is called *nausea*. Who today does not have his heart, mouth and eyes full of nausea? You too! You too!" In fact, the word "nausea" occurs repeatedly near the increasingly giddy conclusion of *Zarathustra*, not only foreshadowing Sartre but commenting on the abyss above which we walk our tightropes, as I'll show in a moment.
56. Ibid.
57. Nietzsche, "The Voluntary Beggar," IV, 8.
58. Nietzsche, "On Old and New Tablets," III, 12, 3.

CHAPTER 6. FROM OLD GOLD TO I.O.U.S: IKE MCCASLIN'S DEBASED GENEALOGICAL COIN

1. Though *The Bear* is part of a larger novel, my response to it has always been that it is a completely self-sufficient piece with more "novel-like" qualities of development, orchestration, and theme than most separately published novels. As a result, I will here punctuate *The Bear* as though it were a novel.

In terms of the double *prosopopoeia* of the epigraphs to this chapter: 1) the personification of the "written and forged thoughts" that transmute into "receding and exhausted thunderstorms and old, yellowed feelings" is wonderfully rich tropic evidence of the linguistic autoaesthetic Nietzsche brings to the power of writing, and which no writer (indeed, no thinker) can ignore (though Faulkner, in his own writing if not in his thematics, does so try); 2) the very interesting and provocative personification of the will, including Kaufmann's use of the impersonal pronoun "he" in the cited passage from *Zarathustra*, is also a transmutation of the force of will into a character (the German of this passage: "Nicht zurück kann der Wille wollen; dass er die Zeit nicht brechen kann und der Zeit Begierde—das ist des Willens einsamste Trübsal," a less dramatic *prosopopoeia* than Kaufmann's translation but one nonetheless). This is precisely the fictive self-invention, at the (gate of) moment of self-awareness, that Nietzschean autoaesthetics strives to demonstrate. Ike McCaslin's melancholy ensphinxedness is an emblem of this autoaesthetic.

2. Faulkner, *As I Lay Dying*, 165.

3. Ibid.

4. Faulkner, *As I Lay Dying*, 165–166. See J. Douglas Canfield's article, cited in the Bibliography, for a fine and full discussion of the theme of emptiness in language suggested here, from a different perspective than mine, in *As I Lay Dying*, but which aids significantly in a reading of *The Bear*.

5. McGee, "Gender and Generation in Faulkner's 'The Bear,'" 54.

6. Irwin among others: see, for example, Douglas Canfield's introduction to his *Twentieth Century Interpretations of Sanctuary* or the epigraph and discussion of genealogy by Philip M. Weinstein in the same volume. André Blaikaston has made some suggestions regarding other Faulkner texts, in his ongoing investigation of Faulkner, as well.

7. Irwin informs us that Faulkner himself seems to have understood the oscillating relationship between a narrator and his story, between a writer and his book, as embodying "the always-deferredness" of meaning, which in addition to its Nietzschean/Derridean overtones acts as a kind of Freudian *Nachtraglichkeit*, in which the act of narration, as a recollection and reworking, produces a story that almost makes sense but not quite, yet whose quality of *almost* being meaningful seems to indicate, indeed, to promise, that meaning has only been temporarily deferred and that some future repetition of the story, some further recollection and reworking, will capture that ultimate meaning (8). This is one of the most subtly powerful autumnal strategies with which Faulkner aligns himself with Nietzschean language strategies.

8. It would be very provocative to see a parallel here between "wood" and "word," as though the former is a slippage of the latter. Indeed, Derrida would certainly permit us this, and famously takes advantage of this sort of semiotic or phonic connection, even across languages. In Nietzschean terms, that is, in German, this will not work, since "Wald [wood]" and "Wort [word]" are close but not linked as the two words are in English. Nonetheless, from Faulkner's point of view, this play might very well be commented on. For Faulkner, the woods is a place in which the lack of words is translated into another dimension, another medium, in which the negation of the ambivalence of language can take place.

9. This Faulknerian ensphinxedness is a central theme of what amounts to Ike's thanatography, which Ike imitates from *Ben*'s ensphinxedness in the stories of which he consists. Insofar as Old Ben the bear is an emblem of life-in-death, Ike's relationship with him, as with any of Ike's symbols, reflects narratized historical self-definition, in just the way that the tombstone of Ike's determination, the doubling of his declared negation ("two ciphers" is both two numbers and two zeros or empty signs) is a monument not only to the beginning of the dialogue

with Ben but also to his own death-wish in language. One must not forget the thanatography inherent in the Dionysian: to live is to embrace death; to live as a human being is to suffer from an awareness of this conundrum. The "old, yellowed feelings" to which Nietzsche refers in *Beyond Good and Evil* are petrified in Ike's tablets, and with almost unbearable (Nietzschean) irony in the yellowed slips of paper he excavates from the tomb of his legitimacy, in the old coffeepot/sarcophagus whose winding sheets have concealed an autoaesthetic treasure heavier than gold.

10. Faulkner, *The Bear*, 10.
11. Nietzsche, *The Will to Power*, 98.
12. Ibid., 127.
13. Ibid., 397.
14. Faulkner, *The Bear*, 195.
15. Matthews, *The Play of Faulkner's Language*, 252–265.
16. This term comes from the seminal passage in Derrida's *Positions*:

> To risk meaning nothing is to start to play, and first to enter into the play of *différance* which prevents any word, any concept, any major enunciation from coming to summarize and to govern from the theological presence of a center the movement and textual spacing of differences. (14)

Derrida uses the word in the context of ironic Nietzschean spirituality.
17. See Canfield, 375–377.
18. "Gender and Genealogy," 47. The Nietzschean implications of Freud's *Civilization and Its Discontents* are unavoidable here. Stretched between the doorways of wilderness and civilization is mankind on his tightrope, asking and answering what Freud calls, in the concluding paragraph of *Civilization and Its Discontents*, "the fateful question for the human species," the question as to "whether and to what extent their cultural development will succeed in mastering the disturbance of their communal life by the human instinct of aggression and self-destruction" (92). Freud concludes the book on the note that this question has special interest for the "present time," in that, given our so-called control over power sufficient to allow us to "exterminate one another to the last man" (not, I assume, a reference to Nietzsche's last man, but all the more prescient since Freud wrote this in late 1929), we experience the anxiety of confusion, caught between cultural development and "human instinct."
19. Stonum, *Faulkner's Career: An Internal Literary History*, 157.
20. Faulkner, *The Bear*, 300–301.
21. McGee, "Gender and Generation in Faulkner's 'The Bear,'" 49.
22. Ibid., 50.
23. Faulkner, *The Bear*, 312.
24. The play here of the Apollinian and Dionysian is worth noting, particularly the way they are "married" by Faulkner. The imagery here suggests that Ike is not and cannot be "the woods" but can only marry them; thus, he is kept in a perpetual state of *étrangeté* relative to the objects of the hunt, just as he proves to be relative to his wife. Ike's ensphinxedness, the heaping together of many contrarities within a single autoaesthetic theme, is a complex language-sin.
25. Ibid., 192–193.
26. Matthews, *The Play of Faulkner's Language*, 259.
27. In this respect, see the comments on silence in *Ecce Homo*, in which Nietzsche claims that "the rudest word, the rudest letter are still more benign, more decent

than silence" ("Why Am I So Wise?" 5). It must not be forgotten that the thanatography of writing is a play with silence, as we saw in *Zarathustra*, Nietzsche's claim notwithstanding. The tendency of all texts to reduce down to silence is a trait particularly associated with the Postmodernist response to Modernist verbosity and the celebration of the exuberance of language.

28. Matthews, *The Play of Faulkner's Language*, 257.
29. Lewis, "The Hero in the New World: William Faulkner's 'The Bear,'" 201.
30. McGee, "Gender and Generation in Faulkner's 'The Bear,'" 46.
31. Faulkner, *The Bear*, 314–315.
32. Ibid.
33. Matthews, *The Play of Faulkner's Language*, 255.
34. Ike's domestic aspect, his "tamed" life in the anonymous rooms to which he retreats, unable to face a fuller, outer life of autoaesthetic power, links him powerfully with Jude. Each of the rooms Ike inhabits, like Jude's, is a new interment—and a new inversion of the "self-space" for which he looks. For Ike as for Jude, the directly aesthetic is not available for a release from this frustrated tension of self-production. One has the feeling with Ike, as with Jude, that if awareness of *art* were to dawn on him, he would be redeemed by it, but this never occurs. Faulkner's richness of language stands always as a high contrast to Ike's un-artful preoccupations, more clearly than was the case with Hardy. Faulkner's orchestral prose, whose never-flagging energy contains a Dionysian power, when juxtaposed with Ike's spare existence, overwhelms it and diminishes it in comparison.
35. Kinney, "Faulkner and the Possibilities for Heroism," 219–220.
36. This is the nature of the *fall* according to Zarathustra: in coming down to life and acknowledging the search—the hunt—for identity, that is, in the *untergehen* by which man associates with his morality, he also associates with death and with *his own* death.
37. Kinney, "Faulkner and the Possibilities for Heroism," 235.
38. Faulkner, *The Bear*, 328–329.
39. Ibid., 254–255.
40. Ibid., 273.
41. Ibid.
42. The doubling, and even the multiplicity, of self-inscription is parabolically investigated in Nietzsche's *Zarathustra*. Not only does Zarathustra converse as an "I" and a "me," but the entire project of Zarathustra's "story" becomes one of effacement in the double, the Shadow by whom the conclusion of Zarathustra's story-book is recounted. Zarathustra's shadow is the ultimate *döppelganger*, against which a self can be sensed and measured, in Ike's case as in Zarathustra's, a word at a time.
43. Irwin investigates the permutations of this thematic strategy in psychological terms (Irwin 33ff). His investigation of the heroic myth of which he wants so badly to be a part begins with the division I have suggested; I want to look at each in turn.
44. Brooks, *William Faulkner: The Yoknapatawpha Country*, 271.
45. Boon is literally the madman in the marketplace, since the forest Ike has associated with the hunt has turned into a stand of saleable trees being turned into rental rooms. The commercialization of the woods is Faulkner's version of the civilizing of the Dionysian in Nietzsche, as in *The Gay Science*, where the madman appears, heralding the death of God. For both of these madmen, we

have killed our own deities, through greed, *ressentiment*, and ignorance. Faulkner's treatment of Boon is a strong link to the Nietzschean themes that lie beneath the shallow topsoil-of-appearance of *The Bear*.

46. Faulkner, *The Bear*, 331.
47. Ibid., 278.
48. Ibid.
49. Millgate, *The Achievement of William Faulkner*, 210.
50. Faulkner, *The Bear*, 275.
51. Ibid., 281.
52. Ibid.
53. Millgate, *The Achievement of William Faulkner*, 207.
54. Faulkner, *The Bear*, 268.
55. Ibid., 269.
56. Ibid., 271.
57. This motif of the equivalency of human life and language is echoed in *Human, All-too-Human*, as for example:

> *Language as an alleged science.* The importance of language for the development of culture lies in the fact that, in language, man juxtaposed to the one world another world of his own, a place which he thought so sturdy that from it he could move the rest of the world from its foundations and make himself lord over it. To the extent that he believed over long periods of time in the concepts and names of things as if there were *aeternae veritates*. ("Of First and Last Things" 11)

58. Ibid., 215.
59. Ibid., 216–217.
60. Canfield, "Faulkner's Grecian Urn and Ike McCaslin's Empty Legacies," 376ff.
61. Faulkner, *The Bear*, 254.
62. Ibid., 318.
63. It is a wonderfully Zarathustran symbolism that removes the "writing hands" of Ben at his conquest. The fact that the de-pawing is an ancient ritual makes it no less rich as a source of Nietzsche interpretation. Just as Ben's power to write himself is transmuted into historical lore at his de-pawing, Ike's truncated autoaesthetic abilities are from the very beginning de-pawed. Ike is always a reader, and never a writer, of the self.
64. Ibid., 323.
65. Ibid., 329.
66. Ibid., 330.
67. Ibid., 235.
68. Boon's knife is only one of the many significant daggers Faulkner weaves into *The Bear*. Boon's seemingly un-artful knife is in fact the appropriate tool for bringing Ben down, since it ironizes the mythic nature of the hunt—the bear *can* be killed. Several knives later, Ike's own autoaesthetic knife is the one that opens the parcel in which his uncle has inscribed his legacy, his history, and his identity. When Ike makes the incision into the parcel, cutting through the twine holding it together, he is the ironized autoaesthetic artist.
69. Ibid., 331.
70. Kinney, "Heroism," 231.
71. Simpson, "Ike McCaslin and the Second Fall of Man," 203.
72. Sam, like Fonsiba and her husband, thus represents the dilemma of free will for Ike. Sam's power is one of the denial of culture's patina and the acquisition of a

deeper and more powerful knowledge, the power of nature, as it were, but which is, because if its very denial of language, unavailable to Ike.

73. Faulkner, *The Bear*, 254.
74. Ibid., 260.
75. Canfield, "Faulkner's Grecian Urn and Ike McCaslin's Empty Legacies," 377.
76. Brooks, *William Faulkner: The Yoknapatawpha Country*, 264.
77. Faulkner, *The Bear*, 283.
78. Ibid., 281.
79. Ibid., 314.
80. Millgate, *The Achievement of William Faulkner*, 210.
81. Nietzsche, *The Will to Power*, 419.
82. Faulkner, *The Bear*, 196.
83. Ibid., 300–309.
84. Ibid., 300–301.
85. Ibid., 306.
86. Ibid.
87. Ibid., 306–307.
88. Kinney, "Heroism," 235.
89. Faulkner, *The Bear*, 291.

CHAPTER 7. NIETZSCHE BEYOND GOOD AND EVIL:
METAPHOR AS POWER

1. Nietzsche, "Beyond Good and Evil," *Ecce Homo*, 1.
2. Miller, *The Linguistic Moment*, xiv.
3. Nietzsche, "The Free Spirit," *Beyond Good and Evil*, 40.
4. Nietzsche, *Will to Power*, 506.
5. Ibid., "What is Noble," 289.
6. Nietzsche has indeed been accused repeatedly of doing just this. He is linked with Hegel and Kant, and even more often with Schopenhauer, in this attempt to conceal but retain his philosophic roots. This "accusation" does not take into account the ironic tone that underlies metaphoricity and that infused everything Nietzsche wrote after *Zarathustra*.
7. Derived in Nietzsche from Heraclitus' polarities, as we shall see in chapter 9, the first manifestation of a purely *metaphoric* tension as a cosmic rationale.
8. Allison, *The New Nietzsche*, xxii.
9. Nietzsche himself tells us this: "In order to understand anything at all of my *Zarathustra*," he says in *Ecce Homo*, "one must perhaps be similarly conditioned as I am—with one foot *beyond* life ("Why Am I So Wise?" 3). "With one foot beyond life": in light of what we have seen of Zarathustra's relationship to his shadow and his book, and to the Overman, this *final step*, one foot beyond life, is to be taken, as I have suggested "beyond" be taken, as the autoaesthetic self-becoming toward which Zarathustra points us, and indeed is the dilemma of Zarathustra's (will-to-)power and of metaphor.
10. "What is Noble" 284. The German *Esel*, literally "donkey," figuratively means "ass," and with several other endings means "stupidity"; all are lumped together here. The word is itself *beyond* denotation.
11. See particularly Lacan's comments on remembering and repeating, very appropriate to Nietzsche, in Chapter Four of *The Four Fundamental Concepts of*

Psychoanalysis, "Of the Network of Signifiers." Lacan links Freud's use of the pleasure principle to a more Nietzschean *topos* than does Freud himself, particularly given the vagaries and comic turns of the standard English translations of Freud, wherein *Treib* (drive) is rendered as "instinct," a dramatic misinterpretation on which Lacan comments extensively in a neo-Nietzschean context in that chapter, in light of the Nietzschean themes of repetition, crossings, and memory.

Lacan continues this investigation of the eternal return of repetition in the following chapter, "Tuché and Automaton," in which he analyzes a dream he has had in light of the "transference" of the so-called real, which "stretches from the trauma to the phantasy" (60), and which is now a function not of "truth" but of "the toils of the pleasure principle" (55). Reality is, for Lacan (translating directly from Freud), *"die Idee einer anderer Lokalität*, the idea of another locality, another space, another scene, *the between perception and consciousness"* (56).

Chapter Five also introduces, at the end, the notion of clinamen, with which Lacan will deal later; see chapter 9, here.

12. Lacan, *The Four Fundamental Concepts of Psychoanalysis*, 49.
13. Ibid., 50.
14. Ibid., 62.
15. This displacement takes differing forms in Freud and Lacan, as it does in various texts and various sections of Nietzsche. One of the most interesting forms of *étrangeté* in Lacan is to be seen in the (very Nietzschean) displacement of *jouissance*, the untranslatable Lacanian word that means something (not) like the "beyond" of pleasure, (not) pleasure (*plaisir*) and not enjoyment. The idea of *jouissance* contains its own subversion, since "the enjoyment of possession of an object [such as a full self] is dependent for its pleasure on others" (Wilden 101) and, so, is a function of *étrangeté*. The *law* Freud defines in the pleasure principle, in which the psyche seeks the most pacific, the most quiescent state of tensionlessness, is a law *jouissance* breaks, by definition, and is thus beyond the pleasure principle (see Lacan, *Four Fundamentals*, 183–185, 281).
16. Blondel's essay, "Nietzsche: Life as Metaphor," seems to be what Alexander Nehamas is doing at greater length in his *Nietzsche: Life as Literature*, but from which he deviates at the conclusion into something less interesting. Blondel points out that Nietzschean man is "nonnatural," based on "distance and scission" (151), and claims that Nietzsche anticipates Freud's "primal repression," what Blondel refers to as Nietzsche's "primal metaphor" (153). Sexuality, for Freud as for Nietzsche, is the meaningful link between the *étrangeté* of body and thought: "By metaphor and its excess, man forgets that he is originally a metaphoric being" (Blondel 173).
17. "What is Noble" 257. The "supra-moral sense," as Kaufmann translates it, or "over-moral sense" referred to here, reminiscent as it is of the title and the content of "On Truth and Lies in a *Nonmoral* Sense," is aimed in a different direction. Here, it is a function of the eternal return's inherent dialectical difference. Now, instead of claiming an *aussermoralischen* sense, Nietzsche claims an *Übermoralischen* sense. The dialogue here of *étrangeté* and *dépassement* is precisely the one Nietzsche wants us to engage and be suspended in, toward a new morality based on the powerful articulation of the self.
18. Ibid., 260.
19. This transcendence is the origin of all autoaesthetic thought, of the "literary," and of philosophy. "A philosopher," Nietzsche says,

is a human being who constantly experiences, sees, hears, suspects, hopes, and dreams extraordinary things; who is struck down by his own thoughts as from outside, as from above and below, as by *his* type of experiences and lightning bolts; who is perhaps himself a storm pregnant with new lightnings; a fatal human being around whom there are constant rumblings and growlings, crevices, and uncanny doings. A philosopher—alas, a being that often runs away from itself, often is afraid of itself—but too inquisitive not to "come to himself" again. (292)

Thus, the basis for the evaluation of "good and evil," as for all evaluation in Nietzsche, insofar as it comes from the higher man, emanates from "crevices," from *unheimlich zugeht*, from "a storm pregnant with new lightnings," as the perceiver of the possibilities of autoaesthetic thought "comes to himself" again, in the eternal return of self-metaphorization.

20. Nietzsche, "We Scholars," 212.
21. Deleuze, *Nietzsche and Philosophy*, 163.
22. Nietzsche, "We Scholars," 212.
23. Lacan, *The Language of the Self*, 3.
24. Ibid., 12–13.
25. *The Will to Power* 818. This passage, in the section entitled "The Will to Power as Art" in Book Three ("Principles of a New Evaluation") of *The Will to Power*, written by Nietzsche in late 1887 or early 1888, is a keystone of the later works, indeed, a kind of gateway to the "tospy-turvy world" Nietzsche was to enter in Turin less than a year later. See a discussion of this very important aphorism in Allen Megill's *Prophets of Extremity* (31).
    This "topsy-turvy"-ness occurs only in the context of Platonic depth-metaphysics with its vertical metaphors; in the aesthetic state of Nietzschean evaluation (from the perspective of the artist/philosopher), as discussed, for example, in the Versuch einer Selbstkritik [Attempt at a Self-Criticism] in the 1886 edition of *The Birth of Tragedy*, Nietzsche says that "it is only as an *aesthetic phenomenon* that existence and the world are eternally justified" (5).
26. "Peoples and Fatherlands" 256. Lest the reader think Nietzsche consists of one-line aphorisms and minimalist condensations, I take the risk of citing this whole extraordinary, Faulknerian *sentence*, 240 words in German, 273 in English (one small omission), to show the way in which Nietzsche so energetically characterizes those models on whom he wants our (his) century to base itself. All of his keywords are here, used rhapsodically; Nietzsche's style in this passage joins and imitates his autoaesthetic models.
27. Megill, *Prophets of Extremity*, 31.
28. Nietzsche, *The Will to Power*, 331.
29. Nehamas, *Nietzsche: Life as Literature*, 234; notice the significantly lower-case "r."
30. Nietzsche, "Our Virtues," *Beyond Good and Evil*, 214.
31. Nehamas, *Nietzsche: Life as Literature*, 234.
32. Nietzsche, "Our Virtues," *Beyond Good and Evil*, 214.
33. *Nietzsche et la métaphore* 36. Kofman's essay also appears in David Allison's *The New Nietzsche* (the translation here is mine). Though I am anticipating chapter 9, the very idea of the *opposition* of concept and metaphor is Heraclitan, as we have seen, as is the origin of the concept or idea of speaking *en abîme*, a chaotic opening that amounts to a reversal, from an Aristotelian point of view, without which Nietzschean metaphor and Nietzschean power are incomprehensible.

Kofman's French is particularly rich and worth citing:

Par-delà la philosophie occidentale héritière d'Aristote, en disciple d'Héraclite auquel il emprunte la métaphore du monde comme jeu, Nietzsche franchît le gouffre creuse, retourne en arrière, pour répéter la philosophie présocratique; dans le tableau même qu'il dessine des Grecs, il dit en abîme l'opposition de la métaphore et du concept et l'éffacement, par le concept et dans le concept, de la métaphore.

Kofman herself, in evoking the overleaping of metaphor, cannot resist the Nietzschean metaphor of the abyss. The "tableau même qu'il dessine des Grecs" is of course *Philosophy in the Tragic Age of the Greeks*.

34. This very serious (Heraclitan) world-game sees itself as the displacement of metaphor by concept, as Kofman has just stated. This is part of the historical (and nostalgic) consideration of the Overman's constitution, and why Heraclitus stands as such a paradigmatic figure in Nietzsche's pantheon, as we shall explore in chapter 9. It is, in fact, the cultural memory of a Heraclitan heritage that makes man capable of even minimally understanding the Overman, according to Nietzsche and Kofman.

35. Deleuze, *Nietzsche and Philosophy*, 49.

36. Deleuze, *Nietzsche and Philosophy*, 163. "The Overman: Against the Dialectic," for a fuller discussion of this idea, as Deleuze perceives it.

37. "What is Noble" 295. *Versucher*, which I have translated as "attempter," is translated by Kaufmann as "tempter" and could also be translated as "experimenter."

38. Hillis Miller's discussion of the Zarathustran Gateway of Moment in "On the Vision and the Riddle" galvanizes this precisely: the Gateway of Moment (which is metaphor), is "so slender and evanescent as never to be experienced as such any more than we are aware of experiencing the darkness and obliteration of our vision that occurs whenever we blink our eyes" (425). The Gateway of Moment is "preface and postface" and also "an interruption" (426).

39. Miller, *The Linguistic Moment*, 425.

40. Haar, "Nietzsche and Metaphysical Language," 35.

41. Miller, "Gleichnis," 83.

42. Blondel, "Nietzsche: Life as Metaphor," 171.

43. Deleuze, *Nietzsche and Philosophy*, 50.

44. Derrida, *Of Grammatology*, 277.

45. Nietzsche, "What is Noble," *Beyond Good and Evil*, 278.

46. Riddel, "From Heidegger to Derrida to Chance," 588.

47. Nietzsche, "The Free Spirit," *Beyond Good and Evil*, 34.

48. Ibid., "Natural History of Morals," 192.

49. Ibid., "Our Virtues," 224.

50. Kofman, *Nietzsche et la métaphore*, 13.

51. While, as we have repeatedly seen, the depth metaphor is subverted by Nietzsche (and, in the Nietzschean mode, by Lacan), it works very well for Freud, for whom the Platonic model of the psychic world holds supreme to the end. Freud, though powerfully influenced early on by Nietzsche, could not accept (among many other things) the Nietzschean idea of surface, which would immediately and fully cancel the "archaeological metaphor" through which Freud validates psychoanalysis: excavating through the layers of metaphoric detritus leads the analyst to the "truth" or "fact" beneath the field of memory and ego. That is, Freud saw Nietzsche's radical reorientation of the "id" (the self) and could not or would not accept it, instead positing the revelation of the scientific methods

by which "self" could be pursued and accrued. Only in the context of the danger of the Nietzschean "self," as the autoaesthetic surface of articulation, can Freud's choice be really understood. In *his* journey beyond good and evil, derived from but divergent from Nietzsche's, Freud must finally insist on closure.

52. Allison, "Destruction/Deconstruction," 308.
53. This is Derrida's contention throughout his *Eperons*, in which he initiates a discussion, consisting of many layers of Nietzschean word-play, and mirroring the themes of *Jenseits*, with the Nietzschean/Goethesque contention that "Vérité, la femme est le scepticisme et la voilante dissimulation [Truly, woman is scepticism and veiling dissimulation]" (56). Derrida's "case" for Nietzsche's styles in *Eperons* is based on just this view of metaphoric centrality, though Derrida's concern does not seem at first (and only at first) to be centrally one of autoaesthetics, as is clearly the case with Nietzsche and Lacan.

CHAPTER 8. THE *JE ME MANQUE* OF JOHN FOWLES' *DANIEL MARTIN*

1. Appropriately, the *corps morcelé* is, according to Wilden in *The Language of the Self*, "originated" by the *stade du miroir*, which never "occurs" at all but which can be "read" in numerous directions. See Wilden's discussion in *The Language of the Self* (159–177, particularly 174).
2. This strategic empowering is precisely what is entailed in Derrida's *différance*, as laid out in *Margins of Philosophy*:

   What I will propose here will not be elaborated simply as a philosophical discourse, operating according to principles, postulates, axioms or definitions, and proceeding along the discursive lines of a linear order of reasons. In the definition of *différance* everything is strategic and adventurous. Strategic because no transcendent truth present outside the field of writing can govern theologically the totality of the field. Adventurous because this strategy is not a simple strategy in the sense that strategy orients tactics according to a final goal, a *telos* or theme of domination, a mastery and ultimate reappropriation of the development of the field. (*Différance* 6–7)

   This Derridean subtext is necessary to understand the grammatological element in the Lacanian adaptation of Nietzschean empowering. The self is always within the field of writing; that is to say, always elsewhere. Both Derrida and Lacan see this Nietzschean theme as a strategic empowering, though they perceive its formulation and implementation quite differently. Because of Lacan's interest in the uttering of the *Verbe*, the Full Word, and his clinical belief (learned from Freud) that such an uttering is feasible, for Lacan, *différance* is experienced as loss, while for Derrida (and Nietzsche) it is experienced as an empowering distance.
3. Fowles, *Daniel Martin*, 405.
4. in this respect, we will see how *Daniel Martin*'s strategy imitates that of *Zarathustra*, in that Dan vanishes into *his* Shadow as well—is "taken up" by the writing hand and revealed as being a function of his own self-novel.
5. This is less overt thematically than it is, for example, in Fowles' *Mantissa*, which is as much a polemic against criticism as it is an exploration of desire and consciousness. This early discussion of narrative theory is invited by the central place Fowles accords the discussion: he is so virulently condemnatory of critical

practice (as opposed to "creative writing") that one is compelled to look further. Dan's comments about Gramsci, about film critics, and about the ancillary place of the critical activity only heighten this interest, which is further developed in all of Fowles' works, particularly the most recent, *A Maggot*.

6. Davis, "Introduction: Lacan and Narration," 849.
7. Ibid., 853.
8. Lacan, *The Four Fundamentals of Psychoanalysis*, 258.
9. "Différance" 12. This is particularly true in light of Derrida's comments on the notion of "abyss structure" in "Coming into One's Own":

> I have never wished to overuse the abyss, nor above all the abyss structure [*mise en abyme*]. I have no strong belief in it, I distrust the confidence that it, at bottom inspires, and I find it too representational to go far enough, not to *avoid* the very thing into which it pretends to plunge us. (120)

Derrida goes on to explain why the concept of the abyss is less interesting to him than is the palimpsestic, *original* idea of the *mise en abyme*, which differs from the *abîme* of Poststructuralist theory in its pedigree and which is, very interestingly from an autoaesthetic point of view, glossed in Derrida's text by a footnote explaining that the *mise en abyme* of French heraldry denotes "a smaller escutcheon appearing in the center of a larger one" (note 7) and going on to explain the genealogy (through Gide) of the contemporary meaning of this homonymic—all within the context of Derrida's distrusting the "confidence" the term engenders. Captured in this abyss-structure monologue is a vital part of autoaesthetic dynamics, which confirms and denies confidence at once.

10. Fowles, *Daniel Martin*, 405.
11. Lacan, *Language of the Self*, 92, note 2.
12. Wilden, "Lacan the Discourse of the Other," 175.
13. This is another way to subvert the Faulknerian idea of the "old truths of the heart," whose veracity purports to lie behind Ike's yearning but which in fact *is* his yearning; he, too, conceives himself in the order of the Real within which he is unable to escape the trap of the Imaginary.
14. Lacan, *Language of the Self*, 73.
15. Nietzsche, *The Will to Power*, 12B.
16. Fowles, *Daniel Martin*, 15.
17. Nietzsche, "On Truth and Lies," 81.
18. Here is introduced that other central element of the Lacanian Real: time (see *Language of the Self* 74–80).
19. Lacan, "Function and Field of Speech and Language," *Ecrits*.
20. Fowles, *Daniel Martin*, 15.
21. Ibid., 17.
22. Ibid.
23. For Lacan, the mirror state is an immensely powerful impetus for life and a first *étrangeté* that is also "the root of all later identifications" (Wilden xiii). Thus, the primary identification is always a schism, a lack, an abyss, which like the Gate of Moment *separates* the self into discourse.

We shall see how in *Daniel Martin* the articulation of this emergence is metaphorized in this same organic way, literally as the "root" of the writing Daniel Martin, who operates at the novel's opening as his own shadow.
24. Bakhtin's definition of the chronotope frames Dan's problem with validification in precise terms, though Bakhtin is caught in the same dilemma as is Dan. According to Bakhtin,

the chronotope in a work always contains within it an evaluating aspect that can be isolated from the whole artistic chronotope only in abstract analysis. In literature and art itself, temporal and spatial determinations are inseparable from one another, and always colored by emotions and values. Abstract thought can, of course, think time and space as separate entities and conceive them as things apart from the emotions and values that attach to them. But living artistic perception makes no such divisions and permits no such segmentation. It seizes on the chronotope in all its wholeness and fullness. (243)

The separation of the living artistic perception, which can claim a time-space continuity and identity, and a non-living one, a structuration in which Bakhtin believes, is of fundamental importance to Daniel Martin and to *Daniel Martin*.

25. Lacan, *Language of the Self*, 15.
26. Fowles, *Daniel Martin*, 3.
27. The notion of coming into one's own, for Daniel Martin or anyone, and addressed by Derrida in his essay of that name, consists of "producing the institution of his desire, making it the start of his own genealogy, making the tribunal and the legal tradition of his heritage, his to delegate, his legacy, *his own*" (116). Mirrored in Derrida's genealogical empowering is each protagonist we have looked at in this book, whose establishment of the "tribunals" for identifying the "legal tradition of his heritage" in self-evaluative and autoaesthetic fictions has been consistently tied to Nietzschean fictionality.
28. Fowles, *Daniel Martin*, 5.
29. Ibid., 9.
30. Ibid., 10.
31. Ibid., 11.
32. Ibid.
33. Ibid., 69.
34. Ibid., 75.
35. The chapter in which this first opening in the wall occurs, called "Games," which because of its purported energy and "innocence" and because of its place in Dan's chronology is in the present tense, ironically fictionalizes the very immediacy of experience Dan aims at and sets the stage for the openings in other walls that will follow, leading to the literal hole in the wall Jane will produce in Dan's hotel room as she renews their relationship later.
36. Fowles, *Daniel Martin*, 19.
37. Ibid., 81.
38. Ibid., 203.
39. Ibid., 207.
40. Ibid., 208.
41. Ibid., 131.
42. Ibid., 239.
43. Ibid.
44. Ibid., p. 552. Given the fact that Daniel Martin is a playwright living in America, it seems likely to me that we might interpret this declaration in light of Eugene O'Neill's *The Iceman Cometh*, whose central thematic metaphor concerns the pipedream. In *Iceman*, the pipedream, whose origin is in opium, is the euphoric delusion by which we evade ourselves. To cancel the pipedream, that is, to live *in* one's life, is the goal of the play's central character, Hickey, who is revealed as being a mad and murderous dreamer, but not until he has destroyed or undermined the enabling pipedreams of everyone else in the play. O'Neill in fact engages in a powerful autoaesthetic strategy in his interpretation of the self-

delusive *epoi* by which we know ourselves and which *must not be destroyed*, lest we cancel our ability to live. The conclusion of *Iceman*, classically tragic, leaves suspended the question of the value of the pipedream and its impossibility.

45. Ibid., 16.
46. Ibid., 273.
47. This is another of Fowles' Nietzschean words, a *pharmakon* in its own right. Parity means balance or equality but also difference; to pare is to cut or slice. Fowles is suggesting that one cannot have balance without difference, no self without *étrangeté*, and that all articulations are dreams of *both* these parities.
48. Ibid., 276.
49. Ibid., 275.
50. For more on counter-transference in light of Lacanian theory, in a very Nietzschean context, see Geoffrey Hartman's discussion of Lacan, Derrida, and Freud, entitled "Psychoanalysis: The French Connection," in *Psychoanalysis and the Question of the Text* (86–112).
51. Ibid., 331.
52. Ibid., 323.
53. Ibid., 325.
54. Ibid.
55. Ibid., 331.
56. Lacan, *Four Fundamental Concepts of Psycho-Analysis*, 48.
57. Fowles' theme of union here, between Dan and Jane, as it will be developed in the novel, is precisely Nietzschean. "The most habitual affirmations of beauty excite and stimulate each other," Nietzsche declares in *The Will to Power*:

> Once the aesthetic drive is at work, a whole host of other perfections, originating elsewhere, crystallize around "the particular instance of beauty." It is not possible to remain objective, or to suspend the interpretive, additive, interpolating, poetizing power (—the latter is the forging of the chain of affirmations of beauty). (804)

The aesthetic sense, thus defined, is for Nietzsche the impetus for the aesthetic sense, as he says in the following section, "On the Genesis of Art":

> (Physiologically: the creative instinct of the artist and the distribution of semen in his blood—) The demand for art and beauty is an indirect demand for the ecstasies of sexuality communicated to the brain. The world become perfect, through "love"—. (805)

Reinterpreted through the lens of autoaesthetics, the perfect world for Daniel Martin is the world of *étrangeté* empowered in the written self; thus, the world Dan discovers with Jane *is* the perfect world.

58. Fowles, *Daniel Martin*, 400.
59. We must also remember the Dionysian element Jane has always offered. Her Rabelaisian motto, *Fais ce que voudra*, "Do what you want," with its implications of a kind of licentious power that Jane acts out in her first lovemaking with Dan, lies as a kind of standard behind what Dan finds most tame and boring in his own life. Even during all the years when they are not together, this side of Jane, an original, energetic side, stays with Dan as a reminder of what is lying under the patina of propriety with which he acts in his own life. Dan's return to Jane, through the unlikely agency of Anthony, is a return to "love" but also a return to the (discursive) Dionysian energy of *radical* energy that permits Dan to reorganize and reorder his life and to write his novel.

60. Ibid., 401.
61. Ibid., 405.
62. Ibid.
63. Ibid.
64. Wilden, "Notes and Commentary," *The Language of the Self*, 92.
65. See further discussion of the irony of this discourse of the Lacanian orders in *Ecrits*, 180–197.

In further ironic, Nietzschean fashion, this non-existence of the materials of the Imaginary is more significant for the apocryphal subject than any reality, since the Imaginary intrudes into the real, Lacan claims; but at the same time, the Real is constructed by the subject of the Imaginary and the Symbolic (corresponding, roughly, to the order of signifiers, such as language and speech). Daniel Martin's *méconnaissance*, his misconstruction, occurs in his confusion of the Symbolic and Imaginary orders. This is a common error, and one Lacan claims psychoanalysis (indeed, modern thought) makes constantly. The error consists of confusing the relation of ego/image with that of subject/signifier.
66. Sheridan, "Translators Note," *Ecrits*, x.
67. Fowles, *Daniel Martin*, 525.
68. Ibid., 524.
69. Ibid.
70. Ibid.
71. Ibid., 542.
72. Ibid.
73. Ibid., 552.
74. Ibid., 558.
75. Ibid., 559.
76. Ibid., 604.
77. Ibid., 597.
78. Ibid., 599.
79. Nietzsche, *The Will to Power*, 821.
80. Fowles, *Daniel Martin*, 87.
81. Ibid.
82. Ibid., 271.
83. Ibid.
84. None of this is in the novel; we must wait for news of it until Dan has confronted his former life and neutralized it. Again, for the reader, that sense of a doubled suspense: Dan is suspended above or beyond his story as the reader waits to hear the outcome of his reunion with Jane, and in our waiting we are aware of the device of denial by which we are suspended. Thematically and technically, as so often before, Fowles' manipulations point to autoaesthetic power.
85. Ibid., 615.
86. Ibid., 628.
87. Ibid.
88. Hartman, *Psychoanalysis*, 92.
89. Fowles, *Daniel Martin*, 628.
90. Ibid., 629.
91. Ibid.
92. Ibid.
93. Ibid., 3.

CHAPTER 9. OPENING THE DIALECTICS OF WRITING:
HERACLITUS/NIETZSCHE

1. References to Heraclitus are to the translation of G. S. Kirk (1962). On occasion, a more recent translation by Charles Kahn (1979) has been employed. Both derive their translations from Diels' Greek text (*Die Fragmente der Vorsokratiker*), though both acknowledge some deviations from Diels. I have employed the English translations as they stand in the translation cited, and have cited each fragment and each instance of a fragment cited. For example, the first fragment cited is Diels' Fragment 41, translated by Kirk; the citation is (D41, Kirk).

    References to the Nietzsche texts are to the Colli-Montinari edition (1968). I have consulted both the Kaufmann and Hollingdale translations, and have adapted them slightly where I considered it appropriate. In the case of both Heraclitus and Nietzsche, I have analyzed the available translated text.

2. This word is itself a "graphting," a collapsing together of graphing and grafting—of charting and of splicing caught somewhere between the semiotic and the organic, writing and "art"—that like Nietzsche's tightrope symbolizes a certain suspense. It is as though the designations with which I am framing the chapter fall somewhere between the two lists by which Ihab Hassan "defines" Modernism and Postmodernism in *The Postmodern Turn* (91–92): the Modernist, concerned with form, genre, determinacy, grafting, overlaps the so-called Postmodernist, concerned with "antiform," text/intertext, inter/indeterminacy, graphing, aware of both paradigms and not able to operate in either.

    I have suggested this altered designation for the Nietzschean interrogative tradition (as, for example, in *Open Letter*, fall 1991, in an essay entitled "Free Fall: The Vertigo of the Videated Image," and in several essays on Beckett), because of the gross distortions inherent in the chronological orientation of the so-called Postmodern, which we all still debate, arguing that the Postmodern supplants the Modern in the thirties, or forties, or fifties, or sixties. . . . This (very Hegelian) chronological view is suitably undermined by the chronotopic dialectics of the Nietzschean critique. I introduce the term "Paramodern" in the following way in the essay cited above:

    > While Kant and Hegel might declare that the world has been seduced by the gross error of radical subjectivity, the free fall of the unconscious, producing the videated image, undermines and disorients the logocentricity of Modernist metaphysics and its inherent cogitocentricity. The paradoxical juxtaposition of hegemonic codes we generally call Modernism and Postmodernism prompts yet another assault on the chronology inherent in that "Post" of the Postmodern; in terms of the videated image; the Postmodern is in fact the "Paramodern."

3. From his earliest essays, Nietzsche refers to Heraclitus as his philosophic forebear. *Philosophy in the Tragic Age of the Greeks* shows this linkage clearly; and Nietzsche refers to the "dark sage of Ephesus" repeatedly in *The Birth of Tragedy*, in terms of Heraclitus' privileging of the chaotic, disruptive nature of that "darkness" of "primordial delight" (Section 24). In his para-doctrine of what Hollingdale calls "the eternal and exclusive becoming, the total instability of all reality, which continually wills and becomes and never is" (93), Nietzsche found the "ancestor" to go with Empedocles, Spinoza, and Goethe, as he points out to himself in a note, (*Musarion* 1920–29, V–XIV, 109). Heraclitus' was, for Nietzsche, "the most profound insight into the Greek soul" (Hollingdale 93)

and by extension into the (Para)modern one.

4. Nietzsche, "We Scholars," *Beyond Good and Evil*, 204.

5. Nietzsche, *On the Genealogy of Morals*, II,16.

6. One of Derrida's most powerful sublimations is that of the *name* of Heraclitus in (but not in) *Dissemination*. The Nietzschean/Heraclitan "rule" with which Derrida opens the dialectics of "Plato's Pharmacy," *beyond* dialectic, addresses this disseminated sublimation: "A text is not a text unless it hides from the first comer, from the first glance, the law of its composition and the rules of its game" (63). The hidden text, here the fragments of Heraclitus, is the *arche*-trace of *différance*, the dissemination of *étrangeté*.

7. Jaspers, *Nietzsche: An Introduction to the Understanding of His Philosophical Activity*, 517.

8. See Alphonso Lingis' "Difference in the Eternal Recurrence of the Same," *Research in Phenomenology* 8 (1978), for a fuller treatment of the "artist thought," which attempts to realize the autoaesthetic potential of a "world full of beautiful things," (re)defined as the forming of perspectives that do not "order" but "stupefy" and "veil" (90).

9. In the following, I will compound Paramodern *étrangeté* by concerning myself with the "standard" English translation of Heraclitus' fragments, not the Greek "original" (which in the sense in which I am using it is no more "Heraclitus'" than is the English or any other translation). This exegesis will include use of the Kirk's English punctuation, absent in the Greek fragments.

10. This organic process-orientation is not modern, of course: see Aristotle's thoughts in the *Poetics* on *katharsis* for a powerful skirmish with the organics of ingestion and purgation. Freud's attention to the expulsive impetus of the poet, and on the pathology of that purgation (as in "The Poet," *Civilization and Its Discontents*, "Jokes and Their Relation to the Unconscious," and elsewhere) is appropriate to this idea, as is Jung's "The Poet." The pathology of art, in terms of its play of forces, is an adumbration of *étrangeté*. This is even evident in Emerson's "The Poet." Equally present here is Derrida's discussion of the *pharmakon*, which is the graphting of ingestion *and* purgation, health and poison.

11. See Chapter One.

12. Salient questions undermine the pre-colon clause: Does Heraclitus intend that wisdom is a single thing? or that wisdom is the thing that is to follow? or that it is in fact a "thing," with the *haeccitas* that implies? some combination, summation, or "heaping" of these? something else entirely contained but not visible in his formulation? something, even, *not* contained in what he has formulated but to which it gives voice, as through a transference, in its physical and its psychoanalytical senses? These questions, along with myriad others and their exegetical responses, remain suspended in Heraclitus' text.

13. One could postulate that the reader needs this "information" sentence to "grasp" Heraclitus' meaning; and yet it is precisely here that meaning is denied: ". . . to be skilled in true judgement, how all things are steered through all"; what does it "mean" to steer judgment through things? Is judgment a thing? If not, can it interact with things? If so, steer it through *all*? And if all things are steered through all things, where is the vantage point from which we "see" this movement taking place, or is it all a function of grammatical parallax: is any steering done (that is, is this not a condition of supersaturation, of a contradictory stasis-in-plenitude)?

Moreover, and most importantly, how are we to treat this *metaphor* (here a metonymy?) of restless steering? Whatever else it is, Heraclitus' steering is unalloyed metaphor: controlled by the *images* of steerage and control, of the indeterminate vehicle moving through "all," it is metaphorical in that it originates and exists only in the tensions of its formulation around the copula. Were it given another form, one might know something else about Heraclitan wisdom. But the epigram's metaphorics are not neat; in their engaged displacement into metonym we discover an interstice, a hiatus between "things" that can only be signified in a chimerical quantum of energy.

14. Nietzsche, *On the Genealogy of Morals*, I,13.
15. Whether or not it is defensible is another matter, since a central Nietzschean doctrine, inherited from Heraclitus, consists of revealing and undermining knowledge's defensive strategies.

    Paramodern science digression: evolving atomic theory applies itself directly to this dilemma of language and knowledge. Its relational application of imagination to knowledge/science occurs in terms of a traditional notion of metaphor as the energy of transference related to the formation—ostensibly beyond metaphor—of "reality" itself in quarks, leptons, and the other subatomic particles, placed in (metaphoric) combination by the four basic forces, the "strong" and "weak" forces within the atom, electromagnetic force, and gravity. Science at the outer limits of such research finds itself in a world increasingly resembling a poem, a world of indeterminacy that Heisenberg or Gödel could only have imagined. Nobel Prize-winner Carlo Rubbia, one of CERN's most energetic and innovative experimenters, who is now one of those searching for a unifying force that "orders" the four known forces, has likened the search for the subatomic particles that provide clues to these forces to "trying to tell the color of invisible jerseys on invisible football players by watching the movement of the ball," a most poetic formulation. Of course, the word "quark," the designation for the "quasi-particle" of which protons, neutrons, and many other nuclear "things" are constructed, comes from *Finnegans Wake* (383). "Quark theory" appropriately restores simplicity to what had become an increasingly complicated nature but simultaneously transfers it to metaphor. Nuclear physics works at a level of the infinitesimal that is unapproachable by (contemporary) instrumentation, and so is purely speculative: tracks in a cloud chamber, ciphers, signs.

    Recent work on what is now called "chaos theory" (a wonderful oxymoron) furthers this argument, as does the sophisticated knowledge we now have of the eighteen-plus "flavors" of quarks. Chaos theory posits a structured but randomized cosmos in which what appear to be laws to us, caught in a limited corner of the total quasi-structure, is no more nor less than local relationality. The idea of "law" in chaos theory must be subjected to the same scrutiny that Wittgenstein applied to the same idea, and with the same result: that any law is determined by local conditions.

    The same is true in the world of subatomic particle physics, where "truth" becomes not only a measure of speculation but of metaphoric interpretation, determined (since Heisenberg at least) by the questions asked in a given context, without the certainty nor even the expectation that the answers to those local questions would or should pertain to other contexts.

16. Vaihinger, *The Philosophy of "As If": A System of the Theoretical, Practical, and Religious Fictions of Mankind*, 347.
17. See Hollingdale for fuller discussion of this issue (91ff). Hollingdale contends

that *The Birth of Tragedy* has value because it "postulates that creation is a product of conflict/contest" (101), and thus furthers what Nietzsche had already begun to (re)discover about the nature of Greek thought as akin to his own graphting.

18. Nietzsche, *Philosophy in the Tragic Age of the Greeks*, 5.
19. Hollingdale, *Nietzsche: The Man and His Philosophy*, 93.
20. At least as laid out by Lyotard in *The Postmodern Condition*.
21. Beckett, *Our Exagmination [sic]*, 14.
22. D124, Kahn 125. This last of Diels' "non-spurious" fragments is referred to in Diels but not analyzed, presumably because he considers it as much a product of Theophrastus as of Heraclitus. Kahn cites it as being found in Theophrastus' *Metaphysica* but as being genuinely Heraclitan. If so, it is among the first uses of *kosmos* as meaning "order" in early Greek, according to Kahn's commentary.
23. See Chapter 10.
24. As discussed in Kirk (220); Kirk points out the historical ambiguity of *kallistene*, which could only have meant "scale" for Heraclitus, according to Kirk, thus radically altering the nature of the fragment. For this etymological reason, Kirk does not treat the fragment as "reliable," as Kahn does.

    And indeed, the heap grows: this great epigram is a citation not of Heraclitus but of Theophrastus' (whose text is itself a corrupt, random heap of sweepings) citation of Heraclitus; the cited Heraclitan declaration is at best hearsay and at worst apocryphal, the articulation of raw autoaesthetics and of the *étrangeté* in which Heraclitus' own rhetoric is generated or cited.

25. Nietzsche introduces this discussion in *Philosophy in the Tragic Age of the Greeks*, when, having completed his treatment of Heraclitus, he opens discussion of Parmenides with this paragraph:

    > While each word of Heraclitus expresses the pride and the majesty of truth, but of truth grasped in intuitions rather than attained by the rope ladder of logic, while in Sibylline rapture Heraclitus gazes but does not peer, knows but does not calculate, his contemporary *Parmenides* stands beside him as a counter-image, likewise expressing a type of truth-teller but one formed of ice rather than fire, pouring cold piercing light all around. (9)

    Nietzsche's assertion is that Parmenides' world view is "completely different" from Heraclitus', and that Parmenides forms his to combat and counteract Heraclitus' (9). Thus, Parmenides and Heraclitus become the originators of a great debate: Heraclitus represents eternal change, Parmenides eternal stasis, a discussion taken up later here as being recapitulated in Heidegger's treatment of Nietzsche.

26. Nietzsche, *Philosophy in the Tragic Age of the Greeks*, 60.
27. Ibid., 62.
28. Ibid.
29. Ibid.
30. See Ramnoux, Chapter VIII, "La Parole et le silence."
31. Nietzsche, *Philosophy in the Tragic Age of the Greeks*, 55.
32. An energetic discussion of this element of Heraclitus' contemporaneity occurs in Clemence Ramnoux, *Héraclite, ou l'homme entre les choses et les mots* (Paris: Société d'édition "les belles lettres," 1968), whose view of Heraclitus and mine are similar. The Preface to this volume, by Maurice Blanchot, adumbrates many of the proto-autoaesthetic themes (for example, of presence and absence, of obscurity, of difference) I have suggested here.

33. Jaspers, *Nietzsche: An Introduction to the Understanding of His Philosophical Activity*, 288.
34. Nietzsche, *On the Genealogy of Morals*, III,7.
35. Vaihinger, *The Philosophy of "As If,"* 360.
36. Here, Heraclitus is linked theoretically with Empedocles, both as historical *tyrannos* of Agrigentum and as the central figure in Hölderlin's *Death of Empedocles*. Empedocles' natural religion, an adumbration of Romanticism, held that the world consists of opposing and disparate forces untamed and uncontrolled except by the poet/priest whose insight, consisting really of a harnessing (but never a quelling) of those forces, takes man to (Zarathustran) heights and, indeed, beyond, into the volcano of fusion-in-difference, Heraclitus' highest goal. Empedocles' "balanced imbalance" of forces, which remain always active even when focused like a laser on the poetic imagination, is a genealogical version of Heraclitan "becoming," another pre-psychoanalytic autoaesthetic ancestor.
37. Socrates' "know thyself," "nothing in excess," and "measure is best" typify this approach to excellence, defining merit in quite a different way from that of the Homeric ideal, which justifies the *aristos* quite apart from any "measure"—until the final 25 lines of the *Odyssey*, when Zeus, through the agency of his moderate daughter Athene, steps in to arrest Odysseus' excesses in a *deux ex machina* quite out of balance with what has preceded it.
38. Socrates' response to Heraclitus' work—Heraclitus' famous "book," which according to Kahn (3–9) was not a series of fragments but a substantial and lengthy text, was available to Socrates, though apparently lost long before the Roman age—was that "what I understand is excellent, and I think the rest is also. But it takes a Delian diver to get to the bottom of it" (Kahn 95). Socrates views Heraclitus as establishing the conditions under which future thought (always deferred) can take place, and every philosophical age, from Cratylus' to the Neoplatonists', indeed, through that of the Church fathers, the Reformation and Enlightenment, and into the nineteenth-century plurality that produces Nietzsche. All these ages not only consider Heraclitus centrally but project their own age and their own philosophical concerns onto the Heraclitan text, to a greater degree than many other antecedents, precisely because of his fragmentary and radical nature. Heraclitus' influence was extensive on Plato, less so on Aristotle (who was, interestingly enough, given Heraclitus' book by Euripides). His influence, particularly in the desire for a unity that is always problematic, is particularly heavy on the Stoics (see Kahn 4ff).
39. Kahn, *The Art and Thought of Heraclitus*, 3.
40. Bataille, *Visions of Excess*, 218.
41. Heraclitus' sense of the fall finds a Modernist/Paramodernist unity in Joyce and Beckett, both of whom overtly declare a longing for the fall into the unorthodox, Joyce in *A Portrait* and Beckett in numerous works from *Murphy* on. It is precisely the mysterious unorthodoxy of articulation and difference that links Joyce and Beckett, through Nietzsche, in an unexpected but inevitable reversal of *doxa*, though, as we shall see in chapter 10, Joyce's redemptive Modernism differs from Beckett's Paramodernism.
42. Derrida, *Dissemination*, 99ff.
43. In this Modern/Paramodern mode, not nearly enough has been done to show the vast differences in grounding assumptions between Nietzsche and Heidegger. Probably because of Heidegger's four-volume *Nietzsche*, in which Nietzsche's work, certainly in terms of the autoaesthetic themes I am exploring here, is

misrepresented or misunderstood, the assumption is made that Heidegger explicates Nietzsche in the French sense of showing what is "going on."

Heidegger's lengthy discussion of Nietzsche centers on a passage from *The Will to Power* in which Nietzsche seems, according to Heidegger, to privilege (a Heideggerian-Parmenidean) Being over the more Heraclitan Becoming. But a glance at the passage in *The Will to Power* will not bear this out:

> To *overstamp* upon Becoming the character of Being—that is the *supreme will to power.*
> Twofold falsification, on the part of the senses and of the spirit, to preserve a world of that which is, which abides, which is equivalent, etc.
> That *everything recurs* is the closest *approximation of a world of becoming to a world of being:—the highest point of contemplation.* (617)

Heidegger quotes only the first sentence of this passage in his "Being and Thought," and is determined that it should demonstrate that Nietzsche has learned from the "error" of Heraclitus, already discussed. But Nietzsche is here doing precisely the opposite of what Heidegger suggests. For Nietzsche, Being is "imposed on" Becoming, not the other way around, and this imposition is, according to the full passage, a twofold falsification, in terms both of the senses and of the spirit, empirical experience and force/energy. Nietzsche's dictum that "everything recurs," while it *is* the insight by which the condition of the Overman is to be reached, confesses at the same time that that condition is *not* "reached," by man nor by language. Nietzsche's dictum is only the closest *approximation* to that "highest point of meditation," a mediation of mediation; not even Zarathustra can reach it. Nietzsche thus confesses his own inability to go high enough and his inevitable fall into literature (adumbration of Joyce in *A Portrait* and Beckett, *passim*). But Heraclitus provides the guideline for a fictional, autoaesthetic Nietzsche concealed by the *méconnaissance* of Heidegger's exegesis, itself a self-creation in which a Parmenidean "that which abides" rules over a self-overturning.

44. Parmenides' theory asserts that the world consists of one unchanging thing, because if change is permitted, then nothing can "be itself"—indeed, cannot have a self, an identity, an existence. Teleologically, Parmenides' theory is born in the "danger" of Heraclitus' dialectical antithesis, whose threat is no less than the murderous one of self-cancellation, from the Parmenidean perspective.

45. See Nietzsche's comment on this phenomenon in the first paragraph of "On Truth and Lies in a Nonmoral Sense."

46. Guthrie, *The Greek Philosophers*, 50.

47. Fragment LXXV; see Kahn, *The Art and Thought of Heraclitus*, 63.

48. Rorty, *Consequences of Pragmatism*, 136.

49. Ibid., 137.

50. Ibid., 135–136.

51. Kahn, Fragment 33; D93. This fragment is discussed by Kirk in conjunction with Fragment D48, "For the bow the name is life, but the work is death" (D48, Kirk 116–123), a pun on *bios*, which designated both "bow" and "life" in Heraclitus' time, without the change in accent that came later (see Kahn 65).

52. That we receive Heraclitus in parabolic fragments while numerous classical philosophers did not, since, assuming it really existed, the full text of Heraclitus' unaphoristic book was available to them, diminishes none of Heraclitus' autoaesthetic power. Like Sappho's poetry, the fact that only cited fragments remain of Heraclitus' work attests to their disruptive and dangerous power.

53. Guthrie, *The Greek Philosophers*, 43.
54. We must remember Socrates' later response to Heraclitus, which follows just this line: "What I understand is excellent, and I think the rest is also. But it takes a Delian diver to get to the bottom of it" (Kahn 95). Here, we find not only the appropriate reverence for the Heraclitan text but an admission of its chimerical interpretive (im)possibilities. Socrates' inability to decipher Heraclitus signals that the fragments contain not revelation and Socratic good sense but parabolic deracination.
55. This fragment (D34), placed near the beginning of the remnant-text (thereby commenting on the remainder of it), is to be found in Clement's *Stromateis* (V.115.3; see Kirk 203). Doubtless, one must ask whether and where the influences on the source, in this case Clement, obscure, cloud, or radically alter what might have been the Heraclitan text. Clearly, the parabolic influence in general and that of Isaiah (6) in particular affects and infects Clement's Heraclitus here. Thus, the nature, or at least the substantiality of the result, of exegesis is thrown further into the abyss.
56. Norris, *The Deconstructive Turn*, 25.
57. Hollingdale, too, acknowledges this genealogical link in Nietzsche's reliance on Heraclitus' teaching concerning "the eternal and exclusive becoming, the total instability of all reality, which continually works and becomes and never is" (93). Jaspers discusses the "metaphor" of exegesis and the "world as cipher" (287ff), and though he shows a heavy Heideggerian influence, Jaspers claims accurately that exegesis is not arbitrary. "Beyond merely conceptual reconstructions," he declares, "there is a higher sense of reinterpretation through *activity*" (293), Jaspers' term for power. "Every center of power has its perspective for all the rest, i.e. its quite definitive evaluation, and its kind of action and reaction. Now there is no other kind of action at all, and 'the world' is but a name for the total play of these actions" (298). Jaspers opens another version of the dialectics of articulation.
58. Nietzsche, "The Birth of Tragedy," *Ecce Homo*, 3.
59. Fragment 67 (Kahn CXXIII; Kirk 184ff). A fuller discussion of Heraclitus and godly *logos*, as in John's gospel, occurs in Ramnoux, Chapters VI–IX and the Introduction. See also Kirk, especially 33–46, 57–63, 65–71; Kahn 93–95, 97–102, 126–130, 175–177, and his introductory chapter; other discussion of this transformation occurs in J. M. Robinson's *An Introduction to Early Greek Philosophy* (Boston: Houghton Mifflin Co., 1968), 87–107, though not in a Nietzschean context.
60. Kirk's analysis of this fragment is one of his most exhaustive; he shows how full of surprises the fragment is, grammatically and semantically. One must remember in this context that the Heraclitus fragments are ordered not by Heraclitus but because of exegetical decisions by H. Diels in his *Heraclitus of Ephesus* (1901). Diels' listing order derives from names of referents to Heraclitus' work in antiquity, since, to Diels, the referent sources and their contexts are more important than the source. Diels calls attention to Heraclitus' aphoristic style, suggesting that Heraclitus had written the phrases and sentences as a kind of notebook or philosophical journal "with," Diels says in one of the supremely ironic phases of modern philology, "Nietzsche's *Zarathustra* in mind" (Kahn 6). Our reading of Heraclitus is determined, according to Diels (who established the authoritative text), by a Nietzschean context in which Nietzsche's diachronic influence is so pervasive that Heraclitus had his writing "in mind." Eternal return, indeed.

61. Breazeale 23. This is not to say that the rational is discredited and discarded: power properly understood, for Nietzsche, results from subjecting even one's deepest beliefs to scrutiny and to constant reinterpretation. Nietzsche distrusts and condemns the irrationality that cannot question systematic premises. As Michel Haar points out,

> Contrary to Plato's method (consisting in gathering sensuous diversity into a unity of essence) Nietzsche's method aims at unmasking, unearthing, but in an *indefinite* way—i.e. without even pretending to lift the last veil to reveal any originary identity, any primary foundation. Thus, the method itself manifests a deeply rooted repugnance toward any and all systematization. (7)

In fact, Nietzsche goes beyond this: for him it is a question of the dialectics of *system* or structure. All systems are themselves at once veils and illuminators, the cruxes of rationality and sense.

62. Bataille, *Visions of Excess: Selected Writings 1927–39*, 218.
63. Ibid.
64. Musarion 1920–29, V. XIV, 109.
65. Nietzsche, *Genealogy of Morals*, III, 7.
66. Nietzsche, *Twilight of the Idols*, 2.
67. Hollingdale, *Nietzsche: The Man and His Philosophy*, 93.
68. Nietzsche, *Philosophy in the Tragic Age of the Greeks*, 8.
69. Nietzsche, *Will to Power*, 481.
70. Hollingdale, *Nietzsche: The Man and His Philosophy*, 93.
71. Nietzsche's famously unproduced, projected magnum opus had two working titles as it evolved: first, *A Transvaluation of All Values*, by which it is generally known, and second (rejected by Elizabeth Förster-Nietzsche and hardly remembered), *An Attempt at a New World-Exegesis*.

   According to Nietzsche, he and Heraclitus are both fictional, textual "hermits of the spirit" (*Beyond Good and Evil*, "We Scholars," 204), eternally returning to "all those fundamental forms of world interpretation devised by the Greek spirit"; in fact, "we are growing more Greek by the day" (*Will to Power* 419).

CHAPTER 10. DIALECTICS OF THE UNWRITTEN SELF: NIETZSCHE/JOYCE/(MALLARMÉ/)BECKETT

1. See Robert Adams Day, 143ff.
2. Nietzsche, *Gay Science*, 261.
3. In my "Father Figures: Nietzsche, Freud, and Autoaesthetic Force," delivered at the University of California at Irvine as part of a symposium coordinated with the visit to the campus of Freud's personal collection of antiquities and *objets d'art*, forthcoming from SUNY Press. The essay's point is that Freud learned his aesthetic sense significantly in a complex reaction to the Paramodern Nietzsche, whose agenda Freud partly assimilates and partly represses.
4. Hugh Kenner discusses this theme in "The *Portrait* in Perspective," in *Dublin's Joyce* (Boston: Beacon Press, 1962), 109–34, as does Stephen Heath, in a more contemporary context, in "Ambivalences: Notes for reading Joyce," in *Post-Structuralist Joyce: Essays from the French*, edited by Derek Attridge and Daniel Ferrer (Cambridge: Cambridge University Press, 1984), 31–68.
5. Rorty, *Consequences of Pragmatism*, xxi.

6. de Man, *Blindness*, 14B. This is what Jean-Louis Houdebine refers to as the *pressant*, the simultaneous confirmation and denial inherent in language. We build a *telos* and then make language confirm it, even while our irony confesses our own tautological (or vortextual) strategy, Houdebine says, in "La Signature de Joyce," in *Tel Quel* 81 (Fall 1979), 52–62.

7. As, for example, that of the snake which has crawled into the mouth of the shepherd and *bitten the inside of his throat* in *Zarathustra*, clearly a comment on the dangers of language; or the, again very consciously literary, references to torture and judgment in *Genealogy of Morals*.

8. Derrida, *Dissemination*, 210.

9. This reply is also a *repli*, a fold in the Derridean sense, as I will show with regard to the highly autoaesthetic fold of Mallarmé's *repli* in "Un Coup de dés," in which the page on which the poem appears is itself implicated in the concealment of self and meaning in the binding of the book. This dramatic and highly self-conscious literary strategy of concealment and (surface) revelation is itself paradigmatic of the Paramodern autoaesthetic and its dialectic with writing.

10. Hugh Kenner has exhaustively demonstrated how the prolegomena to the novel (p)recapitulates it in microcosmic condensations of the themes of the whole. Indeed, this two-page opening section is a *metaphoric* condensation of the whole, a precise poetic synthesis, giving style to Joyce's aesthetic.

11. Joyce, *A Portrait of the Artist as a Young Man*, 7.

12. Derrida, *The Ear of the Other*, 33.

13. Ibid., 50.

14. Like Joyce's sense of epiphany, the thematic "matter" of the novel can be infinitely reduced (conceivably into that initial and initiating "Once"), like the collapsing constellation of Quaker Oats boxes in Derrida's "Double Session," his discussion of Mallarmé in *Dissemination* (265, note 63).

15. See Kenner, *Dublin's Joyce*, 114–116.

16. For corroboration in *A Portrait*, one must look at the pervasive themes of circularity and return that the page itself produces in a reflexive and writerly way in *A Portrait*, and that increases through Joyce's work. These range from Stephen Dedalus' first stabs at poetry in Chapter One, through the villanelle which acts like a transcription of Stephen's inability to clarify his own feelings, to the poetic flights of the last journal/diary entries at the conclusion of Chapter Five; from the first suggestion (on the second page of the text) of the marriage Stephen will make with the first incarnation of E. C. (here, Eileen Vance) to and beyond the merging with the bird-girl on the strand at the conclusion of Chapter Four. This motif of marriage, with its implied union with, interpretation through, and overcoming of the white virgin sheets, reaches a further level of sophistication in *Ulysses*, through the veils of meaning over, as it were, the play of the period itself, in language-play in Molly's character and in such chapter movements as "Nausicaa"—"Circe"—"Penelope." In *Finnegans Wake*, the metaphysical entity of language itself, in such sections as those of H. C. E.'s dreams and A. L. P.'s reveries, which extend and intensify *Ulysses'* rhetoric of desire, Mallarmé's "return of the blanks" is dealt its final blow: *Finnegans Wake* is the Modernist text of the eternal return, as yet unturned to the Paramodern.

17. Said, *Beginnings: Intention and Method*, 9.

18. Putz, "Art and Intellectual Inquiry," 6.

19. Indeed, as Kenner and others have shown, this dialectic is the controlling thematic paradigm of Chapters One, Three, and Five of *A Portrait*.
20. Rey, "La généalogie Nietzschéene," 176.
21. Ibid., 171.
22. Joyce, *A Portrait*, 77–78.
23. Ibid.
24. de Man, *Blindness*, 75.
25. Ibid.
26. It should not be lost on us that the "vicus of recirculation," the eternal return of Giambattista Vico, posits irony as the mode of the era of crisis and world dissolution, the bridge to the new beginning in metaphor in Viconian circulation; Joyce resists that recurrent Viconian age of subversion.
27. In terms of the epiphany, Stephen's *étrangeté* operates in a quite different mode from Nietzsche's; in fact, Stephen is less Paramodern in this respect than either Julien Sorel or Ike McCaslin. Whereas they both have a clear sense of their fundamentally chimerical nature, Stephen feels all too substantial. His is a strategy of certitude, in which the kind of *étrangeté* I have been suggesting has no place.
28. Joyce, *A Portrait*, 59.
29. Ibid.
30. Harry Levin points out that the epiphany concluding each chapter of *A Portrait* leaves Stephen lonelier than the last (409), and here we glimpse a recapitulation of the Paramodern's advent, unbeknown to Stephen: this loneliness is the result of an operating strategy that places him in dialectical opposition to established literary and social normatives. Stephen goes through a process of removal repeatedly, in *A Portrait*, detaching himself not only from church and society but from family, colleagues, and literary associations as well: despite himself, the artist is *para-doxa*.
31. *A Portrait* is in this respect quite different from and darker than the even more Modernist *Ulysses*, which can be seen as a monument and tribute to the history of literature, particularly in such chapters as "Oxen of the Sun," with its recapitulation of the history of the English language, and "Aeolus," with its delicious exploration of the contemporary idioms of "public language" of newspaper and advertising. There is an enormously powerful, reverential fondness for the history of writing in both *Ulysses* and *Finnegans Wake* that does not exist in *A Portrait*, in whose slow build to an experimental detachment in writing is as though Joyce is celebrating not the "being" of written language but the "uninterrupted becoming of realities and meanings" in writing (see Ackroyd 57).
32. Ibid., 72.
33. Ibid., 101.
34. Ibid., 103.
35. Joyce goes even further than this: the epiphanic conclusion of the novel itself, in Stephen's rising from the mundane ground of "unremembered writing" and forging the uncreated conscious of his race, is utterly cancelled in that "stately, plump Buck Mulligan," the narrative of the complacent though frustrated Stephen of *Ulysses*, whose version of the "word bridges" he has so triumphantly forged in *A Portrait* consists of schoolboy jokes about the definition of a pier as a frustrated bridge. The Stephen Dedalus of *Ulysses* is still the autoaesthetic aspirer of *A Portrait*, but one whose autoaesthetic program has been impris-

oned within a dominant English-language code: in *Ulysses* Joyce is no longer interested in exploring the advent of the artist-thought but in the linguistic conditions of that thought *without* the artist, not from the position of the Paramodern but from the Modernist celebration of the "balance and poise of the period itself." This, of course, continues obsessively into *Finnegans Wake*, in which the balance is the perfect circle of the book's continuous and circuitous sentence, without the period. *Finnegans Wake* occupies the same position relative to *Ulysses* as the second part of Goethe's *Faust* does to the first part.

36. Rorty, *Consequences of Pragmatism*, 152.
37. Rorty's undeterminable polarities, in another framework, are what Derrida refers to as "diacriticity," which

> already prevents a theme from being a theme, that is, a nuclear unit of meaning, posed there before the eye, present outside of its signifier and referring only to itself, in the last analysis, even though its identity as a signified is carved out of the horizon of an infinite perspective. Either diacriticity revolves around a nucleus and in that case any recourse to it remains superficial enough not to put thematics as such into question; or else diacriticity reverses the text through and through and there is no such thing as a thematic nucleus, only theme *effects* that give themselves out to be the very thing or meaning of the text. (*Dissemination* 250)

The reversal inherent in Derrida's formulation might well be used as a critique of that formulation: Derrida, too, is dramatically open to Nietzschean questioning and was heavily influenced by his reading of Joyce during his year at Harvard in the 1950s, as Hillis Miller points out in "From Narrative Theory to Joyce: From Joyce to Narrative Theory," in *The Seventh of Joyce*, edited by Bernard Benstock (Bloomington: Indiana University Press, 1982), 3–5.

38. Rey, "La généalogie Nietzschéene," 186.
39. Stephen Heath's formulation of this procedure is in these concise Nietzschean terms. *A Portrait*'s strategy, according to Heath, is

> to rend the blanket of sense through the production of the counter-text of the fiction of the artist and his "voluntary exile"; his para-doxical status forming a contra-position to the realm of the doxa within the interstices of which the writing can, hesitatingly, proceed. (35)

40. Kenner, *Dublin's Joyce*, 117.
41. *Ad Majorem Dei Gloriam*, "To the greater glory of God."
42. *Laus Deo Semper*, "Praise to God always." Stephen surrounds his own writing with the prison house of Jesuit dogma. In every way this page is one of a desperate detachment trying hard to be Modernist.
43. Joyce, *A Portrait*, 70–71.
44. Ackroyd, *Notes for a New Culture*, 54.
45. Rorty, *Consequences of Pragmatism*, 150.
46. Although Jacques Aubert claims that "something happens" in Joyce's mind "under the influence of certain writings of Nietzsche" that reorients his (auto)-aesthetic from the "Neo-Hegelian" to one "radically modern, radically subversive of the concepts initially given" (123), we must still see Stephen's program as a rich metaphysical attempt at forging "the conscience of his race" out of "the chaos of unremembered writing," an alchemical, Modernist privileging of the immanent substance of writing itself. Joyce's metaphorics of transformation do not reach Nietzsche's metonymics, however much they may show us a transitional way.

47. Derrida, *Dissemination*, 297.
48. Kenner, *Dublin's Joyce*, 59–60.
49. Foucault, *Order*, 317.
50. Derrida, *Dissemination*, 221.
51. Ibid.
52. Joyce, *A Portrait*, 154.
53. Ibid., 161.
54. Ibid.
55. Ibid., 162.
56. Ackroyd, *Notes for a New Culture*, 93.
57. Joyce, *A Portrait*, 167.
58. Ibid., 169.
59. Ibid., 172.
60. Ibid.
61. One cannot avoid thoughts here of that other *künstlersroman* of lightness, Kundera's *The Unbearable Lightness of Being*, equally Modernist in its perspective even with the hindsight of Joyce's, and others', projects of self-creation to draw upon. For Kundera, a Nietzschean lightness must be assumed by the writer. The novel's entire framework, in fact, is built on the Eternal Recurrence and its value-statements. The entire notion of the artist, for Kundera as for Joyce, is bound up with the worthiness of the aesthetic vision and with the politics and strategies of self-articulation. This parallel might be extended considerably; what is true of Joyce, in terms of self-creation, is true of Kundera as well. He further explores this theme in his recent critical writings on the novel.
62. In this respect, as in others, the Joycean opus operates precisely according to the structure of Bach's *Musical Offering*, which spirals upward from key signature to key signature, seemingly and potentially without end, toward God.
63. Ibid., 178–179.
64. Ibid., p. 179. This phrase may be the birth of the dripping in the brain with which Hamm is so preoccupied in Beckett's *Endgame*. The emblems of life and death here, blood as the life-fluid but also as the visible signs of disruption, sacrifice, injury, and death, metaphorized in both Joyce and Beckett, are powerful demonstrations of the Modern/Paramodern dialectic. For Joyce, a *consciousness of language* dissipates in the poet, as though he were facilitating his use of tools in such a way as to make their use second-nature, so that in the end, in Joyce's complicated image, the *consciousness* of language occurs only in language itself, a purely Modernist anthropomorphism. For Beckett, on the other hand, as we shall see, no such thing as "consciousness of language" can or could exist; Hamm's dripping is inside a metonymic brain never to be taken as the brain of the poet nor even of the character. Hamm searches through his words for something that will stand for something (always carefully avoiding "meaning"), a sufficient sign. The terms on which Joyce's brain-ebbing and Beckett's brain-dripping occur are located at the Modern/Paramodern membrane.
65. Ibid., 181.
66. Stephen Heath disagrees, declaring that Joyce goes "all the way" to the Paramodern. "Joyce's texts," Heath says, "should not be read as the spiritual biography of a full sourceful subject (the Author) but as a network of paragrammatic interrelations constructed in a play of reassumption and destruction, of pastiche and fragmentation" (34). Although in some respect I wish I'd said

this, I wouldn't say it about Joyce but about the Mallarmé of "Un Coup de dés" and the tradition of the Paramodern, of which I cannot find Joyce a part.

67. Joyce, *A Portrait*, 189.
68. Ibid., 198.
69. Ibid., 203.
70. Ibid.
71. Ibid., 225.
72. Thoth judges by the weight of the heart: too light and one is "wanting"; Stephen's effort to achieve flight makes him a desirer of a light heart; hence, the heavy, fallen Stephen's justified fear of the judge.
73. This effacement brings into high relief the interrelation of writing and the physical existence of character and narrator, another aspect of *étrangeté*. The relationship between language and body metamorphoses, in Joyce as in Nietzsche, into that of language and evaluation itself; the body becomes metaphor, just as it does for Stephen at the end of Chapter Four and in a much more complex way at the conclusion of Chapter Five.
74. Joyce, *A Portrait*, 247.
75. Ibid., 252.
76. Among which is that of Dante Alighieri, whose "spiritual-heroic refrigerating apparatus" (252) is a permutation of Stephen's version of *étrangeté*.
77. Ibid., 78–79.
78. Said, *Beginnings: Intention and Method*, 315.
79. Nietzsche, *Gay Science*, 381.
80. Sollers, *Writing and the Experience of Limits*, 66.
81. This white space is suspended in what Malcolm Bowie, flying by John Fowles' terminology into the nets of the grammatological, calls the "ripeness of silences," always with that "hiatus in which that *supplément* must vent itself, since it cannot in the fullness engendering it" (139).
82. de Man, *Blindness*, 261.
83. Nietzsche, "The Seven Seals," *Zarathustra*, III, 16.
84. This remarkable poem (see my translation of "Un Coup de dés" as Supplement to the chapter) forms a significant part of the basis for Derrida's discussion of Mallarmé in "The Double Session" (*Dissemination* 173–286). It was Mallarmé's last poem, the equivalent in his poetic opus to Nietzsche's *Ecce Homo*, with which it is, in autoaesthetic terms, quite similar. Both are works about "how one becomes what one is" through embracing and avoiding the narrative of the self, by being understood through the unwritten self as a dialectical *écrasure de l'infâme* of Modernist substantiality.

Foucault, discussing the impact on contemporary thought of a Nietzsche/Mallarmé axis in *The Order of Things*, sets the stage for the Derridean redefinition of autoaesthetics:

> Mallarmé's project—that of enclosing all possible discourse within the fragile density of the word, within that slim, material black line traced by in upon paper—is fundamentally a reply to the question imposed upon philosophy by Nietzsche. (305)

In reply to Nietzsche's question, "Who is speaking," Foucault says, Mallarmé replies that "What is speaking is, in its solitude, in its fragile vibration, in its nothingness, the word itself" (306). Foucault goes on to draw the Nietzsche connection more deeply, as a function of *étrangeté*.

Edward Said's treatment of this Nietzsche/Mallarmé connection in its Derridean context, in the chapter of *Beginnings* entitled "Abecedarium Culturæ," places it precisely on the tightrope between the Modern and the Paramodern:

> His work busily traverses the place in mind between structuralism as the alphabet of cultural order on one side, and, on the other, the bare outlines, the traces of writing that shimmers just a hair beyond utter blankness. (343)

In the "nothingness" of the word, just a hair beyond utter blankness, we find both Mallarmé and Beckett, in the (dis)order of the Paramodern.

85. Cohn, *Mallarmé's Igitur*, 102.
86. Kenner, *Pound Era*, 136.
87. Caws, 100.
88. Derrida points out the double-meaning of *plume* in French (feather/pen), then calls attention to its other meaning, once the fold between French and English is crossed, of "effusion of liquid," as in "nightly plumes" for nocturnal emissions (274). Derrida also draws attention to the near-homonym of *plume* and *plus je* ("more I")/*plus de* ("any more," with its implications of both "supplement and lack").
89. Derrida, *Dissemination*, 271.
90. Ibid., 285.
91. Beckett, *The Unnamable*, 291.
92. In fact, Beckett realized, after writing it, that *Murphy*'s *topos* was not that of fiction but of psychoanalysis; Murphy (whose name is derived from *morph*, Greek for "form," and who strives for transcendent *metamorphosis*) is literally *bound* by a seizure: helplessly and monstrously, Murphy is tied to his rocking chair by seven silk scarves preventing *all* movement and catalyzing his hallucinatory "third zone," beyond reason and dialectic.
93. Beckett, *Murphy*, 252.
94. Ibid., 253.
95. See Raymond Federman and John Fletcher, *Samuel Beckett, His Work and His Critics*, 93.
96. Beckett, *The Unnamable*, 308.
97. Rajchman, "Postmodernism in a Nominalist Frame," 51.
98. See Barthes, "The Death of the Author," 142.
99. Ibid., 146.
100. At this point in a production of the play, the entire "action" is repeated, only to reach that imperative stage direction again, whereupon we return to the beginning and start over. When the audience realizes, after a few moments of the second time through, that what they are hearing and seeing they have heard and seen before, identically, an uneasy laughter begins to break out, followed by a profound silence when they realize that the *whole thing* will be repeated. When the play begins yet again, the laughter is more aggressive and less bemused— only when the third repetition comes to a halt partway through, at play's "end," does the audience feel relieved, freed of the potentially endless loop of repetition in which they have been caught.
101. Nietzsche, *Will to Power*, 528.
102. Beckett, "Play," 154.
103. The phrase is Margot Norris', in whose *Decentered Universe of Finnegans Wake* we saw a first Poststructuralist look at Joyce, positing a fall away from the certitude of *Ulysses* in traditional philosophical setting, without being able

to take into account the implications of the Paramodern in Derrida and others.

104. Read, *Icon and Idea: The Function of Art in the Development of Human Consciousness*, 111.
105. Ibid., 117.
106. Barthes, "The Death of the Author," 146.
107. de Man, *Blindness*, 69.
108. Nietzsche, *The Gay Science*, 23.

Selected Bibliography

———◆———

The bibliography contains full documentation for all booklength studies and articles mentioned in the text or the notes.

I. NIETZSCHE'S WORK CITED

A. Editions

Friedrich Nietzsche Sämtliche Werke Kritische Studienausgabe, ed. Georgio Colli and Mazzino Montinari. 15 vols. Berlin: Walter de Gruyter. 1980. This readily available paperback edition offers numerous advantages over the parallel clothbound edition, *Kritische Gesamtausgabe* (Berlin: Walter de Gruyter, 1967ff).

    On occasion, as indicated in the text and notes, I have provided my own translation from Nietzsche's German or have adapted Kaufmann's or Hollingdale's translations. Wherever this has occurred, I have mentioned my reason for so doing in the notes.

B. Other Nietzsche Works in German

"Ueber Wahrheit und Luge im aussermoralischen Sinne." In *Nietzsche Werke: Nachgelassene Schriften 1870–73*. Ed. Georgio Colli and Mazzino Montinari, Berlin: Walter de Gruyter, 1973.

Der Wille zur Macht: Versuch einer Umwertung aller Werte. Stuttgart: Alfred Kroner Verlag, 1964.

C. Translations

Basic Writings of Nietzsche. Trans. and ed. Walter Kaufmann. New York: Modern Library, 1968.

Beyond Good and Evil. Trans. and ed. Walter Kaufmann. New York: Random House, 1966.

The Birth of Tragedy. Trans. Walter Kaufmann. New York: Random House, 1956.

Ecce Homo. Trans. Walter Kaufmann. New York: Random House, 1969.

The Gay Science. Trans. Walter Kaufmann. New York: Random House, 1974.

On the Genealogy of Morals. Trans. Walter Kaufmann. New York: The Viking Press, 1969.

Human, All-too-Human: A Book for Free Spirits. Trans. Marion Faber with Stephen Lehman. Lincoln: University of Nebraska Press, 1984.

On the Genealogy of Morals. Trans. Walter Kaufmann. New York: Random House, 1956.

"On Truth and Lies in a Nonmoral Sense." In *Philosophy and Truth: Selections from Nietzsche's Notebooks of the Early 1870's*. Ed. and trans. Daniel Breazeale. Atlantic Highlands, N. J.: Humanities Press, 1979. 79–91.

"The Philosopher: Reflections on the Struggle Between Art and Knowledge." In Breazeale *Philosophy and Truth*, 3–60.

Thus Spoke Zarathustra. Trans. Walter Kaufmann. New York: Viking Press, 1974.

Thus Spoke Zarathustra. Trans. R. J. Hollingdale. Baltimore: Penguin Books, 1968.

Twilight of the Idols. Trans. R. J. Hollingdale. Harmondsworth, Middlesex: Penguin Books, 1978.

Unpublished Letters. Trans. and ed. Kurt F. Leidecker. New York: Philosophical Library, 1959.

The Will to Power. Trans. by Walter Kaufmann and R. J. Hollingdale. Ed. Walter Kaufmann. New York: Random House (Vintage), 1968.

II. OTHER WORKS CITED

Ackroyd, Peter. *Notes for a New Culture*. London: Vision Press, 1976.

Adams, Robert M. "Stendhal's Use of Names." In *The Red and the Black*. Trans. and ed. Robert M. Adams. New York: W. W. Norton, 1969. 418–420.

Adorno, Theodor. *Aesthetic Theory*. Trans. C. Lenhardt. New York: Routledge and Kegan Paul, 1984.

Afnan, Ruhi Muhsen. *Zoroaster's Influence on Greek Thought*. New York: Philosophical Library, 1965.

Allison, David B. "Introduction," *The New Nietzsche*. 2nd ed. Cambridge, Mass.: MIT Press, 1985.

———. "Destruction/Deconstruction in the Text of Nietzsche." *Boundary 2* VIII, No. 1 (Fall 1979): 197–222.

Ansel, Yves. "'Le Rouge et le noir': Napoléons et Julien." *Stendhal Club* 21 (1978), 42–46.

Aristotle. *The Rhetoric*. Trans. W. Rys Roberts. New York: The Modern Library, 1984.

Aubert, Jacques. *Introduction à l'esthetique de James Joyce*. Paris: Didier, 1973.

Auerbach, Erich. "In the Hotel de La Môle." *Red and Black*. Trans. and ed. Robert M. Adams. New York: Norton, 1969: 435–445.

Bakhtin, M. M. *The Dialogic Imagination*. Ed. Michael Holquist, trans. Caryl Emerson and Michael Holquist. Austin: University of Texas Press, 1981.

Barthes, Roland. "The Death of the Author." In *Image/Music/Text*. Trans. Stephen Heath. New York: Hill and Wang. 1977.

Bataille, Georges. *Visions of Excess: Selected Writings 1927–39*. Minneapolis: University of Minnesota Press, 1985.

Beckett, Samuel. *Endgame*. New York: Grove Press, 1980.

———. *Murphy*. New York: Grove Press, 1957.

——. "Play." In *The Collected Shorter Plays of Samuel Beckett*. New York: Grove Press, 1984.

——. *The Unnamable*. In *Three Novels by Samuel Beckett*. New York: Grove Press, 1965.

——. *Our Exagmination Round his Factification for Incamination of Work in Progress*. New York: New Directions, 1972.

Blanchot, Maurice. "Introduction," *Héraclite: Ou l'homme entre les choses et les mots*. By Clemence Ramnoux. Paris: Société d'éditions "les belles lettres," 1968.

Blondel, Éric. "Nietzsche: Life as Metaphor." In *The New Nietzsche*. Ed. David B. Allison. Cambridge, Mass.: MIT Press, 1985. 150–175.

Bowie, Malcolm. "Jacques Lacan." In *Structuralism and Since*. Ed. John Sturrock. Oxford: Oxford University Press, 1979.

——. *Mallarmé and the Art of Being Difficult*. Cambridge: Cambridge University Press, 1978.

Boyne, Roy. "Alcibiades as Hero: Derrida/Nietzsche?" *Sub-stance* 28 (1980): 25–35.

Breazeale, Daniel. "Introduction," *Philosophy and Truth: Selections from Nietzsche's Notebooks of the Early 1870's*. Atlantic Highlands, N.J.: Humanities Press, 1979.

Brooks, Cleanth. *William Faulkner: The Yoknapatawpha Country*. New Haven: Yale University Press, 1963.

Brooks, Peter. *The Novel of Worldliness*. Princeton, N.J.: Princeton University Press, 1969.

Canfield, J. Douglas. "Faulkner's Grecian Urn and Ike McCaslin's Empty Legacies." *The Arizona Quarterly* 36:4 (Winter 1980): 359–384.

Cohn, Robert Greer. *Mallarmé's Igitur*. Berkeley: University of California Press, 1981. 101–102.

Crouzet, Michel. "Introduction," *Le Rouge et le noir*. Paris: Garnier-Flammarion, 1964. 17–28.

Culler, Jonathan. *Structuralist Poetics*. Ithaca, N.Y.: Cornell University Press, 1975.

Davis, Robert Con. "Introduction: Lacan and Narration." In *Lacan and Narration: The Psychoanalytic Difference in Narrative Theory*. Ed. Robert Con Davis. Baltimore: The Johns Hopkins University Press, 1983. 848–860.

Day, Robert Adams. "Joyce's Waste Land and Eliot's Unknown God." *Literary Monographs* 4. Ed. Eric Rothstein. Madison: University of Wisconsin Press, 1971.

Deleuze, Gilles. *Nietzsche and Philosophy*. Trans. Hugh Tomlinson. London: The Athlone Press, 1983.

——. *Nietzsche et la philosophie*. Paris: Presses Universitaires de France, 1962.

Deleuze, Gilles, and Félix Guattari. *Anti-Oedipus: Capitalism and Schizophrenia*. Minneapolis: University of Minnesota Press. 1983.

Derrida, Jacques. "Coming into One's Own." Trans. James Hulbert. In *Psychoanalysis and the Question of the Text*. Ed. Geoffrey Hartman. Baltimore: The Johns Hopkins University Press, 1978. 114–149.

——. *De la Grammatology*. Paris: Les Editions de Minuit, 1967.

——. "Différance." In *Margins of Philosophy*. Trans. Alan Bass. Chicago: University of Chicago Press, 1972. 1–29.

——. *Dissemination*. Trans. Barbara Johnson. Chicago: University of Chicago Press, 1981.

——. *The Ear of the Other*. Trans. Avital Ronell, ed. Christie McDonald. New York: Schocken Books, 1985.

——. *Eperons/Spurs*. Chicago: University of Chicago Press, 1978.

——. "Force et signification." In *L'Ecriture et la différence*. Paris: Editions du Seuil, 1967.

————. "Freud and the Scene of Writing." In *Writing and Difference*. Trans. Alan Bass. Chicago: University of Chicago Press, 1978. 196–232.

————. *Of Grammatology*. Trans. Gayatri Chakravorti Spivak. Baltimore: The Johns Hopkins University Press, 1980.

————. *Margins of Philosophy*. Trans. Alan Bass. Chicago: University of Chicago Press, 1982.

————. "La mythologie blanche." In *Marges de la philosophie*. Paris: Editions de minuit, 1972.

————. *Positions*. Trans. and Annotated by Alan Bass. Chicago: University of Chicago Press, 1981.

————. "Signature Event Context." In *Margins of Philosophy*. Trans. Alan Bass. Chicago: University of Chicago Press, 1972. 307–330.

————. "Le supplément du copula." In *Marges de la philosophie*. Paris: Les Editions de Minuit, 1972.

————. "The Supplement of Copula: Philosophy *before* Linguistics." In *Textual Strategies*. Ed. Josué Harari. Ithaca, New York: Cornell University Press, 1979.

————. *Writing and Difference*. Trans. Alan Bass. Chicago: University of Chicago Press, 1978.

Diels, Hermann. *Herakleitos von Ephesos*. 2nd ed. Berlin, 1909.

Donato, Eugenio, and Jacques Derrida. Interview. In Jacques Derrida, *The Ear of the Other*. Trans. Peggy Kamuf, ed. Christie V. McDonald. New York: Schocken Books, 1985. 126–128.

Faulkner, William. *The Bear*. In *Go Down, Moses*. New York: Random House, 1973. 191–331.

————. *As I Lay Dying*. New York: Random House, 1957.

Flam, Leopold. "Solitude et 'étrangement' de Nietzsche dans la pensée de Heidegger." In *Nietzsche aujourd'hui, 1: Intensitées*. Paris: Union générale d'éditions, 1973.

Foucault, Michel. *The Foucault Reader*. Ed. Paul Rabinow. New York: Pantheon Books, 1984.

————. *The Order of Things: An Archaeology of the Human Sciences*. New York: Vintage Books, 1973.

Foucre, Michèle. *Le Geste et la parole dans le théâtre de Samuel Beckett*. Paris: Editions A.-G. Nizet, 1970.

Fowles, John. *Daniel Martin*. Boston: Little, Brown and Co., 1977.

Freud, Sigmund. *Civilization and Its Discontents*. Ed. and trans. by James Strachey. New York: Norton, 1961.

————. *Collected Papers (Vols. I–IV)*. London: Hogarth Press, 1933.

————. *Jenseits des Lustprinzips*. In *Gesammelte Schriften*. Vienna, 1924–34.

Gadamer, Hans-Georg. "The Drama of Zarathustra." Trans. Zygmunt Adamczewski. *The Great Year of Zarathustra (1881–1981)*. Ed. David Goicoechea. New York: University Press of America, 1983.

Girard, René. *Deceit, Desire, and the Novel: Self and Other in Literary Structure*. Trans. Yvonne Freccero. Baltimore: The Johns Hopkins University Press, 1965.

————. "Triangular Desire." *Red and Black*. Trans. and ed. Robert M. Adams. New York: Norton, 1969. 503–521.

Giraud, Raymond. *The Unheroic Hero in the Novels of Stendhal, Balzac, and Flaubert*. New York: Octagon Books, 1969.

Golomb, Jacob. *Nietzsche's Enticing Psychology of Power*. Ames: Iowa State University Press, 1987.

Guthrie, W. C. K. *The Greek Philosophers*. New York: Harper and Row, 1950.

Haar, Michel. "Nietzsche and Metaphysical Language." Trans. Cyril and Liliane Welch. *The New Nietzsche*. Ed. David B. Allison. Cambridge, Mass.: The MIT Press, 1985.

Hardy, Thomas. *Jude the Obscure*. New York: Harper and Brothers, 1957.

Hartman, Geoffrey. "Psychoanalysis: The French Connection." In *Psychoanalysis and the Question of the Text*. Ed. Geoffrey Hartman. Baltimore: The Johns Hopkins University Press, 1978. 86–114.

———. *Saving the Text: Literature/Derrida/Philosophy*. Baltimore: The Johns Hopkins University Press, 1981.

Hassan, Ihab. *The Postmodern Turn*. Columbus: The Ohio State University Press, 1987.

Hayman, Ronald. *Nietzsche*. Harmondsworth, Middlesex: Penguin Books, 1982.

Heath, Stephen. "Ambivalences: Notes for Reading Joyce." In *Post-Structuralist Joyce: Essays from the French*. Eds. Derek Attridge and Daniel Ferrer. Cambridge: Cambridge University Press, 1984. 31–68.

Heidegger, Martin. *Introduction to Metaphysics*. Trans. Ralph Manheim. New Haven: Yale University Press, 1959.

———. *Nietzsche*. Four volumes. Ed. David Farrell Krell. New York: Harper and Row, 1961.

———. "The Origin of the Work of Art." In *Basic Writings*. Trans. Albert Hofstadter, ed. David Farrell Krell. New York: Harper and Row, 1977. 149–187.

Heraclitus. *The Cosmic Fragments*. Ed. G. S. Kirk. Cambridge: Cambridge University Press, 1962.

Hollingdale, R. J. *Nietzsche: The Man and His Philosophy*. Baton Rouge: LSU Press, 1965.

Hoog, Armand. "Le 'role' de Julien." *Stendhal Club* 78 (1979): 131–142.

Hornback, Bert. *The Metaphor of Chance*. Athens, Ohio: Ohio State University Press, 1971.

Houdebine, Jean-Louis. "La Signature de Joyce." *Tel Quel* 81 (Fall 1979): 40–62.

Huyssen, Andreas. *After the Great Divide: Modernism, Mass Culture, Postmodernism*. Bloomington: Indiana University Press, 1986.

Irwin, John T. *Doubling and Incest/Repetition and Revenge: A Speculative Reading of Faulkner*. Baltimore: The Johns Hopkins University Press, 1975.

Jarry, Alfred. *Exploits and Opinions of Doctor Faustroll, Pataphysician*. In *Selected Works of Alfred Jarry*. Eds. Roger Shattuck and Simon Watson Taylor. New York: Grove Press, 1965. 173–256.

Jaspers, Karl. *Nietzsche: An Introduction to the Understanding of His Philosophical Activity*. Trans. Charles F. Wallraff. Chicago: Henry Regnery, 1966.

Joyce, James. *Finnegans Wake*. London: Faber and Faber, 1971.

———. *A Portrait of the Artist as a Young Man*. New York: Viking Press, 1970.

———. *Stephen Hero*. New York: New Directions, 1963.

———. *Ulysses*. New York: Modern Library, 1961.

Kahn, Charles H. *The Art and Thought of Heraclitus*. Cambridge: Cambridge University Press, 1979.

Kaufmann, Walter. "Introduction," *Thus Spoke Zarathustra*. By Friedrich Nietzsche. New York: The Viking Press, 1966.

———. *Nietzsche: Philosopher, Psychologist, Antichrist*. New York: Meridian Books, 1956.

Kenner, Hugh. *Dublin's Joyce*. Boston: The Beacon Press, 1956.

————. "Type's Cast." *Harper's Magazine* (June 1986): 58–63.

Kinney, Arthur F. "Faulkner and the Possibilities for Heroism." *Southern Review* 6 (1970), rpt. in *Bear, Man, and God: Eight Approaches to William Faulkner's "The Bear."* Eds. Francis Lee Utley, Lynn Z. Bloom, and Arthur F. Kinney. 2nd ed. New York: Random House, 1971. 235–243.

————. *Faulkner's Narrative Poetics: Style as Vision.* Amherst, Mass.: University of Massachusetts Press, 1978.

Kirk, G. S. *Heraclitus: The Cosmic Fragments.* Cambridge: Cambridge University Press, 1962.

Kofman, Sarah. "Metaphor, Symbol, Metamorphosis." Trans. David B. Allison. *The New Nietzsche.* Ed. David B. Allison. Cambridge, Mass.: The MIT Press, 1985.

————. *Nietzsche et la métaphore.* Paris: Editions galilée, 1983.

————. *Nietzsche et la scène philosophique.* Paris: Union générale d'éditions, 1979.

Kroker, Arthur, and David Cook. *The Postmodern Scene: Excremental Culture and Hyper-Aesthetics.* New York: St. Martin's Press, 1986.

Lacan, Jacques. *Ecrits: A Selection.* Trans. Alan Sheridan. New York: Norton, 1977.

————. *The Four Fundamentals of Psychoanalysis.* Ed. Jacques-Alain Miller, trans. Alan Sheridan. New York: Norton, 1981.

————. *The Language of the Self.* Trans. Anthony Wilden. New York: Dell Publishing, 1968.

Lacoue-Labarthe, Philippe. "La dissimulation (Nietzsche: La question de l'art et la 'littérature')." In *Nietzsche aujourd'hui: 2. Passion* (Paris: Union générale d'éditions, 1973).

————. "Theatricum Analyticum." In *Glyph 2.* Baltimore: The Johns Hopkins University Press, 1977. 122–143.

Levèsque, Claude. *L'Etrangeté du texte.* Montréal: VLB éditeur, 1976.

Levin, Harry. "The Artist." In James Joyce, *A Portrait of the Artist as a Young Man: Text, Criticism, and Notes.* Ed. Chester G. Anderson. New York: The Viking Press, 1968. 399–415.

Lewis, R. W. B. "The Hero in the New World: William Faulkner's 'The Bear.'" In *Bear, Man, and God: Eight Approaches to William Faulkner's "The Bear."* Ed. Francis Lee Utley, et al. 2nd ed. New York: Random House, 1971. 188–201.

Lingis, Alphonso. "Difference in the Eternal Recurrence of the Same." *Research in Phenomenology.* 8 (1978): 74–103.

————. "The Will to Power." In *The New Nietzsche.* Ed. David B. Allison. Cambridge, Mass.: MIT Press, 1985.

Lyotard, Jean-François. *The Postmodern Condition: A Report on Knowledge.* Minneapolis: University of Minnesota Press, 1984.

McGee, Patrick. "Gender and Generation in Faulkner's 'The Bear.'" *The Faulkner Journal* 5. 1, No. 1 (Fall 1985). 46–55.

Magnus, Bernd. "Overman: An Attitude or An Ideal?" In *The Great Year of Zarathustra (1881–1981).* Ed. David Goicoechea. New York: University Press of America, 1983. 142–165.

Mallarmé, Stéphane. "Un Coup de dés jamais n'abolira le hasard." *Oeuvres complètes.* Paris: Pléiade, 1945.

————. "Mystery in Literature." Trans. Bradford Cook. In *Critical Theory Since Plato.* Ed. Hazard Adams. New York: Harcourt, Brace, Jovanovich, 1971.

————. *Selected Poetry and Prose.* Ed. Mary Ann Caws. New York: New Directions, 1982.

de Man, Paul. *Allegories of Reading: Figural Language in Rousseau, Nietzsche, Rilke, and Proust*. New Haven: Yale University Press, 1979.

————. *Blindness and Insight: Essays in the Rhetoric of Contemporary Criticism*. Minneapolis: University of Minnesota Press, 1983.

Manthey-Zorn, Otto. *Dionysus: The Tragedy of Nietzsche*. Amherst, Mass.: The College Press, 1956.

Martineau, Henri. "The Ending of *Red and Black*." In *Red and Black*. Trans. and ed. Robert M. Adams. New York: Norton, 1969. 446–453.

Matthews, John T. *The Play of Faulkner's Language*. Ithaca: Cornell University Press, 1982.

Megill, Allan. *Prophets of Extremity*. Berkeley: University of California Press, 1985.

Miller, J. Hillis. *The Linguistic Moment*. Ithaca: Cornell University Press, 1986.

————. "The Disarticulation of the Self in Nietzsche." *The Monist* 64, No. 2 (April 1981): 247–261.

————. *The Form of Victorian Fiction*. Notre Dame, Indiana: University of Indiana Press, 1970.

————. "From Narrative Theory to Joyce; From Joyce to Narrative Theory." In *The Seventh of Joyce*. Ed. Bernard Benstock. Bloomington, Indiana: Indiana University Press, 1982. 3–5.

————. "*Gleichnis* in the Text of Nietzsche." *International Studies in Philology* XV, No. 2 (1983): 3–16.

————. *The Linguistic Moment*. Ithaca: Cornell University Press, 1986.

————. *Thomas Hardy: Distance and Desire*. Cambridge, Mass.: The Belknap Press, 1970.

Millgate, Michael. *The Achievement of William Faulkner*. New York: Random House, 1966.

————. *Thomas Hardy: His Career as a Novelist*. New York: Random House, 1971.

Nehamas, Alexander. *Nietzsche: Life as Literature*. Cambridge, Mass.: Harvard University Press, 1985.

Norris, Christopher. *The Deconstructive Turn*. New York: Methuen, 1983.

Norris, Margot. *The Decentered Universe of Finnegans Wake*. Baltimore: The Johns Hopkins University Press, 1981.

Pinget, Robert. *Cette voix*. Paris: Les Editions de Minuit, 1975.

Poulet, George. "Stendhal and Time." *Red and Black*. Trans. and ed. Robert M. Adams. New York: Norton, 1969. 470–485.

Prévost, Jean. "Stendhal's Creativity." In *Red and Black*. Trans. and ed. Robert M. Adams. New York: Norton, 1969. 453–470.

Putz, Peter. "Art and Intellectual Inquiry." In *Nietzsche: Imagery and Thought*. Ed. Malcolm Pasley. London: Methuen, 1978. 1–33.

Rajchman, John. "Postmodernism in a Nominalist Frame." *FlashArt* 137 (November/December 1987): 49–52.

Ramnoux, Clemence. *Héraclite: Ou l'homme entre les choses et les mots*. Paris: Société d'édition "les belles lettres," 1968.

Read, Herbert. *Icon and Idea: The Function of Art in the Development of Human Consciousness*. New York: Schocken Books, 1965.

Rey, Jean-Michel. "La généalogie Nietzschéene." *La philosophie du monde scientifique et industriel*. Ed. Francois Chatelêt. Paris: Hachette, 1973. 151–189.

Richard, Jean-Pierre. "Knowing and Feeling in Stendhal." In *Red and Black*. Trans. and ed. Robert M. Adams. New York: Norton, 1969. 485–503.

————. *Stendhal et Flaubert: Literature et sensation*. Paris: Editions du seuil, 1954.

Rickels, Lawrence. "Introduction," *Looking After Nietzsche*. Albany: SUNY Press, 1990.

Riddel, Joseph. "From Heidegger to Derrida to Chance." *Boundary 2*, Heidegger Special Issue (1976): 571–591.

Robinson, John Mansley. *Early Greek Thought*. New York: Houghton Mifflin, 1968.

Rorty, Richard. *Consequences of Pragmatism*. Minneapolis: University of Minnesota Press, 1982.

Said, Edward, *Beginnings: Intention and Method*. New York: Basic Books, 1975.

Sartre, Jean-Paul. *Being and Nothingness*. Trans. Hazel E. Barnes. New York: Philosophical Library, 1956.

de Saussure, Ferdinand. *Cours de linguistique générale*, 3rd. ed., Paris: Payot, 1967.

Schacht, Richard. "Nietzsche's Second Thoughts about Art." *The Monist* 64(2) (April 1981): 241–247.

Shapiro, Gary. "Nietzschean Aphorism as Art and Act." *Man and World* 17 (1984): 399–429.

———. *Nietzschean Narratives*. Bloomington and Indianapolis: Indiana University Press, 1989.

Shelley, Percy Bysshe. "Epipsychidion." In *English Romantic Writers*. Ed. David Perkins. New York: Harcourt, Brace, and World, 1967.

Sheridan, Alan. Translators Note. In *Ecrits: A Selection*. By Jacques Lacan. New York: W. W. Norton and Co., 1977, vii–xii.

Shutte, Ofelia. *Beyond Nihilism: Nietzsche without Masks*. Chicago: University of Chicago Press, 1984.

Simpson, Lewis P. "Ike McCaslin and the Second Fall of Man." In *Bear, Man, and God: Eight Approaches to William Faulkner's "The Bear."* Eds. Francis Lee Utley, et al. 2nd ed. New York: Random House, 1971. 202–209.

Sollers, Philippe. *Writing and the Experience of Limits*. Trans. Philip Barnard with David Hayman. New York: Columbia University Press, 1983.

Sonenfeld, Albert. "Romantisme ou ironie: les épigraphes de 'Rouge et Noir.'" *Stendhal Club* 78 (1978): 143–154.

Spivak, Gayatri Chakravorti. "Introduction," *Of Grammatology*. By Jacques Derrida. Trans. Gayatri Spivak. Baltimore: The Johns Hopkins University Press, 1980.

Starobinsky, Jean. "Truth in Masquerade." Trans. B. A. B. Archer. *Stendhal: A Collection of Critical Essays*. Ed. Victor Brombert. Englewood Cliffs, N.J.: Prentice Hall, 1962: 114–127.

Staten, Henry. *Wittgenstein and Derrida*. Lincoln, Nebraska: University of Nebraska Press. 1984.

Stendhal. *Red and Black*. Trans. and ed. Robert M. Adams. New York: Norton, 1969.

———. *Le Rouge et le noir*. Paris: Garnier-Flammarion, 1964.

Stonum, Gary Lee. *Faulkner's Career: An Internal Literary History*. Ithaca: Cornell University Press, 1979.

Strong, Tracy B. *Friedrich Nietzsche and the Politics of Transfiguration*. Berkeley: University of California Press. 1988.

Tenenbaum, Elizabeth. *The Problematic Self*. Cambridge, Mass.: Harvard University Press, 1977.

Thom, Gary B. *The Human Nature of Social Discontent: Alienation, Anomie, Ambivalence*. Totowa, N.J.: Rowman and Allanheld, 1984.

Ulmer, Gregory. *Applied Grammatology: Post(e)-Pedagogy from Jacques Derrida to Joseph Beuys*. Baltimore: The Johns Hopkins University Press, 1985.

Vaihinger, Hans. *The Philosophy of "As If": A System of the Theoretical, Practical, and Religious Fictions of Mankind*. Trans. C. K. Ogden. New York: Harcourt, Brace, 1935.

Valéry, Paul. "Stendhal." In *Variété II*. Paris: Gallimard, 1930. 85–114.

Weinstein, Philip M. "Precarious Sanctuaries: Protection and Exposure in Faulkner's Fiction." In *Twentieth Century Interpretations of Sanctuary: A Collection of Critical Essays*. Ed. J. Douglas Canfield. Englewood Cliffs, N.J.: Prentice-Hall, Inc., 1982. 129–134.

White, Hayden. "Michel Foucault." In *Structuralism and Since: From Levi-Strauss to Derrida*. Ed. John Sturrock. Oxford: Oxford University Press, 1979. 81–115.

Wilden, Anthony. "Language and the Discourse of the Other." In *The Language of the Self: The Function of Language in Psychoanalysis*. By Jacques Lacan. Trans. Anthony Wilden. New York: Dell Publishing, 1977. 159–311.

———. Translator's Notes. *The Language of the Self*. 89–156.

Williams, W. D. "Nietzsche's Masks." In *Nietzsche: Imagery and Thought*. Ed. Malcolm Pasley. London: Methuen, 1978. 83–104.

Index

◆